D0759142

This is the first book on Andrei Bitov, one of contemporary Russia's most original writers. It plots his evolution from his early publications of the post-Stalin years to his mature masterpieces of the *glasnost* era. Ellen Chances assesses his place both in the Russian literary tradition from Pushkin onwards; and as part of a broader, international cultural heritage.

Chances explores his themes, from the psychological effects of Stalin on Soviet society to universal questions such as the human being's relationship with nature, history and culture, and discovers in his deeply philosophical and intensely psychological writings an innovative methodology, "ecological prose," that goes beyond modernist and post-modernist fragmentation in search of the wholeness of life.

CAMBRIDGE STUDIES IN RUSSIAN LITERATURE

ANDREI BITOV

CAMBRIDGE STUDIES IN RUSSIAN LITERATURE

General editor: MALCOLM JONES

Editorial board: ANTHONY CROSS, CARYL EMERSON,
HENRY GIFFORD, BARBARA HELDT, G. S. SMITH,
VICTOR TERRAS

Recent titles in this series include

Petrushka: the Russian carnival puppet theatre
CATRIONA KELLY

Turgenev: a reading of his fiction
FRANK FRIEDEBERG SEELEY

From the idyll to the novel: Karamzin's sentimentalist prose
GITTA HAMMARBERG

"The Brothers Karamazov" and the poetics of memory
DIANE OENNING THOMPSON

Andrei Platonov: uncertainties of spirit
THOMAS SEIFRID

Nabokov's early fiction: patterns of self and other
JULIAN W. CONNOLLY

Iurii Trifonov: unity through time
DAVID GILLESPIE

Mikhail Zoshchenko: evolution of a writer
LINDA HART SCATTON

A complete list of the books in this series
is given at the end of the volume.

ANDREI BITOV

The ecology of inspiration

ELLEN CHANCES

Professor of Russian literature and culture
Princeton University

Studies of the
Harriman Institute

CAMBRIDGE
UNIVERSITY PRESS

Published by the Press Syndicate of the University of Cambridge
The Pitt Building, Trumpington Street, Cambridge CB2 1RP
40 West 20th Street, New York, NY 10011–4211, USA
10 Stamford Road, Oakleigh, Melbourne 3166, Australia

© Cambridge University Press 1993

First published 1993

Printed in Great Britain at the University Press, Cambridge

A catalogue record for this book is available from the British Library

Library of Congress cataloguing in publication data
Chances, Ellen B.
Andrei Bitov: the ecology of inspiration / Ellen Chances.
p.   cm. – (Cambridge studies in Russian literature)
Includes bibliographical references.
ISBN 0-521-41897-6
1. Bitov, Andrei – Criticism and interpretation   I. Title.
11. Series.
PG3479.4.18Z6   1993
891.73′44 – dc20   92-33565
CIP

ISBN 0 521 41897 6 hardback

Studies of the Harriman Institute
Columbia University

The Harriman Institute, Columbia University, sponsors the Studies of
the Harriman Institute in the belief that their publication contributes to
scholarly research and public understanding. In this way, the Institute,
while not necessarily endorsing their conclusions, is pleased to make
available the results of some of the research conducted under its auspices.
A list of the Studies appears at the back of the book.

SE

To Troup

In any case it is perfectly clear that the goal for all art
. . . is to explain to the artist himself and to those around
him what man lives for, what is the meaning of his
existence. To explain to people the reason for their
appearance on this planet; or if not to explain, at least
to pose the question.

Andrey Tarkovsky, *Sculpting in Time*

Contents

Illustrations

Preface

I became interested in the giants of Russian literature – Chekhov, Dostoevsky, Tolstoy – because those writers removed the veils from the routines of everyday existence and dealt starkly and powerfully with the fundamental issues of making sense of a world of paradox and injustice. The books struggled with the basic questions. They often offered no simple answers, but, rather, especially in the case of Dostoevsky, they posed more questions. They challenged me to ask deeper questions of the world and of myself. Most importantly, the books told stories of people who had the courage, strength, and integrity to keep searching, no matter how difficult the task, for a life of meaning and value. The Russian literary giants taught of the necessity of feeling the pain of others. They spoke of the artist's obligation to act as society's conscience. They sang songs of tribute to the life-affirming force, "the sticky green leaves" that grow even in the face of intense suffering.

The books reflected the wide expanses; the deep, dark crevices; the wildness; the tenderness and vulnerability; the fanaticism; the violence and gentleness of the human soul. Russian literature taught me a great deal about life.

Much of Russia's – indeed, the world's – greatest literature grapples with questions about how to live one's life. People read books in order to help them live. Many of the best books have been propelled by writers' own fears, despair, conflicts, and dreams.

The power of Andrei Bitov's writings lies in his capacity to face head-on the necessity of the quest for a life of integrity, no matter how gut-wrenching that path may be. He documents the dignity that accompanies the ability to face reality as it is rather than as one might want it to be. He documents the distortions that accompany a life of lies, self-generated or externally imposed.

Bitov abstracts to a philosophical plane the experiences of a generation born during Stalin's purges. The desire for integrity/wholeness/integration becomes a major driving force of Bitov's works. Thematically and stylistically, he reflects the life process, the way that organisms relate to one another, to themselves, to their society, to the universe. In his prose, he shapes the life processes of expiration and inspiration.

NOTE ON THE TEXT

I use the Library of Congress transliteration system (Natalia instead of Natalya, Iurii instead of Yury). However, when a proper name has a commonly used spelling in English (Dostoevsky rather than Dostoevskii), I retain that variant. I spell the name Asya instead of Asia, since Asia would be confused with the name of the continent.

The following journals have graciously granted me permission to include, in my book, versions of material that originally appeared in articles: *Armenian Review*, *Canadian-American Slavic Studies*, *The Harriman Institute Forum*, *Russian Literature* (North-Holland), *Slavic and East European Arts*, and *Slavic Review*.

Acknowledgments

I wish to express gratitude to the following institutions and organizations for their contributions to this book. I am very thankful to Columbia University's W. Averell Harriman Institute for the Advanced Study of the Soviet Union for a productive, pleasant, and intellectually exciting year there as a Senior Fellow. I am grateful to Harvard University's Russian Research Center; to the staff of Harvard's Widener Library and Princeton's Firestone Library; and to Princeton University's Committee on Research in the Humanities and Social Sciences for summer grants. I am thankful to the American Council of Learned Societies/USSR Academy of Sciences exchange program of the International Research and Exchanges Board, and to the Fulbright-Hays Faculty Grants Abroad program, for their support of my research in the Soviet Union. Thanks also go to the American Philosophical Society for a grant.

Thanks go to Orest Pelech and Alan Pollard, former Slavic Bibliographers of Princeton's Firestone Library; to Effie Chen of Firestone's Interlibrary Services and Mary George of the Reference Division, for their help in tracking down hard-to-find research materials. I thank the library staff of Leningrad's Pushkin House and the staff of Leningrad's Saltykov-Shchedrin Public Library and Moscow's Lenin Library.

I am extraordinarily thankful to Princeton University's Anne Chase for her remarkable typing abilities, patience, conscientiousness, and good cheer in the typing of revised versions and variants of *The Ecology*. Several Princeton University student assistants made my life easier, and I thank them: Andrew Wilson, Michael Bott, Radmila Grin, Richard Grimes, and

Kirsten Hildebrand. I am grateful to Isobel Abelson for her able typing of an earlier version of the manuscript.

I have benefited from stimulating conversations about life and literature with friends and colleagues: Nadezhda Azhgikhina, Galina Belaia, Robert Belknap, Aleksandr Chudakov and Marietta Chudakova, Edith Clowes, George Gibian, Judith Gross, Stevan Harnad, Natalia Ivanova, Amy Mandelker, Robin Miller, Catharine Nepomnyashchy, Maria Tatar, Carol Ueland, Mark von Hagen, Michael Wachtel, and Thomas Winner. I appreciate tremendously the generous sharing of Bitov materials and their own writings by Priscilla Meyer, Ronald Meyer, Kurt Shaw, and Sven Spieker. I thank Michael Wachtel for his help.

I am enormously grateful to my editor, Katharina Brett, for her enthusiastic support of this book, from the moment she heard about it, to the final stages of production. Her expertise, keen mind, and excellent judgment guided me to a better finished product. My thanks also go to Janet Hall for her sensitive copy-editing of the manuscript.

Several very special acknowledgments are in order. Elena M. Soloveitchik, my great aunt, deceased, of Leningrad, first introduced me to Andrei Bitov's writings in 1970. I am extremely grateful to Andrei Bitov for his generosity of time and for offering to provide photographs for my book. I am thankful to him that he writes. I am extremely thankful to Dr. Edwin Kroeker and to Evangeline Peterson for always being there. I am thankful to Aaron Lemonick for his unswaying faith in my abilities, for his wisdom, and for his constant support and encouragement. I am grateful to Robert Maguire for sharing his knowledge of literature, for his conscientious and thoughtful reading of an earlier version of my book, and for his wise and helpful comments. I thank my family for encouraging the pursuit of questions, and for fostering a deep respect for culture, values, and education. I thank Troup Mathews, who shared the agonies and ecstasies of the ecology of inspiration, in literature and in life. I dedicate this book to him.

CHAPTER I

Andrei Bitov's ecological prose

Given a choice of societies, I would only join an
ecological society.[1]

Andrei Bitov, letter, 1978

Language . . . is a body, . . . one unified text . . .
that will change tomorrow . . .[2]

Andrei Bitov, "Ecology of the Word"
("Èkologiia slova")

It seems to me that everything that I am writing
is one unified house.[3]

Andrei Bitov, "Diverse Days of Man"
("Raznye dni cheloveka")

[The trees – E.C.] are all connected . . . and they
represent a unified system.[4]

Andrei Bitov, "The Forest," in *Days of Man*
(*Dni cheloveka*)

INTRODUCTION

Andrei Bitov is an important writer. He is a complicated,
original writer. Bitov's books tackle questions that have driven
great Russian writers: What is the meaning of life? Who are we?
Why are we here? The nature of reality, of the creative process,
of human consciousness, history, culture, science, and life – these
are Bitov's themes. His foci are boundaries and the dissolution of
boundaries – of the ego, of genres, of time and space, of the
human and the divine, of life and death, of life and art, of
biological species. His genres are the short story, novel, poetry,[5]

I

philosophical essay, travelogue, literary criticism, film essays and scenarios.

His writings encompass nineteenth- and twentieth-century Russian literature, contemporary Soviet life, art, and history, the films of Federico Fellini, Alfred Hitchcock, Georgian film, Lamorisse's "The Red Balloon," ecology, Armenian and Georgian culture, human and animal behavior, Buddhism, Icelandic prose, Japanese poetry, medieval Arabic philosophy, mining expeditions in Uzbekistan, ice motorcycle racing in Ufa, and so on.

Structurally, Bitov's works are often shaped like circles. Endings repeat beginnings. He frequently uses circle imagery – wheels, balloons, spheres, spirals, rings. During the late 1950s and early 1960s, he emphasized expanding circles, each circle intersecting others in order to enlarge one's capacity to experience life. During the mid to late 1960s, Bitov began to write about contracting circles, wheels of death, vicious circles. Upward spirals are replaced by downward spirals.

In his brilliant tour de force, *Pushkin House*, Bitov plots the circles of endless humiliation and self-destruction. He documents one person's struggle to break out of those circles and to find personal and artistic integrity and authenticity. Bitov speaks, in *Pushkin House*, about the damage that Stalin inflicted upon everyone who lived through and beyond the nightmare years of the 1930s, 1940s, and early 1950s. The raw power of Bitov's novel explodes into our consciousness, whether or not we lived in the Soviet Union of the Stalin years. Bitov speaks to all of us as he identifies, unwittingly, the Stalinist elements in many human lives, those negative forces that prevent people from escaping self-destructive circles and living lives of personal freedom.

In the early 1980s, Andrei Bitov's name had all but disappeared from the pages of Soviet publications. *Pushkin House* (*Pushkinskii dom*, 1964–71), his major novel, had been rejected by Soviet publishers (although some of the novel's less provocative sections had appeared in Soviet journals). During the years that the Russian press now refers to as the Brezhnev era of stagnation, Bitov acted in ways that hardly endeared him to the Soviet authorities. In 1978, *Pushkin House* was published in the United States by Ardis Publishers.[6] A year later, Bitov was an editor of and contributor to *Metropol*, an anthology that represented what, under Gorbachev, was known as glasnost, or openness, in the arts.[7] Under Brezhnev, many of the contributors were punished.[8] Because of the confluence of these events, Bitov suffered during the late 1970s and early 1980s; from that time until Gorbachev's ascent to power, Bitov had almost nothing published. One book, *Sunday* (*Voskresnyi den'*), consisting of almost all previously published materials, appeared in 1980, as did a few short pieces, articles, and a story, "The Taste" ("Vkus") (1983). During that period, Bitov's name was not mentioned as frequently in Soviet articles and books as it had been before 1978 and 1979.

In the Gorbachev era, Bitov's fortunes changed dramatically. Under the liberalized cultural atmosphere that prevails, *Pushkin House* was serialized in *Novyi mir*,[9] and the novel was published in the USSR in book form in 1989.[10] In 1986 alone, two of his books, *Articles from a Novel* (*Stat'i iz romana*) and *Book of Journeys* (*Kniga puteshestvii*) were issued. The year 1987 marked the publication of three of Bitov's short fictional works in the journals *Znamia, Novyi mir*, and *Iunost'*.[11] Two collections of short Bitov works, *Man in the Landscape. Tales and Stories* (*Chelovek v peizazhe. Povesti i rasskazy*) and *Tales and Stories. Selected Works* (*Povesti i rasskazy. Izbrannoe*), saw the light in 1988 and 1989, respectively. His novel, *Vanishing Monakov. A Novel with Ellipses* (*Uletaiushchii Monakhov. Roman-punktir*), came out in 1990.[12] He travelled West many times during Gorbachev's reign, for instance to a West Berlin cultural festival; to the Wheatland Foundation's International Writers' Conference in the United States; to Wesleyan University as writer-in-residence; to Finland; to England, for a writers' conference; to Paris, to accept a prize for the French translation of *Pushkin House*.[13] He is interviewed in newspapers and journals, and his opinion sought, in printed discussions, on literary and cultural topics.[14] He acted in a film, S. Soloviev's "Chuzhaia belaia i riaboi," and is featured on television programs.

Increased freedom in the arts in Gorbachev's USSR is well

documented. It is important to realize that advocates of increased cultural freedoms were also active between the 1950s and the current glasnost era. Stephen Cohen addresses the issue of diversity of opinion within Soviet political culture.[15] Even during the most stifling years of Brezhnev's regime, asserts Cohen, forces for liberalization were at work within Soviet society.[16]

The same tendency held true for the arts. Literature printed in official Soviet publications, even in the late 1960s and the 1970s, was divided between works that adhered to old-guard Socialist Realist ideology and more eclectic, experimental, and individualistic works.[17]

Socialist Realism, the method imposed upon the arts in the early 1930s, demanded that literature include ideologically positive heroes promoting the collective interests of Soviet society. Socialist Realist works were to serve the Communist Party in advancing its ideology. They were to be written in a simple "objective" style that the masses would comprehend. Authors were to ignore, in their writings, concentration upon an individual's consciousness. Socialist Realism was to depict socialist society optimistically.[18]

Under Khrushchev, authors were allowed more flexibility, and they could, for the first time since the NEP period, write more experimentally. This tendency continued, albeit with greater obstacles than in the Khrushchev and Gorbachev eras, to exist in the Brezhnev period. Both Socialist Realist advocates and advocates for greater freedom in the arts influenced what could or could not be published in official Soviet publications.

As an eclectic writer, Bitov had difficulties getting published but, significantly, his works appeared in official Soviet publications throughout the 1960s and 1970s. While Socialist Realism prevailed in the literary arena during the Brezhnev years, other more liberal voices were allowed to be heard.[19]

Bitov and other liberals, whose works did not fit Socialist Realist formulae, battled old-guard ideologues in order to get published. Bitov's heroes are complex human beings. Bitov presents reality as the subjective reflection of an individual's consciousness. The essence of that reality is often depressing, a far cry from the optimistic depiction required by Socialist Realism. His style is difficult and dense, a fact that elicited objections on the part of old-guard critics who accused him of elitism.

If Bitov is not a Socialist Realist, where are his roots? Like others (Vasily Aksenov and the "Young Prose" movement) who began writing in the 1950s, he is a continuator of the tradition of Soviet experimentation of the 1920s. His spiritual fathers include fellow traveller Iurii Olesha and absurdist Daniil Kharms.

Olesha serves as one of Bitov's spiritual fathers in his use of the technique of a first-person narrator's acutely sensitive thoughts interwoven into a narration of a set of actions, as, for example, in Olesha's "The Cherry Pit" ("Vishnevaia kostochka"). Bitov's "Jubilee" is like Olesha's "Love" ("Liubov'"), where a character in bed experiences an adult existence and childhood sensations on the borderline between wakefulness and sleep. The sharp powers of observation of Olesha's narrators, as, for example, in the description of the bandage in "I Look to the Past" ("Ia smotriu v proshloe") are brought into the world of Bitov's narrators, as is Olesha's merging of the inanimate and animate worlds. The description in *Envy* (*Zavist'*) of the frosted oval glass that becomes an egg comes to mind as we read Bitov's "The Wheel," where a motorcycle race track becomes, for the narrator, a nest with an egg.[20]

Bitov's first stories were short absurdist pieces whose child-like logic and simple narration are reminiscent of Kharms' mini-stories. Bitov claims that these stories were not influenced by Kharms, but rather by contemporary Soviet writer Viktor Goliavkin, whose humorous short stories contain direct simple narration and child-like logic.[21]

"The People Who Had Shaved on Saturday" ("Liudi, pobrivshiesia v subbotu"), Bitov's first story, written on October 5, 1958, was published, without his knowledge, in an émigré literary almanac.[22] The light-hearted story concerns a narrator, on a trolley car on Monday morning, observing his fellow passengers as they make the difficult transition from Sunday to Monday.

Another early story, "The Story" ("Rasskaz"),[23] is as reminiscent of Kharms as of Goliavkin. The story line repeats itself. A man hands a saleswoman an envelope that contains a story called "The Story," the name of the Bitov story that the reader is reading. This is like the Kharms story, "The Fairy Tale" ("Skazka"), in which Vania, a little boy, writes a story, and Lenochka, a little girl, says that a story like that already exists. The story, we are told, is in the magazine that the reader has just read.[24]

Bitov explains that he soon abandoned this absurdist direction.[25] Yet the playfulness and humor remain embedded in Bitov the writer and Bitov the person.[26] Bitov's literary roots also extend beyond the Soviet period, to nineteenth- and twentieth-century Russian and Russian émigré literature. His wit and irony are in the tradition of Pushkin, Gogol, Bely, Nabokov, Zoshchenko, and Kharms.[27]

In important ways Bitov continues the great tradition of Russian literature from Pushkin to Nabokov. His works, like those of his distinguished predecessors from Pushkin to Dostoevsky to Blok to Bely to Mandelstam, are filled with references to literary progenitors. He is part of the Petersburg tradition that began with Pushkin and Gogol and found haven in Dostoevsky's and Bely's novels.[28] His writings bear the imprint of the clarity of prose of Pushkin, Tolstoy, Chekhov, Mandelstam, and Nabokov. The precision of documenting nuanced feelings he inherits from Lermontov, Tolstoy, Chekhov, and Nabokov. In tracing the psychological movements of the individual consciousness of a twentieth-century young man, Bitov reflects the tradition of Pushkin's and Lermontov's nineteenth-century superfluous man.

The ability to integrate within a novel social, historical, psychological, scientific, moral, and ethical questions Bitov inherits from Tolstoy, Dostoevsky, Bely, and Pasternak. The enormity of scope and breadth of vision that mark *Pushkin House* can be found in Tolstoy's and Dostoevsky's major novels.

In discussing old issues, Bitov sees the relevance of placing them in new frameworks, appropriate to the new, late twentieth-century context. Thus, when asked about his understanding of the contemporary superfluous man, he explained that circumstances have changed since the time of the nineteenth-century superfluous man in his particular societal context. Now he regards the superfluous man within a global context: ". . . To what end," he asks, "does Man exist, to what extent is he indispensable (or useless) in relation to his environment, to the system that governs life?"[29]

In looking at the way in which Bitov fits into the contemporary political and literary context, we should keep several factors in mind. He is among those writers who insisted on writing according to their own individualized voices rather than adhering to ideological formulae. He belongs to the "Khrushchev literary generation" ("children of the Twentieth Party Congress") that began to write in the liberalized "thaw" atmosphere of widened perspectives and freedom of the immediate post-Stalin years of the 1950s and 1960s. Although often stifled in the Brezhnev years, "it was already too late," states Bitov, for the writers' "literary personalities had had time to hatch."[30] He is among those "Leningrad writers," émigré and Soviet – like Joseph Brodsky, Aleksandr Kushner, and Evgenii Rein – who felt themselves strongly attached to the Petersburg literary tradition, from Pushkin to Mandelstam.[31]

Bitov is from a society where the very act of marching to one's own drummer, of writing in an apolitical, nonpolitical way, was considered a politically anti-Soviet act.[32] Bitov says, "I've never been political, I write about ordinary people, Soviet people and their psychology. But I suffered censorship at the hands of the editors; they would often be afraid to publish, or they'd want to delete a paragraph here, a passage there . . . One editor said to me, 'You know, I can't understand what's wrong with you. When I read your book, it seems perfectly all right, and yet I want to cross out every word!'"[33] Indeed, he got into trouble, especially after *Metropol*, because the ideologues thought that by not being pro-Soviet, he was "anti-Soviet," "anti-social," although, he admits, he educated himself as an "extra-societal" ("vneobshchestvennogo") person.[34] He believes that freedom for a writer is an internal rather than an external matter.[35]

Most important, when discussing Bitov's place in contemporary literature, is that he does not fit into facile categories or pigeonholes. His greatest strength as a writer is that he has his own unique voice, one that spans centuries and "schools of literature," but one that, in the final analysis, stands out from less talented writers. Like other great writers, he writes things that surprise, that delve into unexplored territory. They challenge the reader to think.

When addressing Bitov's cultural context, we must investigate important formative factors in his intellectual development. Bitov was trained as a geologist. He has not worked as a geologist since graduation from the Leningrad Mining Institute,[36] and while there, he was far from being a stellar student. Nevertheless, I believe that the geologist's vision of the world – as the formation of layers of past moments of the earth's history within the present – contributes to Bitov's views on life.[37] The ability to see the present world as an accumulated history of layers of past experience contributes to Bitov's complex vision of life.[38]

We must also acknowledge film's importance for Bitov. He thought about a writing career after reading the novel *The Atom Station* by Halldor Laxness, Icelandic Nobel Prize-winning author, and, significantly, after seeing Federico Fellini's film *La Strada.* [39] (In the next chapter, I discuss the relationship of *La Strada* to Bitov's "One Country.") Beginning in 1965, Bitov spent two years studying in Moscow's Graduate Courses for Screenwriters and Directors.[40] Since then, he has written film essays, where he speaks of movies' capturing life in movement.[41] He has written film scenarios.[42] Bitov, in his own prose, emphasizes movement, by placing previous works in the context of new ones. In the medium of literature, he uses a principle he learned from cinema.

We must consider, as a contributing factor to Bitov's intellectual development, literary scholar Lidiia Ginzburg's influence on him. He studied with her,[43] and he inherits, in broad outlines, her approach to literature, which she, in turn, had inherited from her teacher, Iurii Tynianov. (Tynianov, it should be noted, wrote on the dynamic qualities of film.)[44] Ginzburg, like Tynianov, emphasizes the relationship, in literature, of a word to the words around it. A word changes meaning depending on its context. In her essay, "Tynianov – Literary Scholar" ("Tynianov – literaturoved"), she speaks of her teacher's emphasis upon the function of parts of a literary work in their dynamic relationship to other parts of the work.[45] Here, and elsewhere, Ginzburg, like Tynianov, emphasizes the word "unity" ("edinstvo"), the system as a whole, the dynamic wholeness of a work, its "integrity" ("tselostnost'"). She, like Tynianov, highlights the importance of studying a work of art in the *context* of other works of art of that period.

Bitov is a direct Ginzburg–Tynianov descendant in essays on Pushkin where he urges the study of the poet in his cultural context, and where he accentuates connectedness and the unified system of Pushkin's oeuvre. He uses the same words – "unity" ("edinstvo"), "unified" ("edinyi"), "integrity" ("tselostnost'") – as analytic criteria as had Tynianov and Ginzburg.[46] He shows his indebtedness to Tynianov in direct and oblique ways that I shall address in my chapter on *Pushkin House*.

More importantly, it is the general world outlook that, I believe, Bitov shares with Ginzburg. She concurs. In a 1986 interview, she named two writers whom she considers as her pupils – Bitov, and Leningrad poet Aleksandr Kushner.[47] She regards her scholarly work and her original literary compositions as parts of one unified system. She believes that some of her reading that seems irrelevant to her scholarly work ends up being more relevant than books that would, at first glance, seem to be more scholarly. She believes in the dissolution of barriers among seemingly unrelated, disparate realms of life.[48] In her studies of the psychological novel and literary hero, she dips into fields that are, at first glance, unconnected to literature, in order to set up analogies to the literature she examines.[49]

THE ECOLOGY

Beyond his position as an inheritor of the legacy of Russian and Soviet literature through the 1920s, Bitov contributes something new to literature. He writes a fragment/short story/essay which is (1) in one context, an independent, self-sustained entity and which becomes (2) in another context, part of a new, larger work. He changes the name of his main character when the same short story appears in different collections. The meaning of the story changes, depending on the material that flanks it. His earliest quasi-travelogue/quasi-speculative, philosophical essay provides a model for an examination of later Bitov works. "One Country" purports to be a series of loosely constructed episodes during the main character's sojourn in Uzbekistan. By the end, the fragments cohere into a larger meaningful whole.

Bitov deals with the same concerns, protagonist, consciousness and voice of that protagonist. The narrator's voice often merges with the major protagonist's, and the voice becomes familiar as we follow it from one work to another, whether travelogue, essay, short story, or novel.

In the past, Bitov has written that he divides his works into two distinct categories: (1) short stories about a contemporary young man and (2) travelogues. I believe that there is a unity, in all his works, from the outset of his career.[50]

One work merges with another, as, for example, when a section of *Pushkin House*, embedded in the English version of *Apothecary Island*, changes the name of the hero Leva Odoevtsev to Aleksei Monakhov, the name of the main protagonist of the rest of *Apothecary Island*. There is a thematic emphasis, throughout Bitov's writings, upon the merging of one realm of life with another. My conclusion, after many years of studying Bitov's works, is that the works must be viewed as one unified whole.

Examining Bitov's artistic concerns, techniques, and thematics, I concluded that Bitov is writing what I call "ecological prose." Ecology is the study, in biology, of the interrelationships of organisms with other organisms and with their environment. Bitov has always been acutely aware, whether consciously or unconsciously, of interrelationships. Thematically, his works include an awareness of the relationship of the human being to his/her natural environment, culture, biological niche. His focus is always on relationships and connections – of the human being to animals, to art, to society, to the corrosive effects of living in the politically unhealthy environment of Stalinist society. He addresses the relationship of life to art, of life to our preconceived notions about life, of present life to past life. He addresses issues of ecology in the literal sense – the necessity of the human being to respect the interconnectedness of nature's ecosystem. He discusses, in his story, "The Forest," the relationship of one tree to the forest as a whole and makes analogies to the human situation. He refers, within his writings, to the Nobel Prize-winning ethologists Konrad Lorenz and Nikolaas Tinbergen, who have studied patterns of animal behavior that enable animals to occupy a niche in the larger ecological whole. These scientists study the interrelationship of the organism and its environment.

I have come to the conclusion that Bitov models some of his works on other principles of science – molecular biology's upward and downward spirals of DNA; organic chemistry's emphasis upon the interrelationships of chemical elements. He presents microcosms in his works – the tiniest units of life, the cell and the atom, and he presents macrocosms in his works – the overarching ecosystems of one organism's relationship to other organisms. He writes an essay, "The Ecology of the Word," in which he discusses contemporary language in ecological terms – which words are dying, the reciprocal relationship between a word and life, words in their environmental and cultural context.[51]

Bitov's ecological system extends beyond thematics and structure. In the very way in which he writes, he creates his ecological prose. One fragment/organism/short story exists as an individual entity in a larger whole/collection of works/ecological system. Bitov is always aware of the interrelationships of each individual organism to the larger ecosystem. All of the living entities (his individual novels, stories, essays, travelogues) are parts of a larger ecological whole (his works as a whole). All are intertwined with and interconnected with each other. Each individual unit is at once an individual, separate segment and an integral part of a larger unit. Together, they form a larger whole. We the readers experience the creative process as we follow the shapes of Andrei Bitov's writings. He keeps linking one work to another, thereby dissolving the boundaries between one work and another.

Bitov has been consistent in describing a field of human endeavor or an individual's artistic output as a unified whole. In 1965, he described the economy as one organism whose parts are interrelated.[52] Five years later, he asserted that, in his writings, author Gennadii Gor was building a house.[53] A discussion of artistic method leads Bitov, in 1981, to say that in all he creates, a writer writes but a single book.[54] New York City reminded Bitov of a biological organism,[55] as did a description of Leningrad under siege.[56]

Bitov describes Pushkin's works as one unified text,[57] one ". . . indissoluble whole . . ."[58] He comments that we could compile editions of Pushkin's works – by date instead of by genre, by passages that he had deleted, and so on.[59] Bitov's 1987 review of Tengiz Abuladze's film "Repentance" and the trilogy to which it belongs emphasizes the trilogy's structural and thematic unity. Bitov suggests seeing the films not in chronological order; to him, they make up a spherical whole.[60] Speaking about his own oeuvre, Bitov has stated that he is building a house.[61]

What do we learn from reading Bitov's works? We learn to look at contemporary Russian literature in new ways. We learn that the categorization of contemporary Russian literature must be reassessed. I have argued for the establishment of ecological prose as a descriptive term for Bitov's prose. Russian and Western scholars alike have begun to re-evaluate the categories as they see new directions emerge in recent Russian writings.[62] For example, Anatolii Bocharov ponders the categories, philosophical prose, and intellectual prose, for discussing prevalent tendencies of recent Russian literature.[63]

At certain points, tendencies that are thought of as distinct from one another intersect. We see, for example, the ecological concerns of Bitov, an "urban" writer, and Vasilii Belov, a "village prose," or "derevenshchik," writer. Belov's *Harmony. Essays on Folk Aesthetics* (*Lad. Ocherki o narodnoi èstetike*) treats the eternal cycles of nature, the old, the new, the eternal. He discusses the sense, in the countryside, of viewing the world as a unified whole. He discusses the interrelationships of all parts of life. He includes, within his ecological whole, essays and photographs.[64] These themes resemble some of Bitov's concerns. In fact, in his essay, "The Ecology of the Word," Bitov praises Belov's *Harmony*.[65]

Most of all, when we read Bitov, we learn about the human condition, about the pains, the struggles, the thoughts, the internal battles that one human being has lived through and given shape to in the multiple forms of his writings. When we read one short story, essay, or travelogue, it is as if we were being introduced to a person. Reading many Bitov works is analogous to the experience of getting to know a person over a long period of time. For over thirty years Bitov has been documenting his discoveries about himself and about life. In the process, we learn more about our lives and about life in general.

On the level of plot, Bitov drags a character's past (from previous short stories) into the present (new story). Incidents, personality characteristics, favorite songs, speculations about life, details of setting repeat themselves. New incidents and speculations about life emerge. This is analogous to being with a person with whom we have interacted in the past. Some personality traits remain as the essence of that person; others change, as the person's experiences affect him. On the level of text, Bitov reproduces this changing, growing process, for each individual story/essay/fragment represents a moment in life, and each individual fragment, in its interrelationship to the larger whole, is ever changing as fragments/moments/stories are added.

In form and in content, Bitov reproduces the process of life. Physical life consists of breathing in and breathing out – of inspiration and expiration. Spiritual fulfillment can be linked to divine inspiration, and artistic creativity, to inspiration. Bitov collapses the distinctions and, in his works, examines the forces that create or destroy the integral nature of inspiration. He examines life as a dynamic, living, breathing, moving whole. It is for this reason that I call my book *The Ecology of Inspiration*.

STEPS TOWARD THE ECOLOGY

The Ecology of Inspiration approaches Bitov's prose from two vantage points. I show the way in which Bitov shapes his ecological whole. To this end, I examine predominant themes in "One Country," the travelogue that opens his first published collection, *The Big Balloon*, and then demonstrate the way in which, together with "One Country," other works within that collection form a unit. These themes – the focus upon a person of Bitov's generation, an emphasis upon boundaries, a concern with values, and a connection with contemporary cinema – repeat themselves in later works.

They also assume new dimensions as the ecological whole grows. Thus, focus on the childhood of a person of Bitov's generation shifts to focus on an adolescent, a young adult, and an older man. An emphasis upon the dissolution of geographical boundaries shifts to discussions of boundaries in other contexts. Discussions about values describe a person's development of ethical and spiritual values and later address a person's failure to live a life of values. Values are seen through the lens of one human being and are later discussed as a nation's cultural attribute. Focus on personal life shifts to focus on Soviet history, in the Stalin era, as a cause of one individual's problems. A concern with motion results in the use of cinematic technique.

The themes overlap. In "One Country" and in *Such a Long Childhood*, Bitov's focus on values is intertwined with the idea of motion and with the idea of expanding one's boundaries. There is value in the movement, which brings with it an expansion of world outlook.

"Journey to a Childhood Friend," the opening work of *Dacha District*, shows a young adult as he discovers values on a journey to his past. Bitov, for the first time, involves the young man in writing professionally, for the hero is a journalist. Moreover, the first intimation of a critique of Soviet society emerges as Bitov debunks Socialist Realist "positive heroes." Values are spot-lighted in "The Garden," as Bitov pits truth against the idealized version of reality, and as he points out the distortions that result from a refusal to confront the truth. "Life in Windy Weather," with, for the first time, a hero-creative writer, demonstrates that the creative process of writing matches the creative process of living. A contemporary of Bitov's discovers that by living a life freed from habit and conventions, he can tap into the universal values of a sense of oneness with people, nature, and the universe. The theme of values, the dissolution of boundaries, and the importance of motion – away from the ossified habitual forms of life and of writing – take on new dimensions, as the boundaries between artistic, spiritual, and personal inspiration (breathing, moving) melt.

Some stories emphasize a person of Bitov's generation who, instead of finding a life of values by expanding his boundaries, builds barriers between himself and life, and behaves in self-destructive ways. His motion is toward death. "The Idler" and "Penelope" star young men who never get beyond a mechanized response to life. Sometimes a person on automatic pilot can change, as does the hero of "Infantiev," who travels a path from a routinized, empty life to a life that dissolves the boundaries between this world and an other-worldly, spiritual dimension.

In *Image of Life*, Bitov's next book, the author describes the disparity between life and a person's images of life. He continues to deal with a person of his generation and with the questions of values, boundaries, and film (motion), but he shifts his focus. Following the precepts of his nonfictional essay, "The Boundaries of Genre," where he advocates the necessity of freeing oneself from conventional genres, he sets himself free from the fetters of his own old forms. "The Wheel," a hybrid form – an essay cinematically constructed as a collage, a montage – concerns the circular motion of life. Boundaries between past and present disappear as Bitov discusses the similarity in societal function of two phenomena, horses (past society) and cars (present society). His discussion of values includes the question of the nature of reality. "Armenia Lessons" addresses questions of value. Here Bitov discusses culture and values – specifically, the importance of the past for the present. The chief concern is no longer the individual looking into himself and finding essential eternal values. Rather, culture as a whole, we read, must be preserved and must live in the present. By tapping into a work created by an authentic person, one thereby feels the boundaries melt between oneself and all other authentic people. Values include the value of the creative person who is authentic and who is thereby preserving and transmitting culture.

In *Seven Journeys*, his next collection, Bitov continues his search for individual values. In "The Gamble," he documents a journalist's movement toward discovery of his inner voice. He plays with the theme of the boundary between author, narrator, and protagonist, between reality and fiction/film, as he describes the interpenetration of the layers of being and non-being, reality and illusion. "Choice of Location" interweaves film and life, images of life and life. The boundary between art and life is of significance as Bitov explains that our knowledge of life comes from books, as he explains that art captures the essence of life.

The next volume, *Days of Man*, includes a novel, *The Role*, where the main protagonist's lack of values issues from living a life devoid of feeling. He cannot escape the vicious circles that lead to spiritual death. One of the stories, "The Forest," includes the image of a film going in reverse direction, away from life toward death. Here, for the first time, Bitov bases his story on a biological ecological model, as he plots the dying of a tree in its forest ecological system. "The Taste" plots the path of a man deadened to life and trapped in a downward spiral. "Birds," part of *Days of Man*, is an essay on the borderline between literature and philosophy. It explores the positive features of respecting the distinct boundaries between one living being and another.

The *Metropol* stories plot movement toward death as Bitov links the theme of biological cessation of movement (extinction of a species) to political, social commentary on the Stalinist past. *Sunday* repeats themes from earlier collections.

Pushkin House addresses the question of values of a person of Bitov's generation denying himself a life of integrity. The novel deals with the negative effects of the melting of boundaries between past and present, in terms of the main protagonist's past, present, and creative gifts. Bitov's concern with motion assumes the form of a philosophical discussion of Zeno's paradox.

Bitov's latest works explore the existence of life in literature, as he continues to tear down the boundary between life and literature.[66]

I offer a detailed investigation of the repetitions, the shifts in focus, and the intertwining themes in each work. This approach alerts the reader to the way in which Bitov shapes his ecological prose. I show the way in which boundaries between and among his works disappear. I guide the reader to what is new in each work, what is old, and where relevant, I point out the ways in which Bitov's concerns will be repeated in later creations. I show the ways in which the structure and technique of Bitov's writings reflect the ideas he sets forth.

My approach is two-pronged. I document the workings of Bitov's ecological prose. I chronologically present the writings, work by work, in each of his published collections.[67]

Bitov's practice of inserting, sometimes, with changes, a previous work of his into a new collection, raises thorny problems of chronology for the scholar. Bitov rewrites works, too, so that sometimes a story or essay, in its new incarnation, will bear two or three dates. Sometimes the same story will appear in two or more collections. Within a collection, sometimes the works are not arranged chronologically according to the date of writing. I offer an intensive analysis of each work and, when appropriate, place it in the context of the oeuvre as a whole. Where relevant, I show the way in which Bitov responds to Russian, Soviet, and foreign literature and culture – Pushkin, Lermontov, Gogol, Dostoevsky, Tolstoy, Chekhov, Socialist Realism, Olesha, Mandelstam, Pasternak, Nabokov, Solzhenitsyn, Dickens, Proust, Zeno, Fellini, Greek myth, and Avicenna.

My goal, in this first book on Bitov, is to present a comprehensive study of the author's writings to the scholarly community. I include in the discussion of his works references to the critical literature that has appeared so far. There have been two American doctoral dissertations on Bitov and a British master's thesis on the early stories. Other dissertations, British and German, are in progress. Most articles on Bitov have been Soviet. Scholarship includes Czech, Yugoslav, Danish, German, South African, and American responses to his writings.

My hope is that by the end of the book, the reader of *The Ecology of Inspiration* will better understand the methods, ideas, and shapes of the difficult, stimulating world of Bitov's books.

CHAPTER 2

"The Big Balloon": *terrestrial and celestial spheres*

"ONE COUNTRY"

Bitov had not always planned to be a writer (Figures 1–7 show moments from Bitov's early life). After high school, he drifted from job to job. He then entered the Leningrad Mining Institute's Geology Prospecting Department, not out of love of geology, but from a passion for travel that his mother had ignited in him by taking him on a journey every year from the time when he was ten years old. He pursued his study of science with a decided lack of enthusiasm.

In 1956, for the first time, as Bitov explains in an autobiographical essay of January 25, 1974,[1] he perceived ". . . the possibility of a contemporary reflection of contemporary life . . ."[2] when he, by chance, saw Fellini's *La Strada*. Bitov continues, "And from then on everything somehow started rolling inexorably and on its own."[3]

He accidentally ended up at a literary association meeting of Mining Institute amateur student-poets. The circle included Aleksandr Kushner and Gleb Gorbovsky, who have become important Leningrad poets. Bitov ". . . was simply stunned by the fact that there were people who write about what they feel and what they see."[4] He was asked whether he, too, writes. Fear of expulsion from the group drove him to claim as his own some verses that his older brother had written. The verses were imitative of Igor Severianin, of whom D. S. Mirsky, in his book on Russian literature, has written this memorable sentence: "The moment came when vulgarity claimed a place on Parnassus and issued its declaration of rights in the verse of Igor Severyanin . . ."[5] Without equivocation, Bitov asserts, "Thus, my literary path began with plagiarism."[6]

18

1–7. Bitov's pre-literature life. Captions based on Bitov's words.

1 Before World War II, with brother Oleg (on right).

The terror of being found out propelled Bitov to write "bad poetry"[7] with such fervor that he was dismissed, not from the literary circle, but from the Mining Institute, for neglecting his studies.

He then became a stevedore, lathe operator, and soldier. His military service he spent in construction brigades, continuing to compose verses. After being discharged for medical reasons (a "heart neurosis"),[8] he married, in the autumn of 1958, poetess Inga Petkevich[9] and was reinstated as a Mining Institute student. He gave up writing poetry and turned to prose. His first story was published in 1958.[10] He worked on his own stories during institute lectures. Summer expeditions gave Bitov experience and material. Impressions from these trips, writes Bitov, form the basis for his first works, "One Country" ("Odna strana"),[11] *Such a Long Childhood* (*Takoe dolgoe detstvo*), and a film scenario, "Draw It, and Live in It" ("Narisuem – budem zhit'").

In 1962 his daughter Anna was born, he graduated from the

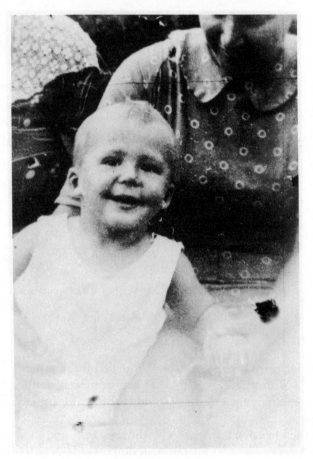

2 Before the war. A happy boy. At the dacha; and he even has a nanny.

Mining Institute, and negotiations for the publication of his first book, *The Big Balloon* (*Bol'shoi shar*) were completed. Since 1963, he has devoted himself exclusively to literature. In 1970, he was a delegate to the Writers' Congress of the RSFSR (Russian Soviet Federal Socialist Republic).[12]

The year 1963 marks the publication of *The Big Balloon*. Bitov's major concerns are present, in embryonic form, in his earliest writings. "One Country" (1960)[13] is a travelogue/fictional first-person narrative based on a young geologist's four-month

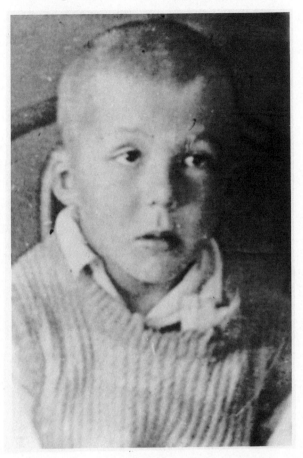

3 Bitov, aged 5, during the war. Summer of 1942. After the siege winter, in March, 1942, his mother had taken Andrei and Oleg along the "road of life," to Revda, in the Urals, where their father was working. The photograph was taken for some document.

working expedition in Uzbekistan. The parallels to Bitov's life are unmistakable. Boris,[14] the Leningrad protagonist, is twenty-three years old, Bitov's age in 1960, the year that "One Country" is dated. Like Bitov, he is a member of the intelligentsia. The place he describes is familiar to Bitov, for he had spent two years in Uzbekistan as one of the children evacuated from Leningrad during the siege of that city in World War II.[15]

4 Bitov's mother, aged 36, showing the strains of wartime life.

Boris wanders aimlessly through life just as the reader wanders
aimlessly through the pages of "One Country." By the end of the
work, Boris attaches meaning to what had seemed to be disjointed impressions and experiences. By the end of the reading
experience, the reader attaches meaning to what had seemed to
be disconnected vignettes.

Near the end of "One Country," the narrator describes one
moment during which he was rendered speechless. He saw the
sky "as Prince Andrei had seen it on Pratzan Heights" (p. 80).
The allusion to *War and Peace* (*Voina i mir*) is to the moment when

5 After the war, 1950, in the middle of the century. A happy Stalinist childhood. Vacation in Odessa. A trip on a ship with the symbolic name "Russia" (a former German ship, obtained through reparation, perhaps the "Germany" or the "Adolf Hitler"). It's doubtful whether the boy (Bitov) understands what a heavy lifesaver he has in his hands.

eternity opened up for Prince Andrei as he lay wounded at Austerlitz and gazed at the sky. Bitov's present real moment is thus linked to a past fictional moment in nineteenth-century Russian literature. The present moment (time) and the sky (place) plus the reference to the fictional moment introduce the realm of infinity to the reader by linking past, present, reality, and fiction.

6 Here's a genuinely historic picture. Summer, 1952. The great leader is still alive, and this is his Mecca in Gori. The little boy, who looks so much like Mao, in a Mao jacket, is me (Bitov). Under him (bottom, third from left) is his Mom, for some reason, in a turban. Surrounding them are pleasant faces from that era. It is obvious that they are all nice people. The picture is puzzling: if the people in back are standing up, and the ones in front are seated, then how are the people in the middle row arranged? It seems to me that I am on my knees.

Boris broadens his vision of the world through the moments of new experiences which he assimilates and conjoins with the repository of moments of imagination, dream, and past experience. He is engaged in an ongoing process of creating new shapes out of the moments.

In the form of "One Country," Bitov recreates that same life process – the experiencing and conjoining of seemingly separate moments in the text. The reader, along with the author, creates the larger shapes of life out of the individual moments of "One Country." Bitov's message emerges slowly as we journey through the sections and subsections of the text.

In the sky scene, Boris is happily surprised at the expansion of a moment into infinity. By contrast, sometimes he is disappointed because moments do not meet expectations. For instance, Boris orders a telephone call to Leningrad to speak

7 1955. A student at the Mining Institute. After the death of Stalin,
the author devoted himself to physical training. A year after this
photograph was taken, he began to write. For the time being, he doesn't
have an inkling of this.

with his mother and with "her" (pp. 55–63). As he waits, he
rehearses his side of the anticipated conversation. The conversation is different from the one Boris had imagined.[16] Each party
can hardly hear the other.

The form and words of the conversation did not meet
expectations. Boris concludes, "And in my ears and within me,
her laughter has still been sounding for a long time. And nothing

else really matters" (p. 63).[17] The *essence*, her laughter, is what counts. What is important are substance, value, and meaning in life. The human bond between these two people transcends the words they say to one another.

The subsection "Letters Are Written" repeats the discussion about values and the inadequacy of words. One week elapses between the moment when a letter is written, with the concerns of that moment, and the moment when Boris receives it. Boris answers the outdated questions and sends these stale answers and his own present questions in his letter. By the time the letter is received, its concerns are no longer part of the present. In the letter-writing process, explains Bitov, one always paints what one has left behind in rosier colors than it is. Letters are not truth, writes Bitov. Even so, he continues, they are necessary, for what matters is the essence of the letter. One person loves another and wants to know about him or her.

Bitov points out that one's concept of homeland can change, depending on where one has been (p. 98). He is Russian, he says, yet his Russia does not include Central Asia. But if he had gone around the world, Russia, perhaps, would have begun in Kushka (Turkmenia). He continues, "and if I had returned from Mars and had landed in Africa ... Where do familiar places end and begin?" (p. 98). Everything depends on our perspective, which can expand and shift its borders.

One important literary device here is what Formalist critic Viktor Shklovsky called "defamiliarization," "making it strange" ("ostranenie"). Tolstoy, as literature scholars know, used the device to break down our conventional perception and to offer a fresh perspective on a literary scene. The famous example is, of course, that of Natasha Rostova at the opera, seeing, instead of the "reality" of the make-believe scene, a fat lady shouting. German scholar Wolf Schmid, in an excellent article on Bitov's travel literature, sees "ostranenie" as central to his art. Bitov's journeys, writes Schmid, are primarily journeys of self-discovery. For Schmid, Bitov makes "ostranenie" an organizing principle for perceiving the world, life, time, and space. Schmid concentrates on the way in which "ostranenie" awakens the characters' consciousness and knowledge of self.[18]

For Bitov, the act of perceiving anew is not limited to the aesthetic realm. It propels us into the sphere of values.[19]

To look at our old patterns from a fresh perspective is to shake us out of our old patterns. The narrator of "One Country" writes, "Separation results in a revaluation of values ... More correctly, not a revaluation, but a return of values" (p. 103). We leave in order to return. By returning, after having distanced ourselves from our surroundings, we see those familiar surroundings from a fresh perspective.

Each person, explains the narrator, is given one country, one language, one city, one occupation, one beloved person; it is impossible for a person to have two countries, languages, cities, beloved people (p. 97). This seems to run counter to Bitov's arguments in the rest of the book. However, the next paragraph helps us to place the "one country" sentiment expressed here into the larger framework of "One Country." Bitov's narrator admits that we grow so accustomed to our own country that we do not notice it (p. 97). The only way to see our *"one"* is to distance ourselves from it. What we are can be grasped only by understanding "what we are not." To know what we are entails the injection of the fresh perspective of "separation" into our familiar surroundings.

By the time we have finished "One Country," we realize that we have grappled with fundamental questions about life. Bitov claims that we must transcend fixed concepts of time, place, and attitude in order to arrive at an integrated view of life. The process of integration of the seemingly scattered, separate pieces and moments of experience is what gives life meaning. The process is ever in motion, and Bitov captures that ongoing process in "One Country."

The epilogue to this work begins with an epigraph from a book about the nineteenth-century Russian explorer, Nikolai Przheval'skii. Part of it reads: "Upon his return from the journey, he [Przheval'skii – E.C.] sank into a deep longing for the boundless expanses of his wilderness" (p. 103). Boris is at home and, like Przheval'skii, longs for the exotic haunts he has left behind in Central Asia.

The end of Boris' journey and of our own returns us to the

beginning. We have come full circle. At the beginning of "One Country," Boris, in Leningrad, had brought a book about Przheval'skii to his mother. The child longed to go to Asia. At the end of "One Country," the reader is presented with the epigraph from a book about Przheval'skii, describing his longing to return to Asia. The description fits Boris' mood after his own return home. The last scene of Bitov's work almost parallels the first, for Boris is sitting at home with his relatives, longing for Asia.

For Bitov, part of the process of the motion of life is that everything becomes everything. Place becomes time. Place remains place. Time becomes place. One place becomes another place. One time becomes another time. And everything depends on our perspective to give it its trajectories of motion.

By the end of the epilogue, we have returned to the departure point of the journey. Everything is the same, yet everything is different, too. When Boris had originally read about Przheval'skii, he was a child. The epilogue does not mention his childhood. When Boris had originally dreamt about Asia, Asia had existed only as a fantasy. In the epilogue, his longing for Asia is based on real-life experiences, new experiences, which are now old experiences, part of his past.

In his 1974 autobiographical statement, Bitov expressed thoughts about his writing in general, but they are particularly important in coming to grips with the central methodology of "One Country." Bitov wrote,

I am interested in those authors and those books in which *knowledge of life in the very process of creation* [My italics – E.C.] takes place. That is to say, not what the author intended, not what he knew, not his already ready-made experience, even the most valuable – but what he himself got to know in the process, what he had not known before, what he never would have gotten to know in another way. The creative process seems to me to be alive precisely when it itself is a method of knowledge for the person who is writing. Such a writer evolves, such a person creates something new; only in this way does that unique outpouring of language which one can call artistic prose emerge.[20]

Meaning for Bitov, emerges from experiencing life. In his own statements, Bitov asserts that good literature is written as the writer discovers meaning in the writing process. The process, for Bitov, of discovery in life, and that in writing literature, are the same. The boundaries between life and literature, between living life and writing literature, dissolve. In the same way, boundaries between beginnings and endings, between different times, between reality and fantasy melt as we examine the workings of "One Country."

Only in the broadest terms can "One Country" be described as a cohesive unit. It has a beginning, middle, and end. It plots Boris' departure for Central Asia, his arrival there, his experiences and observations while in Uzbekistan, and his return to Leningrad. With the exception of the departure and arrival scenes, it seems as if any section could have been placed in any other order.

Even the initial scene does not concentrate exclusively on Boris' departure. The first chapter, "The Gates to Asia," consists of four subchapters. "The Beginning", the first of these, reveals, in the two introductory paragraphs, the narrator's childhood fascination with Asia. He writes that he had been in awe of great nineteenth-century explorers like Przheval'skii, whose travels had included rides on camels and great geographical discoveries. Bitov's narration recreates a child's fantasies of growing up to be a famous explorer. The distinction between the voice of the adult narrator and that of the child dreamer fades. The child makes up a last name for himself that sounds suitable for a great explorer. The narrator continues, "Przheval'skii places his hand on my shoulder, and with his other one, he motions to the distance. There is the Boris Murashov Mountain Range. The great explorer Murashov-Mongolskii against the background of the wild camel that he had discovered. A book from the series, 'The Life of Remarkable People' – the photographs: the explorer's mother, ... father, the great explorer as a child" (pp. 7–8).

Another part of "The Beginning" switches abruptly to the present, as the narrator states that he is a Mining Institute student. The reader is then whisked off to Boris' current daydreams – Japan, its ancient customs, beautiful Japanese clothes, a woman – and then back to Boris' present-day life. The

last words of "The Beginning" deal with the present, but then
return us to the beginning point of "One Country": "I am going
to work. But I am going to the Asia with which childhood
connects me" (p. 9).

In "The Beginning," the past fantasies of the child Boris,
thinking about his own future, include historical figures of the
nineteenth century. Thus, the protagonist's *past* encompasses at
once a *future* and a *far-gone past*; his *dream-fantasy world* includes
bits of historical *reality* and his past *Leningrad* dreams center on
faraway *Asia*. Boris' present Leningrad dreams are directed
toward Japan, a more distant Asia, and toward knowledge of its
present customs which derives from a familiarity with its thousand-year-old *past*. The narrator is speaking about the *present*,
yet the piece begins and ends with *childhood*. The second word of
the first sentence is "childhood" ("detstvo"): "From *childhood*
[My italics – E.C.] I was crazy about Asia" ("S *detstva* [My
italics – E.C.] ia bredil Aziei") (p. 7). The last sentence, as we
have seen – "But I am going to an Asia with which childhood
connects me" ("No edu ia v Aziiu, s kotoroi menia sviazyvaet
detstvo") (p. 9) – ends with the word "childhood" ("detstvo").
Past, present, and future merge into one another, as do imagination and reality.

The beginning of Boris' trip to Central Asia does not, for
Bitov, remain the simple beginning of a trip to Central Asia.
"Three More Beginnings," the third subchapter, focuses on
three different ways of conceiving of the place where Asia begins
– the first, in Moscow, at Kazanskii Railroad Station; the
second, during the train journey; and the third, at his destination point, when Boris gets off the train. Even the first beginning
("For the first time Asia *began* [My italics – E.C.] in Moscow at
Kazanskii Railroad Station" ("V pervyi raz Aziia *nachalas'* [My
italics – E.C.] v Moskve na Kazanskom vokzale") (p. 9)
contains within it additional beginnings – "*At first* [My italics –
E.C.] in the line for tickets. Then on the platform, near the
train" ("*Snachala* [My italics – E.C.] v ocheredi za biletami.
Potom na perrone, u poezda") (p. 9).

Boundaries are the focus of Bitov's attention in another
respect. The boundaries between literature and film dissolve, for

Bitov models "One Country" on a Fellini movie. It is important to realize that Bitov's travelogue is both a part of a rich literary tradition and a work dependent on Fellini's *La Strada*.

Some critics expressed admiration for Bitov's poetic style. V. Ermilov described "One Country" as a lyrical journey in the tradition of Laurence Sterne.[21] A theme common to several appraisals of "One Country" is its formal similarity to Soviet "Young Prose" ("molodaia proza") writings of the 1950s and 1960s. Aksenov's technique of "chopped up prose" ("rublenaia proza") is mentioned in this regard, as are the similar features of his American models J. D. Salinger and Ernest Hemingway. Bitov's explorations of an individual's internal world, the capturing of people's natural speech patterns, and the self-ironic wit, critics trace back to these "Young Prose" characteristics.[22]

Soviet critics Lev Anninskii and V. A. Apukhtina write about the mosaic-like structure of Bitov's prose. Apukhtina regards this as reminiscent of Aksenov's works, while Anninskii traces the practice to prose of the 1920s, in particular to Dos Passos, with the insertion of pieces of nonfiction into the fictional work.[23] The influence of Soviet prose of the 1920s, in the form of ornamental prose and of the 1920s "chopped up prose," is also discussed in analyses of Bitov's "One Country."[24] A Czech article on Bitov considers that his prose is strongly reminiscent of the 1920s, in its fragmented, mosaic construction, its collage effects, and its cinematic montage-like features.[25]

The statements tracing Bitov's roots to Soviet literature of the 1920s and post-Stalin "Young Prose" of the 1950s are valid. However, we must recall that Bitov had spoken of his indebtedness to *La Strada* for giving him the idea that ". . . a contemporary reflection of contemporary life" was possible.[26]

An examination of *La Strada* reveals that the structure of "One Country" coincides with that of Fellini's masterpiece. The Italian film, whose English title is "The Road," is a travelogue of sorts, a number of scenes held together only by the presence of the two main characters, Zampano, the thick-skinned roving circus performer, and Gelsomina, his pure-hearted assistant. Each episode, only vaguely related to other episodes,[27] fits into the overall framework of the journey along the road.

Fellini uses the journey motif as a backdrop against which to show aspects of the human condition. He depicts the clash between good (Gelsomina) and evil (Zampano). He conveys a philosophy of the dignity of human life and, indeed, of all of existence. One character, the Fool (Il Matto), tells Gelsomina that everything in the world, even a stone, serves a purpose. If anything is useless, he continues, then everything is.

The audience catches glimpses of the villages, countryside, and ocean as Zampano and Gelsomina travel from one place to another. We are given flashes of seemingly disconnected scenes – a lone horse wandering through the streets as a forlorn Gelsomina waits for Zampano; an ant crawling on Gelsomina's hand; a boisterous wedding; Zampano's theft of silver hearts from a convent; a murder; the circus.

The journey ends, as it had begun, near the ocean. The place is the same. The acquaintance with Gelsomina has affected Zampano. In certain ways, he is not the same person that he had been at the commencement of his journey with her. By the end of the film, we feel that we have examined deep issues of what it is to be human. Fellini accomplishes his ends by linking together realistic pieces of the everyday life of Zampano and Gelsomina; scenes of nature; philosophical passages; the repetition of a lyrical musical refrain; the viewing of the world through the eyes of the child-like Gelsomina.

The evidence – Bitov's statement about the significance of this film in pushing him toward a writing career; the journey motif; the open-ended form; the descriptions of life along the road; and the inclusion of grander statements about values – argues, it seems to me, for considering *La Strada* as a model for "One Country."

Bitov has spoken of the importance of the oeuvre of Pushkin and Lermontov for him.[28] An imprint of their journey literature is faintly visible in Bitov's novella, although the imprint is not as strong as is Fellini's. "One Country" shares features with another fictional "travelogue," Lermontov's *A Hero of Our Time*, where an account of a journey does not depend on the chronology of its parts. The time sequence is scrambled, as Vladimir Nabokov's introduction to an English translation forewarns us.[29] The tone of Pechorin's journal is often ironic. The chief purpose of the "travel notes"[30] is not to reveal new information about the places visited. As students of Russian literature know, a standard interpretation of *A Hero of Our Time* is that the journey is primarily through the nooks and crannies of Pechorin's psyche. The discoveries are insights into the protagonist's personality. Bitov's travelogue, also fictional, shows us some of the sights along the way, but it, too, has, as its main purpose, a discussion of something other than geography. By the end of the trip, the reader has gained more knowledge about the philosophical rather than the psychological realm of life.

"One Country" shares less common ground with Pushkin's *Journey to Arzrum* (*Puteshestvie v Arzrum*) than with Lermontov's novel. Bitov's descriptive style is reminiscent, in several passages, of Pushkin's clarity and simplicity of language in descriptions of nature, his "stylistic neutrality," in Iurii Tynianov's words.[31] The playful irony of Pushkin's tone is also present in Bitov's work.

In "One Country," Bitov wrote a work reverberating to other works of art. That fact does not detract from the distinctiveness of his own literary voice. As Iurii Trifonov wrote, "... he knows how to see in his own way. In him, imitation, ... so characteristic of many young people [writers – E.C.], does not make itself felt."[32]

THE STORIES

The nine stories that follow "One Country" in *The Big Balloon* develop major themes that the opening travelogue highlights. The emphasis upon a person of his own generation, be it child, adolescent, or young adult, preoccupies Bitov, as do values and boundaries.

"Grandmother's Uzbek Cup"

"Grandmother's Uzbek Cup" ("Babushkina piala"), the first story, was written in 1958, the year, it will be recalled, when Bitov began writing prose. It is his earliest work to appear in a collection of his writings. The author's inexperience shows. The story seems immature, tentative, and experimental, as if Bitov were searching for, but not yet finding, his own literary voice.[33] The Bitov signature is there – the intertwining of past and present; the linking, by the end, of seemingly disparate incidents; a description of his experiences in Uzbekistan; a first-person narrative; a youthful protagonist.

Bitov combines (1) a description of events and objects in the physical world with (2) an account of memories triggered by seeing one of those objects with (3) ruminations on memory, the nature of the present, the aging of older generations of one's family, and the particular material objects that carry people's experiences. Bitov describes a day in the life of Alesha. As workers install new pipes in the apartment of Alesha's family, their everyday routine is disrupted. Life's usual rhythm is also broken by clearing out an oak wardrobe that had belonged to Alesha's deceased grandmother. An object that comes to light in the process is his grandmother's Uzbek cup. He had first seen the cup, as a five-year-old, during his stay with his grandmother in Tashkent during World War II. The reader is transported to Alesha's childhood perceptions of her and of the cup. After the flashback, Alesha visits his girlfriend. In Alesha's brief absence, his father falls ill.

On one level, "Grandmother's Uzbek Cup" is the straightforward rendering of the events of Alesha's day. On another, it is a philosophical discourse on the relationship between objects and people, between present time and other time. Special objects and events of the physical world acquire meaning only when human consciousness assigns a significance to them. Seeing the object later causes the person with whom it is associated to be remembered and to live again in the present.

By seeing his grandmother's Uzbek cup, Alesha relives his past experience of his grandmother. He is the child, bedazzled, after wartime food shortages, by the magic of sugar in Tashkent. He is the young Alesha, captivated by the design on the Uzbek cup: pairs of strange little hedgehogs with red tummies and green backs standing on their back paws.

The cup, Alesha observes, is the same, down to the same dark crack that he remembers from childhood. But time makes a difference. His grandmother has been dead for three years. And when Alesha carefully examines the Uzbek cup, he discovers that the design has nothing to do with hedgehogs. It is, rather, "... some Asiatic flower or fruit, drooping on a stalk ... Unintelligible and quite tastelessly painted."[34] The creative powers of the child's imagination are gone. Red-tummied little hedgehogs have, through an adult's perception, become ugly, cheap flowers, whose identification in Latin and whose growing patterns the grown-up Alesha discovers in encyclopedias and atlases. Aging makes a difference, in one's perception and in one's life. Past reality and one's present view of the past are very different.

Alesha tells us that his father had once painted and papered the rooms where the pipes were now being changed. The illness and aging of Alesha's father are surely associated, in Bitov's mind, with Alesha's grandmother's death. This hypothesis is supported by the message of the epigraph to the *Big Balloon* version and to the version of "Grandmother's Uzbek Cup" which appeared in *We Are Young* (*My − Molodye*), a 1969 anthology of young Soviet writers: "Towards evening I was sitting in the room without light/And I suddenly look:/Father and mother/Are coming out of the wall,/Leaning on canes."[35]

Before his father becomes ill, Alesha does not attach significance to his father's painting of the new pipes. These painted pipes are part of the present. In the future the pipes will remind Alesha of his father, just as the Uzbek cup now reminds him of his grandmother. By the end of the story, Bitov interweaves two layers of memories, for Alesha's memory of his grandmother becomes intertwined with his future memory of his father's illness and the freshly painted pipes. The present is the present – the ongoing narration of the day's little events. The present also contains the past, in the form of objects whose existence triggers one's consciousness to remember. The present also contains the future's past, which is the present. Seemingly insignificant separate episodes of a mundane nature, when tied together by memory and consciousness, acquire significance and lose their quality of separateness. Alesha's father's illness assumes a new shape – the shape of possible death – in the reader's mind because that incident in the story has been shaped by Alesha's memory of his dead grandmother. And his memory was, in turn, shaped by the discovery of the Uzbek cup. The boundaries melt between past, present, and future.

"A NOTHING"

In "A Nothing" ("Fig"), a story written in 1959, a year after "Grandmother's Uzbek Cup," child perception is Bitov's central focus.[36] The protagonist is again called Alesha. "A Nothing" is a vignette about young Alesha's afternoon as he does, or rather, does not do, his homework. Alesha's emotional state and imagination are traced in his interactions with his mother, with "uncle," and with the family cat.

We see the child's heightened awareness of the sounds, smells, tastes, sights, and textures of the world. We read, for example, "If you chew on the shaving [from sharpening a pencil – E.C.] – such a fresh taste . . ."[37] We see Alesha's attempts to catch the cat, whose previous experience with the little boy one can easily surmise from the cat's hissing and hiding. We follow him as he opens the garbage chute and listens, then waits for the echo from the phrase he has directed into the chute: the famous proverb, "Learning is light, and ignorance is darkness" (p. 118). We hear, with him, the garbage chute's murmured reply, the rustle of the pencil shavings as they go down the chute, and the clatter, as it quickly goes down the chute, of a knob Alesha had, minutes before, knocked off a sideboard in his relentless pursuit of the cat.

Then Alesha thinks, "If I'd throw away the cat down there, . . . That would really be a symphony!" (p. 118). He later hears the music notes "do," "re," "mi," and "fa" issue from the razor he is sticking into an edge of the table at which he is supposed to be doing his homework. The narrator writes, "He couldn't get 'sol' at all" (p. 119).

In his story, Bitov does not offer an idealized picture of a child's behavior. Alesha bangs on the sideboard to get the cat to come out from under it. He calls it a "worthless beast" and "repulsive animal." He lies to his mother.

For the literary scholar, the importance of "A Nothing" lies in its rendering of a child's sensibility and its introduction to a character who will play a significant role in *Pushkin House*. "Uncle" has many features in common with that novel's "Uncle Dickens" ("diadia Dikkens").[38] Both swear and return home smelling of liquor. Both live in the same house as the protagonist's family. Both write. Both are linked to the protagonist's grandfather. (In "A Nothing," "uncle" is writing a book about Alesha's grandfather and is working on the section having to do with the grandfather's attitude toward the revolution.) Both lend their "nephews" books.

In *Pushkin House* the character of "Uncle Dickens" becomes a part of Bitov's larger discussion of fathers and sons, Russian culture, and Russian literature. In Bitov's early story, "uncle" figures exclusively as an older person who treats the child affectionately.

"A Nothing" spotlights the child's reactions to life. The next story in *The Big Balloon* emphasizes a youthful protagonist's reactions to life and extends still further Bitov's interest in the question of boundaries.

"THE SUN"

"The Sun" ("Solntse")[39] has gone largely unnoticed in the critical literature about Bitov. The only scholars to praise the story have been Wolf Schmid, Stephen Hagen, and Kurt Shaw. Schmid treats the story as part of Bitov's travel literature, for the main protagonist, walking through a city on a sunny day, sees everything from his individual perspective. Schmid compares Bitov's dissection of actions into their constituent parts to Iurii Olesha's documentation of the process of an action. The "defamiliarization" effects of light and shadow in Bitov and in Olesha interest Schmid. Hagen emphasizes the lyrical elements in the story. He speaks about the sun's symbolizing the essence of life. He alludes to cinematic devices in the story and to Bitov's experimentation in theme and style. Like Schmid, Hagen remarks on the similarity of Bitov's "Sun" to Olesha's prose. Shaw analyzes the main character's psychological isolation from reality.[40]

The plot of "The Sun" is simple. One sunny morning, Vitia

Tamoikin, an institute student, gets up. He has many things to do, gets distracted by random scenes of everyday life that he observes on his way to class, thinks about what he has to do, and decides not to do those things. The narrative tone is a matter-of-fact. The sentences are often short, sometimes with only a noun and a verb. Some paragraphs contain one word. The narrator's and Vitia's voices are indistinguishable.

The first few paragraphs are filled with descriptions of objects, often reduced to simple geometric shapes. Bitov writes,

Four golden rectangles extended from the window to the bed . . .
  The sun.
  On the blue screen [as in television or movie screen – E.C.][41] of the window a gray sparrow appeared and enthusiastically began to twirl its head. A tall factory smokestack – permanent scenery – was a cheerful brick color. (p. 124)

We then read about Vitia's body describing an arc as he sits down on the bed and lets his feet land in a golden rectangle. His toes, we read, leave ". . . dark hyphens on the dusty floor" (p. 125). Outside, the air jumps, workers seated in a row on a log sunning themselves are compared to sparrows on a branch. A board being lifted on a hoist is said to look down at everything from above. One paragraph reads, "A balcony" (p. 125).

Often the images link inanimate objects and natural phenomena to the human world of people and feelings. The four golden rectangles of the sun are inside a person's room. A window pane and frame against the sky become a television screen on which a bird performs. A shoe wants to hide. In part of the description of a construction site, the sentence, "The hoist was standing" ("Lebedka stoiala") (p. 125), refers to a machine, but the word "lebedka" also means female swan. A burner licks the asphalt with a pale tongue. A board looks. Workers on a log are sparrows on a branch. The sun beating against the glass of a bus window is compared to a big, warm bird and is said to pulsate like a heart.

Bitov's technique of frequent word repetition links parts of the story that would not otherwise be connected in the reader's mind. The repetition bridges different realms of life, as did the comparisons of human and nonhuman qualities. The hoist, three bystanders, people, a worker, and Vitia are, at different times, described as standing. Vitia's toes create a new pattern, the dark hyphens, on the already dusty floor; pieces of plaster from a house under repair are reduced to dust as they hit the asphalt below. The air jumps, as do Vitia's things to do. Man-made plaster and nature-made snow fall down. A woman has a pale face, and a burner at a construction site has a pale tongue (flame).

Intricate patterns emerge as Bitov weaves interconnecting threads of images. Bird imagery is an example of such patterns. The second paragraph of the story is one word, "The sun" (p. 124). In the third sentence, the reader is introduced to a gray sparrow, seen in nature (against the sky), through the window (the boundary between the human being's home and a bird's habitat). These distinctions collapse, for the sky and window are metaphorically dubbed a television screen on which the sparrow appears. A few paragraphs later comes the scene where people (the workers sunning themselves on a log) are seen as sparrows on a branch. Still later the sun beating against the bus window is likened to a big, warm bird. The next sentence states that it (the sun) was throbbing like a heart. The very next paragraph is, "The sun" (p. 128).

The sun, human beings, and birds are common to all three passages. Each of these repeated clusters brings into the picture new images, some of which forge new links to other parts of the story. The sun was described as a warm bird. Bitov's only other use of the word warm had been in speaking of the warm air which jumped. And the only use of the word jump had been in reference to Vitia's things to do, which jumped.

The sparrow was gray. Gray is used only one other time, to describe the lumps of snow which were flying. A form of the verb to fly had been used once before, to describe the sparrow's departure. The word lumps is used once more, in the final sentence, to refer to "lumps of houses" which are swimming and soaring in the air because of the omnipresent sun. Everything is connected to everything. Repeated words set up associations of images, and these new associations create their own reverberations rippling through the story.

Why Bitov would resort to such intricate word patterns will

become clear when we examine the significance of one of the key passages of "The Sun." As Vitia is on his way to the institute, he observes a group of people who, in turn, are looking at something. The narrator writes, "A crosswalk for pedestrians was being created. People, from among the pedestrians, were standing and looking at how it was being created" (p. 126). Workers were affixing ". . . wide sparkling knobs." In each new knob a new sun was catching fire" ("V kazhdoi novoi knopke zagoralos' novoe solntse") (p. 126).[42]

Upon reflection, we see that the grand pattern of "The Sun" shines through. The story is about life's creative processes, about creation, about destruction, about life in movement. The same seeing consciousness of the human being (Vitia, the narrator, Bitov) creating/destroying his life/work/things to do is no different from the acts of the workers who destroy parts of the building being repaired, or the workers who create knobs in which new suns shine, or from the movement of the sun that creates golden rectangles, or of the setting sun that is pierced by the point of a prospect going off into the distance. The sun, life, the life-giving force, is everywhere. The penultimate sentence of the story reads, "The sun was in front and, at the same time, on all sides" (p. 129).

The workers were creating a crosswalk for pedestrians, a "transitional road" ("perekhodnaia dorozhka") for people to cross from one side of the street to the other, and people were watching the process of the road's being created. Through the workers' work, new suns caught fire in the knobs, the products of their work. In the same way, Bitov, the writer, is a worker, the creator of a crosswalk, a "transitional road," a work of art, for people to cross from one realm of life, the everyday world, to another, the world of the imagination; and the people (we readers) watch the process of the road's being created. Through Bitov's work, a new sun, "The Sun," caught fire in the product of his work, the written page.

Realms of life merge into one another as we follow the creative and destructive processes of Vitia's seeing and thinking, of people's actions, and of the sun's presence. At the beginning of the story, in the morning, Vitia mentally breaks up his day into hours and into the things he has to do. He has created a pattern. On the balcony of a house under construction, a worker with a sledge hammer destroys a pattern, as pieces of plaster fall onto the asphalt and dissipate into dust. As Vitia observes the worker on the balcony of a house under construction, he waits, hoping to see the balcony fall and wondering what the worker will do. In the same sentence in which the narrator informs us that the balcony held up, we read that Vitia's things to do ". . . crowded into a shapeless heap . . ." (p. 126). Vitia's imagination had destroyed the balcony. The balcony, in real life, retains its shape, but Vitia's things to do lose their shape. Vitia then watches another set of workers constructing the crosswalk. A few paragraphs later, Vitia "built" (p. 126) his things to do ". . . like knobs" (p. 126). Vitia's being distracted by a woman who gets on the bus on which he is riding destroys the sequence of his things to do that he has built. He again begins, mentally, to put them in order. They jump, thereby destroying the order. Two pages go by before Vitia even thinks about his things to do, and then he does not even attempt to create a pattern for them. He just remembers that he has things to do. The next reference to them is only a reference. The things to do never get done. One destructive process in life, the destruction of potential, has been documented here. What has also been registered is the ongoing process, or movement of life, even if, in this instance, the movement was toward destruction.

We have ample opportunity to watch the creative process at work. The sun assumes many different shapes – the four golden rectangles; new suns in the crosswalk; dry sunny asphalt winding itself around the wheels of the bus; a pulsating heart; a big, warm bird. It, of course, destroys, too, blinding the narrator's eyes; causing a worker to assume the shape of a black shadow; making a flame grow pale. Whether destructive or creative, the forces described are those of the movement of life, which, of course, includes both forces. In the same way, the same Vitia who destroyed his things to do created the dark hyphens on the sunny dust, created the "crosswalk" from his consciousness to people's activities to nature's world. Some workers reduced part of a balcony to dust. Others created the crosswalk of new suns.

We the readers have traversed a path, our own crosswalk, from simple geometric shapes to repeated words to a merging of the human and nonhuman worlds. Everything merges into everything else. At the beginning of the story, the sun enters the man-made room through its own "crosswalk," the window. At the end, the setting sun is pierced by a man-made object, an avenue. Chunks of houses (which contain rooms) are flying in the air. We have witnessed one day in the life of the sun and one day in the life of Vitia's consciousness. Objects are torn down and built up, they disperse and come together, they decompose and fuse. The creative process in the artist, in the worker, and in the nonhuman world of nature produces the same patterns.

"A FOREIGN LANGUAGE"

The short story, "A Foreign Language" ("Inostrannyi iazyk"), 1959, centers on a young man on the last late-night train into Leningrad. The protagonist's thoughts merge with the narrator's voice and with sounds from the environment – the rhythm of the train's wheels and the sound of his feet hitting the ground as he runs to catch the train.

He had given an English lesson to a young woman to whom he was attracted. She had just rejected his advances. He now stares at the only other passenger in the train car. He shows an interest in her, and she looks the other way. When she initiates a conversation, his interest in her wanes. Ironically, she, too, studies English.

By the end of the train ride, and of the story, Genka decides not to pursue the nice woman. He wishes that he had offered to walk her home. He mentally replays the scene, adding a different ending. He had missed his opportunity. Genka mentally repeats the phrase, "Nature abhors a vacuum."[43] He is left with a vacuum by his refusal to respond to someone kind. He creates the difficulties/vacuum of communication in a "foreign language" when he speaks one "foreign language" to a woman who does not wish to communicate in the same "language" as he, and when he fails to communicate in the same "language" as his sympathetic fellow train-passenger.

The appeal to the senses, the creation of a desolate atmosphere, the focus on missed signals between people, the capturing of a moment in mid air, the emphasis upon the ordinary rather than upon the melodramatic – these elements in "A Foreign Language" suggest Chekhovian or Kazakovian resonances in the story.

There are also familiar Bitov traits. The author is concerned with what a moment is. We see a moment collapse into nothingness, a vacuum. The author again uses the technique of a character's mentally going through an action and then physically acting in another way. In "One Country," Boris imagines himself leaving a place where he feels unwanted. He keeps staying, though. In "The Sun," Vitia imagines following a young woman, but he remains seated on the bus. The theme of potential other moments instead of that moment which has transpired will continue to preoccupy Bitov. In *Pushkin House* he will return to the issue of the boundary of a moment. *Pushkin House* will also return to another theme in "A Foreign Language," that of unrequited love.

"MY WIFE IS NOT AT HOME"

"My Wife Is Not At Home" ("Zheny net doma"), 1960, rehearses the missed signals between man and wife. The story is told from the point of view of the nameless husband who, one evening, is waiting for his actress wife to return home from her film-shooting session. The husband, like Alesha in "A Nothing," spends his time drifting aimlessly from one activity to another rather than studying. His wife comes home late, and neither one believes the other when the subject of the evening's activities arises.

Most of the story is either the narrator's stream-of-consciousness thoughts or a dialogue between the narrator and others. The style is realist. V. Geideko praises Bitov for describing life as it is without condemnation or defense of the protagonist. Geideko presents Bitov's philosophy: ". . . It's my business to show, but why [I show – E.C.] what, you figure out for yourselves . . ."[44]

The story is a Bitov excursion into a young man's psychology, but it adds nothing new to the annals of Russian-Soviet literature. Its roots are fixed in "Young Prose" writings of the 1950s and 1960s with their cynical young urban protagonists and their explorations into psychology. The nonjudgmental presentation of human behavior is reminiscent of Chekhov's.

Of significance to Bitov research is the function of "My Wife Is Not At Home" and "A Foreign Language" as a creative workshop for *Pushkin House*. A man–woman relationship based on lack of trust will form the core of Leva's and Faina's "love."

"A TERRIBLE FORCE"

"A Terrible Force" ("Strashnaia sila"), 1961, is a first-person narrative, starring an adolescent, Vitia, a student spending four months away from home on a work expedition. Bitov's focus is a realistic rendering of a young man's interactions with people. In this story, he pays attention to the nastier sides of human nature, as people torment the nonconformist.

The character Bitov describes, the outsider, is an example of the superfluous men inhabiting the world of Russian literature since the days of Chatsky, Onegin, and Pechorin. It was often the case, in nineteenth- and twentieth-century portrayals of superfluous men, that the authors implicitly condemned their nonconformist protagonists.[45] Pushkin's "Gypsies" ("Tsygany"), for example, tells the story of the outsider, Aleko, who cannot adapt to the gypsies' peaceful customs. It is he who is at fault (Pushkin even has him commit a murder). The group of gypsies is shown to be good. "A Terrible Force" reverses the assignment of guilt. The outsider, Vitia, is blameless for not submitting to the collective mentality. The collective is wrong for hounding the nonconformist.

Bitov reverses the pattern of many Socialist Realist novels where the collective is praised and the individual condemned. In an early model for Socialist Realism, Gladkov's *Cement* (*Tsement*), 1925, Gleb Chumalov assumes greater stature as he sheds his individuality and merges with the collective. Fellow-traveler literature of the 1920s defended the nonconformist individual as opposed to the group-minded person, but the dominant pattern of the Stalin era was that literary characters who join the collective are heroes and those who exhibit individuality are villains. During the Thaw period of the 1950s and 1960s following Stalin's death in 1953, authors were finally permitted to write about the positive characteristics of individuality. "A Terrible Force" is an example of the new emphasis upon the individual.

As Vitia travels to his destination, he takes mental notes on the landscape: "The terrain was bare, stony, and there were not any beautiful things at all."[46] The rest of the paragraph sounds a thematic chord that is repeated as the action unfolds: a person's idealized version of reality – of natural surroundings, animals, and people – is drastically at odds with reality.

The dichotomy between what is imagined and what is real surfaces as Vitia thinks about and then, in reality, associates with, his new fellow workers. "After all, there really are no bad people, I reasoned ... This was my own idea, and I was happy with it" (p. 151). His experience belies these thoughts.

Vitia is persecuted for being a student and is ostracized by his new companions for associating with Iura, whose work abilities the group envies. The pack mentality is vicious in its techniques for torturing people who are different from the pack. When Vitia walks into the club to join a game of billiards, silence descends upon the group. In another scene, Kolia, one of the group, explains to Vitia that Iura is persecuted because "he's not a collective person ..." (p. 165). When Vitia, a new person, arrived, the collective had to test him. Kolia comments, "The collective is a ter-r-rible force ..." (p. 165).

Bitov introduces an episode in the animal world to parallel the human traits he catalogues. Vitia describes four dogs that associate with his fellow workers. Their personalities are described in human terms. One night, three of the dogs tear a stray dog to pieces. Dogs, it turns out, are just as cruel as people in their attacks on those who are not in their group.[47]

"THE DOOR"

"The Door" ("Dver'"), 1960, is a psychological study of a nameless boy with a crush on an adult woman. She had agreed to meet him, but did not show up at the appointed time. Waiting in a hallway from evening until mid-morning the next day, he believes he will intercept her as she goes to a friend's apartment. The door to that apartment is the door after which the story is named. The boy vacillates between the expectation that she will appear at any moment and the certainty that she is in the apartment. At 4 a.m., a man emerges from the apartment, and the boy is convinced that she had let him out.

At approximately 10 a.m., when the woman leaves the apartment, the boy says that he knows she had stayed there all night. She offers her own version of the events: she had stayed at her girlfriend's apartment, the man was the friend's brother, and that very night he had gone off on a trip.

At first the boy does not believe the woman's explanation. As he walks home on a foggy day, he concludes that the woman must have been right. He mentally castigates himself: "And I'm a swine. I am to blame with respect to everyone ... A swine."[48] Critic V. Geideko argues that the boy was incorrect in his assessment of events.[49] In contrast, O. H. Bakich writes, "It is obvious that she is deceiving him but he would rather believe her than face reality."[50] Bakich's approach to "The Door" is compatible with a frequent Bitov theme. The main protagonist idealizes people. Their true natures do not match his dream-spun versions; their cruelty disillusions the protagonist.

Bakich's argument is bolstered by evidence from "The Door." Although the story is open-ended – the author does not bluntly state that the woman was lying – Bitov's imagery and tone point us toward concluding that the boy's initial reactions were correct. First of all, Bitov keeps emphasizing the boy's heightened powers of observation. He is sensitive to and aware of his surroundings: the sounds of door latches being fastened for the night; the crack on the wall that resembles an ox; the felt-strip on the door; and so on.[51]

Secondly, it seems to be no accident that the description of a foggy day immediately follows the woman's version of the night's events and immediately precedes the boy's acceptance of her explanation. Blurring the outlines of physical reality parallels the boy's psychic fogginess, caused by the woman's lies. Her

lies confuse the boy, just as the foggy day makes everything seem
dim. The boy then doubts his own perceptions of reality,
exonerating the woman of blame, and instead, taking upon
himself the role of wrongdoer.[52] Thirdly, the tone of the boy's
final thoughts – that everything *must* have been as the woman
had described it – sounds as if he is trying to convince himself
that she is right.

In "The Door," Bitov demonstrates the human psyche at
work. He presents the boy's incipient sexual awakening, as he
stands on one side of the door; the woman, on the other. He
shows the boy's Oedipal desire for a mother figure. The author
maps out the process by which children, faced with authority
figures' lies, believe those authority figures. Children learn to
deny the truth in order to keep authorities on their pedestals.
The adult/parent figures are necessary to a child's survival.
Therefore, in the child's psyche, they are right, and the child,
wrong. The result is, as with the boy in "The Door," that
children psychically damage themselves. They needlessly
assume a burden of guilt. They deny and repress the truth.[53]

In this reading of the story, the image of the door is the defense
mechanism the boy builds in order to shield himself from the
truth.[54] At one point, he wants to "... rush to the door, to burst
in – in order to see."[55] He does not. He does not want to know
because, unconsciously, he already knows the cruel truth.

In "One Country" and in "The Sun," Bitov showed the
processes of the dissolution of boundaries. In "The Door," he
plots the process of the construction of barriers.

"THE JUBILEE"

In "The Jubilee" ("Iubilei"), 1960, Bitov's protagonist is
elderly. Seventy-one-year-old writer Boris Karlovich Vagin
lives a dual existence, a solitary external life of physical decline
and a rich internal life of imaginative flights into childhood.
Bitov captures the elderly person's proclivity to live in the past.
Lying awake at night, Boris Karlovich observes the same
reflection on the ceiling as he had seen in childhood. He
transports himself to his past and to his mother's caresses.

Defensive in his behavior toward adults, he finds solace in observing children in a playground. He identifies with small children. The boundaries between childhood and old age dissolve – in his mind alone, for he cannot become a child again.

"The Jubilee" begs for comparison with another story of old age, Chekhov's "A Boring Story (From the Notes of an Old Man)" ("Skuchnaia istoriia [iz zapisok starogo cheloveka]"). Neither Chekhov nor Bitov had reached the age of thirty (Chekhov was twenty-nine; Bitov, twenty-three) when they wrote about old men. Both stories concern intellectuals – Chekhov's Nikolai Stepanovich is a professor; Bitov's Boris Karlovich, a writer. Both characters are acutely aware of their physical deterioration – Nikolai Stepanovich, when he compares his present bumbling lecturing style to his past energized style; Boris Karlovich, when he stoops down, with difficulty, to retrieve his hat. Both protagonists, near the beginning of the story, lie awake at night. Both characters dip into their past. Both are dissatisfied with the adults with whom they come into contact.

Typical of Chekhov characters, Nikolai Stepanovich cannot transcend his isolation even when another person, Katia, reaches out to him. Nothing provides solace for Nikolai Stepanovich in his loneliness. Bitov's elderly man is isolated from other adults, but he finds comfort. His imagination and his ability to merge with the world of childhood save him. In reality, he is isolated, even from children. During the scene at the playground, he is the observer. When anyone intrudes upon his privacy, he feels disturbed. The point is that he treasures the privacy which allows him to go off into his own imaginative world. Nikolai Stepanovich had rejected any possibility of transcending his isolation. Boris Karlovich transcends his isolation by retreating further into himself. He derives pleasure from his ventures into dreams.

Boundaries, borders, and barriers continue to figure prominently in *The Big Balloon*. In "The Jubilee," Bitov demonstrates that a person can dissolve boundaries in one facet of his life and can, simultaneously – in fact, by that very act – build barriers in another.[56]

"THE BIG BALLOON"

In "The Big Balloon" ("Bol'shoi shar"), 1961, the last story in the collection of that name, readers come full circle from the beginning of the journey through that collection. The same themes dominate. As in "One Country," "The Big Balloon" centers on the experiences of someone of Bitov's generation. (In making the major protagonist a girl, Bitov is, perhaps, alluding to the universality of childhood experience. Thus, there is a dissolution of boundaries between one gender and another.) Boundaries melt between the material and the spiritual worlds, as Bitov examines the spiritual values that infuse the small girl's experiences on earth. Knowledge of film, as in "One Country," enhances our understanding of Bitov's writings.

"The Big Balloon" is a short story that recounts the adventures of Tonia in her quest for ". . . the biggest, reddest, roundest [balloon – E.C.] in the world – the one with the little golden ship on the top."[57]

From the first, Bitov contrasts earthly reality and an otherworldly dimension of life. Within the opening paragraphs, we read, "The window gave out onto the courtyard, and it was gray and empty there. Higher up was the blue, blue sky" (p. 197). Throughout the story, the realm of the "gray and empty" is symbolically juxtaposed to that of the "blue, blue." And throughout the story, Tonia attunes herself to the spiritual frequencies of the blue skies above.

The story's plot is simple. Tonia watches, then joins the ranks of a passing holiday demonstration, then leaves the column of demonstrators. She finds herself on an unfamiliar street, sees a woman with a red balloon with a little golden ship on top. She asks where the woman had found the balloon.

With the required information, she sets off to find the street and the house where the balloons are sold. While in line, she discovers that she has no money, runs home to get some, returns, only to discover that there are no more balloons. She waits in front of the closed door of the balloon-vendor's apartment, saying to herself, "it could not be that there was no balloon" (p. 208). Her unwavering faith is rewarded as the vendor opens the door, sees Tonia, and produces a balloon for her. Tonia, cherished balloon in hand, successfully maneuvers her way home, undaunted by the taunts of small boys in her courtyard. When her father arrives home, she tells him the story. The story ends as she asks him where "Notlong Lane" is. He does not know, nor has he ever heard of the street where she had bought the balloon. He asks, "And why do you want to know?" (p. 214). "Tonia looks out the window – and suddenly smiles. At what, she alone knows ..." (p. 214). The closing words which immediately follow are "Ding-dong-dang" (p. 214), the magical musical notes that have accompanied Tonia on her quest for the balloon.

Tonia's search for and acquisition of the balloon reveal a series of miracles, as she focuses on the realm of the heavenly spheres. She hears music coming from within herself, as if a little bell were ringing. When a soldier breaks off from the parade, she follows him onto a half-sunny side street, strange in the stillness and light of its sunny side. The soldier notices that she is following him, laughs, reaches into his pocket, and gives her a spool with thin, silky red thread.

Tonia discovers another street, almost fairytale-like in description: "... to the left was a park behind a beautiful lattice, and to the right, a very long building with white columns, and ahead, a church cupola, and there was not a single demolished building on that street. And not a single person" (p. 201). She thinks that perhaps this city, so sunny, beautiful, and empty is not her city, but a magic city where extraordinary happenings take place. It is at this point that she sees a woman with a child and "higher ... higher ... in the blue sky – an enormous ... red balloon. Ding-dong-dang. Ding-dong-dang ..." (p. 201).

Tonia perceives beauty and steadfastly follows it. She insists upon finding out where the woman got the balloon and does not give her peace until she finds out. This part of the story, too, reads like a tale of miracles. The house where the beautiful balloons can be bought is green. "And in the middle of the courtyard, surrounded by a round railing, big old trees grew in a circle ... And in the very center was a round fountain, and in the center of the fountain was a beautiful white bird." For Tonia, the spiritual dimension lives on earth.

In "The Big Balloon," we see the seeds of what will emerge in full blossom in Bitov's later works. As do so many Russian and Soviet writers, the author includes a past piece of culture in his conception of the present. The cultural string to which "The Big Balloon" is most attached, it seems to me, is Albert Lamorisse's "Le Ballon Rouge" ("The Red Balloon"), a 1956 French movie and book.[58] Bitov claims not to have seen the film or read the book,[59] but there is evidence that the film "The Red Balloon" ("Krasnyi shar") was known in the USSR as early as 1958.[60]

Bitov has written of the importance of film for his development as a writer, as we saw in our discussion of "One Country." References to films (for instance, Hitchcock, St. Matthew Passion, contemporary Georgian films) pepper his texts. In the final analysis, it is not essential to know whether or not Bitov was familiar with Lamorisse's work (although I would be *very* surprised if he were not), or, if so, to know whether or not he was consciously aware of modelling his "Big Balloon" on "Le Ballon Rouge."[61] What is important is that a comparison of the two works highlights Bitov's affirmation of the existence of a spiritual dimension on earth.

The adventures in Bitov's and Lamorisse's balloon creations are set in cities, Paris and, presumably, Leningrad. Both star small, red-haired children. Both children are lonely. Pascal has no brothers or sisters; Tonia's mother has died. Both children are outside when, for the first time, they catch sight of a red balloon. It is through the child's efforts that the balloon comes into his/her possession. Pascal climbs a lamp-post, and Tonia finds the balloon vendor. Both balloons are endowed with magical qualities.

A scene with the red balloon outside the child's window figures prominently in each work. So does a scene where a gang of neighborhood bullies attacks the small, vulnerable protagonist as he/she, accompanied by the balloon, walks home. Pascal and Tonia and their balloon companions escape unharmed. In these ways, the two works are similar.

In other ways, the two works are distinctly different. Lamorisse's protagonist is a boy; Bitov's, a girl. Lamorisse's balloon has human attributes. The emphasis in the French work is upon the development of a friendship between Pascal and the red balloon.

When he first finds his balloon, he refuses to abandon it when a busdriver will not allow the balloon on the bus. The balloon, in return, does not fly away when Pascal's mother releases it out of the window. Lamorisse writes, "But Pascal's balloon stayed outside the window, and the two of them looked at each other through the glass. Pascal was surprised that his balloon hadn't flown away, but not really as surprised as all that. Friends will do all kinds of things for you. If the friend happens to be a balloon, it doesn't fly away."[62] Like a playmate, the balloon teases Pascal. Bitov's balloon does not manifest human attributes. The balloon's magic consists of the ethereal qualities with which Tonia invests the balloon.

In both works, there is a second confrontation scene between the child protagonist and the neighborhood ruffians. In "The Red Balloon," the boys steal the balloon, Pascal recaptures it and attempts to escape. The bullies surround and then attack Pascal. The balloon refuses to abandon its friend even though the nasty gang starts to throw stones at it. One stone hits and bursts the red balloon.

We read, "While Pascal was crying over his dead balloon, the strangest thing happened! Everywhere balloons could be seen flying up into the air and forming a line high into the sky."[63] The book ends with these words, "And all the balloons of Paris came down to Pascal, dancing around him, – twisting their strings into one strong one and lifting him up into the sky. And that was how Pascal took a wonderful trip all around the world."[64]

Bitov's second confrontation scene between Tonia and the nasty neighborhood boys takes place in a dream sequence once she has the balloon safely at home. In her dream, Tonia's deceased mother has sent her a pair of red slacks that do not fit because Tonia has grown since her mother died. Tonia cannot take a step because of some ugly, horrible turkeys. More turkeys approach as she walks along the street. They grab at her red slacks and cluck offensively. Tonia runs, and they chase her. They grab her slacks and painfully pinch her legs. She cannot walk any more quickly, and her slacks fall down (pp. 213–14).

Bitov writes, "And these very turkeys – the very same little boys from her courtyard, the two gypsy women – peck, jump, and burst her biggest and reddest balloon" (p. 214). Tonia shouts, "No! No!" (p. 214), wakes up, and in horror, looks out through the window. Her balloon is still there. It was only a bad dream. Her father is sitting next to her, smiling. The world of magic balloons and music triumphs in Tonia's waking life.

One might argue that both Bitov's and Lamorisse's second confrontation episodes are similar. They both encompass both death and hope. Pascal's balloon dies, yet his new balloon friends comfort him. In the dream, the reader is made aware of the death of Tonia's mother, yet after the nightmare, Tonia's father is there to comfort her. The similarity does not go any further.

Lamorisse's message is not a happy one for earthlings. Non-earthly playfulness and fidelity get one into trouble on earth. Pascal's mother, the busdriver, school officials, the church, as well as the younger generation do not allow the magic red balloon into everyday life. Magic is possible only in other spheres, only when the balloons lift Pascal out of the earthly realm into the sky. This world is cruel.[65]

In Bitov's story, beauty, goodness, and purity, in the form of the "biggest, reddest balloon in the world," are brought into a child's everyday life. From Tonia's dream, we understand that, in her unconscious, the magic balloon is a gift from her dead mother. The reader wonders whether the spirit of Tonia's mother has paid her daughter a visit. The creation of beauty and the spiritual in life is within Tonia's power. She trusts and believes, and we see the result.

The terrestrial sphere includes the celestial sphere. The earthly sphere ("zemnoi shar") is a celestial sphere ("nebesnyi shar"). These spheres, these worlds, represent the realm of Bitov's "big sphere" ("bol'shoi shar"), and, ultimately, of our own.

THE BIG BALLOON – CONCLUSION

Bitov's first volume traces the path of many spheres of life. The earth and the heavens, the circular sun and a round balloon, round-trip journeys, vicious circles of behavior, dream bubbles of children's fantasies and of an old man's past, a realist fragment of everyday life and the creative flight of fantasy of a sensitive individual, intersecting worlds of time and space, past and present, time and memory, reality and dream – these are the spheres which contribute not only to Bitov's creation of one country or of one foreign language or time of life, but to his creation of one big sphere/world ("shar") which encompasses, includes, and reverberates with all the others.

CHAPTER 3

"Such a long childhood": growing pains

The important thing . . . [is – E.C.] your distinctness
from other people . . .
    Andrei Bitov, *Such a Long Childhood (Takoe dolgoe
                                             detstvo)*[1]

. . . Sometimes a special condition visits a person . . . It is
an upward flight, an illumination. It lights up a person
from within . . .
    And suddenly everything opens up . . . The smell of the
forest, the smell of the earth, . . . The grass and the sky.
Their smell. Their taste and their significance . . . The
grass and the sky – an instantaneous world and an
eternal world, an insignificant world and an infinite
world. And the first world is equal to the second
world . . .
    And suddenly it seems that a person's life in this world
can be measured only by such an upward flight. This is
the beginning of everything creative in the world. This is
such an individual and solitary feeling, but it is precisely
this that links us to the world. And this is what makes
one person distinct from another.
    Andrei Bitov, *Such a Long Childhood* (pp. 198–9)

Bitov's introduction to an English translation of Armenian
writer Grant Matevosian's *Bread and Word (Khleb i slovo)* explains
Matevosian's method:

A tremendous number of similitudes [*sic*] exists in this world. A blade of
grass, a tree, night and day, the seasons, the emotions – all these
different things have something in common, and this common denomi-
nator is the basic quality, the law governing each of these various
objects and phenomena, i.e., life itself. Grant Matevosian has the
ability to discern this common heartbeat of all living things. The prose

he brings forth is like life. It is life.... Matevosian's narrative is unhurried. One story follows another, one description follows another, one character follows another, and the logic of the ties between them is not always apparent until the end ... The various chapters ..., which at first seem disconnected, become ever more essential to understanding the story as a whole, for the whole reflects its every part and produces a telescopic effect, so to speak, with one section moving out after another, so that the star you are watching grows ever brighter and larger.[2]

Bitov's remarks about Matevosian's art describe perfectly his own methodology in "One Country" and in *Such a Long Childhood* (*Takoe dolgoe detstvo*). To reproduce the dynamics of life in motion, Bitov places together pieces of life which, at first glance, seem to be disconnected. The process of assimilating experiences and of placing them into some larger context comes only after the "isolated" events have transpired.[3] In "One Country," Bitov followed the process with respect to Boris' discovery of values in the *external* world. In *Such a Long Childhood*, the author follows the process with respect to the main protagonist's discovery of values in his *internal* world.

It makes sense to view "One Country" and *Such a Long Childhood* as companion pieces. Critic Lev Anninskii points out that the two were written simultaneously.[4] "One Country" is a journey that expands Boris' vision to include new perspectives gained from his contact with a strange new place; *Such a Long Childhood* is a journey that deepens Kirill's knowledge of himself as he comes into contact with new people and experiences. "One Country" describes the exotic Central Asian atmosphere in detail. *Such a Long Childhood* describes the backdrop for the action, the exotic polar regions ("68° 37'"),[5] almost not at all.

Instead, it details the main character's separation from childhood. In articles discussing *Such a Long Childhood* – it is one of the Bitov works that has received the most critical attention – the work is characterized as a farewell to childhood,[6] a journey away from childhood,[7] and a journey into oneself.[8]

The process of moving away from one stage of life to another[9] is shown by following the actions, reactions, and thoughts of Kirill Kapustin, whose name, with its combination of Cyril and cabbage, Bitov makes quintessentially Slavic. (Kirill was the name of an inventor of the pre-Cyrillic, or glagolitic alphabet [the oldest Slavic alphabet], as is well known, and "kapusta," of course, is the Russian word for cabbage.) The action begins as Kirill is trying to decide whether or not to accompany his Leningrad schoolmates north to work in the mines for the summer, in spite of the fact that he has just been expelled from the institute. (The work has autobiographical overtones with a situation paralleling Bitov's expulsion from a mining institute.) Several of the novel's opening words, the locomotive's onomatopoeic puffing, "Too-oot-toot! ... To go-o – or-not to go-o-o?" ("Tu-u-tu! ... ekh-khat' – ne ekh-kh-khat'!") (p. 5), refer to Kirill's immediate dilemma and, implicitly, to his internal conflict as he travels away from childhood. To grow or not to grow is the central question of the book. The reader accompanies Kirill on his quest for the answer to that question.

Two brief sections set the stage for the journey. The first is the aforementioned scene of Kirill's indecision. The second is an exchange of letters between Kirill and his parents in which he informs them of his expulsion and his journey and in which they answer. The letters are not reproduced verbatim in the text. Rather, they are filtered through Kirill's consciousness as if he were writing or reading the letters. Of this passage, Deming Brown writes, "Intimacy in third-person narration, no less than first-person, was achieved through interior monologue, constructed so as not only to convey ideas but also to suggest thought processes themselves."[10] The thoughts are those of the fearful child, resolving to go north, more out of a desire to escape his parents' opprobrium for his dismissal from the institute than out of a wish to seek adventure and independence.

Kirill's experiences in the north are documented in the bulk of the book, two large parts entitled "Three Days of an Insecure Person" and "Grass and Sky." The first part is subdivided into sections, "Saturday," "Sunday," and "Monday," which are in turn divided into subsections. Part One deals with several episodes from the early part of Kirill's stay in his new surroundings. He makes friends with Kolia, one of the experienced workers with whom he works in the mine. He attends his first dance. He is betrayed by his best friend Mishka, who steals a young woman away from him, and who later, with no explanation, leads a movement to ostracize Kirill from his friends. He experiences exhilaration and renewal when he jogs to the top of a mountain. He develops a relationship with Valia, a friend of Liusia, who had become Mishka's girlfriend.

Throughout Part One, the delineation of Kirill's experiences is merely an interesting excursion into Soviet youth mores of the late 1950s and early 1960s. We read about the youths' discussions – someone asks Kirill what he thinks about A. J. Cronin, Böll, and Hemingway. We read about the way in which Kirill and his colleagues amuse themselves – by going to the movies and dances, by playing soccer, by getting drunk. The pieces of the three days' events are not given any profound significance.

It is only at the end of Part One that the reader discerns that some maturation has taken place. While Kirill is jogging, he sees Valia, who asks why he had not visited her that day. He lies, saying that he could not. Then, as he runs up the mountain, a group of children asks him from whom he is running away, and he replies, "From myself" (p. 96). The children begin to taunt him. Undeterred, he continues his trek upward. From the summit, he sees that the city has flowed together, and that the lake is a drop ("kaplia") (p. 98). We read, "And beyond those mountains – there are more lakes and more mountains. And all of this – is without end. And on the right – without end. And on the left – without end. And ahead – without end. And behind – without end" (p. 98).

On the way back he cannot find secure footing. He thinks, "'Every lack of equilibrium takes away a lot of energy. The important thing is to maintain one's equilibrium ...'" (p. 99). By persisting in his task of climbing the mountain, reaching its summit, and climbing down again to complete the journey, he feels a sense of strength and renewal. He feels that his body is "well-balanced" ("stroinym") and "his own" ("svoim") (p. 99).

The inner peace and harmony/equilibrium that come from being oneself is what Kirill experiences during his trek to the mountain.[11] That sense is what Kirill learns to look for as he begins, in Part Two, to search for life's meaning rather than to allow himself to be buffeted by events. The description, in Part One, of disjointed events, devoid of deeper philosophical significance, reflects Kirill's immature state of mind as he lives, childlike, from one episode to the next. Part Two of *Such a Long Childhood* reveals the wisdom Kirill begins to acquire as he slowly gains a foothold on the other side of the mountain of childhood.

Indicative of the changes being wrought in Kirill, the titles of the main subsections of Part Two are no longer days – entities through which any nonthinking or thinking person, child or adult, animal or vegetable passes – but are abstract concepts ("Equilibrium," "Events," "Parting," and "Along the Road") from which Bitov's protagonist learns new lessons about life.

He gains further equilibrium after his schoolmates depart for Leningrad and he establishes a closer relationship with Valia. For the first time, he takes the initiative, in suggesting that the two spend a day along the river. He gains stability as he settles into the rhythm of his job and his relationship with Valia. The serious injury of his work companion, Kolia, and Kirill's conversation with him in the hospital trigger his reflections on mortality, values, and the meaning of life.

Kolia tells him that each day in life is long, but that life as a whole goes by in a flash. He states that he has been thinking, during his hospitalization, that people are always discontent. They believe that what is happening now is not real life, that real life will begin tomorrow. Meanwhile, explains Kolia, they exist in a constant state of anticipation and end up not living at all. He continues,

"I suddenly understood that one's circumstances don't matter . . . Life is the same everywhere – so it now seems to me. I did not know a good life, but to recollect now – I had everything: I had love and wine and friends . . . *and* work! And there was freedom and grief . . . There was everything . . . That's what I now think, that to understand this *is* freedom." (p. 171)

The rest of the book consists of Kirill's struggle to attain that freedom. Bitov places Kolia's revelations in the subsection entitled "The Day After Tomorrow," which is followed by

"Tomorrow" and "Today." Kirill's task is to get from tomorrow to today, from dreams of how life might be to the reality of life as it is. The lesson is brought home as he prepares for the final day before his departure as a draftee. He plans what the special last day will be like. Other events intrude. As he goes through the day, he keeps thinking of the way it was supposed to be. The day is, therefore, spoiled for him. At the last minute, the draftees are given a twenty-four-hour reprieve before their departure. This time, Kirill does not waste the precious moments by thinking about what a final day should be. Instead, he lives every minute of it. By the end of the book, Kirill is beginning to understand what it means to live a life with meaning, to live creatively, to find oneself, to be oneself.[12]

In *Such a Long Childhood*, Bitov's focus is on the process of going from one side to the other of the borderline between childhood and adulthood. We witness the expansion of Kirill's consciousness, as he separates himself from one stage of life in order to arrive at the next. He leaves the world of his parents. His schoolmates leave him. He leaves the world of sexual inexperience as he and Valia draw closer to one another. He leaves the familiar world of work and his involvement with Valia as he sets off for life in the military. The question of whether Kirill will continue to grow Bitov leaves unresolved. Earlier on, the narrator had explained that there are stages one must move through in order to become oneself: repeating what one has learned, dissolving and intermingling with others, and then singling oneself out. Many people remain in the second stage, he goes on. It is premature, he says, for us to speculate on whether Kirill will get to the third stage, the stage of individualization described in the passage quoted in the epigraphs to my analysis of *Such a Long Childhood*.

In the final episode, whose title, "Along the Road" ("Po doroge"), recalls "Doroga," ("The Road"), the Russian title of Fellini's *La Strada*, Kirill merges into a column of marching soldiers-to-be. At the beginning of the novel, the locomotive sounded the word "to go" ("ekhat'"). At the novel's end, a column "goes" ("idët"), and Kirill "goes away" ("ukhodit") (p. 205). The closing shot is cinematic, as Kirill's figure in the column becomes smaller and then fades away. He has reached the second stage of blending with others. We, like Kirill, cannot know whether he will continue to grow.

Artistically, *Such a Long Childhood* is less successful than "One Country" and most of the stories in *The Big Balloon*.[13] The philosophical passages (Kolia's discourse on living, Kirill's revelations about self-identity) are powerful, but in other sections, the imagery is heavy-handed. For example, Bitov "happens to" introduce three different scenes in which the word "naked" ("golyi") plays a key role. In the first, as Kirill is exercising, naked, in the dormitory, some children look through the window. He decides not to exercise until the next day. (Later we realize that one of the points of the book is to show Kirill leaving the state of immaturity where one would always post-pone living until the next day.) The next passage in which nudity plays a role involves a letter Mishka writes after his return to Leningrad. In it, he asks Kirill why he thinks that Rodin depicted Hugo in the nude. Mishka's question invites readers to ask why another artist, Bitov, would make Kirill, the person he created, naked. For we read again, in a third scene, during Kirill's induction into the military, that Kirill must appear nude before a series of doctors. In this scene, Kirill keeps looking at himself in mirrors. Kirill sees himself as he is, without hiding behind layers of clothing. Given the broader context of the book, we conclude that it is only when a person dares to look at himself in the stark, naked reality of what he is, that he can begin to disentangle himself from layers of immaturity. The scenes mesh well with the progression of the book, but are too self-consciously rendered.

The introduction of other images is smoother. One example is the word play which evolves naturally out of a conversation Kirill has with Valia. They see a cat, who, they surmise, has become confused by seeing them occupy its usual place on the staircase. Kirill asks Valia how to spell "katavasiia" ("confu-sion"), playing on the word "kot" ("cat"). After more twisting of the syllables, the two conclude that the word is for them. (Bitov's narrator fails to include the slang word "kotovat'": ["to be courting"], yet this word describes their activity, and the word is close to "katavasia" in sound.)

The grass and sky imagery, and the way in which it is woven

into the second part, is beautifully rendered. What Bitov has attempted to do on the pages of *Such a Long Childhood*, to convey the pulls and tugs of Kirill's growing up in a way that would duplicate the pulling and tugging of real-life growth, was a challenging goal. Not every risk into new territory results in the discovery of a new country. However, Bitov should be given credit for setting off into the unknown, for without taking a risk, one will never discover anything new, about countries or about selves.

CHAPTER 4

"Dacha District": automatic-pilot living and creative living

"JOURNEY TO A CHILDHOOD FRIEND"

"Journey to a Childhood Friend (Our Biography)" ("Pute-shestvie k drugu detstva [Nasha biografiia]"), 1963–4, continues Bitov's examination of fresh perspectives as a way to gain greater wisdom about life. It is the second selection in Bitov's 1967 book, *Dacha District. Stories (Dachnaia mestnost'. Povesti).*[1] The first is "One Country." It is easy to understand why the author places "Journey to a Childhood Friend" after "One Country," for both, under the pretext of being travelogues to the eastern regions of the Soviet Union, deliver similar philosophical messages. In "Journey to a Childhood Friend," Bitov implies that the act, in the present, of returning to a person from one's past, is valuable, just as the act of going to distant places had, in "One Country," triggered a re-examination of one's values. In "One Country," Bitov had concluded that by traveling and seeing what we are not, we come to a definition of what we are. The same mechanism is at work in "Journey to a Childhood Friend." Through our evaluation of another person, an evaluation of who we are not, we come to discover the value of who we are.[2]

Bitov's principle of the dissolution of boundaries operates here as boundaries melt between "separate" works of his. "One Country" is a separate work, but it can also be seen, for the reasons elucidated above, as a part of a larger work that includes "Journey to a Childhood Friend." It makes sense to place these two works together with *Such a Long Childhood*, as Bitov did in his 1976 *Seven Journeys*, where *Such a Long Childhood* is the first section; "One Country," the second; and "Journey to a Child-

63

hood Friend," the third. *Such a Long Childhood* demonstrated a character's going forward in time, gaining a new perspective on himself. "Journey to a Childhood Friend" focuses on a character who goes back in time, thereby gaining fresh insights into himself.[3]

In a discussion of "Journey to a Childhood Friend," *Such a Long Childhood* deserves to be kept in mind for another reason as well. Bitov's definition of achieving greater maturity focused on one's capacity to distinguish oneself from others. Bitov discussed distinctiveness as a positive quality. In "Journey to a Childhood Friend," he shows us that the quality is not necessarily a positive one. In a sense, then, "Journey to a Childhood Friend" is a dialogue with and/or continuation of *Such a Long Childhood.*

Having connected Bitov's first three journey works, we must now examine "Journey to a Childhood Friend" on its own terms. This fictional travelogue covers much territory. It is an examination of the narrator's childhood attitudes, as seen by the adult. It is a discourse on the concept of the positive hero. It is an attempt at "documentary prose" and a mockery of that form.[4] It is an analysis of the psychology of the success-driven personality type.

In its simplest form, "Journey to a Childhood Friend" is the first-person tale of an anonymous narrator, on assignment to visit and write about his childhood friend, the successful volcanologist, Genrikh Sh. The journey focuses on the narrator's thoughts as he makes his trek east, waiting in airport lounges; thinking about Genrikh, whom he has not seen in years; reading articles he has collected about Genrikh; and observing the activity in the airport and on the airplane.

The beginning of "Journey to a Childhood Friend" is spiced with humor. The narrator is called into an editorial office and is asked to write something on assignment. He is told, " 'A hot topic like the construction of cow sheds . . . should be of interest to you . . .' "[5] The narrator explains that this topic is far afield from his interests, whereupon another is suggested, the problem of the economy of leather in shoe manufacturing. This, too, the narrator explains, is not within the scope of his expertise. The editors assert that they want to preserve the narrator's "creative individuality" (p. 74). They want him to apply his style to material that is unfamiliar to him.

They ask, "'Does the positive hero and his problem really not excite you?'" (p. 74). The narrator replies that all his heroes are positive. He says, "'People live – and by virtue of that, they are heroes'" (p. 75).[6] The editor asks the narrator to consider writing about a positive hero. The narrator recalls that his childhood friend Genrikh is precisely that type and agrees to write about him.

The passage is humorous, with its ironic reference to the kind of "hot topics of the day" that often filled the pages of Soviet publications about smiling tractor operators and superhuman factory workers. At the same time, Bitov sets the tone for his ironic, skeptical attitude toward the "perfect" positive hero that will prevail in "Journey to a Childhood Friend."[7]

This tone is reinforced by the reader's first glimpses of Genrikh's character. Before introducing Genrikh, the narrator presents hyperbolic newspaper headlines about his activities: "A DWARF BECOMES A GIANT"; "ON THE BRINK OF THE PRECIPICE"; and so forth (p. 77). Soon thereafter an excerpt from an article, "WHO WILL BE CHAMPION?" (pp. 78–9), about Genrikh's athletic prowess, is inserted into the text. Following the hyperbolic terms in which Genrikh is described in a newspaper come the real-life facts in an episode which the narrator recalls about the real-life Genrikh.

After years of not hearing from Genrikh, the narrator suddenly receives a telegram from him. Genrikh wants the narrator, who knows English well, to cheat by taking an English examination in Genrikh's place. The will of the "perfect" positive hero to excel is so strong that he will stop at nothing to achieve his goal. Morality is irrelevant. Luckily, the examiner is the narrator's former English teacher, and the narrator refuses to honor Genrikh's request. Instead, he coaches him and agrees to speak to the teacher about Genrikh's dilemma. In spite of Genrikh's sketchy knowledge of the language, he manages to pass the examination. His competitive nature surfaces, and he tells the narrator that he regrets that he did not receive an "A." This is the reader's introduction to the positive hero, a driven man whose only concern is to win, no matter what.

The next newspaper clipping describes a New Year's mishap when Genrikh was seriously wounded while working in a volcano. The narrator contrasts his own paltry life, recalling that at the time he had been at home, arguing with his wife. Genrikh's courage places the narrator's domestic quarrels and ordinary life into a shadow. However, because of the strategic placement of the cheating episode, the reader is not as impressed by Genrikh's gargantuan achievements of bravery heralded in the newspaper account as he/she might have been without Bitov's clever insertion of the English examination incident.

After a description of another of Genrikh's heroic deeds, the narrator explains that he calls the sections of his narrative dealing with Genrikh's stupendous achievements "GENRIKH'S TWELVE EXPLOITS" (p. 86). He compares Genrikh to Hercules because both performed their first feat at a very young age. By comparing Genrikh to Hercules/Heracles (their names in Russian even sound vaguely alike – "Genrikh" and "Gerakl") and by referring to Genrikh's twelve exploits, the same number of "labors" that Hercules had performed, Bitov casts the positive hero as a superhuman character of legend rather than of life. At the same time, Bitov chips away at this larger-than-life monumental figure by questioning the concept of the positive hero. The personality traits of the likes of Genrikh may constitute the material for legends about a superhuman Hercules, but they are not the stuff out of which sensitive human life is molded.

For example, Genrikh's first exploit took place while he and the narrator were ten-year-olds at the same pioneer camp. Genrikh, of course, always won the sports competitions. One day, there was a contest to see how many times the children could lift a crowbar. Most stopped before the count of thirty-seven. The narrator felt that he had won when he reached one hundred fifty times. Suddenly Genrikh stepped forward to say that he would lift it one thousand and one times. Straining himself beyond his capacity of physical endurance (he becomes ill after the contest), Genrikh reaches the designated number of times. He must win, even if, in the process, he causes himself physical harm.

The perfect movie hero, positive hero, and legendary mythical hero, Genrikh keeps performing superhuman feats and, as a result, getting broken bones, concussions, loss of blood – and rave reviews in the press.

The narrator deals with his past feelings of inadequacy when, for example, Genrikh had been captain and hero of the soccer team and the object of admiration of the young women in whom the narrator had been interested. The narrator admits that he had always been jealous of Genrikh. One section of "Journey to a Childhood Friend" is called "My Jealousy" (pp. 100–5).

As he relives his past, the narrator realizes that the qualities he had once envied in Genrikh, he no longer envies. In a passage significant for understanding the truth about Genrikh, the narrator writes,

And even when he [Genrikh – E.C.] had already, ages and ages ago, proved to others and when he had no rivals and when there could be no rivals, he would feel the constant need to try to prove, by now only to himself, by now almost abstractly, so to speak, out of a love of the art. And it now begins to appear as if he, more than anyone, was unsure of himself and weak; otherwise, why keep trying to prove one's strength so uninterruptedly and endlessly? (p. 87.)

It later occurs to Bitov's narrator that maybe he, and not Genrikh, is the victor. Genrikh's goal had always been to win for the sake of victory whereas the narrator had always set concrete goals for himself. It occurs to him that in the final analysis, the so-called strong Genrikh is weak whereas he, the so-called indecisive one, is strong.[8] He did not cheat; he did not push himself beyond his physical limits; he did not attempt the daredevil acts which repeatedly landed Genrikh in the hospital. In reassessing his past attitude toward Genrikh, the narrator discovers his own value.[9] He comes to believe what he had told the editor – that people are heroes in that they live. The view recalls Tolstoy's philosophy of history in *War and Peace*. The true heroes are not the heroes of history like Napoleon, but the nonheroes, the ordinary people living out their lives. For both Tolstoy and

Bitov, when one consciously strives to be a hero (Andrei Bolkonsky and Genrikh), this is not true heroism.

Bitov struggles with the question of what is real and what is not. In a seemingly unrelated section of "Journey to a Childhood Friend," "The Time in Flight," as an apparent diversion from the analysis of Genrikh, the narrator relates his observations of the stewardesses on the airplane. While preparing the flight snack, they are standing behind a partition that does not reach the floor. The narrator watches their legs. It seems to him that he is in a puppet theatre, watching the action on a stage with a curtain. Another "troupe" makes its appearance when the airplane stops in Omsk, and new feet act in the play. As they leave to make room for the third shift, the narrator wishes that they, like actors, would disappear rather than be observed as they disembark from the airplane. In that way, declares the narrator, he would be able to preserve the illusion that one gets in the theatre, that actors are special people.

The light-hearted scene is a comic interlude. It is more than that, too, for it brings us back to the question of mythmaking which has been occupying Bitov in "Journey to a Childhood Friend." The twelve stewardesses – Bitov's selection of this number links them to the number of Genrikh's twelve heroic deeds – become special creatures, actresses in a play, only when the narrator designates them as special people. In the same way, Genrikh becomes a larger-than-life Hercules figure only when the narrator, the newspapers, whoever, make him into one. When the narrator stops making life into theatre, when he sees the reality of Genrikh's character, he understands himself, too.

The narrator's relationship to Genrikh and his final evaluation of his positive-hero friend are more complicated than a purely negative approach would suggest. The narrator also admires the famous volcanologist. He declares that Genrikh accomplishes amazing feats in that he risks his life each time he descends into a volcano's crater.

By the conclusion of the narrator's ruminations, he discovers that in certain ways, he and Genrikh are friends. They have lived through the same experiences. They are of the same generation. They have shared the same time span, an important characteristic which neither later nor earlier generations can boast. Whether or not the shared time was spent pleasurably – and the narrator's memories of Genrikh consisted of his envy of him and his own feelings of incompetence – the fact of their common past establishes a bond.

"Journey to a Childhood Friend" ends as Bitov's narrator reaches his destination and is reunited with Genrikh. He gives him letters and gifts from home, and Genrikh, in turn, asks how the narrator's parents are. Genrikh's and the narrator's shared journey through childhood in Leningrad cements the friendship.

The conclusion is an interesting one, and it can be interpreted on more than one level. O. H. Bakich remarks that positive heroes such as Genrikh were "... childhood model[s – E.C.] to the generation portrayed in Bitov's works. They read about such heroes in books, discussed them at school meetings, and watched films about them."[10] The narrator's return to the positive hero of his past can signify his return to the Stalin-era models of positive heroes in life and in literature.

Bitov implies that the narrator, by delving into his past, can accept it and can grow from the experience. He sees Genrikh in a new light and can be at peace with his past. They lived through the past together, and the past is part of the narrator, no matter what his attitude, then and now, is toward it. Bitov takes these implications much further in *Pushkin House*, where he declares that it is wrong to deny a piece of the past to anyone. The parents of the main protagonist, Leva, live in hypocrisy as they hide the truth, the fact that Leva's grandfather is not dead, but has been serving out a sentence in Stalin's concentration camps. After Stalin's death, Leva's grandfather is embittered because the act of rehabilitation has denied the existence of the thirty years of his life that he had spent imprisoned in Siberia. On a larger plane, the implication is that it is necessary to admit that the Stalin era, no matter how horrible it was, did exist. It is healthy, says Bitov, to accept the past rather than to attempt to deny it.

The montage of newspaper excerpts and wanderings of the narrator's mind, the mosaic of psychological portrait[11] and philosophical essay, the trip far to the east and deep into the past map the circuitous route through Bitov's "Journey to a Child-hood Friend." T. Khmel'nitskaia, in an essay on contemporary Soviet literature, calls this work a "story-meditation."[12] In his "semiphilosophical, semiessay 'autopsychological'"[13] works, she writes, Bitov "... pointedly raises the question ... of the multi-layered, heterogeneous nature ..."[14] of man. As we have seen, Bitov seeks truth and reality beyond the facades, beyond the borders of literary conventions, and beyond the present into the past.

"THE GARDEN"

Bitov's 1962–3 "long short story," "The Garden" ("Sad"), again highlights the problem of the incompatibility of truth with an idealized version of reality. This time, Bitov attacks the issue from the perspective of an amorous relationship. Aleksei, the main character, wishes to hold onto his idealized picture of Asya, the woman he loves, in spite of the ugly truths which distort that picture. In "Journey to a Childhood Friend," Bitov had studied the consequences of the narrator's decision to face reality. In "The Garden," he analyzes a young man's refusal to confront the truth.

Aleksei is fond of Asya, who is separated from her husband. He knows, on an almost conscious level, that she deceives him, yet he pushes that information away from his consciousness. She tells him that she had bumped into her husband, that they fell asleep together, but that nothing else had happened. Aleksei vaguely senses that she is lying, but does not insist upon getting at the truth. She wheedles money out of Aleksei for a New Year's celebration and then sends him home early. He feels that she has arranged for a later party with her friends, but without him. Aleksei keeps ignoring his doubts about Asya's fidelity and integrity.

Aleksei is not a positive hero. The first few paragraphs of "The Garden" introduce the themes of betrayal and lies which will play a significant role in the story. Aleksei, at home awaiting a telephone call from Asya, deceives his mother, who does not like Asya. He pretends to have a telephone conversation with a male friend about electromagnetic fields, solenoides, and somisoids because he knows his mother is pleased with such serious conversations. In fact, there is no one at the other end of the line; Aleksei just needs an excuse to hang around the telephone in anticipation of Asya's call. Asya, instead of asking to speak to Aleksei, has her husband make the telephone call so that Aleksei's mother will not know that Aleksei is talking to Asya.

The fabric of the story continues to be woven by lies. When his mother walks into his room, Aleksei hides the cribnotes he is writing for an examination. He cheats on his examinations. He steals bonds from his aunt – immediately after which he eats some tasty pâté that she has made – and then cashes in the bonds in order to pay for his and Asya's New Year's celebration.

Only gradually does the point of the story become clear. During one episode, Aleksei is in bed, reading Herman Melville's *Moby Dick*. Bitov quotes a passage[15] whose gist is that one cannot know what warmth is without experiencing cold, that is, not-warmth. Aleksei reads, in Russian translation, Melville's words, "'... truly to enjoy bodily warmth, some small part of you must be cold, for there is no quality in this world that is not what it is merely by contrast. Nothing exists in itself.'"[16] He then opens his bedroom window and climbs under the blanket in order to experience warmth. The scene is light-hearted. His mother asks him why he is lying in the cold, and he, in response, quotes Melville, "'The one warm spark in the heart of an arctic crystal ...'" ("'Edinstvennaia teplaia iskorka v serdtse arkticheskogo kristalla ...'").[17]

The passage is much more than a peripheral comedy scene. Melville's words provide the key to understanding "The Garden," a key that will later open the reader's door to comprehension. By experiencing not-love, Aleksei also experiences the category of love, which cannot be known without its contrast, not-love. The concept of something equals, for Bitov, its being *not* its opposite.

We, together with Aleksei, learn of the significance of the *Moby Dick* excerpt in the final pages of "The Garden." Aleksei's parents have discovered that he had stolen his aunt's bonds. His mother scolds him. After Aleksei confesses to his aunt that he had robbed her, he goes into his room. He vaguely remembers that a book he has not read for nine or ten years would, he believes, be appropriate now. He finds the book, dust-covered and hidden, on his bookshelves. The book, which Bitov does not identify, is tattered, and some of its pages are missing. Nevertheless, in it, Aleksei discovers thoughts that apply to his current situation.

The "strange author"[18] views jealousy as the opposite of love. He explains that when he is jealous, he does not dare ask questions because he does not want to know the truth. Aleksei feels that his relationship with Asya replicates the author's description. Aleksei knows that he had not dared to ask questions, for fear of learning the truth. He knows that had he done so, nothing would have remained of his relationship with Asya. Aleksei continues reading. The strange author states that each person is a bundle of opposites: he/she is loved by someone and loves someone, is great in one person's eyes and insignificant in another's, lies to someone and tells the truth to someone else.

The strange author ends with questions and statements about the nature of love. He asks whether love comes from the person who loves, or from the person who is loved, or whether it originates elsewhere. He declares that once one has loved, one becomes less of what one was without love. Suddenly there is a passage about a beautiful garden, but sections of this passage are missing from the book. Aleksei does not quite grasp the meaning of what he has read. He skips a part about God, but is haunted by the question of the origin of love. He ponders that thought.

The thoughts in the strange author's book are incomplete. There are, on Aleksei's and the reader's part, glimpses of clarity and clouds of confusion. Since pages of the strange author's book have been ripped out, the thoughts are not in logical sequence. Aleksei seems to fit together the pages which follow one another in his reading only because the pages in between are missing.

What is Bitov trying to say in "The Garden?" Why link the Aleksei/Asya line of narrative, the Melville excerpt, and the strange author's disconnected thoughts? Bitov's point is that Aleksei is learning about love through its opposite, jealousy. In a state of unlove or untruth, he can experience love, since things cannot exist without reference to their opposites. Bitov describes

Aleksei's process of discovery of truth through lies; of love, through unlove; and of religious faith,[19] through unbelief. The discovery, for Aleksei, comes in fits and starts. He has not found a direct path to truth, yet the values of love, truth, and faith are securely in place within Aleksei's being.

Bitov emphasizes both the incomplete state of Aleksei's growth and his underlying solid values by means of the structure he imposes upon "The Garden." Unbeknownst to Aleksei, he unconsciously repeats lines from the strange author's book even before he decides to reread it. In an earlier part of "The Garden," he had been in a beautiful garden and had been overwhelmed by the experience. It is to be recalled that the strange author speaks about a beautiful garden.

The process of Aleksei's discoveries is similar to his process of reading the book with the missing pages. Some insights are clear, some are not, and some he knows on an intuitive level without consciously understanding them. By the end of "The Garden," Aleksei has not resolved his problems, nor has he eliminated the character traits which produce his lying. His experiences, his reading, and his contemplation of the origin of love contribute to his becoming a wiser person capable of understanding the deep significance of contrasting philosophical and emotional concepts.

Some critics have spoken of Bitov's main protagonists' resemblance to one another. Priscilla Meyer explains that the book, *The Days of Man (Dni cheloveka)*, a 1976 collection of Bitov stories which includes "The Door" and "The Garden," "... chronicles the development of Aleksei Monakhov (monakh in Russian means 'monk,' and the name suggests a special sort of isolation) and of Bitov himself. . . . The subject of the book is the growth of Monakhov's self-awareness ..."[20] Meyer speaks here[21] and elsewhere of the strong autobiographical flavor of Bitov's works.[22] For example, Bitov's aunt's desk from his Leningrad apartment plays a role in "The Garden."[23]

In his afterword to *The Days of Man*, V. Gusev comments, in another context, that Bitov keeps returning to the same kind of hero.[24] V. Oskotskii sees "The Garden" and two later stories, "The Image" ("Obraz," also know as "The Third Story"

["Tretii rasskaz"]) and "Vanishing Monakhov" ("Uletaiushchii Monakhov"), also known as "The Forest" ("Les"), as a
trilogy.[25]

Adol'f Urban notes the similarity of Bitov's heroes and the
repetition of situations in his works.[26] For example, the protagonists of "Journey to a Childhood Friend" and "The Garden"
share the same favorite song from childhood, "When I Served as
a Mail Coachman" ("Kogda ia na pochte sluzhil iam-
shchikom").[27] Urban finds the repetitions tedious.[28] There is, to
be sure, a familiarity about many Bitov protagonists. Their
names, thoughts, reactions, and the situations in which they find
themselves repeat themselves. The device, I believe, is not a
defect. Instead, the method is at the heart of the innovative
nature of Bitov's prose. Let me illustrate.

Aleksei, in "The Garden," unconsciously relives the scattered
portions of the book he had read a decade before. In certain
ways, the story "The Garden" "relives" scattered portions of
other Bitov works.

"One Country" includes the thought, repeated in "The
Garden," that a person can contain only one instance of any
category of things (country, love of one other individual and so
on) in oneself. When one thing is there, another is not. One
learns about what one is from discovering what one is not. This
idea, developed with respect to one's culture in "One Country,"
is applied to the psychological and personal realm in "The
Garden."

In "Grandmother's Uzbek Cup," something reminds Alesha
(the diminutive of Aleksei), of the past. In "The Garden,"
Aleksei's aunt's desk opens his consciousness to the past, just as
Alesha's grandmother's dresser had done in the earlier story.
Another Alesha, in "A Nothing," hides something from his
mother as he is studying. The scene is virtually duplicated in
"The Garden."

"The Sun" concentrates on life's destructive and creative
forces. In "The Garden," we witness the opposing negative and
positive emotional forces of "not-love" and "love," "cold" and
"warmth." In like fashion, in "A Foreign Language," we read
about the negative and positive potential of a moment. Bitov

concentrates, as he does in "The Garden" (albeit with different emphasis), on the expanding and contracting qualities of life, specifically, in "A Foreign Language," of a moment.

"My Wife Is Not At Home" resembles "The Garden" in its focus on lack of trust in a love relationship. "A Terrible Force" stars a protagonist who, like Aleksei in "The Garden," places people on a pedestal. As in "The Garden," the author points to human cruelty and to the difference between what one longs to believe and what is true.

As in "The Garden," the main protagonist of "The Door" wishes to believe lies rather than to admit the truth to himself; and as in "The Garden," the hero sometimes tunes out rather than facing reality. He exists as in a fog, and when he chooses to deny reality, he lets his imagination create fish out of people. In "The Garden," as Aleksei's parents upbraid him for stealing, he mentally transforms the television in the room into an aquarium and the people on TV, into men-fish. The room is cast in a strange greenish, aquatic color. Aleksei, thus, distances himself from the truth.

The elderly writer in "The Jubilee" is transported to childhood as he lies in his bed and, in the room familiar to him since childhood, free associates. This Proustian device of eliciting distant memories from a familiar object is present, as we have seen, in "Grandmother's Uzbek Cup." Bitov's use of a *room*, known since childhood, which calls forth bygone days, is repeated in "The Garden." Aleksei sees a room in his family's apartment with the eyes of a seven-year-old child. The child's irrational faith in the existence of good, so central to "The Big Balloon," is reproduced in "The Garden," in Aleksei's steadfast, illogical belief in love.

Scattered threads of every Bitov work preceding "The Garden" are woven into its text. But it is *Such a Long Childhood* that has the most in common with "The Garden." Both works describe a youth's maturing. Both include the discovery of betrayal as a step in the growth process. Both emphasize the passage of time. Part One of *Such a Long Childhood* has chapters called "Saturday," "Sunday," and "Monday." "The Garden" is divided into sections entitled "On December 29th," "On

December 30th," "On December 31st," "On January 1st," and "On January 2nd." Both works include a scene in nature which serves as an epiphany in the character's life. The grass and sky trigger the awakening in *Such a Long Childhood*. A snow-covered garden and the sky (plus the description of a garden in the "strange author's book") lead Aleksei, in "The Garden," to contemplate universal values.

Bitov plants hidden or not so hidden pieces of his previous works in "The Garden." In like fashion, Aleksei replays, on an unconscious level, thoughts and episodes from the book he had read a decade before. Upon rereading the "strange author," Aleksei discovers new insights into life. Bitov, like Aleksei, returns to the same point, but that point, spiral-like, is different each time one returns to it – because of the movement of everchanging, evolving life.

"LIFE IN WINDY WEATHER"

In "Notes from around the Corner" ("Zapiski iz-za ugla"), the linked variant to the story "Life in Windy Weather" ("Zhizn' v vetrenuiu pogodu"), Bitov writes, "... the lulling of the consciousness, ... the substitution of reflex for consciousness, ... so very characteristic of our times – all this has been a theme of mine for a long time ..."[29] "Life in Windy Weather" explores the process, in life and literature, of escape from ossified forms of existence and art. Bitov plots the path toward creative living and creative writing. For him, one cannot divide the creative process in life from the creative process in literature.

In its barest outline form, "Life in Windy Weather" concerns a writer, Sergei,[30] who, with his wife and infant son, has arrived at the family dacha. He has escaped the bustle of the city and expects to settle down to work in the peaceful countryside. He is restless and craves the empty clutter of his city life. He goes to the city for a day, knowing that he is wasting time. By the end of the story, Sergei finds, in the "dacha district," tranquility, satisfaction in work, and purposefulness in life. He discovers spiritual harmony. He discerns the meaning and value of his life. The process comes about in a series of epiphanies in which Sergei discovers his bond with nature, his son, his father, his wife, his work, and the universe.

"Notes from around the Corner," as Priscilla Meyer comments, is a companion piece to "Life in Windy Weather," providing the alleged diary entries of the author Bitov as he is working on "Life in Windy Weather."[31] Meyer writes, "By pairing the two . . ., ["Life" and "Notes" – E.C.] Bitov sets up a series of oppositions which are complementary: while the first text moves toward life and affirmation, the second dwells on death and despair."[32] In "Notes," Bitov speaks of death as the end of man's cycle (from birth to death) and of nature's (from spring to winter). The dates of the "Notes" entries correspond to the movement toward death in nature, for the first entry is dated June 18th and the last, October 27th.

"Life in Windy Weather" is one of the Bitov works that has received the most critical attention. In a 1973 interview, Vasilii Aksenov spoke of Bitov as one of the most interesting contemporary Soviet authors and "Life in Windy Weather" as one of his "most interesting works."[33] Deming Brown calls the work ". . . the most mature and generally the finest story of Bitov to date . . ."[34] Brown writes that the story can be read on many levels, as the account of a young urban man experiencing an identity crisis, as a work on the psychology of creativity, as a story about the issue of aesthetics, as a contribution to the literature of the isolation of the artist.[35]

Indeed, the critical literature contains a variety of approaches to the story. Several critics emphasize Bitov's concern with values. Lev Anninskii speaks of Sergei's spiritual emptiness.[36] Viacheslav Ivashchenko writes that "Life in Windy Weather" teaches us values. We learn to appreciate the good in ourselves and in others, and we learn to appreciate these values in the present moment.[37] V. Kamianov highlights Bitov's careful monitoring of Sergei's spiritual state.[38]

Other critics single out Bitov's introspective protagonist. Anatolii Bocharov describes the recurring circles of self-analysis through which Bitov's heroes pass.[39] Adol'f Urban emphasizes Sergei's psychological revelations and his propensity to self-analysis.[40] Vsevolod Sakharov finds self-analysis to be at the heart of Bitov's story, but in contrast to other critics' enthusiasm for the story, his conclusion is that this characteristic results in a static, lifeless quality.[41] While focusing, like Sakharov, on the lack of action in "Life in Windy Weather," A. A. Terpelova, declaring that the story is one of Bitov's best, praises the author for his descriptions of Sergei's soul-searching attempts to find himself.[42] Quoting Bitov's words in "Notes from around the Corner," George Gibian is astute in pointing the reader in the direction of one of Bitov's key issues connected with his in-depth analysis of character, the issue of the deadening of one's reflexes.[43] Igor' Zolotusskii focuses on the interplay between the protagonist's inner world and the world of the external.[44]

In coming to grips with "Life in Windy Weather," I shall turn to the interpretations of the four scholars who have written the most extensively on the story. Wolf Schmid, declaring it to be one of Bitov's best works,[45] considers it a travelogue of sorts, a journey of self-discovery. Bitov, according to Schmid, describes the process by which Sergei, his consciousness freed from habit, perceives the world anew. Schmid equates the wind with Sergei's change in consciousness. The wind cleanses the air and allows for clear perception just as Sergei's consciousness, cleansed of busywork, apprehends the world in a fresh way.[46] In the calm of the country, Sergei learns to look at the world through his child's eyes. With his new eyes/perception, cleansed of habit, Sergei finds harmony in the world of nature, family, and friends.[47] Schmid's emphasis is on Sergei's journey toward the development of heightened powers of consciousness that enable him to see the harmony around him. Near the end of his essay, the German scholar links Sergei's heightened aesthetic powers of observation to his maturing. Schmid speaks of the ethical effect of Sergei's new defamiliarized world. Without the fetters of habit, Sergei, with his new vision, can respond to life in ways that are not mechanized reflexes.[48] For Schmid, then, the journey traced by Bitov leads from a defamiliarized aesthetic vision to an ethical one.

Priscilla Meyer's interpretation of "Life in Windy Weather" and of "Notes from around the Corner" focuses on literary creativity. For her, Bitov's concern is with the nature of literary truth.[49] The wind image, for her, represents creative inspiration.[50] The wind episodes "... map a progression containing the crucial components of creativity: the artist; his images; the joy of intensified vision; his battles internal and external; synthesis in epiphany; and the creative distance to explicate this synthesis."[51] Priscilla Meyer sees as key to the story Sergei's brief discourse on new literary forms. To write creatively, he says, one must free oneself from formalism (forms, preconceived arbitrary conventions) and through formlessness, through the newness of open spaces, the writer will "... come closer to the living truth ..."[52] and therefore be able to create something new. Priscilla Meyer links Sergei's discussion of literary open spaces and creativity to the new vision/epiphany Sergei experiences when he is in the open spaces of a field with his son.[53] For Meyer, "Life in Windy Weather" plots the process of achieving the aesthetic ideal, from the disconnected, fragmentary images of raw experience, through the refracted lens of the artist who is true to his own aesthetic vision and experience.

"Notes from around the Corner," according to Priscilla Meyer, shows the author's so-called journal notes, thus providing a different reading of the same raw materials of life. The truth of the experiences, according to Meyer, differs from the fictionalized version in "Life in Windy Weather." In the fictionalized version, a rainstorm results in Sergei's heightened awareness of individual leaves, and the leaf imagery is connected to artistic inspiration and to his renewed tender feelings toward his wife.[54] In the real-life version, "Notes from around the Corner," raindrops on the leaves cause the author to respond automatically with a reflex action and are therefore part of the movement toward death that he describes.[55] Meyer writes that the two sections of "Dacha District" present a "... cycle of life and death, of artistic and divine creation, and their complementary truths merge in religious love."[56] The emphasis for Meyer has been on literary creativity, but she alludes, in the passage just quoted, to the connection Bitov makes between creativity and the religious impulse.

Ronald Meyer speaks of the theme of the continuity of generations (Sergei's father, Sergei, and Sergei's son) in the story. His essay, like Priscilla Meyer's, highlights the creative process of the writer, as described by Bitov in "Life in Windy Weather" and "Notes from around the Corner."[57] Ronald Meyer, like Priscilla Meyer, links the wind metaphor to artistic creativity. For him, each wind episode pushes the writer further along toward the heightened perception Sergei deems necessary for writing.[58]

While Priscilla Meyer and Wolf Schmid briefly touch upon the spiritual dimension of "Life in Windy Weather," Stephen Hagen makes it the centerpiece of his discussion of the story, which he calls the most significant mid-1960s Bitov story.[59] He draws parallels between Sergei's steps toward "cosmic consciousness" and features of Zen Buddhism. Hagen declares that he is the first critic to discern the similarity between the perspective of Bitov's writings and that of Zen Buddhist thought.[60]

In Hagen's reading, the wind, seen as a force of life[61] shaking Sergei loose from his mechanized response to life, enables Sergei to come to a deeper understanding of himself and of his place in the world and in the universe.[62] The act of being liberated from routine in life is connected to Sergei's ideas about being free from conventional forms in literature in order to be closer to life and truth.[63] For Hagen, a central message of the story is the importance of being truly alive rather than of living a deadened life of mechanized reflex.[64] Hagen declares that Sergei's journey toward vitality parallels Zen Buddhist ideas. Hagen does not claim that Bitov is a Buddhist. He acknowledges that although Bitov was aware of Buddhist ideas, and therefore, perhaps unconsciously,[65] infused the story with them, the author was concerned with "self-realization" ("samoosoznanie"),[66] with self-realization through self-perception.[67] Hagen shows the way in which Zen Buddhist ideas duplicate Sergei's discoveries about life. Sergei's discoveries come, not through intellect, but through intuition. He transcends a sense of time and space and attains a new state of consciousness. This, according to Hagen, is like the Zen concept of "satori" in which a sense of time and space dissolves, revealing a higher state of consciousness.[68] For Bitov, people usually exist in a state of not being fully awake to life.

Hagen points out that the Buddhist concept of "Avidya" ("ignorance")[69] describes the "fetters" one places on oneself in order to hide from oneself the true nature of life and conscious-ness.[70] Sergei, for Hagen, moves toward self-enlightenment, just as Buddhist doctrine traces a path away from "Avidya" toward greater knowledge of self and the universe, toward spirituality.

In his mystical view of life, which Hagen likens to Buddhist expanded consciousness, Sergei experiences a oneness with the universe, with other people, and with nature. Hagen connects Sergei's epiphany, Buddhist doctrine, and the transcendental spheres of life described by Proust.[71] For Hagen, then, the metaphysical, spiritual dimensions of Bitov's "Life in Windy Weather" are paramount.

How are we to reconcile the interpretations of Schmid, Meyer, Meyer, and Hagen? Which is the correct approach to Bitov's "Life in Windy Weather," one that spotlights fresh, individual perception, one that underscores literary creativity, or one that focuses on spirituality?

Each of these approaches is correct. Each scholar examines a vibrant quality that motivates Bitov's story. These approaches are not mutually exclusive. After all, Schmid and Priscilla Meyer conclude their essays by affixing their interpretations to the larger moral framework constructed by Bitov, and Hagen, in the course of his comments, connects the spiritual dimension of Bitov's story to the aesthetic process of literature described by Sergei in his search for truth.

During one of his epiphanies, as he is taking a walk with his son, Sergei feels, for one instant, an utter harmony, an "acciden-tal symmetry" ("... simmetriia ... sluchainaia ...")[72] in which everything – his son with his outstretched hand, a cow, a train, the meadow, a little boy on the meadow – "... everything ... as if on one axis, coinciding with his glance and with the wind, everything was united by the cupola of the sky" (p. 214). It is possible, it seems to me, to connect Hagen's, Schmid's, Meyer's, and Meyer's interpretations and, as Bitov's protagonist does, to find harmony in the "accidental symmetry" of disparate pheno-mena of life.

It seems to me that Bitov, in "Life in Windy Weather," is

capturing the creative process of life, which includes both life
and art, which includes perception and the creative process of
literature and the process of metaphysical awakening to a higher
dimension of reality. The process is the same, in life, art, and
religion. Bitov shows the way in which the destructive and
constructive aspects of life are inextricably bound with one
another. Sergei's restlessness, his escape to "unproductive" city
life, his not-working are necessary for working. Bitov demonstrates that the cycle of creativity (in literature, human life, and
nature) includes the fallow and the blossoming times. Note, for
instance, that after Sergei's intense experience of harmony in the
accidental symmetry scene, he speaks of his sense of "devastation" (p. 214). Throughout the story, Bitov refers both to
sensations of emptiness and to bursts of joy.

For Bitov, being in balance, in harmony – which means
accepting the city and the country, the wind and the calm, the
rain and the sun, the role of father and that of son, the periods of
lack of artistic productivity and of productivity, death and life –
happens, but only if life is accepted in its totality. Accidental
symmetry comes only by looking beyond the narrow forms of
convention, in life and in art. Sergei attained it only by living
beyond the confines of the city and becoming "... master of his
own personal transportation ..." (p. 190) rather than being
connected to the rhythm of other people's transportation in the
city. One must become free in order to make connections with
the essential ingredients of life, or, rather, one must allow oneself
to be free in order to enable the connections, the accidental
symmetries, to be made. Bitov states elsewhere how important
the creation of the process of life is to him in his literary works.[73]
The entire story, it seems to me, is about the process of getting to
the deepest essential truths of creativity in the domains of life,
art, and spirituality.

This is demonstrated from the beginning of the story. The title
is "*Life* in *Windy* Weather." It focuses, therefore, on life, and it
focuses on life at moments – its windy episodes – when life is in
motion. The first words of the story emphasize movement:
"Finally they *moved*" ("Nakonets oni *pereekhali*") [my emphasis –
E.C.] (p. 189). Furthermore, Bitov keeps repeating verbs of

motion and verbs with the prefix "trans-" ("pere-"), as if, in his use of verbal prefixes, to encourage motion, moving, transition. The last words of the story also emphasize life in its moving, changing aspects: "... after all, no one knows what turns life will take" ("... ved' zhizn' neizvestno kak eshche mozhet povernut'-sia") (p. 222).

The wind image can be seen as central to the story's focus on the creative aspects of life. Hagen, as we recall, had spoken of the wind image as a life-force, and Priscilla Meyer had spoken of it as a metaphor for artistic inspiration.[74] We can look at it as the equivalent of *breath*, breathing life into everything. As in the Latin, both the English and the Russian words for breath, inspiring ("v*dokh*," "v*dykh*at'/v*dokh*nut'"), are etymologically related to artistic inspiration ("vdokhnovenie") and to the religious spirit ("dukh"). Bitov, in speaking of creativity, deals with the necessity of breathing (of the necessity of the wind) rather than stagnating in frozen, conventional forms of life, art, and spirituality. For Bitov, all aspects of being alive, all aspects of creativity – in living, art, and spirituality – are intertwined.

At the beginning of "Life in Windy Weather," Sergei sits down in his study on the second floor of his dacha.[75] He does not feel like working. Suddenly a wind and rain storm begins. The wind shakes his study, and he feels that he is on a boat. He thinks that his second floor is flying. The rafters and columns become, for Sergei, masts, the strings of a musical instrument, a ship, an organ. The narrator describes the "ribs" of the house. Suddenly the wind dies down. "Sergei lifted his head and it was as if he had seen for the first time that there was no ceiling over him – right away there was the roof" (p. 191). The roof assumes the shape of a cathedral for him, and this merges with the idea of an organ. Gazing at some jars which had caught the raindrops, Sergei feels a sense of permanency and of stability. He goes outside and sees that each leaf seems more separate than before the rain and that bending and straightening out, as if coming to life, the leaf sheds an enormous drop of water, as if it were discarding a heavy burden, and it *breathes* with joy (p. 192).

The wind has stirred up Sergei, the study, and the leaves. It has shaken up life, just as moving from the city to the country stirred up Sergei's life patterns. After the turmoil, peace and calm descend upon Sergei and upon nature (the leaf). Sergei has noticed that there is no ceiling between him and the roof. This impulse, the figurative ability to notice that there is no ceiling between himself and the roof, later enables him to see the world through the eyes of his baby son. This impulse enables Sergei to unleash the creative images that come to him in the storm. This impulse enables Sergei to conjure up the "accidental symmetry" of the artistic images of cathedral, organ, ship, and strings. This impulse of removing the forms and boundaries enables Sergei to see beyond the awkward form of his father's conversation and to apprehend the substance, which is his father's love for Sergei. Personal serenity, a sensitivity to the calm in nature, and increased powers of artistic creativity are merged in this initial scene describing the wind.

The images which come to Sergei in this scene and in the later scene of accidental symmetry have significant subtexts from literature and from the Bible. (Priscilla Meyer has established that oblique references to literature are a part of Bitov's method in "Life in Windy Weather." Meyer unearths a hidden reference to Pushkin's *Eugene Onegin* [*Evgenii Onegin*] in an episode in which Sergei is playing with a toy gun. She points out a similar reference in a similar scene near the beginning of *Pushkin House*.)[76]

It seems to me that a Pasternak poem called "The Wind" ("Veter"), appropriately enough, has left its imprint on the wind passage in "Life in Windy Weather" which is described in the paragraphs above. The relevant lines of the poem (one of the poems at the end of *Doctor Zhivago* [*Doktor Zhivago*]) are:

And the wind, crying and complaining,/Is rocking house and forest, straining/Not every pine tree, singly bending,/But all the trees together, one/With unlimited space extending./They rock like hulls of sailboats on/A harbor's mirrored surface

(I veter, zhaluias' i placha,/Raskachivaet les i dachu./Ne kazhduiu sosnu otdel'no,/A polnost'iu vse dereva/So vseiu dal'iu bespredel'noi,/Kak parusnikov kuzova/Na gladi bukhty korabel'noi).[77]

Bitov's and Pasternak's images of the wind, the shaking up of the dacha and the forest, the merging of all the trees, the use of the word ship as part of the scene, all coincide.

The same image cluster marks Pasternak's poem and Bitov's wind episode. Moreover, many of the same words are used: "veter" ("wind"); "dereva" ("trees") [Pasternak]/"derev'ia" ("trees")[Bitov]; "les" ("forest"); "otdel'no" ("separately") [Pasternak explains that the wind rocks all the trees not individually, separately]/"otdel'nyi" ("separate, individual") [Bitov speaks of each leaf's being more separate after the wind has ceased]; "raskachivaet" ("rocks") [Pasternak]/"pokachivaetsia" ("is rocked slightly")[Bitov]; "parusnik" ("sailing vessel") [Pasternak]/"parusnyi korabl'" ("sailing ship")[Bitov]; "korabel'noi" ("ship" – adjective) [Pasternak]/"korabl'" ("ship" – noun)[Bitov]. In the Pasternak poem, the "wind" ("veter") rocks the "dacha" ("dacha"), and curiously enough, the subtitle of Bitov's story "Life in *Windy* Weather" ("Zhizn' v *vetrenuiu* pogodu") is "*Dacha* District" ("*Dachnaia* mestnost'") [Emphasis mine – E.C.].[78]

That Bitov was familiar with the Pasternak poem "The Wind" becomes clear when we read Bitov's later story "The Taste" ("Vkus") (1966, 1976, 1979). In that story, where Pasternak's death and a visit to the poet's grave are central to the plot, the main protagonist quotes several lines from the poem, including the lines referring to the wind, the dacha, the pine, and the trees.[79] The next line in "The Taste" includes the narrator's statement, "Everything was especially *windless* and silent" ("Bylo osobenno bezvetrenno i tikho") [Emphasis mine – E.C.].[80] Ronald Meyer identifies the source of the quoted poetry in "The Taste" as Pasternak's "The Wind" (no mention of poet or title of the quoted lines appears in "The Taste").[81] Meyer explains that a consideration of Pasternak's *Doctor Zhivago* – in which, we will recall, the poem appears – is crucial to an understanding of "The Taste," for both contain the themes of life and death, artistic immortality and resurrection.[82]

The same might be said about the relevance of Pasternak's novel to "Life in Windy Weather." *Doctor Zhivago* is about a man whose surname derives from the word "life" ("zhizn'"). The novel concentrates on Zhivago's quest for life's essential values, which, he finds, reside in the realms of life (his love for Lara), art, and religiosity. Like Zhivago, Sergei is a writer. Like Zhivago, Sergei moves between city and country. Pasternak writes a novel and affixes to it the poems that its hero has allegedly fashioned out of the raw materials of life presented in the novel. Bitov writes a story and affixes to it the alleged diary events which shape the fictional story that the reader has just read. Both authors deal with the triad of art, life, and spirituality. Both deal with the cycle of life and death in physical, artistic, and religious terms.

Although this is more problematic, it might make sense to consider other intimations of Pasternak in our discussion of "Life in Windy Weather." Another poem of his entitled "The Wind (Four Fragments about Blok)" ("Veter [Chetyre otryvka o Bloke]") contains the image of the wind penetrating under the ribs and into the soul ("... veter, pronikshii pod rëbra/I v dushu, ...").[83] (The etymological roots for "dusha" ["soul"] and "dukh" ["spirit"] are the same; this brings us back to the breathing/inspiration metaphor.) In the Bitov wind scene in which allusions to Pasternak's *Doctor Zhivago* wind poem appear, we read about the "ribs" of the house (p. 191). Ribs and wind bring us back, once again, to our breathing/inspiration image. Some of the other imagery in the Pasternak wind poem about Blok finds its way into Bitov's story. The wind, writes Pasternak, is everywhere – at home, in the trees, in the village, in the rain, in Blok's poetry, in death.[84] He speaks of a little river, a meadow, childhood, the forest, the sky, a storm, Blok's life, and his poetry. Much of this imagery appears in Bitov's accidental symmetry scene, which the narrator links with the wind scene in the second-floor study of the day before.

The accidental symmetry scene, in which Sergei shows his son the little river, tells him what it is and goes through the naming of objects for his son, is reminiscent of a scene in *Doctor Zhivago* which, as in Bitov's later scene, contains the images of a train, a carriage, a meadow. As Lara breathes in the air of the meadow, the narrator writes, "For a moment she rediscovered the purpose of her life. She was here on earth to grasp the meaning of its wild enchantment and to *call each thing by its right name* [Emphasis mine – E.C.], or, if this were not within her power, to give birth out of love for life to successors who would do it in her place".[85] In the Bitov story, Sergei, the father, names things for his son, and through seeing the simplicity and joy of the world through his son's eyes, he discovers the meaning of life.

Just as the quoted lines in Bitov's later story "The Taste" led us to the hidden references to Pasternak's poetry in "Life in Windy Weather," so, too, an examination of a quotation that Bitov uses in another later story, "The Forest" ("Les") (1965, 1972) leads to the discovery of another important subtext for "Life in Windy Weather." The epigraph to "The Forest" is from the Book of Psalms: "The days of man are but as grass: for he flourisheth as a flower of the field" ("Dni cheloveka, kak trava,/ Kak tsvet polevoi, tak on tsvetet").[86] The "days of man" ("dni cheloveka"), the first two words of the epigraph, also serve as the title of Bitov's collection of short stories in which "The Forest" originally appeared.[87]

If we look at the psalm from which the quotation comes and at the psalms immediately before and after, we find that they are relevant to an analysis of "Life in Windy Weather." Psalm 101 (in the Russian version of the Bible) speaks of David's sense of grief and hopelessness, of his sense that his days are disappearing like smoke, of the drying up of his heart and, finally, of the endurance of the children of God's servants. The next psalm, 102 in the Russian version, 103 in the English – the one in which the days of man quotation appears – deals more with hope and life than did the preceding psalm. Before, David had compared himself to a lonely bird; now, he speaks of his feeling that his youth, like an eagle's, is being renewed. He recounts the blessings bestowed upon man if he lives according to God's law. In the verse immediately following the "days of man" line, comes a line about the wind passing over the field ("for the wind passes over it [the field – E.C.], and it is gone, and its place knows it no more" ("Proidet nad nim veter, i net ego, i mesto ego uzhe ne uznaet ego"]).[88] In the verse immediately preceding the "days of man" line, the word "sostav" ("make-up, composition, structure") is used. Bitov uses this word, after a sentence in which he describes the windy days ("vetrenye dni"), in the accidental symmetry scene with Sergei's son (p. 213). God's love, the psalm continues, will endure for man and for his children when man has faith.

The next psalm, called, in Russian, the psalm of David (103) "... about the creation of the world" ("... o sotvorenii mira"), is of particular relevance for our purposes. The psalm has to do with the creative process, the central issue of "Life in Windy Weather." The imagery bears a striking resemblance to that of the wind/epiphany scenes in Bitov's story. One of the first verses of that psalm speaks of God's going on the wings of the wind ("... na kryl'iakh vetra");[89] the next verse says that God creates breaths/spirits ("dukhov")[90] as His angels. Here, then, the wind is associated with life's spiritual dimension. Later in the same psalm, we read about God's having created the grass for cattle and about His having created small animals. We read about chamois and about the verdure. We read about the ships that sail and about God's stretching out His hand. These images play an important role in the episodes in which Sergei stands in awe of the wonder of life. When he and his son are in the meadow, Sergei sees the verdure, a cow, a goat, and a cat. When he is in his study, the room is transformed into a sailing ship. When Sergei is in the meadow, his son stretches out his hand.

Near the end of the psalm, the act of singing, in praise of God, is mentioned. Near the end of Bitov's story, the girlfriend of a friend of Sergei's is urged to sing. The song, not identified in Bitov's text, is, according to Stephen Hagen's insightful chapter on the story, by Soviet poet and singer Novella Matveeva.[91] The part of the song sung by the woman is: "What a big wi-nd/ descended on our is-land/and removed the roofs from the houses,/like fo-am from milk ..." (p. 218). The words of her song tie in directly to the theme of "Life in Windy Weather." During the first episode of windy weather, as we will recall, Sergei notices that there is no ceiling between him and the roof. The wind had removed a layer between him and life and had thus shaken free his creative impulses. Similarly, in the song, the wind removes the roof, the layer between the sky and the house.

In all scenes in which Bitov describes the removal of ossified perception, he demonstrates that the removal of such forms, structures, conventions results in Sergei's capacity to make connections. "Connection" ("sviaz'") is a word Bitov repeats in this context. Hagen sensitively points out Sergei's emphasis, as a result of his newly experienced revelations about life, upon union with other people, with nature, and with the lofty dimensions of reality.[92] Sergei, for instance, feels that an invisible, but real thread connects him to the woman singing the song. At the end of the story, Sergei feels a close connection with his wife and son.

The direction taken by Sergei has been from death to life, in constructing a creative personal life, spiritual life, and artistic life for himself. In "Notes from around the Corner," the trajectory is the same, going from the narrator's discussions of dead life and literature to his feelings of terror that his own death is imminent, finally to his being freed of terror. Having faced the possibility of his death, he can live in peace, confident that the dimensions of his life have changed. Nothing, he says, in his external life has changed as a result of his epiphany. He realizes, though, that his attitude toward life has wrought a profound change in the way he will live.

In like manner, the psalms that make their presence felt in Bitov's "Life in Windy Weather" begin with a feeling of man's deadness (feeling withered, isolated; understanding that he is dust) and end, through man's discovery of his spirituality, with a song to God. (In "Life in Windy Weather," as Sergei is riding into the city with his father, he fantasizes that an atomic bomb drops and imagines that the car in which they are riding is a speck of dust ["pylinka"] [p. 206]. During the same ride, Sergei's father explains that in the event of a war, the most important military tactic will be communication ["sviaz'"] on the second day. Sergei points out that this is ridiculous since no one will be left after the first day. The conversation demonstrates the importance, brought out in other ways throughout the story, of establishing true communication/connection ["sviaz'"] and the consequences of not understanding what makes for real communication.) With his song, David creates, with God, a world filled with meaning.

The narrator in Pasternak's "Wind" poem begins by declaring that he is dead and ends by speaking of the wind's creating a song for his lover. *Doctor Zhivago* begins with the death of Iurii Zhivago's mother and ends with Gordon and Dudorov holding a notebook of Zhivago's writings. Feeling at one with the present, the future, the past, their children, the city (holy city), the earth, they are surrounded, describes Pasternak's narrator, by the ". . . inaudible music of happiness"[93] and are supported in their feelings by the book of poetry in their hands. The meanings of life and art and spirituality are merged into one. Connections have been made.

We have seen how the words and thoughts of Pasternak and of the Bible make their presence felt in Bitov's story. One could argue that Pasternak's works are also infused with Biblical references. The poem "The Wind," for instance, and the novel *Doctor Zhivago* as a whole, including the other poems in the Zhivago cycle, contain explicit and implicit Biblical references. Where, then, do we draw the line between what Bitov absorbed from the Bible and what he absorbed from his reading of Pasternak? And how do we reconcile the fact that Bitov's "message" can be analyzed as stemming from both the Judeo-Christian tradition and from the Buddhist tradition; that it can be viewed as the discoveries about artistic creativity of one individual human being; that it can be understood as one person's clarification about a meaningful way to live his life?

For a clue to an answer to these questions, we must turn to Bitov's own words, stated in another context. Priscilla Meyer explains that he denies all influences on his work. A scene of a horse in his story "The Idler" ("Bezdel'nik") has been traced to Raskolnikov's dream about a horse in Dostoevsky's *Crime and Punishment* (*Prestuplenie i nakazanie*). Meyer writes, "While he has of course read *Crime and Punishment*, Bitov explains the similarity by a kind of collective unconscious: the ideas, myths and symbols of a culture are in the air, and the fallen horse is part of a shared imagery."[94] In one sense, for Bitov, the boundaries among different works of art are discarded as the writers make contacts/connections with other writers, ideas, and cultures, with one another, in the realm of the collective unconscious that exists beyond the boundaries that separate individual images into arbitrary categories.

In like fashion, as we move toward an understanding of Bitov's "Life in Windy Weather," we must acknowledge that the seemingly discordant interpretations of the story are harmonious when we look beyond the boundaries of individual religions; of individual aspects of artistic creativity; of individual processes of perception of one individual human being. In *all* respects, Bitov's message is the acknowledgment of the existence of the invisible threads of commonality that extend farther and farther when human beings decide to live and act creatively. Bitov is speaking, in the broadest sense, of the creative processes of life. His method underscores his message. Ronald Meyer describes the "unit" of "Life in Windy Weather" and "Notes from around the Corner," in its attempt at creating true literature, as "... plotless prose ...," "... a lyrical-philosophical narrative with some semblances of plot ... testing, straining at the boundaries of genre ..."[95] Bitov's boundaries of genre, then, are dissolved, just as boundaries melted as Sergei came closer to dealing with life more truthfully. In our search for an interpretation of Bitov's story, we, too, must acknowledge that the boundaries of interpretation among the separate consciousnesses of Meyer, Meyer, Hagen, Schmid, and Chances are not really boundaries at all, for together they attain the truth about Bitov's story about truth.

During Sergei's moment of greatest harmony, when he sees the "accidental symmetry" of life, Bitov's narrator speaks of the "... endless continuation of the axis *beyond visible boundaries* [Emphasis mine – E.C.] ..." (p. 214). Seeing beyond visible boundaries to the essence that ties one seemingly disparate realm of life to another is the key to Sergei's discovery of the meaning of his life, to his discovery of the harmony in life. The boundaries have been removed between him and the roof, between him and other people, between him and nature, between him and the conventional forms of dead literature. Only in this way can he get to the real connections with other people, with real literature, with the eternal verities of life. Only in this way can he get to the truth about life and literature. If one is honest and not afraid of the wind, one will feel the wind shake the house. The wind will breathe movement into you. The wind might carry you to the edge of the abyss. In "Notes from around the Corner," the narrator feels that he will die. If you are willing to take this step, to move with the wind, to be inspired by the wind, you will get to creative inspiration, epiphany, and harmony. If you refuse to breathe and move, and instead stay frozen in conventional, dead forms, if you refuse to change, expiration will take place. Bitov gets to his own accidental symmetry of life, literature, and the life of the spiritual. For him, all of these realms are intertwined. All lead to a true harmony and, as Bitov writes, in daring to look beyond visible boundaries, one gets closer to the truth.

In the scene in which Sergei and his father are driving to the city, the narrator uses the word "ploughing" ("pakhoty") (p. 204) in describing the landscape. A Pasternak poem, "Ploughing" ("Pakhota"), appropriately enough, from the cycle entitled "When the Weather Clears" ("Kogda razguliaetsia"), begins like this: "What happened to the familiar district?/The earth's and sky's border has been erased" ("Chto stalos' s mestnost'iu vsegdashnei?/S zemli i neba sterta gran'").[96] The dissolution of boundaries, according to Bitov, is what true living is all about.

DACHA DISTRICT — CONCLUSION

One can speak of the dissolution of boundaries between "Life in Windy Weather" and other stories that appeared together with it in the collection *Dacha District*. Boris, in "One Country," by escaping his routine patterns of living, gets to know himself. By accepting his past (the part of himself that is dead), the narrator of "Journey to a Childhood Friend" can live more freely. He forges connections to the past, erasing the boundaries that he had erected between himself and that past. In "The Garden," Aleksei realizes that knowledge of love can come only by knowing what not-love is. "Life in Windy Weather," together with its companion piece, "Notes from around the Corner," links these themes in teaching that life's creative cycle follows a path of death (not-life) to life, that the human being, like the wind, must accept the movement of breathing in and out in order to live a meaningful life, filled with inspiration.

CHAPTER 5

"Apothecary Island": "I-lands" of existence

"APOTHECARY ISLAND"

As much as "The Big Balloon" hints at the presence of a spiritual dimension in everyday reality, "Apothecary Island" ("Aptekarskii ostrov")[1] smacks of real events of life on earth in the "Apothecary Island" section of Leningrad.

It is an unpleasant day for second-grader Zaitsev. The story contains references to Bitov's childhood, for young Zaitsev, like Bitov, returned to Leningrad after having been evacuated during World War II. Bitov had spent the first year of the Leningrad siege in that city. In March, 1942, his mother took him and his brother Oleg along the "road to life," first to the Urals and then to Tashkent. In 1944, Bitov returned to Leningrad and entered the first grade.

In an autobiographical statement, Bitov explains that the stories "The Big Balloon" and "Apothecary Island" were among the rare instances of works of his that bear the stamp of his childhood experiences during the war.[2]

In "The Big Balloon" and "Apothecary Island," the narration is a blend of third-person and first-person. As in "The Big Balloon," Bitov uses third-person narration, and as in "The Big Balloon," the stream-of-consciousness, interior monologue thoughts of the young protagonist often make it appear as though the narration were first-person, from the child's point of view. As in "The Big Balloon," the reader witnesses one event in the life of the child protagonist.

Bitov's theme in "Apothecary Island" is childhood isolation. The focus is the psychology of a small boy. Zaitsev, having returned from evacuation three months before the events of

"Apothecary Island" unfold, feels alone. His schoolmates shun him. Bitov's narrator explains, ". . . Zaitsev would go out with everyone after classes, and everyone would . . . go off in groups, . . . and Zaitsev . . . would walk alone. His school bag would become heavy and alien, and Zaitsev was miserable" (p. 24).

One day, after school, two schoolmates invite Zaitsev to play with them. That morning, his mother had told him to be home early since it was his father's birthday. Because of his desire to make friends, Zaitsev, with a fleeting thought ("What would it have cost papa to have been born tomorrow?") (p. 25), joins the two boys. Zaitsev feels more isolated, for "the two" make fun of him when he cannot find his way home. They are unsympathetic when he hurts his foot.

Bitov reproduces well the rejection a child feels as he seeks approval from playmates whose reason for being with him is to give their own psyches the security of lording it over the weak. The theme is repeated in Bitov's works. It surfaces in "Journey to a Childhood Friend," where a "strong" character is pitted against the "weak" narrator. The psychology of the insecure person is replayed in *Pushkin House*, for the indecisive Leva Odoevtsev is duped by the domineering personalities of his colleague, Mitishatiev, and his lover, Faina.

In "Apothecary Island," Bitov sensitively records a child's psychology. Zaitsev talks to his wounded foot, cajoling it to do his bidding. When he reaches his building, the pain is too acute for him to climb the stairs. He sees his father enter the building and wants more than anything else to cry out to him. He remains silent. Zaitsev's father stops climbing the stairs, turns around, and begins to climb down. Zaitsev says nothing, suddenly recalling the earmuffs with which his father had hit him.

In this scene Bitov presents the full gamut of emotions as he catalogues the young boy's longing for and fear of his father, his guilt at not having come home earlier, and his breaking into sobs. The older Zaitsev's wide range of reactions and feelings is also sensitively registered. His worry, anger, regret, and tears are recorded, simply and succinctly.

"The Big Balloon" and "Apothecary Island" present vistas of childhood. The former describes hope and good. The latter focuses on children's physical and psychic pains. In most anthologies of his stories except *The Big Balloon* ("Apothecary Island" had not then been written), Bitov places the two stories back-to-back.[3]

"THE IDLER"

Bitov states that in *Dacha District* and *Apothecary Island*, he examined "... the theme of self-realization or its absence ... I was interested in the question of how a supposedly intelligent man could manage to avoid a confrontation with his own experience, in what intricate way his self-awareness could be bent in order to avoid self-realization".[4]

"The Idler" ("Bezdel'nik") 1961–2[5] features a character "without" ("bez") a sense of himself. Vitia, the "hero," fails to meet his responsibilities at work. One day he cannot even bear to go to work and wanders aimlessly through the city. He goes to a movie, gets drunk, wants to play with a little boy building a snow city in a park, feels ashamed at his irresponsible life, lets his thoughts wander, and generally avoids actions that would assure him self-respect.

Vitia has no sense of who he is. His boss says that Vitia creates the impression of being solid, but is not. Vitia, who, during the conversation, escapes into fantasy, ruminates over the fact that he produces many different impressions on people. In a revealing statement, he admits, "Exactly what kind of person I am ... I cannot say" (p. 51). His thoughts drift as he thinks about looking in a mirror to see how other people see him. Again, he speaks about not knowing himself. "I rarely recognize myself in the mirror" (p. 51), he thinks.

Wolf Schmid characterizes many Bitov works as journeys of the protagonists' self-discovery.[6] Bitov takes us on a journey through Vitia's consciousness, as his mind flits from one topic to another.[7] Many of Vitia's thoughts bear the imprint of adolescent rebellion.[8] As the boss reproaches him for his irresponsible work habits, Vitia thinks of hurling a bottle of ink toward the boss' bald spot or of throwing a grenade at him. Other thoughts reveal the adolescent's childish nature. In the scene with his superior, he imagines that after he is fired, he will become invisible, take over the PA system, and play lively music on it.

Vitia feels that he was most alive in childhood. At one point, he wants to play with a little boy. The boy sees that the adult is drunk and does not want to play with him. Priscilla Meyer remarks that Vitia's dilemma ". . . is to reconcile the demands of responsible adulthood with the values represented by childhood."[9]

Vitia catches glimpses of the values that would make for a more meaningful life. The recognition of values does not lead Vitia toward a spiritually fulfilling existence. After work, as he leaves the office, he notices the vitality of colors in the world – the blue sky; the sun; the red tram with its white roof; the "red, green, and blue children;" and a blue church dome. This sense of happiness, beauty, and aliveness makes no lasting impact on Vitia. In fact, in the next scene, Vitia thinks,

It seems to me that in a hard, transparent stone, narrow canals are etched for each person. Each person has . . . a lonely path, and one can only look with sadness and pity, as another alone-person passes by behind the transparent wall and also looks at you with sadness and pity, and we don't even stop, neither you nor she, we don't knock at the wall . . . – we walk past . . . One alone-person plus one alone-person equals two alone-people. (p. 61)

In another episode, as he is gazing out of the bus window on his way to work, he imagines that he sees a woman being murdered in an apartment building. After pondering the obligation of responsibility to another person, he thinks of telling a policeman, even if he turns out to have been wrong about a murder taking place. The scene ends, ironically, as Vitia, shirking his own responsibility, decides not to go to work.

Vitia feels good, during that day, as he, with others, encourages a fallen horse to stand up. He speculates about the notion of freedom and decides, "Perhaps the only genuine feeling of freedom is when a human being realizes that he has just acted humanely . . ." (p. 78). He imagines being imprisoned and suddenly understanding the meaning of life. He thinks that one day, he might wake up, by some miracle, ". . . in equilibrium and simplicity" (p. 79). He realizes that he is not imprisoned, that he is free to do as he pleases, and he then goes off to a beer hall to get drunk! He never acts in a way that would free him from his idling life.

Priscilla Meyer asked Bitov about the similarity between this scene and Raskolnikov's dream about the horse in Dostoevsky's *Crime and Punishment* (*Prestuplenie i nakazanie*). Bitov denied the influence, although he explained the coincidence as the result of the "shared imagery" of a culture.[10] Meyer quotes Bitov: "'It's funny, everyone asks about that horse.'"[11]

Other critics have traced the scene to the same Dostoevsky episode.[12] B. Bursov mentions similarities with horse scenes written by Mayakovsky and Nekrasov, too.[13] Although he does not specify, Bursov, no doubt, has in mind Mayakovsky's portrait of the fallen horse in his poem, "Good Relations toward Horses" ("Khoroshee otnoshenie k loshadiam"). In "The Idler," Bitov describes a horse as a "remarkable person." Mayakovsky writes that we are all horses. Both, then, identify human and horse attributes.

If we compare Bitov's horse scene with Dostoevsky's, we can understand why people have assumed a Dostoevsky influence. Each horse is pulling a cart ("telega"). Dostoevsky's cart has "wine casks" ("vinnye bochki"); Bitov's is filled with bottles ("butylki"). Dostoevsky's horse has fat legs (". . . s *tolstymi* [my italics – E.C.] nogami . . ."); Bitov's cart has thick wheels (". . . s *tolstymi* [my italics – E.C.] kolesami . . ."). Each passage contains the word mountain (Dostoevsky: "goru"; Bitov: "goroi"). In Dostoevsky's scene, the child Raskolnikov cries ("plachet"); in Bitov's scene, the horse cries ("plachet"). Dostoevsky's peasant painfully ("bol'no") beats the horse. Bitov's Vitia says that looking at the horse is painful ("bol'no") for him. In the Bitov scene, the driver flogs his horse mercilessly; the horse's owner in Raskolnikov's dream beats his horse. After his dream, Raskolnikov gets up and goes to a bridge ("most"). The Bitov scene takes place on a bridge ("most"). Raskolnikov utters the word "freedom" ("svoboda, svoboda!"). Vitya speaks about "freedom" ("svoboda").[14]

Reverberations from *Crime and Punishment* are felt in other scenes in "The Idler," too. Vitia ponders the issue of responsibility as he thinks that he sees the woman being murdered. In *Crime and Punishment*, Raskolnikov sees a man making lewd advances to a young girl and wonders whether or not he should help. In each scene, the protagonist deals with thoughts about a policeman. In both works, the main character feels acutely isolated. In "The Idler," Vitia thinks that if he were imprisoned, he might find the key to the meaning of life. Raskolnikov does just that. As in *Crime and Punishment*, freedom entails, for Bitov's Vitia, responsibility toward other people.

At the end of "The Idler" the possibility of spiritual transcendence surfaces. Vitia's boss is again speaking to him about his work habits, and Vitia again tunes out of the conversation. At that moment, the "accidental symmetry" (to borrow Bitov's expression from "Life in Windy Weather") of meaningful life appears as Vitia gazes at a green cactus with red needles on the window sill, at the blue sky and the sparkling snow outside the window, a red trolley car, and a blue dome. The combination of colors is the same as those which had made him feel so happy and alive before. (He notices that it is the same park that he had enjoyed after work before.) He then notices a bubble in the windowpane, and he observes that the sky, snow, trolley car, trees, and church dome all fit in the bubble. This discovery of a joyful state of being has no positive effect on Vitia. Instead, he is caught up, again, in the question of how others see him. We come full-circle, to the beginning of the story. In the first paragraphs, as Vitia sat with his superior, he pondered how others saw him and as we recall, admitted to little knowledge of himself. Here Vitia imagines that a tiny person lives in the snow city he sees in the windowpane bubble. The last line of the story is, "I wonder, what kind of person does he see me as from there?"(p. 85). Instead of finding himself, Vitia loses himself and moves away from growing.

The loose structure of the story matches the loose structure in Vitia's life. In "Life in Windy Weather," Bitov speaks of the dangers of remaining confined, within structures, without the wind to stir one out of a routine existence. In "The Idler," the author demonstrates the dangers of living without structures. In *Apothecary Island*, "The Idler" is placed directly before "The Door." In the latter story, Bitov demonstrates the danger of being trapped by the structures of one's past without the ability to transcend them. Bitov continues to dip into other works of his in order to create the one big work, almost, which can be said to consist of all of the little, overlapping products of his creativity that have been labelled, in turn, psychological *études*, philosophical excursuses, travelogues, short stories, and essays. Thus, "The Idler" and "The Sun" star main protagonists, Vitia, who wander aimlessly through the city. Vitia is also the main character of "A Terrible Force," and like Vitia in "The Idler," he feels different from the people around him. The English translation of "The Idler" changes his name to Alesha, presumably to emphasize that the character in "The Idler" is the same as the character, Monakhov, in "The Leg" (whose name changes from Zaitsev in the original story entitled "Apothecary Island" to Monakhov in the same story, called "The Leg" in the English and in other Russian editions); "Penelope;" "The Soldier" (the name is Leva Odoevtsev when this section appears in *Pushkin House*); "Life in Windy Weather;" "The Garden;" "The Third Story;" "The Forest;" and "The Taste." An Alesha stars in "Grandmother's Uzbek Cup" and "A Nothing," both stories that share details with "The Idler." Alesha's child-like reactions, captured in "A Nothing," play a prominent role in "The Idler." "The Idler" shares with "Grandmother's Uzbek Cup" thoughts of regret that Alesha's parents are growing old. As in "My Wife Is Not At Home," the main character is a drifter who cannot force himself to act responsibly. The same is true of the main characters of "The Garden" and "A Nothing." As in "The Garden," Alesha turns to his inner thoughts and imaginative flights as an authority figure upbraids him for irresponsible behavior. As in "Life in Windy Weather," childhood, in "The Idler," represents vitality. As in "Life in Windy Weather," there is a discussion of the aftermath of modern technological warfare, when life will cease to exist. As in "The Garden," a scene of a garden in the snow energizes the protagonist.

"PENELOPE"

"Penelope" ("Penelopa"), 1962, is another Bitov story about how not to act. It is a story of betrayal, of oneself – in behaving in an undignified way – and of another person, in acting deceitfully. One might link several stories written within the same period, 1960 to 1963, and devoted to the same theme. "The Garden" (1962–3) and "The Door" (1960) (grouped together under the heading *The Lover [A Novel with Ellipses]* in the English *Life in Windy Weather* and under the heading, *The Role, A Novel with Ellipses [Rol', roman – punktir]* in the Russian *The Days of Man [Dni cheloveka]*) deal with the main character's disappointment in a lover's deceit. "The Idler" (1961–2) and "Penelope" (1962), paired under the heading *Apothecary Island* in the English *Life in Windy Weather*, deal with the protagonist's betrayal of himself and, consequently, of other people. The cluster of "betrayal stories," "The Idler," "The Door," and "Penelope," is brought together in the 1968 collection *Apothecary Island.*

Penelope is the symbol of fidelity,[15] the opposite of the characteristics displayed by Lobyshev: he ducks out of work and goes to a movie, *Odysseus*, in which the wanderings of Homer's Odysseus (to whom Lobyshev compares himself) and the fate of his faithful wife Penelope are re-enacted. Upon entering the movie theater, Lobyshev and a nameless young woman strike up a conversation. To Lobyshev's dismay, the woman attaches herself to him. He is ashamed of being seen with her because she is not dressed elegantly. Earlier, he had worried about his own physical appearance (since he had just returned to Leningrad from the country).

Lobyshev lies to the woman, promising that he will help her get a job and arranging a future meeting at a location that he has fabricated. The story ends with Lobyshev's thought that this is typical of his daily behavior. He realizes that this honest thought about his behavior contains a long-forgotten sensation, clarity. The ending is inconclusive. Acknowledgment of a life of lies might lead to change. The reader is not told the outcome, though.

The critical response to "Penelope" was, on the whole,

positive. Vadim Kozhinov[16] was enthusiastic. He wrote that
Bitov is ". . . the most mature and profound prose writer of his
generation."[17] He addresses Bitov's ability to depict, in Lobyshev, the lack of internal freedom that propels people's actions.
According to Kozhinov, Bitov shows that personal responsibility, a trait lacking in Lobyshev, is a prerequisite for freedom.[18]

Many scholars focus on the main character's mechanized,
automatic reflex responses to life. Bakich discusses Bitov's frequent explorations into the psyches of characters who ". . . have
well-developed mechanisms for suppressing all unpleasant and
disturbing thoughts."[19] S. Sergeev, in a review of *Apothecary
Island*, focuses on the automatization of feelings and thoughts in
"Penelope."[20] Lev Anninskii regards "mechanical reflex living"
as the key dilemma facing the protagonists of "Penelope," "The
Garden," and "Life in Windy Weather."[21] He explains that
Bitov's idea is that ". . . the source of moral values . . ." resides in
the individual.[22] Steven Hagen discusses the psychological
intricacies of the story which, for him, reproduces the pattern of
"The Idler" and "Apothecary Island": an external event upsets
the equilibrium of the protagonist's mind.[23] Moreover, for
Hagen, the section on the epic movie, *Odysseus*, criticizes the
positive hero, akin to protagonists in Socialist Realist works. He
explains Bitov's purpose as a plea for literature to include the
stories of everyday life and characters.[24]

Another interpretation of the story emerges as one contemplates the subtitle Bitov affixed to "Penelope" in the English
translation: "Nevsky Prospect" ("Nevskii Prospekt"). In so
doing, Bitov alerts the reader to Leningrad's main thoroughfare
and to Gogol's "Nevsky Prospect."[25] The Gogolian backdrop, it
seems to me, infuses the Soviet story with one of Gogol's major
themes. All is deceit. Nothing, according to Gogol's narrator, is
what it seems, as one traverses the mysterious Nevsky Prospect.
In the same way, deceit and illusion mark Lobyshev's travels
along Nevsky Prospect, where the action of "Penelope" unfolds.

When a woman is attracted to Lobyshev, as in the Gogol short
story, she turns out to be someone with whom the main
character would rather not associate. As in the Gogol short
story, the protagonist prefers looking at the woman (Penelope)

of the dream/illusory world (of film, in Bitov's story) to relating to the real-life woman (in Bitov's story, sitting next to him in the theater). Lobyshev's promises of a job are illusory; he plays tricks on his companion. Lobyshev's thoughts about the epic film include skeptical illusion-puncturing comments. He thinks, for instance, that Odysseus' so-called altruistic act – to fasten himself to the mast so that he could listen to the Sirens – was not so much a noble deed as thirst for daredevil adventures. The epic hero, then, is not what the illusory world of the epic film would have us believe. Although the epic hero, muses Lobyshev in a passage that recalls the narrator's musings in "Journey to a Childhood Friend," looms large in physical strength, he is stunted in terms of essential human qualities.

When the reader turns away from the unreal epic world of the film and looks for humanness in the ordinary character of Lobyshev, the result is also deceit and illusion. Lobyshev lies to his mother. He leaves work during business hours. He deceives his new acquaintance.

Gogol's "Nevsky Prospect" concludes as the narrator bemoans the fact that everything is deceitful, that Nevsky Prospect always lies. Bitov's "Penelope (Nevsky Prospect)" ends as Lobyshev admits that he always lies. The one potential slice of hope, in Lobyshev's case, is that he admits, at the end of the tale, that he lies.

"INFANTIEV"

"The Idler" and "Penelope" focus on death in life. While the main protagonists go through the motions of being alive, their inner beings are dead. The story "Infantiev" ("Infant'ev"), 1961–5,[26] which immediately follows "Penelope" in two out of the three collections of Bitov's stories in which the two stories appear together,[27] deals with life in death.

The main hero, Infantiev, is a reserved, deadened person to whom no one at work pays attention until he becomes head of department. He has no friends at the research institute where he works. His wife and he have a lacklustre marriage.

Our introduction to Infantiev comes through the narrator's

observations of Infantiev's fellow workers. Our information –
about Infantiev's marriage and about his cold manner with his
wife Natalia during telephone conversations – comes in snatches
from others. We are introduced, in the same fashion, to Natalia's
fatal illness. We find out, through the impersonal means of the
workplace grapevine, that he must be suffering, for he now
leaves work in the middle of the day, and he speaks more
tenderly to his wife on the telephone. The fact that no one at
work knows what the problem is indicates to the reader that
Infantiev lives in isolation. Infantiev has been living a dead life
that, in other stories, Bitov described as resulting from a
mechanized response to life.

Unlike Lobyshev and "the idler," Infantiev sheds his dead
skin and finds meaning in life. In this way, he is like another
idler, Sergei, of "Life in Windy Weather." Infantiev, through
experiencing his wife's death, transcends his isolation and
routine, and finds communion with people and nature. He
discovers a spiritual dimension in life. Given the pattern of the
protagonists' lives, it is not surprising that in a 1980 collection of
Bitov's stories, *Sunday* (*Voskresnyi den'*), under the heading
"Island" ("Ostrov"), the last three selections are "Penelope,"
"Life in Windy Weather," and "Infantiev," in that order.

While Infantiev is still living a habit-filled life devoid of
meaning, the narrative is third-person, describing events from
the outside and from others' points of view. When Infantiev
begins to grow, the narration switches to third-person narration
that seems to merge with the first-person thoughts of the chief
protagonist's psyche.

As Infantiev allows himself to feel more, the story, more and
more, loses its sequential order. At the beginning, one section,
followed by a blank space, presents Infantiev's behavior at work.
The next section, also followed by a blank space, tells of the
diagnosis of breast cancer, Natalia's worsening condition, the
spread of the disease, and her death. The third section, also
followed by a blank space, describes the cemetery. Here, for the
first time, the theme of life in death emerges. The cemetery is a
place of death, yet the qualities described are those of life. There
are pine trees, a lake, and an old church. The narrator says that

this cemetery is "living" ("zhivushchee") (p. 131). He continues, "And if the sky is clear, and it is sunny, and the pines rustle, and masses of clouds are reflected in the water, there is no death here" (p. 131). These, then, are three distinct sections, crisply marked off as separate entities.

The next section of the story deals with the day of Natalia's burial. Here, too, three distinct episodes are marked off, this time by Infantiev's memory. The day, for Infantiev, was divided into three frames, always in the same sequence. First came his discovery, through accidentally observing another funeral procession and following it into the cemetery church, of a community created by grief. The priest's voice floated into a narrow column of light that illuminated the church interior. Infantiev notices that the people are as one, and that there is, at that point, no longer any grief. The second episode concentrates on Natalia's burial, on the light, sun, snow, and music that Infantiev senses as he is about to place the first handful of earth on the coffin lid. Infantiev feels that with the mysterious internal music comes a sensation of people's moving off into infinity. The third episode describes a third death scene. Infantiev notices that on the tombstone next to Natalia's burial spot, a "living sparrow" ("... zhivoi vorobei") (p. 136) is pecking at a piece of candy. All three instances of death bring Infantiev a sense of the bond of life that, through grief and loss, can link person to person, person to nature, and person to the eternal.

The beginning of the story through the sparrow scene encompasses a little less than half of "Infantiev." The remaining half deals with the one day when Infantiev, for the first time since the burial, visits his wife's grave. This half of the story is structured more loosely, coinciding with Infantiev's own loosening structure of life. The process, for Infantiev, is an awakening to a meaningful life. It is not coincidental, I believe, that this half of the story takes place during spring, the time of the awakening of nature, whereas Natalia's death took place during winter, the season of nature's death.

In the second half of the story, logical sequences dissolve to reveal the hidden essence of life to Infantiev. On his trolley-car ride to the cemetery, he sees his wife. They converse. He asks her what is "there ("tam"), and in response, she tells him to look at the blue sky. Infantiev dissolves the boundaries between life and death. For him, his wife, a dead person, is alive in the present. She also appears to him at home. After her death, they communicate in a deep way that had never occurred before she died. Infantiev, through her death, allows true communication to take place and allows a spiritual dimension to enter his life.

The final pages of "Infantiev" record the titular hero's acquaintance and conversation with "... the strange woman" (p. 141) whose husband's tombstone is in the plot adjoining Natalia's gravesite. He listens to her illogical, inconsistent conversation about her husband, and he realizes that she is conveying something important to him. He discovers that by placing a premium on logical consistency and sequence, he had missed a great deal of what is of value. Infantiev thinks that perhaps, "... all his life he had been listening to a great deal that ... he had not grasped because he had considered understanding to be only clear sequence, only the flow of one thing out of another. But right now, he needed precisely this running, nonsequential story because in rejecting sequence, he was expressing the essence" (p. 143). During his conversation with the woman Infantiev notes, as a heavy downpour has given way to sun, that "... everything had been extraordinarily transformed" (p. 141).

It turns out that the strange woman also communicates with her dead husband. Infantiev realizes, by the end of the story, that a spiritual dimension exists in his present life on earth – in the living presence of his wife, in his ability to communicate with the strange woman on a deep level, in his capacity to appreciate nature. What makes this possible is Infantiev's capacity to be open to true communication (love – "liubov'" in the *Sunday* version of the story),[28] to be open to life in its truest manifestations.

The spiritual dimension is made more explicit in the subtitle to the story, "son of a priest." According to a Hagen conversation with Bitov, the subtitle, deleted by the editors, is essential to understanding the story.[29] The significance of the subtitle and of the main protagonist's name is explained in a section of the story that is not in the 1968 *Apothecary Island* version, but which has subsequently been included in all published versions.[30] In that sequence, the strange woman asks whether Infantiev was the son of a priest. He insists that he was not, although he then recalls that his father had attended seminary for a while. The woman explains that the root of the name Infantiev is from the French and Spanish Infante, "... royal child, heir."[31] She explains that in the past, Russian provincial priests had made up unusual names for themselves – Resurrection, Transfiguration, Assumption, Epiphany, and that when these names were used up, they resorted to more unusual names. In this way, she explains the origin of the name Infantiev. Infantiev retorts that the same phenomenon occurs in the circus. (The reader might note that the Russian circus is often the home of bears, who are often called "Misha" in Russia. Misha was the name of the woman's dead husband.) In response to Infantiev, the woman agrees, giving her own circus example: "Here's something interesting: Monakhov is just this sort of an actor name, but after all, it must come from priests. Probably there, too, the father was a priest; the son, an actor. Can you imagine the drama? The conflict?"[32] Of course, the Monakhov comment is not directly relevant to the plot of "Infantiev." It serves, however, to remind the reader of the lines that Bitov is always forging among his stories.

What Bitov means is not clarified. In what way is Infantiev – who insists that his father was not a priest, but a "metal-worker"[33] – the son of a priest? And why is the parallel with the origin of actors' names drawn? Why does Bitov place Infantiev, son of a priest, together with the woman, wife of Misha, together with the beauties of nature, and Infantiev's memories of child-hood? (The woman offers Infantiev "Misha of the North" chocolates that remind him of childhood. He realizes that he could have, every day, eaten these chocolates that give him joy, but that he has not had one since childhood.)

The question of why Bitov makes Infantiev a priest's son is, perhaps, easier to answer than the other questions. In the context of the story, he is the heir, the continuator, the preserver – not literally, since his father was not really a priest – of the spiritual dimension of life. By tapping into life's eternal verities, he, as "son of a priest," preserves an essential dimension of human existence. Bitov deals with this idea in greater detail in "Armenia Lessons" and in *Pushkin House*.

The question of why the author links the actor and priest is more problematic. The connection between the realm of art and the spirit was made by Bitov in "Life in Windy Weather." Knowing that Bitov was working simultaneously on these stories, we can surmise that he treats, in a sketchier fashion, the same interrelationship in "Infantiev" that he addresses, in a more focused way, in "Life in Windy Weather." In "Infantiev," Bitov places his protagonist in nature – the sun, the sky, the pine trees, the rainstorm that cleanses. He places him together with a strange woman who exudes childhood, playful qualities. She feeds chocolates to the sparrows and rides a bicycle to the cemetery (she had wanted to ride a motorscooter, but figured that it would be stolen). The illogical, unpredictable nature of her speech, for Infantiev, captures the essence of life. As in "Life in Windy Weather," Bitov combines the domains of nature, art, a childlike innocence, and spirituality as the major ingredients of a life with meaning. For Bitov, as we have seen in our examination of "Life in Windy Weather," when one gets beyond the distinct categories of the creative in various dimensions of a person's life, the essence is the same. This point is not explicitly made in "Infantiev," but this is the direction in which Bitov vaguely points. His emphasis, though, differs from that of "Life in Windy Weather." In "Infantiev," Bitov emphasizes the texture of the vague qualities of the mysteries of life, whereas in "Life in Windy Weather," he shows the way in which, once those mysteries have been lived, they can be harnessed to creative action in one's life.

Almost nothing has been written about "Infantiev." The most extensive treatment of the story appears in Hagen's fine analysis of "Infantiev." He is the first fully to investigate its mystical elements, its treatment of religious awakening, and its attention to the theme of life after death.[34]

Alla Marchenko, in her review of the *Apothecary Island* collection, declares that "Infantiev," in her view, does not belong with the rest of the stories.[35] Other responses, by Hagen and by Priscilla Meyer,[36] point out links between "Infantiev" and other *Apothecary Island* stories. Both Hagen and Meyer refer to the similarity between Infantiev at the beginning of the story and Bitov's other protagonists. Priscilla Meyer writes that Infantiev "... is even more emotionally isolated than Monakhov."[37] Hagen states, "... Infantiev initially displays the same symptoms as Lobyshev; he exists without thought or feeling."[38]

Scholars mention other connections between "Infantiev" and other Bitov works. Priscilla Meyer links the deaths in "The Taste" to those in "Infantiev" and "The Soldier." She writes that "Infantiev" and "The Soldier" contain older people as major protagonists.[39] Hagen connects the story to "The Jubilee," where death is central to the plot.[40] He explains the typical Bitov emphasis upon the "... psychological processes going on inside a single character ..."[41] He sees the parallel between "Life in Windy Weather" and "Infantiev" in their inclusion of a character's great insight into himself, at the beginning of the story, as distinct from the pattern of other Bitov stories where the discovery of self-awareness tends to take place toward the end.[42] He writes that both "The Forest" and "Infantiev" consider the possibility of life after death and "... mystical communion with the dead ..."[43]

Hagen refers to "Infantiev" as the only Bitov story thus far to concentrate on the existence of life after death.[44] A page before, however, Hagen had quoted the epigraph to Bitov's "Grandmother's Uzbek Cup" (where the dead father and mother come through the wall) as an illustration of the theme of life after death.[45] In his discussion of "Infantiev," Hagen also writes that the titular hero is as sure that his wife had appeared to him as Tonia is of the existence of the big balloon, in the story of that name.[46]

It is fitting that "Infantiev" is the last story in *Apothecary Island*. It is also fitting that Bitov begins the volume with "The Big Balloon," the final tale in *The Big Balloon*. Whether consciously or unconsciously, Bitov underscores the lack of seams between one collection of his stories and another. It can be argued that "Infantiev," a tale about an older man whose spouse has died, is tied to "The Big Balloon," a story about a young girl whose mother has died. (The English version of "The Big Balloon" gives Tonia the name Asya. Priscilla Meyer's introduction to *Life in Windy Weather* explains that Infantiev is Asya's father-in-law.)[47] The point of these tales is that a spiritual domain exists in our life. In both stories, Bitov does not explain – consistently or in sequence – the possible existence of the dead person's presence, yet in both, that presence is experienced as the main character looks to the blue sky and hears the mysterious music of the spheres.

CHAPTER 6

"Image of Life": life and images of life

"THE WHEEL"

Image of Life (*Obraz zhizni*), 1972[1] begins with "The Garden," to which Bitov affixes "The Door" as a prologue. "Life in Windy Weather" follows. As his final selections of the book, Bitov includes two works never before included in a collection of his writings: "The Wheel (Notes of a Novice)" ("Koleso [Zapiski novichka]"), 1969–70,[2] and "Armenia Lessons" ("Uroki Armenii"), 1967–9.[3]

The narrator of "The Wheel" declares that when we talk about ourselves, ". . . we are always dealing not so much with life itself as with an image of our life, with a representation of it" (". . . my vsegda imeem delo ne stol'ko s samoi zhizn'iu, skol'ko s obrazom nashei zhizni, predstavleniem o nei") (p. 139). This sentence can serve as a key to approaching *Image of Life*, for we come to understand the "images of life"[4] which are born of different perspectives on life.

If one refuses, or does not want to see, that lies are lies, one remains in a fixed position, as had Bitov's little boy in "The Door." That story begins with the words, "The boy had gotten completely frozen under the arch" ("Mal'chik promerz pod arkoi").[5] The description of the boy's physically "frozen" condition duplicates his rigid psychological state. The second part of "The Garden" (containing the whole of "The Garden" as it appeared in the 1967 collection *Dacha District*)[6] demonstrates the necessity of expanding our perspective: to define love, we must also approach it, shows Bitov, from the perspective of what it is not. The third section of *Image of Life*, "Life in Windy Weather," urges us to transcend the limited perspective of conventional forms in life and art in order to see life from a fresh perspective.

"The Wheel," in form and subject matter, can be read as an extension of Bitov's discussion of literary forms and creativity in "Life in Windy Weather." Write, he had said, and, out of formlessness, a form will emerge on its own. This method of living and creating was, for Bitov, the way to arrive at the essence of reality, at the truth in life and art.

This point of view he supports, in an important theoretical statement on genre, published in the same year, 1969, in which he was working on "The Wheel." In "The Boundaries of Genre" ("Granitsy zhanra"), printed in *Questions of Literature* (*Voprosy literatury*), one of the Soviet Union's most distinguished literary criticism journals,[7] Bitov writes that the story has become deadened by adherence to a form that has outlived its time. According to Bitov, the most interesting contemporary literature is the prose that exists ". . . at the junction of genres, on the boundary of transition from genre to genre . . ."[8] Prose writers should not, he says, think about what genre they are writing in, but rather about what they are writing, and to what end. If this is clear, Bitov continues, what issues forth will be prose. He concludes, "But what precisely, – a novella, novel, or 'fragment,' – this is not so very important. Perhaps suddenly you'll get a short story."[9]

The results of Bitov's excursus on literary form are borne out in "The Wheel," a work whose genre is difficult to pinpoint. Critics have devoted much attention to determining the nature of "The Wheel." Wolf Schmid refers to its Olesha-like unusual perspectives and to the Futurist, Cubist reduction of human beings to technological mechanisms.[10] George Gibian astutely categorizes it as an analogue to the American genre of "New Journalism" and discusses the vitality of this genre of nonfiction, documentary, semijournalism in contemporary Soviet prose.[11] He also speaks of its being an example of documentary prose.[12] T. Khmel'nitskaia praises the originality of Bitov's "sketch" ("ocherk"), constructed, she notes, almost cinematically out of individual frames.[13] N. A. Kozhevnikova, although not speaking specifically about "The Wheel," describes the genre of documentary literature, popular in the Soviet Union in the 1950s and 1960s, in which fragments of documents are inserted into a fictional text.[14] Sylva Tvrdíková notes the variety of material that Bitov includes in his innovative prose – cinematic effects, philosophical discourse, documents, diaries, travelogue – to make up what the Czech scholar refers to as a cinematographic montage of fragments of thoughts, or an artistic collage.[15]

Mikael Klefter points to the fragmentary nature of "The Wheel" and sees it as Bitov's attempt to reflect, in writing, a reality without logical continuity.[16] The editor of a collection in which three Bitov works, including "The Wheel," appeared in 1974, describes Bitov's originality in splicing philosophical essay, travel sketch, sociological commentary, and diary to produce a form outside the usual categories of genre.[17] Soviet Uzbek writer Timur Pulatov emphasizes that "The Wheel," like "Armenia Lessons," differs from Bitov's earlier creations, for he is now ". . . seeking . . . a more spacious framework for the short story."[18]

V. Turbin discusses Bitov's utilization of the fragment to convey many aspects of the world – literary genre, sports, the human being, the perception of the world.[19] Vladimir Kantorovich views "The Wheel" as an essay on the wheel, symbol of movement.[20] Vsevolod Sakharov describes "The Wheel" and "Armenia Lessons" as works on the border of many genres, as parodies of contemporary journalism, and as fragments resembling film montage.[21]

There are elements of the travelogue in "The Wheel," for the narrator, a journalist, goes off to Ufa, capital of the Bashkir Republic, to report on the world semifinals of motorcycle racing on ice. The external form, although somewhat resembling previous Bitov travelogues, is more daring. There are "entries" ("zapiski"), the narrator's reflections on Ufa's local sport of motorcycle racing on ice, on the role (pun intended) of the wheel in life; on the meaning of life; on the image of the circle.

On the surface, "The Wheel" follows the mental and physical wanderings of a journalist covering a sports event. His "entries" take us from a frivolous song whose lyrics include the word

"Ufa;" to the airport; to the racetrack; to technical descriptions, quoted from books, of motorcycle parts, and parts of a horse's body; to a tram ride from Ufa to the track; to the sports commentator's words; to the center of the track; to the awarding of medals; to a description of champions; to the art of racing on ice; to a visit with a former champion; to speculations on and an imagined film scenario about children would-be motorcycle-racing winners; to an interview with the director and founder of Ufa's motorcycle club; to the journalist's relationship to the races and to their role in the world; to the press coverage of the Ufa semifinals in major Soviet newspapers; to the deaths of former champions.

"The Wheel" is, however, about much more than ice motor-cycle racing in Bashkir. Interwoven into the "entries" are discussions about reality. What is it? Why does it take the shape that it does? What is my world? What is the meaning of being in a circle or outside the circle? These questions are woven into the discussion of wheels and are formulated by the author's repeated use of wheel and circle imagery. The issues Bitov treats are replicated in the devices and stylistic techniques that his readers encounter along their spin on his "wheel." The result is a brilliant, idiosyncratic masterpiece. In its broadest sense, "The Wheel" concerns the wheel, or circle, as a metaphor for life.[22] Circles of the past intersect circles of the present. In an early scene, hearing the strains, at the Ufa airport, of a tune[23] popular several years ago prompts the narrator to recall hearing that melody years ago on an ice-skating rink. He then hears the same music at the racetrack. The circle of the ice-skating rink becomes the circle of the motorcycle racetrack. Circles of the present incorporate circles of the past.

The first word of "The Wheel," "Omsk," begins with the letter "O," a circle. The last entry, "Epigraph to Everything as a Whole" ("Èpigraf ko vsemu v tselom") (p. 163), begins with the narrator's thoughts on epigraphs. He says that although authors decide upon the epigraph after finishing a work, the epigraph is always placed at the beginning. By placing his epigraph at the end, Bitov makes the end the beginning.

The text of the epigraph is a quotation, which, Bitov's

narrator explains, a reader acquainted with the manuscript of "The Wheel" had brought him in an open book. The quotation is from Goethe's *Italian Journey* (*Italienische Reise*): "And ... the world is only a simple wheel, equal to itself along its whole circumference; it seems extraordinary to us simply because we ourselves are spinning together with it" (p. 163).[24]

Our perspective on the world, writes Bitov, is limited because although in motion, we move in a fixed circle of people, events, and attitudes toward life. Our lives, therefore, exist in a closed circle, wheel, system. It is surprising to us, Bitov writes, when we realize that not everyone shares our opinion.

Bitov is also concerned with the phenomenon, in our lives, of contracting and expanding circles, for he points out that the tiniest of worlds – the world of motorcycle racing – has the potential, if one explores it thoroughly, to become boundless. Everything depends on one's perspective. Before arriving at the motorcycle track, the narrator considers it a long distance from – on the outside of – Ufa's center. Once he becomes a part of that world, physically located on Ufa's outskirts, he feels as if the whole world belongs to and depends on the track.

Bitov addresses questions about primary causes and prime movers. What causes the circles? Who plotted the earth's orbit? What causes the earth to move in its particular orbit? What moves us to take one direction in life and not another? How, asks Bitov's narrator, did it become inevitable that he would travel to Ufa? His quest for the answer to this question leads him to the cold night when he had been ill and when his car engine had frozen. Therefore, he had had to go to car repair shops. Therefore, he had met people from the Ufa Motorworks, where the engines for his model of car were made. Therefore, his high fever had caused his presence at the Ufa motorcycle racing semifinals. The search for primary causes, Bitov writes, can lead us to a point where we would question the reason for our birth. Some things just are, he declares. If we do not accept them as facts, he decides, we end up spinning in circles from which there is no escape. Why, asks Bitov's narrator, is Ufa the center of ice motorcycle racing, the home of so many world champions of the sport? He understands, in his circular reasoning, that the fact that so many world champions have come from Ufa has made that city stand out. He determines that the reason for Ufa's success is Anshel' Lvovich Baloban, the executive administrator of the Number 3 Trust of the Ufa Motorclub. Baloban had arrived in Ufa from Odessa in 1956 and had founded the motorclub that had sponsored the ice racing sport ever since. Without his dedication and creative energy, the motorclub would not have existed. He nurtures the sportsmen's talents. Bitov's impulse, after discovering Baloban's role in the creation of champions, is to take the matter a step further. Why, he ponders, did Baloban come to Ufa in 1956? The narrator's mind moves, but the motions of recurring questions end up in spinning closed circles that keep him in a fixed position, no closer to the answer to the deeper implied question: why is life the way it is, what causes one's life to move in a particular direction? Posing these questions does not result in one's going forward. One ends up trapped, in the same twirling wheel.

Bitov deals with still other aspects of wheels and circles. The narrator recalls his experience with a car wheel. Thinking himself clever, but in the reader's mind showing the narrow circle/perspective in which he is enclosed, he cannot imagine what passions had obsessed little boys before the invention of the car. His driving teacher points out, from a perspective that includes a different circle of experience, that in the countryside, where he had grown up, horses had played the same function in little boys' lives that cars now play. To drive home his point, Bitov inserts excerpts from two parallel scientific texts: one, a description of a motorcycle engine, taken from a 1969 book, *Racing Motorcycles*, and the other, a description of a horse's body, from a 1921 book, *Horses* (pp. 120–1).

The passages show, predictably, that there is an enormous difference between a machine and an animal, but that there are striking similarities, too. Bitov displays two columns of texts (side by side, one on the left side of the page and one on the right), in which one finds parallel concepts and words. The passage about the machine includes the word "valves" ("klapanov") (p. 120). Valves, of course, can be parts of mechanical engines and of an animal's anatomy, the living heart. The function of each is the same. The word "motor" ("motive force") ("dvigatel'") (p. 120) is used in the passage about the horse. The term "cylinder head" ("golovka tsilindra") (p. 120), while used to describe the motorcycle engine, contains the word for an anatomical part of an animal body, the head. "Golovka," "little head," is derived from "head" ("golova") (p. 121), a word used in the parallel text about horses. The word "parts" ("chasti") (p. 120) appears in both texts. Both texts describe the way that the individual parts are intermeshed in order to make the motorcycle/horse move.

The first word of the horse text is "movement" ("peredvizhenie") (p. 120), and the last word in the column about motorcycles, a paragraph of the narrator's, is "MOVEMENT" ("DVIZHENIE") (p. 121). Here, the narrator takes us into another recurring circle of "The Wheel," for he asks how the motor moves. We are back to the question of primary causes.

The first word of the motorcycle text is the adjective, "general" ("obshchaia") – with its first letter "o," another circle – and the first sentence in the column of the horse text begins with the letter "o" ("from" ["ot"]). The last few words in the column of the horse text are "... that its [the head's – E.C.] halves be completely symmetrical, like one anoth- ..." (p. 121).

The texts Bitov places side by side, one written in 1969 and one in 1921, display a striking similarity. The "entry" in which the two columns of texts appear begins with the narrator's wondering whether Bashkir motorcycle racers are successful because they are descendants of ardent horsemen. The horse functioned in the past as the motorcycle now does. Functions recur. Bitov's implication is that one entity is unique to its time and place and that if we widen our perspective, we see that a later entity, unique to its time and place, serves the same function. Concepts are reborn in different forms, but turn out to be the same form. Circles recur. In the passage following the parallel columns of motorcycle/horse texts, Bitov returns to a normal page format, but continues to quote the sentence from the horse text that he had interrupted midstream. The end of that sentence explains, "... each ... organ [of the two halves of the horse's head – E.C.] would accomplish its physiological purpose in an appropriate manner" (p. 121). Individual parts fit together to make the larger organism work. Everything is connected, just as, throughout Bitov's "The Wheel," all parts of the text are connected.

The next paragraph contains a description of a horse's eyes. Eyes are circles, the same shapes Bitov keeps describing in the larger text of "The Wheel." One thing is another, Bitov again emphasizes in his next entry, "How many motorcycles are there in Russia? . . ." The entry, presumably a response to the question posed in the entry title, is a quotation from the book *Horses*, quoted in the previous entry. The entry consists of two sentences in which statistics on the number of horses in Russia are given. In this entry, then, horses are motorcycles.

One thing is another, Bitov keeps demonstrating. The passage about horses in the parallel text entry contains a description of a horse's neck as a "swan's neck." Elsewhere Bitov likens a motorcycle driver and his motorcycle in a racetrack pile-up to a centaur. Here is another version of animal/machine clusters. Circles intersect as the motorcycle (compared to a horse in the parallel texts) becomes, together with a human being, the legendary horse/human being figure of the centaur.

Philosophical issues are discussed in "The Wheel." The narrator's tone, though, is often playful. When describing a sports commentator's words at the speedway, Bitov presents the words spoken by the commentator and then explains that words and parts of words wrap around each other, one part of a sentence absorbing, "biting" its end, because of the presence of loudspeakers at the track. He includes a description of a bird's-eye view of the track, a gray nest with a big shiny egg. Salt-flats are described as having hors d'oeuvres of five-ton cucumbers on one large plate. The narrator points out that from the perspective of the rider on the motorcycle, nothing is moving. All he sees is the wheel. At one point, the narrator describes life as a closed figure, like an egg. The egg image recalls the narrator's humorous bird's-eye view of the speedway. (Some ancient Greek cosmogonies speak of the World-Egg, created by Chronos, containing the seeds of life. Other cosmogonies – the Japanese, the ancient Indian, and the Egyptian, among others, include the concept of the "cosmic egg," tying, as Bitov does, the idea of life to the image of the egg.)[25]

Wheels, Bitov writes, go around each other and around themselves. This principle certainly holds true for "The Wheel." The points the author makes about recurring and intersecting circles, the interlocking patterns he weaves, are themselves the patterns that he weaves in his works as a whole. In the same way that he says that this tiniest of worlds of ice racing becomes immense, we, the readers, can see that this tiniest of worlds of one Bitov work, "The Wheel," replicates and intersects the individual circles of other Bitov works, and the larger circle of his works taken together. As we know, Bitov keeps using circle images. We think of "The Big Balloon," with its otherworldly sphere. We think of the life-giving circle of "The Sun." We think of the roundtrip circle of "One Country." The protagonists of "The Idler," "Penelope," "The Door," and "The Garden" exist within the limited circle of fixed patterns of behavior.

Hagen highlights the Buddhist tendency in Bitov's stories of 1958–66. "The Wheel," written slightly later, suggests several Buddhist concepts, the most important of which is the symbol, in Buddhist thought and art, of the wheel of life. Time is seen as a recurring cycle. Past lives influence people in their present incarnations. There is the belief in recurring rebirths and the idea of the inability of escaping one's fate. The Buddhist wheel of the Law is the chain of causes and effects. The wheel of life is ever moving.[26]

A discourse on the motorcycle thus becomes connected to thoughts on Buddhism. In a remarkable instance of life's intersecting circles, it is germane to mention another work about motorcycles, the nature of reality, and Buddhism. *Zen and the Art of Motorcycle Maintenance. An Inquiry Into Values*, by an American former philosophy professor, Robert M. Pirsig, came out in 1974, not long after the appearance of Bitov's "The Wheel."[27]

In "Armenia Lessons," the twist of Bitov's wheel takes different turns. The narrator there declares, ". . . there is no old and new in the world because in it [the world – E.C.] *everything is now*."[28]

"The Wheel," although not directly related to Tolstoy,

contains features that are strongly reminiscent of him. In *War and Peace*, Tolstoy, in his discussion of history, uses machine imagery to convey his point that one cannot find a primary cause for an historical event. He emphasizes the interdependence of parts of a machine, of parts of history (the intertwining of people's wills), of people's actions as a cause of anything. Tolstoy speaks of fatalism, the Buddhists include the concepts of fatalism in their wheel of life (incidentally, Tolstoy wrote a very short piece, "Karma"), and Bitov, in "The Wheel," talks about fatalism. Circles of themes and images keep recurring. Bitov presents us with overlapping orbits, intersecting circles, circles that beget circles, links in a chain of circles. He does not lead us out of the circle. He merely points out the existence of circles in our lives.

Bitov leads us to ideas and images of his previous works, to Buddhism, to Goethe and eighteenth-century Europe, to Tolstoy and nineteenth-century Russia.

"ARMENIA LESSONS"

"... and what is the use of a book," thought Alice, "without pictures or conversations?"[29] (Lewis Carroll, *Alice's Adventures in Wonderland*)

The times are connected only by that which always was, that which does not have time and that which is common to all times.[30] (Andrei Bitov, "Armenia Lessons" ["Uroki Armenii"])

"Armenia Lessons" is a brilliant, original, powerful essay/meditation/travelogue on culture and values. Most of the critical reaction to it has been enthusiastic. (Soviet scholarship has given the work more attention than has Western.)[31] Expressions such as "brilliant book,"[32] great stylist and psychologist,[33] "profound and outstanding work,"[34] and "a lesson for contemporary prose"[35] pepper the discussions about Bitov's travel essay.

Although "Armenia Lessons" ("Uroki armenii"), 1967–9,[36] was written before "The Wheel," it is placed afterwards in *Image of Life*.[37] "The Wheel" ends with a discourse on the epigraph, which discourse includes an epigraph from Goethe's travelogue,

Italian Journey. "Armenia Lessons" begins with an epigraph from Pushkin's travelogue, *Journey to Arzrum*. Mandelstam's travelogue, "Journey to Armenia" ("Puteshestvie v Armeniiu"), first published in 1933, was re-issued 1967, the same year that Bitov was writing his own account of Armenia.[38] In "Journey to Armenia," Mandelstam asserts that the only book he had taken on his journey was Goethe's *Italian Journey*.

For Bitov, past culture is as alive as present culture. In "The Wheel" the past as part of the present becomes a larger social issue when Bitov speaks of the matching functions in society of past phenomena (horses) and present ones (cars). Bitov declares, in "Armenia Lessons," that a culture as a whole, with its accumulated tradition of books and cultural monuments, contains the eternal values which a society must preserve. According to Bitov, these eternal cultural values, embodied in specific literary, artistic, and architectural monuments, in places, in objects, in traditions, and in people, are what connects one age to another. He is concerned with a nation's preservation and transmission of values that transcend history, that reside in certain cultural monuments of each era.

Bitov had already dealt with narrators and protagonists whose profession was writer or journalist. In "Armenia Lessons," the author discusses the role of created products, the role of creativity in the life of a people, and the relationship of the created products (from many ages) to the life of an individual in the present. Bitov continues, in "Armenia Lessons," to include themes he had used before. He says that the past and present – everything – is contemporary. "Armenia Lessons," one of Bitov's best works, is an impassioned cry for the preservation of culture in contemporary life.

Bitov's observations are divided into eight "lessons," each containing several sections. In the course of his Armenia lessons, Bitov's narrator, Andrei Bitov, describes, in the first person, his experiences and thoughts about Armenia, about culture, and about life. His are observant eyes and open ears, as he leads the readers through a ten-day adventure in the unfamiliar terrain of Armenia.

Bitov's epigraph, taken from an early variant of the first

chapter of Pushkin's "Journey to Arzrum," is worth quoting in full since it contains, in embryonic form, themes that are central to my analysis of "Armenia Lessons." Pushkin writes,

... The slight, solitary minaret attests to the existence of a settlement that had disappeared. It [the minaret – E.C.] rises harmoniously among piles of stones on the bank of a dried up stream. An interior staircase has not yet collapsed. I climbed up [the stairs – E.C.] onto a landing from which the voice of a mullah no longer resounds. I found there several unknown names that had been scratched on the bricks by officers who were passing through. Vanity of vanities! Count *** followed me. He inscribed on the brick a name dear to him, the name of his wife – the lucky man, – and I [inscribed – E.C.] my own.

Love yourself,

My dear, lovable reader. (p. 166)[39]

The solitary minaret, built as a place of worship, stands as a present-day reflection of a dead culture. Time has allowed it to remain. People in the present, however, desecrate the age-old monument by scratching their names into its bricks. The quotation ends with Pushkin's admonishment to his readers to love themselves. These themes – the existence of past culture in the present, lack of respect for culture, and the importance of loving oneself – are played out in "Armenia Lessons."

Upon arrival in Erevan, Bitov is impressed with the ties that bind Armenians to their national cultural heritage. What immediately strikes him is the alphabet. It remains as it had been 1,500 years ago when invented by Mesrop-Mashtotz, one person, a genius, who was, writes Bitov, like God in the days of creation.[40] The letters, Bitov notices, reflect the life, landscape, and feelings of Armenia. He admires Armenians for preserving, unchanged, a piece of culture that reflects their national characteristics so precisely. (In an analogous manner, Russia's ancient alphabet seems to him to reflect Russia's landscape, architecture, and personality [p. 10]. Bitov points out the dangers of reforms that may be good from an economic standpoint, but that tamper with the natural unfolding of a nation's culture. He brings up the Russian alphabet reform which, although advantageous for the promotion of literacy, was not, he says, advantageous for the preservation of culture. For example, *War and Peace*, without hard signs, is not the same *War and Peace* that Tolstoy had written, although, he humorously adds, the elimination from the novel of the hard sign considerably reduced the number of pages. Like nature and historical monuments, language, he reflects, should be preserved.)

Bitov is impressed with the Armenians' sense of the continuity of history: "... the impression that in Armenia there is no beginning of history – it has always been. And during its eternal existence it has consecrated each stone and each step" (p. 20). All Armenians have read the works of Leo, an ancient historian of Armenia. All can tell Bitov details of history and of the history of culture whereas Bitov realizes that among the Russians he knows, only his deceased grandfather had had that ability.

Bitov's description of one place that preserves culture, the Erevan Matenadaran Repository for ancient Armenian manuscripts, is powerful. He admires the building for its simplicity, taste, and elegance. It serves its purpose without calling attention to itself. He admires a sculpture that is being chiseled. Its shapes, human forms, emerge naturally from the stone, thereby preserving the "... natural integrity of the stone" (p. 24). He lovingly describes the display of books, some more than one thousand years old: a biography of Mesrop-Mashtotz; a schoolboy's notes, one thousand years old, about botany, with a tiny flower drawn in the margin; and an ancient sketch of the heavens (p. 24). Bitov comments that although these manuscripts are ancient, a sense of life, "... simple and clear ..." (p. 26), emanates from them.

Bitov visits ancient Armenian temples and admires the structures' simple and pure lines. At a friend's house, he opens, at random, a book on the genocide of Armenians in the late nineteenth century. The book, issued by Armenia's Academy of Sciences, preserves the unpleasant part of Armenia's past.[41] The materials document brutal murders, rapes, tortures, burnings, and sufferings that Armenians had endured. This, too, is a part of the nation's past that the culture carries with it into the present.

Wherever he turns, Bitov sees that the Armenians accept themselves – with their particular past and their particular national features – as they are. Bitov sees Armenians flock, from all over the world – French popular singer Charles Aznavour, writer William Saroyan, Australians, Poles – to see their ancestral home. Bitov explains that people accept their national identity not because one nation is better than another, but because it is theirs, just as your mother, no better or worse than other women, is special precisely because she – and no one else – is the one who gave birth to you (pp. 44–5).

At his friend's house, Bitov notices an historical atlas of Armenia. As he turns the pages quickly, from past to present, the colored circle that represents Armenia becomes smaller. By turning the pages the other way, the circle becomes wider. Bitov tells us that one's perspective broadens if one includes the past in one's purview of the present.

In the same way, he begins to understand Erevan only when he broadens his perspective by exploring the surrounding areas. He complains that the modern convenience of air travel deprives people of the understanding of a new place that would come from seeing its border and experiencing the countryside bit by bit, instead of being deposited, by airplane, in the middle of "the book," without people's having "read" the beginning.

His visit to the arch of Charents imparts to him a sense of the harmony of perfect creation. The lines, the simplicity, the sense of infinity, a feeling of the "music of the spheres," of creative soaring, of majesty, penetrate his every pore as he gazes at the panorama that spreads out before him and above him. He is reminded of his Armenian friend's definition of a master: "The creation must be loftier than his hands. He'll take the clay into his hands – and it will flutter out of his hands ..." (p. 57). Bitov feels himself soaring and quotes, without identification of the source, a line of poetry: "'The heavenly flight of angels ...'" (p. 20). The line he quotes is from Pushkin's poem "The Prophet" ("Prorok"). The theme of the poem is the divine inspiration that is given to a poet.

At Lake Sevan, Bitov perceives the precision of lines and colors, of lines and light; the perfection of the landscape exactly

as it is. At an ancient monastery, the wind reminds him of the
wind in Chekhov's short story, "The Student" ("Student"),
which, writes Chekhov's narrator, had been the same wind that
had blown in the times of Riurik, Ivan the Terrible, and the
Biblical Peter (p. 66). As in "Life in Windy Weather," Bitov
associates wind with creativity and spirituality. After the Chekhov passage, without citing the source, he quotes one of
Mandelstam's Armenia poems.[42]

Bitov's visit to the "expanse" surrounding Erevan, his visit to
the monasteries and his feelings of holiness about these ancient
monuments and their close ties with their natural surroundings
infuse him with the eternal values preserved in these monuments. At those moments, he writes, he is in touch with the
boundlessness of nature's beauty and with the eternal verities
preserved in the great monuments by creative masters of his own
culture, Pushkin, Chekhov, and Mandelstam, one of whom was
speaking about the divine inspiration of the artist; another,
about the collapse of time between Biblical times and the
present; and a third, about Armenia, the place where he is
experiencing the ties between past and present culture. Bitov
ends this section with lines reminiscent of Mandelstam: "Great
poetry is always concrete. And there are no images" (p. 66).[43]

He had come to Armenia with certain ideals (images) of what
Armenia would be like. When he looked for these (for instance,
Ararat), he could not find the essence of Armenia. When he
stopped anticipating and started to experience what he himself
was experiencing, he began to grasp the true nature of Armenian
culture, a delicate, quiet, unassuming attunement to eternal
values. For Bitov, finally, the best word to describe Armenia is
"authentic" ("podlinnyi") (p. 71).

About halfway through his journey, Bitov speculates about
the nature of ideals. He wonders where they come from since, by
definition, they are not a part of the world in which we live. He
concludes that there must exist, within us, an ideal world that
forces us to compare our lives with the ideal life, that forces us to
experience shame and pangs of conscience when we do not
measure up to that ideal. He wonders where and how an image
had arisen in him "... of some heavenly country, a country of

real ideals" (p. 70). He realizes that that country had always been there, no matter where he had been: "This was a country where everything was what it was: a stone was a stone, a tree was a tree, water was water, light was light, a wild animal was a wild animal, and a human being was a human being" (p. 70).

Bitov comes to realize, gradually, what he has been learning from Armenian culture – that authenticity rests in reducing everything to its simplest elements. Only in this way can one reach the essence of an object or an experience. Life's deepest meaning emerges, naturally, without calling attention to itself. It comes from people, objects, history, being what they are and accepting who they are. It comes from "being attentive." Bitov, in the language "lesson" entitled "Allusion," explains that the Armenian word "ush" is not "ear" (the Russian word for ears is "ushi"), but "being attentive." The opposite, he says, is not "inattentive," but idiot.

As the Armenian lessons proceed, we, the pupils, together with Bitov, the teacher, learn that culture consists of "being attentive." He titles the subsection "Allusion," perhaps because it is an allusion, at the beginning of his journey, an allusion quietly waiting to show him what is being alluded to – if he is attentive and not an "idiot," "abush," which in Armenian is the opposite of being attentive. It is appropriate here, to recall Mandelstam's thought about Armenia, in his "Journey to Armenia": "... 'To see,' 'to hear,' 'to understand' – all these meanings coalesced at once into a single semantic bundle.'"[44]

From the quality of being attentive, from being oneself, Bitov realizes, emerge the self-respect, dignity, simplicity, harmony which mark off the great human beings, the highest, noblest creative acts of which people are capable, the lasting created products – architectural monuments, letters of the alphabet, churches, city buildings, books, paintings. The creators of these objects, created once and for all at one particular time, were not creating with any ideal in mind. The creations were a reflection of the creators being who they were. In being true to themselves, the creators lost a sense of themselves (that is, they had the courage to let go of the ego that tried to shape the material according to a certain image and were able to let themselves be guided by their creative impulse – in other words, "the clay fluttered out of their hands") and they thereby gained access to the "heavenly flight of angels," to the eternal values of truth, authenticity, and love that transcend any one era and that join age to age.

Bitov does not limit his discussion to high culture. Culture, he claims, exists in any realm of life. There is, for example, a culture of food and of eating. He observes, while in an Erevan bazaar, that Armenians treat their food with respect. Two plums fall from a pile of fruits, and the people's attitude toward those plums is dignified. People respect the value of the earth and of the labor that went into growing the plums (p. 75).

This brings Bitov to a key passage in "Armenia Lessons," to his discussion of the definition of culture. He does not tie it to education, for the most highly educated person, for Bitov, can be uncultured, and an illiterate person can display traits of what he defines as culture. He defines it as "... the capacity to respect." "The capacity to respect the other, the capacity to respect what you do not know, the capacity to respect bread, land, nature, history, and culture; consequently, the capacity for self-esteem, for dignity ... [,] ... the capacity not to gorge oneself" (p. 77). For Bitov, the uncultured person is a glutton. No matter how much he has consumed, he will always crave more. He will always plunder.

Bitov illustrates a lack of respect for culture in scattered incidents in "Armenia Lessons." One episode reads like a replay of a scene in the Pushkin epigraph. Pushkin describes modern visitors' scribbles on the bricks of the ancient minaret. Bitov speaks of finding tourists' scribblings at Geghard, one of the most awe-inspiring sacred churches of ancient Armenia. Bitov explains the tourists' disrespectful behavior by their being overwhelmed by, unaccustomed to, and untrained for the experience of majesty. The "... sight of true grandeur and beauty is as irritable to the untrained eye as is harsh light or sound, and all reactions that follow from this are Pavlovian..." (p. 115). Bitov explains barbarians' plundering in the same way.

Contrasts between the cultured and uncultured person emerge in the final "lessons" of Bitov's book. He describes his interview with an urban planner/"city builder" ("gradostroi-tel'"). The urban planner speaks of his goals (ideals), of the necessity of building for the future, of the necessity of building a sculpture that will stimulate curiosity in passersby to find out more about the sculptor. He speaks about "... architecture as a means of educating people ..." (p. 132). The planner will, he says, fashion what the city looks like, what people will think in the future, and the way in which people will perceive the city's "look." But, Bitov points out to him, a distinguishing feature of Erevan is its lack of one coordinated look. Since it has existed for so many centuries, it has evolved its own unique character precisely because time has shaped it. The urban planner, to Bitov, does not understand the nature of authenticity. He wants to impose his own will, under the guise of ideals, upon the shape of the city.

Bitov declares that one of the few examples he knows of one person's will being imposed upon the shape of a city is the case of Peter the Great and Petersburg. The urban planner's face lights up at the comparison. Bitov explains, later, to an acquaintance, that he had not brought up the example of Peter in a positive light, but that the urban planner had not cared what he had meant. He had wanted to impose his own ideas upon his environment.

After the interview, Bitov walks down the street about which the urban planner had declared that people would see the new structures and be inspired to ask questions about them. Bitov finds no inspiration there, and he resents being told what and how to think. Only when he wanders along century-old side streets does he feel himself in the presence of authenticity. These streets had not been planned to teach anyone anything. The buildings had been built for housing, yet because genuine life went on there, Bitov feels inspired. There is no pretense, but rather, he finds there a respect for the continuity of life and for the unfolding of life in all its multifarious, complicated, chaotic shapes and moods.

Do we appreciate, questions Bitov, what has evolved "... without our participation, – the great harmony and art of nature and time?" (p. 153). Bitov tells his acquaintance what he had

had in mind in bringing up Peter and Petersburg in his conversation with the urban planner. The passage is relevant to Bitov's points in "Armenia Lessons," about culture and lack of culture. It is crucial, therefore, to quote Bitov's own words:

... when the power of inertia of Peter's idea finally dried up, Petersburg ... in its form, entirety, and uniqueness, dictated the laws of continuation. In Russia, a few ideas, like Petersburg, like the Soviet regime, were embodied in this kind of sequence and concreteness. The commonality, of course, is purely external because the sources of these ideas are opposite, but there does exist a commonality. It is even possible that only Petersburg could have become its [the Soviet regime's – E.C.] cradle. (Only in this city, in this idea that turned to stone inevitably and purposefully, like its prospects, could the idea of ... order and harmony be incarnated.) And here is Petersburg, the most unRussian city, the triumph of Peter's idea, here it stands to this day ... And it will keep standing because Petersburg cannot be changed gradually; it can only be destroyed, ... together with the idea that created it, and the two together, city and idea, will disappear. Other beautiful Russian cities grew in a gradual ... way. They were built through the centuries by life itself, and their unique and elusive harmony and charm ... are defenseless against any constructive idea. Moscow is disappearing in this way ... In recent times, the word "construction/building" sounds more and more lofty ... whereas it is a profession, work. The builder should not be seized with arrogance. He builds something, and he builds it for someone. While he puts up a dwelling and temple, ... – he builds for himself and outside time. But as soon as he begins to build for someone else: a palace for the tsar; a private residence for the great man; a hut for the slave; he ... belongs only to his own time. And no matter how much of a genius he is, he will be outlined by the trait of his time, and he will not build for all times. Only time itself builds for all times. And it is precisely time, preserving one thing, burying another, and erecting a third, that imparts to a city its unique and beautiful features ... And if we build a city over the course of a few years (and we build it properly and as we should), then we must at least be aware that the work of centuries is not within the realm of our possibilities, and we must not flatter ourselves in this respect ... For, proceeding from even the most beautiful, but single idea, won't we foist it, already unwelcome and unsuitable, upon subsequent generations? One shouldn't build for the future, but for the present, with deep love for it. (pp. 147–9)

Here Bitov could be making a thinly veiled political allusion, as he argues for a society's evolution rather than (as in the case of

Peter the Great and that of the Soviet regime) for revolution. The question of the continuity and the violent destruction of culture will preoccupy Bitov in *Pushkin House*.

In the same section, a little later, Bitov writes, "The great textbook of harmony is given away to us by life, free, gratis. And we should remember that if we rip out all the pages, we won't have anything to study from" (p. 154). Immediately after this sentence follows a quotation, unidentified, from one of Mandelstam's Armenia poems.[45] In Erevan's narrow streets, Bitov found authenticity, the same authenticity Mandelstam, identified as "the poet" by Bitov, had found. Bitov, Mandelstam, and the old quarter of Erevan had tapped into the qualities that last and that provide continuity from one age to another.

Bitov is speaking about much more than one particular person or culture or time or place. He is sounding a warning to modern man not to violate the very earth upon which we stand. In this instance, his ecological prose begs for human beings to be attentive to, to respect nature, the land, evolution, and the ability of time to impart its own shape to the world.

The affirmation of his ideas about culture Bitov finds in a visit to an "elder," as uplifting as the immediately preceding interview with the urban planner had been disappointing. Bitov describes the characteristics of the elderly Armenian painter Martiros Saryan. He does not name him, but from his description, it is clear that he is speaking about Saryan.[46] What impresses Bitov is his youth, spontaneity, and *joie de vivre*, despite his chronological age of ninety. According to Bitov's definition, he is cultured. With a child's unsophisticated straightforwardness of expression, the artist speaks about the possibility of the annihilation of humanity by an atomic bomb. He says, simply and directly, that if people on earth do not join together, everyone will die (p. 167). He talks about the cosmos as the hope of mankind.

During the visit, Bitov contemplates Saryan's art and painting in general. He realizes that, for him, the definition of painting is "movement" (p. 167). If the movement is beautiful, the painting will be beautiful (p. 167). The reader realizes that as in other works – "Life in Windy Weather," in particular, comes to mind – Bitov connects aesthetics and ethics. Without the creator's authenticity, he believes, the resulting art cannot be genuine.

Bitov's conclusion to his "lessons" is appropriate: ". . . life dictated its own precision . . . That's the thing, that life has but a single precision – that precision which is, and all the rest is imprecise" (p. 171).[47]

The concluding section, "After the Lessons," contains Bitov's speculations after the completion of his journey. He is interested in the interrelationship of life and art. In Bitov's words, ". . . if a person writes, then he himself gets to know what he had not known before. That is his method of cognition – writing" (p. 174).[48]

He talks about the absorption of his past experience into his writing. After completing a book, he declares, the author ends up in the world he had described and he realizes that in his life, he experiences events he had described in his book (p. 175). The book, then, anticipates his personal experience (p. 174). The boundary between book and life is erased.

The final section of "After the Lessons," "Recollection of Agartsina (Three Years Later)" ("Vospominainie ob Agartsine [Cherez tri goda]") (pp. 178–83), pursues themes Bitov addresses throughout his cultural journey through Armenia. He remembers his visit to an ancient monastery, Agartsina, where he had felt dissolved into the world in which he had always lived. He had tapped into the roots of his own creative powers. The world expanded before his eyes. He felt his presence melt into the rest of the world (p. 180). There were no boundaries between him and the rest of the world. The temple, writes Bitov, showed ". . . the idea of dissolution in creation" (p. 182). Never, writes Bitov, had he experienced such humility in the "builder" (p. 182). Instead of calling attention to his own structure, the builder had directed attention to the place ". . . so that we would perceive *where* it [the temple – E.C.] was standing, where we live, the reflection of God's face in his own creation" (p. 182).

With the principle of "dissolution in creation," Bitov highlights the principles he has been enunciating all along. Only with respect for himself could the temple builder have been humble enough to lose himself and thereby gain access to the eternal. At the point at which "the clay fluttered out of his hands," the power of seeing life from multidimensional perspectives shines through, and only then is it possible to gain access to the "reflection of God's face in his own creation." These, for Bitov, are the true products of an authentic culture. And these products are the sacred manifestations that tie one genuine human being to the sacred and therefore to the qualities of the genuine and the sacred in every other culture and time that has been and will be. This "dissolution in creation" comes about for Bitov when he gains respect for himself.

The experience brought him, figuratively, to his knees (p. 183). Life was reduced to its most basic elements. He must begin from the beginning. He must learn the language anew. He must pronounce the first word, once he has gained this breadth in his life. For Bitov, the first word is "world" ("mir") (p. 183): ". . . th–is the world. It is whole. It is everything. Everything is before me. The world – is everything. The world opened up before me . . . The gateway to the world. The gates of the world. I stand at the threshold. It is I who is standing. It is I" (p. 183).

The interrelationship of the individual person, Bitov, with authentic culture, with the capacity to respect the other, brings Bitov to a respect for himself. By the end of "Armenia Lessons," we have come full-circle from the beginning. The Pushkin words quoted in Bitov's epigraph had been: "Love yourself;/My dear lovable reader."[49] In a typical Bitov merging of endings and beginnings, Bitov says, in another context, in the beginning of "After the Lessons," "I had thought that this was the end. Not at all. Right here is where everything begins" (p. 172).

In "Armenia Lessons," Bitov utilizes a technique he had used before. In "Life in Windy Weather," he had interwoven images from the Book of Psalms and Pasternak's poetry into his text and had thereby reinforced, on a stylistic level, the point he was making thematically. In "Armenia Lessons," the technique becomes a part of the message he imparts. Bitov writes, ". . . there is no new and old in the world because *everything* in it [the world – E.C.] is now" (p. 175).

Authenticity lasts, and the eternal connects one age to another. Bitov writes, "The eternal has no history. History is only for the transient. Biology has a history, but life has none. The state has a history, but a people has none. Religion has a history, but God has none" (p. 35). Particular human beings, governmental structures, and religions are time-bound, but the essence of life, of a people, and of God is eternal.

Bitov illustrates his point by weaving into his text quotations, patterns, images, and resonances from pieces of past culture that are eternal. By the end of "Armenia Lessons," Bitov has referred to ancient temples and books; Ecclesiastes; the Armenian French chansonier Charles Aznavour; the Armenian American writer William Saroyan; Jonathan Swift's *Gulliver's Travels*; Lewis Carroll's *Alice in Wonderland*; Osip Mandelstam's "Journey to Armenia" and his poems about Armenia; Pushkin's "Journey to Arzrum," "The Bronze Horseman," "The Prophet"; Turgenev's "Russian Language" ("Russkii iazyk");[50] Chekhov's story "The Student"; Soviet Mikhail Kol'tsov's travelogues; science fiction writer Ray Bradbury; Armenian customs; the inventor of the Armenian alphabet, Mesrop-Mashtotz; the Armenian historian, Leo; the contemporary Armenian artist Martiros Saryan; contemporary Armenian writer Grant Matevosian; and Dutch Renaissance painting.

Pushkin and Mandelstam play important roles in this respect. Pushkin's *Journey to Arzrum* plays a larger part in Bitov's "Armenia Lessons" than to serve as a source for its epigraph. Pushkin begins his 1829 journey to the same geographical location in which Bitov's travelogue takes place by explaining that the poet does not seek inspiration, but that inspiration seeks out the poet. This duplicates a major realization to which Bitov comes while in Erevan. It was only when he stopped searching for the essence of Armenia that the essence of Armenia found him.

Pushkin explains that during his travels, he found a copy of his "Captive of the Caucasus" ("Kavkazkii plennik"). One of the sections of Bitov's "Armenia Lessons" is entitled "Captive of the Caucasus" and the incident Bitov relates in "The Little Song," one of its subsections, replicates, in general outline, the plot of Pushkin's "Captive of the Caucasus." In both, a local woman is attracted to the "captive" Russian man. Near the end of his journey, Bitov speaks about living the experiences that he has described in his book. Here, he is living the experience which Pushkin, who had written his own travelogue, had described in one of his works. Bitov removes the boundaries between life and literature.

In *Journey to Arzrum*, Pushkin describes an incident in which poets and dervishes are deemed to be equal to political leaders, and it is the poets, he explains, to whom the political rulers bow. Bitov, like Pushkin, emphasizes a poet's exalted status. Pushkin's poem, "The Prophet," includes the theme of inspiration that Bitov discusses in his travelogue. Pushkin's "The Bronze Horseman" is discussed, revealing Pushkin's ambivalent attitude toward Peter the Great's city. Through his reference to Pushkin and through the prominent place Pushkin and Pushkin's thoughts occupy in Bitov's epigraph and essay, the reader can see that nineteenth-century culture is alive (we recall Bitov's words, "everything is now") in the present.

Mandelstam's works are equally important for "Armenia Lessons" in this respect, although his "Journey to Armenia" is not explicitly mentioned in "Armenia Lessons."[51] Bitov's original title for his Armenian travelogue was "Journey from Russia" ("Puteshestvie iz Rossii"),[52] a title that more obviously connected it to Mandelstam's "Journey to Armenia." Even without that title, "Armenia Lessons" demonstrates that the past culture of Mandelstam "lives" in the present work of Bitov. Bitov's "Armenia Lessons" seems to converse with Mandelstam's "Journey to Armenia."

As Bitov later does in "Armenia Lessons," Mandelstam begins his ruminations with a tribute to the Armenian language. Mandelstam serves as Bitov's model when he writes that he is impressed with the Armenians' ". . . magnificent familiarity with the world of real things . . ."[53] Mandelstam speaks of a "deafness" ("glukhota")[54] that he notices in speaking about Armenian culture. Bitov describes a "muteness" ("nemota") (pp. 119,174). Early in his visit, Bitov speaks of Armenia as being like the convex planes of a beer bottle, a polyhedron. The shape, he says, reminds him of Armenian churches (p. 52). Mandelstam writes about a scientist who had explained convexity and the polygon to him.[55] Mandelstam remarks on the shapes and colors of Armenia; Bitov does, too. Mandelstam declares that there is no perspective – one cannot see the horizon – in Armenia. Bitov writes that there is perspective. Mandelstam writes that he wants to live ". . . in the 'what ought to be.'"[56] Bitov writes that instead of living in the world of ideals, he wants to live life as it is.

Mandelstam describes ancient Armenian cultural monuments, and so does Bitov. Both speak of the country's sensual nature. Mandelstam describes his "sensual encounter with an Armenian church."[57] Bitov asserts that he wants to merge with the feminine landscape. Mandelstam writes that he wants Ovid, Pushkin, and Catullus to live again. One of Bitov's major points is the existence of past culture in present life. Mandelstam speaks about the state's hunger and the writer's responsibility to treat the state with compassion. Bitov speaks of the cultural person's capacity to respect the other and to understand those who feel uncomfortable in the presence of true culture. Of course, one of the major themes of Mandelstam's works was the writer's importance as the force that preserves and transmits a culture's ethical values from generation to generation. This, of course, is a major theme of Bitov's "Armenia Lessons."

Bitov preserves and transmits pieces of Mandelstam's poetry about Armenia. Without attribution, he quotes from Mandelstam's poem cycle, "Armenia" ("Armeniia"). The first line he quotes, "'Armenian speech is a wild cat'" ("'dikaia koshka – armianskaia rech''") (p. 7), appears in Bitov's first "Language Lesson" and in two out of the three final Mandelstam Armenia poems.[58] In typical Bitov fashion, beginnings are endings, and endings are beginnings. In these poems, Mandelstam asserts that the Armenian language reflects the country's landscape and history, a point Bitov emphasizes in the "language lesson."[59] Mandelstam refers to Armenia as a book, thus intertwining the concepts of culture and country, language and landscape. Bitov's longstanding theme, here and elsewhere, is the interrelationship of life's seemingly disparate dimensions.

Bitov begins his journey by reducing the culture to its simplest elements – language and alphabet. He brings into his discussion one of the eternal genuine masters about whom he later speaks with such admiration. At this incipient stage of his knowledge of Armenia, he does not yet understand or experience authenticity and its effect on him.

Bitov does not yet see the real Armenia. This fact is bolstered by the next line of Mandelstam's Armenia poems quoted in Bitov's text: "'Oh, nothing do I see, and my poor ear has gone deaf...'" ("'Akh, nichego ia ne vizhu, i bednoe ukho oglokhlo ...'").[60] A few lines after this second Mandelstam quotation, Bitov writes that he could not see Ararat when he first arrived in Erevan (p. 66).

The quotation of this line of poetry ties in with another Bitov theme, that of "being attentive," which, as we recall, is "ush" in Armenian. "Ush," we know, is not "ushi," the Russian word for ears (p. 19). By using the line of poetry which includes the Russian word "ukho" ("ear"), Bitov interweaves his words and Mandelstam's, both in direct and in more subtle ways. And we must recall that Bitov's play on the word "ush" and "ushi" in Armenian and Russian is found in the subsection entitled "Allusion," an allusion, perhaps, to the discoveries of the many layers of culture that Bitov and the reader who "sees" and "is attentive" can learn from "Armenia Lessons."

Bitov's explorations lead him from not seeing the essence, at the start of his journey, to seeing, by the end. The "Geography Lesson," in which this Mandelstam line is quoted, contains instances of Bitov's not seeing: "In no way can I believe that I *do not see* anything, ... My perception is forced, I want to see Armenia in everything – and *I do not see*" ("Ia nikak ne mogu poverit', chto *nichego ne vizhu*, ... Vospriiatie moe natuzhno, ia vo vsem khochu uvidet' Armeniiu – *i ne vizhu* [Italics mine – E.C.]") (p. 52).

Another Mandelstam Armenia poem, not cited in Bitov's text, begins with a similar line: "I will never catch sight of you,/ Near-sighted Armenian sky" ("Ia tebia nikogda ne uvizhu,/ Blizorukoe armianskoe nebo").[61] In this poem Mandelstam refers to the land as a book which the ancient Armenian people studied. Bitov makes extensive use of this concept. He compares Erevan to a book from which he is learning. He writes that the city is his alphabet, his dictionary, his conversation book. He

speaks of reading the country of Armenia. Bitov, following
Mandelstam's lead, learns the spiritual values which the sacred
ancient culture of Armenia teaches to those people who are
attuned to the melody of eternal values.

By the end of Bitov's journey, he has learned what the books,
real and metaphoric, old and new, have taught him. We must
respect "the great textbook of harmony," he writes, for if we rip
out its pages, we will not be able to study from it. At this point,
Bitov again quotes from Mandelstam, from one of the same
poems he has already cited: "'Oh, Erevan, Erevan! Or did a bird
draw you?/Or did a lion, like a child, color you with a colored
pencil case?'" ("'Akh, Èrivan', Èrivan'! Il' ptitsa tebia risovala,/
Ili raskrashival/lev, kak ditia, iz tsvetnogo penala?'").[62] Significantly, Bitov's next paragraph contains these words, "... I
finally caught sight of this Erevan. The poet could not be
inaccurate ..." ("... ia uvidel nakonets takoi Erevan. Poèt ne
mog byt' netochen ...") (p. 154).

This passage, and the episode in which Bitov walks through
the old quarters of Erevan where he finds life, occur in the
subsection he calls "Traces on Stone" ("Sledy na kamne") (pp.
143–54). One of Mandelstam's poetry collections was entitled
"Stone" ("Kamen'").[63] One of Mandelstam's "Stone" poems
speaks of "Tsarskoe Selo," a place associated with Pushkin.
Three of the poems, "The Lutheran" ("Liuteranin"), "Hagia
Sophia" ("Aiia-Sofiia"), and "Notre Dame" ("Notre Dame"),
intertwine architecture and spirituality. Many of them treat
cultural themes – Bach, Beethoven, Dickens, Racine, and so
forth.

The more we broaden our perspective, the more we are
attentive to the lessons of geography, history, and life, the more
we use the binoculars of history to extend our circles of vision, the
more we will see the underlying interconnections of particular
people and cultural monuments and places, the more we will
understand the ways in which life can be a "textbook of
harmony." As we, the readers, learn more from Bitov's lessons,
we, like Bitov, discover the ways in which Armenian culture,
Russian culture, Soviet culture, and human culture, when the
authentic people create it and see it, are one and the same. They

all, according to Bitov, contain the sacred harmony of life's most essential values.

For example, the linking of bird imagery, creativity, and divine inspiration occurs in Bitov's travel essay as his friend explains to him the definition of a master, which, as we will recall, is the person who takes the clay into his hands and then allows it to flutter out of his hands. Mandelstam, in one of the "Stone" poems, writes, "God's name, like a large bird,/Flew out of my breast" ("Bozh'e imia, kak bol'shaia ptitsa,/Vyletelo iz moei grudi").[64] Pushkin's poem, "The Prophet," quoted by Bitov in "Armenia Lessons," includes the image cluster of poet, bird, and divinity. Pushkin writes that the angel touched the poet's "ears" ("ushei")[65] and that God demanded that the prophet see and hear ("... vizhd', i vnemli,").[66] Through the intertwining and repetition of images from Pushkin, Mandelstam, and Bitov, we return to the theme of "being attentive." When we are attentive to life's allusions, we discover the world as it is, and with that discovery we come to know our true selves: the world is what it is, and I am what I am.

Pushkin's and Mandelstam's eternal voices, part of a past, continue to exist in Bitov's work. What is authentic, writes Bitov, will last, if man respects himself and others, if there is no distortion in history or personality, if man does not distort himself. It is significant that Bitov chooses Pushkin and Mandelstam, for the fate of each in contemporary life represents a major point Bitov is making. The reader knows that Pushkin's works continue to live. The reader knows that Mandelstam's fate represents part of the rupture caused by Stalin's repressive policies. As we know, Mandelstam fell victim to Stalin's paranoia, and his works began to be published again only after Stalin's death. Since Mandelstam's was an authentic voice, though, it continued to live.

Bitov's call is for the authentic, the genuine, the honest, the truthful. He believes that the only way to get authenticity is to let people, things, and cities evolve naturally. If you let things grow and flow freely and with continuity, you will, according to Bitov, get "the reflection of God's face in creation." In this he sees the only hope for the continuation of the genuine in the world. In the preservation of culture in its highest sense, he sees the only possibility for the preservation of mankind's eternal values.

At the beginning of Bitov's sojourn in Armenia he had visited the Matenadaran Repository for ancient manuscripts. The manuscripts were propped up on stands, imparting eternal wisdom to those people who listen, who are attentive. One of the manuscripts was a biography of the divinely inspired creator of the Armenian alphabet, a representative of Bitov's eternal category of a people. A second manuscript, the thousand-year-old schoolboy's botany exercise book on which he had drawn a little flower, represents Bitov's eternal category of life. A third, an ancient sketch of the celestial spheres, is symbolic of Bitov's eternal category of God. The spiritual dimension in man, the life-force, and a people's values will endure, says Bitov, as long as there are people who respect what is and what has been, for that is the only way to guarantee that the genuine, the honest, the good, and the true will endure.

Most of the sparse criticism that exists on "Armenia Lessons" concurs that the work is one of Bitov's best. One of the few dissenters is Vsevolod Sakharov, who is troubled by what he sees as the inaccessibility of "Armenia Lessons" to the average reader. In claiming that one needs a "dictionary–commentary" to unravel obscure literary references, in claiming that Bitov can be understood only by an erudite audience,[67] Sakharov misses the point of Bitov's tour de force.

Igor' Zolotusskii is more perceptive. He is, I believe, right on target when he writes that Bitov is in the tradition of Dostoevsky in constantly speaking about the big, eternal questions.[68]

IMAGE OF LIFE – CONCLUSION

Vsevolod Sakharov spoke with greater acumen than he had about "Armenia Lessons" when he discussed the unity of *Image of Life*, seeing the book as a sort of Bildungsroman whose individual pieces, although written at different times, come together to form a new whole.[69] Another critic, V. Gusev, sees all of Bitov's heroes as one person, deeply troubled by moral questions, in a constant search for what makes life worth living.[70]

Bitov's quest, in *Image of Life*, is to get beyond the image, to life itself. At the beginning of "The Door," the door is closed to reality. The focus is on the personal, psychological plane, as Bitov shows the dangers of believing in an idealized version of reality rather than seeing life as it is. By the end of "Armenia Lessons," Bitov extends his perimeters to include sociological, cultural, and historical dimensions. He opens the door to reality, and he knows, finally, who he is. "In front of me the world opened up . . . I'm the one who is standing. It is I."[71]

CHAPTER 7

"Seven Journeys": journeys to the other and journeys to the self

SEVEN JOURNEYS – INTRODUCTION

Bitov's next collection, *Seven Journeys (Sem' puteshestvii)*[1] contains, as the title indicates, seven works that concern travel. Most had appeared in earlier Bitov collections, but this is the first time that he groups his travel literature together.

Several scholars have written on the travel theme as a continuing preoccupation of Bitov's. Schmid maintains that the journey serves as the basis for most, if not all, of Bitov's works.[2] For Mikael Klefter, Bitov's central premise is that life is a journey; he divides the people in Bitov's works into those who travel (move, change place) and those who remain in a fixed position.[3] One critic observes that Bitov's works always deal with characters who change place and always focus, in the journey structure, on psychology and ethics rather than on external features of the landscapes.[4]

Five out of the seven journeys – "Such a Long Childhood," "One Country," "The Wheel," "Journey to a Childhood Friend," and "Armenia Lessons" – I have discussed in the context of earlier Bitov collections. We learn new things by examining their function in the new setting. In *Seven Journeys*, we follow the progress of Bitov's journeys. He orders his journeys chronologically, by date. What unites the journeys is Bitov's attention to change, to movement from one state of being to another.

"THE GAMBLE"

The journey in "The Gamble (The Journey's Seamy Side)" ("Azart [Iznanka puteshestviia]") (1971–2)[5] reminds us of other Bitov journeys. "Armenia Lessons" teaches us that the path to authenticity lies in the capacity to be attentive, to see, to listen. "The Wheel" shows repetitive circles from which there is no escape. "The Gamble" teaches the human being to be attentive to, to listen to, his own inner voice.

Bitov connects this journey to his journey to Uzbekistan, described in "One Country." He does this by changing the name of the protagonist in the *Seven Journeys* version of "One Country" to Karamyshev, the name he uses for the main protagonist of "The Gamble." The author comments that his journey to Uzbekistan a decade ago ("One Country" had appeared a decade before) had been made at a time when he had observed reality not as it is, but as an "image" ("obraz") (p. 479). The author links his previous works to "The Gamble," for the reader who knows other Bitov writings can immediately relate this to *Image of Life* and to the themes of illusion and reality that he addresses there.

The interplay between illusion and reality captures Bitov's attention in "The Gamble." He writes that the convention of a travelogue demands that the author write not about what happened to him – i.e., about what *was* – but about events that he witnessed without participating in them. In "The Gamble," Bitov defies the convention and writes, instead, about what happened to him when he traveled to another geographical location and made discoveries about his own life.

In the past, Bitov had merged first-person and third-person narration. In "The Gamble," voices also merge. There is a first-person narration. The narrator speaks of writing a story about a character, Karamyshev. The events of the story's plot then take place in the narrator's life. The narrator then declares that he believes in the existence of creative imagination. From that point on, some of the action is described in the first person, and some as happening to Karamyshev. The boundaries between the protagonist created by the narrator and the narrator created by Bitov are blurred. Bitov addresses the question of the illusion of fictional time in *Pushkin House*. There, he also discusses the relationship of authorial time to the hero's time. In "Armenia Lessons," Bitov, as we know, speaks of the blurring of boundaries between books and life, for his narrator discovers that what he writes about then occurs in life.

The theme of illusion and reality appears humorously, in a sense of "The Gamble" in which an old building, used as part of a movie set, is decorated – in the present – in order to make it look old for the movie. Bitov is playful as he muses that he had been freer during his previous trip to Uzbekistan, for he had not had the "luxury" of access to a car. This time, his greater status affords him the illusory sense of greater convenience. In reality, trying to get a car and driver when he needs them proves to be complicated and burdensome. He writes that he had been freer a decade before because he had been free of reality, which, at the time, he had not known.

Change continues to preoccupy Bitov in the sixth of the seven journeys, "The Gamble." His tale begins with an epigraph explaining that there is a time during which things exist in a state of non-being before they exist in a state of being, "'for time and matter precede everything whose existence has a beginning in time ...'"[6] The quotation is from "The Book of Salvation" by Avicenna, the renowned medieval physician and philosopher who had lived, for a time, in Uzbekistan (near Bukhara), the setting for "The Gamble."[7]

The aspect of change that concerns Bitov in "The Gamble" is the movement away from a human being's self-destructive behavior toward a self-affirming approach to life. The motion described is, first, motion backwards, away from the positive, and then, forward, toward healthier living. Bitov's narrator describes the state of not listening to his inner voice and then, during the course of "The Gamble," plots the journey toward his decision to live guided by the dictates of his inner voice. The events described in "The Gamble" are connected to Avicenna's passage from "The Book of Salvation." The way to "save yourself," for Bitov, lies in the capacity to trust one's inner voice. He shows that the capacity had existed, within the narrator, in a state of non-being before it had begun to exist in a state of being.

On the surface, "The Gamble" recounts the adventures of the narrator as he accepts a writing assignment – and the promise of forty-five rubles as payment – to travel to the city of Khiva, Uzbekistan. His intuition urges him to stay home, out of worry that his lover will betray him. He realizes, ironically, that his willingness to go to Uzbekistan means that he values a paltry forty-five rubles more than his life and that he is more hesitant about saying no to strangers than he is about ensuring his own personal happiness by staying with his lover.

His arrival in Khiva, the brief descriptions of his hotel room, of the city, of the people he first meets, of his visit to a cotton-growing kolkhoz, are tangential to the central incident of "The Gamble," an actual gambling game upon which the narrator accidentally stumbles during his wanderings through the city's bazaar. Bitov masterfully describes the psychology of the gambler; his description differs from other descriptions of gamblers in Russian literature. The narrator first evokes Pushkin's notorious gambler, Hermann, of "The Queen of Spades" ("Pikovaia dama"), as he comments that he, like Hermann, watches every move of the game without participating in it. He, like Hermann, then begins to play.

The similarity between the Bitov and Pushkin works stops at this point, for their emphases are different. Pushkin poses, but does not answer, questions about the relationship between the conscious and unconscious worlds, between the rational and the irrational, between an externally motivated, supernatural force and the force of a crumbling psyche of an individual compulsively driven by an obsession. Dostoevsky, in *The Gambler* (*Igrok*), concentrates on a compulsive gambler's psychology.

Bitov emphasizes psychology, but his perspective is different. He speaks about the game between the player (himself) and the "croupier." He focuses on this rivalry with him and his attraction to him as to authority figures upon whom, in childhood, he had had crushes. The narrator imagines the special knowledge that he thinks he and the croupier share as beings superior to others in the game. He imagines that the croupier favors him because he, unlike other players, understands the game. On all these counts he is wrong, for he notices that he has begun to lose and that the powerful croupier can do anything he pleases. During his musings, the narrator thinks about the special bonds among the players, for they share the same feeling at the same moment and cannot therefore be lonely.

The narrator comes to the realization, as he is losing, that he knows that he is destroying himself. He is not losing the *game*, but is losing to the other more powerful *person*. This partner's strength is what appeals to him. In life, too, muses the narrator, people act self-destructively, fully conscious of what they are doing. They then forget and become unaware of what they are doing (p. 506). Bitov analyzes the automatic-pilot response to life, documented in "Penelope," "The Door," and "The Garden." In "Journey to a Childhood Friend," he describes a rivalry between two personality types. In "The Gamble," Bitov's narrator maintains that the awareness of non-self-destructive behavior existed all along – "in a state of nonbeing," in Avicenna's words – even as he was acting against his own best interests.

What the narrator learns about his psychology during the game of "Italian lottery" in Khiva is the first of a set of major revelations that jolt him out of his self-destructive behavior. Having lost forty-eight rubles (we recall that he was paid forty-five rubles), he goes to a restaurant. Along the way, he decides to write a story in which the character will see the croupier sitting at a table in the restaurant. He rejects this thought since there would not have been enough time for the croupier to get to the restaurant before the narrator. The narrator walks into the restaurant, and his "rival," the person to whom he had lost the game, is already there.

The croupier leaves, and the narrator becomes involved in an unpleasant conversation with a restaurant patron who does not believe him. (The pretext for the altercation is amusing, for the man who picks the fight insists on seeing the "poetry" in the narrator's notebook. The narrator keeps telling him that it is not poetry [it is a list of his expenses], and the man, for some reason, becomes irate.)

The narrator's initial reaction to the possibility of the trip to Khiva had been negative. What happens next confirms the fact that he should have acted according to his intuition. After he leaves the restaurant, he is accosted and almost dies. His savior – this part of the story is told in the third person, about Karamyshev – is the person to whom he had lost in gambling.

The incident shakes the narrator to his core. He realizes that he must always listen to his inner voice, and he decides that he must immediately leave for home. While waiting the extra days for the next flight out, he becomes friends with the person who had saved his life. He visits several minarets. Like the protagonists in many Bitov works, the narrator experiences moments of oneness with the universe. Gazing at the landscape – "sky" and "desert" (p. 516) – he realizes that Uzbek cupolas are the color of the sky, and the yellow houses and walls, the color of the desert. He senses the ". . . interpenetration of the spheres and the surroundings because of the absence of a boundary . . ." (p. 516). Despite other people's advice that he will not find a particular minaret interesting, he acts according to his own wishes and climbs that minaret.

He realizes that he has always allowed himself to be drawn into people's games. He realizes that he had not controlled his life and that when he listens to his own voice as a guide to live his own life, he feels at one with the world.

True connections with people and with the world come about only when he makes a connection with himself first, i.e., when he trusts himself. One should do this, he says, even when this flies in the face of rationality. (The idea is reminiscent of "Infantiev," where the protagonist is not certain whether to trust what he sees, although his rational mind rejects the mystical evidence.) Bitov again cites Avicenna, who felt that ignorance makes us reject things which do not seem possible. According to Avicenna, one should not turn away from knowledge acquired through the gift of prophecy (p. 520).

Bitov's journey in "The Gamble" takes him into the interpenetration of the journey's non-seamy and seamy sides, of the layers of non-being and being, of illusion and reality, of game and life, of objective reality and mystical other-worldly reality. He pursues, vigorously, the proposition that life is a growing, changing phenomenon whose separate categories spill over into one another and form an interdependent whole. The substance of separate Bitov works bears this out. The "how" of his works – the way he links work to work, narrator to character, narrator to previous narrators – attests to his underlying premises about life. Throughout his works, he maintains that personal integrity, to oneself and to others, is the foundation upon which all else rests.

"CHOICE OF LOCATION"

Of central import to Bitov is the relationship of life to images of life. The relationship of art to life is of prime concern to him in "Choice of Location (Three Georgians)" ("Vybor natury [Tri gruzina]"), (1971–3),[8] a speculative essay/travelogue about the Soviet Republic of Georgia. The title provides the first indication to the reader of the direction in which Bitov will be going. "Vybor natury" ("Choice of Location") refers, in Russian, to the choice of location for filming a movie "na nature" ("on location"). The word "natura" ("nature"), in Russian, refers to nature or to an artist's model; "risovat' s natury" means "to paint from life." The subtitle, "Tri gruzina" ("Three Georgians") refers to three people. (The three Georgians whom Bitov discusses are involved in creating the art of the cinema; they produce artistic images of life.) The choice of location for the film is a place in nature, in life. The live human beings about whom Bitov speaks are artists. The title, then, interweaves art and life.

Bitov's choice of literary location for his essay underscores the same principles. Appropriately, he chooses an epigraph from Mikhail Lermontov's *A Hero of Our Time*, an artistic work set in the Caucasus, which purports to contain its protagonist's real-life journal. Bitov's narrator, also a traveler to the Caucasus, relates his purported real-life meetings with three artists. Lermontov's narrators and his fictional protagonist, Pechorin, relate their alleged real-life experiences.

Bitov's epigraph constitutes the first paragraph of Lermontov's "Bela." Its first words, "I was going" ("ia ekhal"),[9] are linked to the last words of Bitov's introductory remarks: "... I am going" ("... ia edu") (p. 526). The Lermontov passage ends with the word "whole" ("tsel").[10] Bitov's introductory section, which immediately follows the epigraph, begins with the word "whole" ("tsel'nyi") (p. 525).

The noun to which Bitov's adjective refers here is "image"

("obraz") (p. 525). He states that the Russian's image of Georgia, culled from literary images created by Pushkin, Lermontov, and Tolstoy, is accurate, for these authors, in their images of Georgian life, had captured the Georgian soul in a way that even a prolonged stay, on the part of a Russian reader, would not have been able to produce. Thus, the real knowledge of the Caucasus comes from books. Bitov writes that art is "... the homeland of the original image" ("... rodina pervonachal'-nogo obraza") (p. 525), that it conquers the "... inexactitude of our ideas..." ("... netochnost' nashikh predstavlenii...") (p. 525).

The rest of "Choice of Location" notes the ways in which art and life are, during Bitov's trip to Georgia, inextricably bound. Structurally, in each section of "Choice of Location," Bitov alternates the focus of his observations between art and life. Each section devoted to life is shown to correspond to art, or our images of life, and each section whose focus is art is shown to capture the essence of life.[11]

First come his observations about Tbilisi, a city which, for Bitov, is alive because it has taken shape organically. The "living rhythm" of the city, he writes, "... begins to coincide with your breathing..." (p. 529). Bitov's idea is that the city, a created product of people, corresponds, in vitality, to the living organism of a human being.

Bitov pursues the idea of the erasure of boundaries between biological life and the created products of a human being as he speculates, in the next section of "Choice of Location," on "the phenomenon of the norm" (p. 535). He repeats principles enunciated in "Armenia Lessons" and in "Life in Windy Weather," for the realms of art, nature, and the divine are shown to correspond to one another. In "Choice of Location," Bitov speaks of the "divine norm" (p. 537) that characterizes Mozart's music, the created products of a human being: "The same [norm – E.C.] as in nature, – the norm of creation" (p. 537).

The first Georgian artist whom Bitov describes, film director Otar Ioseliani, embodies in his work the qualities Bitov admires in Tbilisi. Two of Ioseliani's movies, "The Falling of the Autumn Leaves" ("Listopad"), 1967, and "There Lived a

Singing Thrush" ("Zhil pevchii drozd"), 1972, explains Bitov, contain incidents that seem to be haphazardly thrown together. By the end of the films, though, the viewer realizes that these seemingly haphazard incidents have produced a strong impression of life. We, the readers of Bitov's essay, understand that what attracts Bitov to Tbilisi, the feeling of vitality that emerges from the organic shaping of the city, is the same impulse that draws the author to Ioseliani's films. Bitov's observations of Ioseliani, the man, bear out the qualities he has found in the films of Ioseliani, the director. Bitov writes that it is as if Ioseliani, in his works, had not discovered anything, but that, rather, everything had come about of its own accord. The author wonders, "Is the world in the reflection or is the reflection that is familiar to us in the world?" (p. 548).

The next Georgian cinematic hero is scenario writer Revaz Gabriadze, whose "wholeness, integrity" ("tsel'nost'") as a person Bitov admires. He admires Gabriadze's capacity, in his work, to create his own world, the world of Gabriadze and of Georgia, whether the material be French (Claude Tillier's "Don't Grieve" ["Ne goriui"]), Italian (Luigi Pirandello's "The Jar" ["La giara"], ["Kuvshin"]), or Soviet (Zoshchenko's "Serenade" ["Serenada"]) (pp. 558–9).[12] Bitov is impressed by the mythic, folk quality of Gabriadze's works and by the fact that they can be widely understood. The implication is that by being himself, Gabriadze can forge bridges to the universal, can tap into the qualities of all of these films that create a "fusion" that is universally understood.

The third Georgian whom Bitov spotlights is Erlom Akhvlediani, writer of the script for the film, "Pirosmani," about Georgian artist Niko Pirosmanashvili, and of a cycle of stories about two friends, Vano and Niko.[13] Bitov admires Akhvlediani's ability to free his works of any imprint of a particular author – in other words, the capacity to free himself from himself. Bitov declares that a prominent Soviet professor of literature, N. Berkovskii, had expressed disbelief when told that these stories were written by one author (p. 580).

The section of "Choice of Location" concentrating upon Akhvlediani is sandwiched between two episodes that focus on experiences from the narrator's life. The first is his visit to Svetitskhoveli, one of Georgia's oldest temples. The narrator experiences a sense of silence and stillness that differs from the kind he had experienced in Armenian temples. The unique quality of silence in the Georgian temple was, he realizes, familiar to him only from the sensation he had experienced, not in life, but as he had watched Akhvlediani's film "Pirosmani." Another instance of the intertwining of life and art occurs in the section preceding the scene describing the visit to Svetitskhoveli. He speaks of visiting a village where wine is produced. As he is eating with a Georgian friend, he feels that their tables are fusing, that the friend has stepped out of the Pirosmanashvili painting, "The Princes' Banquet" ["Pir kniazei"].[14] The friend assumes the characteristics of the narrator's father in his youth, familiar to the narrator from a photograph. Everything, he writes, seemed to merge; he even understood the friend's toast, pronounced in Georgian.

This episode is strategically placed in "Choice of Location," for it links the episode that precedes it, the description of Gabriadze's art, and the one that follows it, the section about Akhvlediani. What Bitov notices in Gabriadze's films, the director's capacity to dissolve the boundaries between French, Italian, and Russian films, he experiences in his life. He experiences the dissolution of boundaries between himself, other people, the Georgian and Russian languages, his father and his friend, the Georgian painting of Pirosmanashvili and Russian life, images of life and life (Figure 8 shows "Georgian Bitov").

Just as this episode becomes entwined with Bitov's previous remarks about Gabriadze's art, it becomes entwined with the part of the essay that treats Akhvlediani's film scripts, for, it will be recalled, Akhvlediani had written the script for the movie "Pirosmani," about the artist's life.

The conclusion of "Choice of Location," placed after the Akhvlediani section, repeats the art/life merging that has functioned as the unifying principle of construction and theme in Bitov's travelogue/essay. Entitled "Leaving the Movie Theatre" ("Vykhod iz teatra"), this section records the narrator's sensations as he leaves the theater where he had seen Akhvlediani's

8 Bitov's friend, Revaz Gabriadze, head of the Puppet Theater in Tbilisi,
made this puppet of Bitov as a Georgian prince, for Bitov's fiftieth birthday
in 1987.

film. The first words, "I" and a verb of motion: "I walked out of
the movie theater" ("Ia vyshel iz kinoteatra . . .") (p. 590), take
us back to and provide links with the first words of the epigraph,
"I went" ("ia ekhal") and to the last words of the introductory
section, "I am going" ("ia edu"). One of Akhvlediani's creations seems to accompany the narrator as he emerges from the
theater into the street. The sense of silence that he experiences is

one that he is aware of having felt before – "... not in a movie," he writes, "... but in life ..." (p. 591).

The final words of the essay, an unidentified couplet of poetry written by Bitov,[15] note that the success of art cannot be fully explained (p. 591). These words, too, reverberate to another part of the essay, for in the introductory section Bitov had said that he would attempt to find reasons for the success (the same word for success, "udacha," is used in both instances) of art by focusing on three examples "... in order to elucidate its nature and source" (p. 526).

We are left with the idea that the true nature of successful art cannot be fully explicated, yet in the course of Bitov's reflections on life and art he has explained what makes the films of Otar Ioseliani, Revaz Gabriadze, and Èrlom Akhvlediani come alive for him.

Furthermore, in his ruminations on Georgian art and life, Bitov has set forth the very priorities about art and life that inform his own works. The descriptions of Tbilisi and of Ioseliani's films suggest a principle according to which Bitov had been constructing his own works from the earliest stages of his career. Follow whatever life offers, and the artistic shape will emerge of its own accord. Live life in its seemingly asymmetrical pieces, and the meaning will emerge that ties the separate fragments together.

Bitov's description of the major protagonist of one of Ioseliani's films, "There Lived a Singing Thrush," presents us with a portrait of a spiritual brother of some of Bitov's creations. Like Bitov's Lobyshev (in "Penelope") and his idler (in "The Idler"), Ioseliani's character is an aimless drifter. As in many Bitov stories, the protagonist acknowledges the existence of a loftier dimension in life. For Ioseliani's hero, a musician, music fulfills this function. (Significantly, the section about this Ioseliani film immediately follows the passage in which Bitov discusses the "divine norm" of Mozart's music.)

When Bitov praises Gabriadze's "wholeness" as a person and as an artist, rich connections can be made to observations Bitov had made in another context. In "Armenia Lessons," he had concluded that when people and cultures are who they are, they are linked to all other authentic people and cultures across time and space. When authentic artists, he had written, create authentic works of art, those works of art are vital, alive, living beings. Bitov says the same thing about an individual person's being true to himself. In "The Garden," as Alesha learns to live a life of authenticity, he finds that there is a correlation between his thoughts and the thoughts in the mysterious sacred book he peruses.

Bitov's analysis of Akhvlediani's writing focuses on the set of characteristics he had outlined in "Armenia Lessons" to describe a master – someone who, when he takes the clay into his hands, allows it to flutter out of his hands – and to describe one of the genuine Armenian temples – where the personality of the builder had dissolved in order to allow the place to be focused on. In the case of Akhvlediani, Bitov speaks admiringly of his ability, in his works, to efface his personality.

In "Armenia Lessons," Bitov had spoken about how genuine past art (Pushkin's, Mandelstam's) lives in the present. In "Choice of Location," he emphasizes the lack of boundaries between art and life. True art reflects true life. Living honestly (i.e., true life) is necessary to create true art.

In previous works, Bitov had been preoccupied with the dissolution of boundaries. In "Choice of Location," the boundaries between art and life are mercurial, slippery – if not impossible to fix – as they, too, dissolve.

CHAPTER 8

"The Days of Man": roles and rhymes

THE DAYS OF MAN – INTRODUCTION

Bitov's book *The Days of Man. Tales (Dni cheloveka. Povesti)* 1976,[1] contains a novel, *The Role, Novel with Ellipses (Rol', roman-punktir)*; one hundred pages entitled "The Young Odoevtsev, Hero of a Novel" ("Molodoi Odoevtsev, geroi romana"); and a philosophical essay, "Birds, or New Information About Man" ("Ptitsy, ili Novye svedeniia o cheloveke"). These "days of man" include a "roman," which, in Russian, as in French, can mean either a novel (a piece of literature, an image of life), or a romance (a piece of life). The novel *The Role* documents, chronologically, at different times in his life, one man's love for a woman. "The Young Odoevtsev" is connected, in title, to *The Role*, by the use, again, of the word "novel." This section is connected, with a "dotted line," to another novel, *Pushkin House*, for it is, in substance, five chapters of *Pushkin House*. Finally, "Birds," an essay about birds, discusses some of the issues that preoccupy Bitov in his discussions about human beings in the rest of the book.

THE ROLE: "THE THIRD STORY"

The first part of *The Days of Man* consists of *The Role. Novel with Ellipses*. The novel, as published in *The Days of Man*, is made up of five short stories, three of which ("The Door," "The Garden," and "Infantiev") had been published, years before, as separate short stories and in previous collections of Bitov's and two of which ("The Third Story" ["Tretii rasskaz"] and "The Forest" ["Les"]) had recently come out in journals, under different titles, as separate short stories.[2]

153

The novel has undergone name changes. In the English translation, in *Life in Windy Weather*, it is called *The Lover. A Novel with Ellipses*. Priscilla Meyer explains that Bitov titled it anew because *The Role* sounded awkward in English. The titles he contemplated, besides *The Lover*, were *The Twin* and *The Double*.[3] Revaz Gabriadze, a close friend of Bitov's, asserts that the novel is called *Vanishing Monakhov* (*Uletaiushchii Monakhov*).[4] Bitov referred to the Russian title of the novel as *Uletaiushchii Monakhov* in a talk at Columbia University,[5] and it came out under that title in the USSR in 1990. The last three pages of the 1990 edition constitute a new section, a poem entitled "The Staircase (The Sixth Story)" ("Lestnitsa [Shestoi rasskaz]").[6]

The Role first came out, in *The Days of Man*, without "The Taste" ("Vkus"), the story that was originally going to end the novel. Bitov states that the publisher insisted on replacing "The Taste" with "Infantiev."[7] The English translation of the novel includes "The Taste" as the final story. The story first appeared in Russian, as a separate story, with Gabriadze's explanatory note about its relationship to the novel, in the Soviet publication *Literary Georgia* (*Literaturnaia Gruziia*).[8]

All the titles Bitov chose for his novel contain a reference both to a person and, by implication, to an "other" person. The notion of lover implies the existence of another person. The concepts of a twin and a lover assume the existence of another person, a mirror image, a person who is you and yet not you. A vanishing Monakhov, one who is flying off, could imply someone who is there and yet not there. A role implies the existence of an other. An actor plays the role of a "someone-other-than-himself." In a play, a role is an image of life.

The implications embedded in Bitov's titles fit into a pattern that Bitov often weaves in his works. It is to a major concern, the relationship of an image of life to life, that the author addresses himself in the first three stories of *The Role*, "The Door," "The Garden," and "The Third Story" (originally titled "The Image").

The novel plots Aleksei Monakhov's journey, as he moves from one stage of life to another. Priscilla Meyer speaks of the derivation of the name Monakhov from the Russian word "monakh," or "monk," and of the state of isolation associated with being a "monk."[9] "The Garden," she explains, concerns adolescence. "The Third Story" demonstrates the character's awareness, a decade later, of the subjective quality of love.[10] Hagen, too, speaks of the stories in *The Role* as centering on one person's maturation. He connects the first four stories by explaining that each highlights a formative episode in Mona- khov's life from adolescence to middle age.[11] He speaks of the increasing pessimism of "The Third Story" in comparison with the preceding two stories.[12] Ronald Meyer's work on *The Days of Man* focuses on the move from the protagonist's innocence in "The Door" to his discovery, in "The Garden," that people play roles (Asya deceives him), to his change in attitude toward Asya in "The Third Story."[13] Gabriadze identifies love as the major theme of this novel that centers on one hero over a span of twenty years.[14]

In the author's preface to *Life in Windy Weather*, Bitov writes, "Perhaps these stories [the stories in the English collection – E.C.], my proto-novel, were in part about how a person is unable to evaluate the *present*, tied as he is to the undigested past."[15] In *The Role*, Bitov demonstrates that his character's present is cluttered with the debris of an undigested past. The character, Aleksei Monakhov, is familiar to readers of Bitov works. He aimlessly wanders, as do the idler and Lobyshev. He lies, as does Alesha of "A Nothing." Like Lobyshev, he deceives others.[16] Betrayal and deception between a man and a woman connect Monakhov to the "star" of "My Wife Is Not At Home."

Monakhov's patterns follow him from one story of *The Role* to another. I have noted, in an earlier section of this book, the interrelationship of "The Door" and "The Garden." "The Door" featured a boy deceived by an older woman. "The Garden" concerned a slightly older young man, Alesha, who knew that Asya, the older woman with whom he was involved, was deceiving him. In "The Third Story," placed by Bitov as the third story, following "The Door" and "The Garden," in *The Role*, Aleksei Monakhov accidentally meets Asya on a bus ten years after the incidents recounted in "The Garden."

"The Third Story" self-consciously repeats incidents from "The Door" and "The Garden." As in "The Garden," Aleksei tags along as Asya does errands. A key scene in "The Third Story" takes place in a kindergarten; the word "garden" ("sad") in the Russian phrase for kindergarten, "detskii sad," repeats the title of the story of Alesha's previous encounter with Asya. As in "The Door," Aleksei waits for Asya in a cold stairwell as he glances at the closed door behind which Asya is hidden.[17] Bitov underscores the parallel. While waiting, Monakhov speculates that passersby might "... think that he was waiting, like a boy, ... for someone," ("... podumat', chto on zhdët ... kogo-to, kak mal'chik").[18] (The main protagonist of "The Door" was "the boy" ["mal'chik"].) When he smokes, he recalls a similar incident, recounted in "The Door." Monakhov is transformed, for an instant, into his former self. He muses, "... everything repeats itself ... All situations are the same. Like offprints. Word for word. Only paler. Or like a broken record. Everything is the same; only the sound worsens with each turn. The wheezes, the crackles ... Everything is the same; only we are no longer the same ..." (p. 88).

Everything is, at once, the same and different; and this is one of Bitov's major points in "The Third Story." Asya has not changed, yet the changed Monakhov sees her differently. He is now married, and his wife is about to give birth to their first child. Asya continues to be enmeshed in divorces and extramarital affairs. (In "The Garden," Asya was about to be divorced. In "The Third Story," she is divorcing a man whom she was getting to know in "The Garden," and she now has a new fiancé.) Monakhov is now indifferent to her flirtations and sexual advances to him. He sees that she plays roles. He observes that she seems to hold up different masks to her face. He now sees through her deceitful behavior.

Monakhov realizes that the Asya he had known had never existed. "It had been an image, ..." ("Byl obraz, ...") (p. 75). In using the word "image" ("obraz"), Bitov links this story to *Image of Life*, the first story of which is "The Garden." He introduces a principal theme of "The Third Story," originally entitled "The Image," and of Bitov's work in general. The boy in "The Door" clings to his image of life; there is a disparity between the boy's image of life and life. In "The Garden," we learn about the experience of love. Bitov traces a move away from a life of lies toward a life of honesty and authenticity. The direction had been from the negative to the positive. The ecological system Bitov was building was an expanding one, since Alesha's growth was linked to a positive value, that of love.

"The Third Story" presents a much more negative view of life. Monakhov does not respond to Asya's advances to him, but he does not see this as a healthy sign of maturity. Instead, he realizes that the reason for his lack of response is his numbness to feeling. He comments, "When, in childhood, feelings were real, people were unreal: they were ... images" (p. 95). When we began to see people for what they are, Monakhov continues,

... our feelings became unreal. Now feeling has become an image, the image of a feeling. There is no feeling, just its image, no love – just the image of love, no betrayal – just the image of betrayal, the image of friendship, ... etc. And a person with experience has begun to understand the world even less than a child; he has become even more entangled in it [the world – E.C.] because of the lack of reality of his own feelings. (p. 95)[19]

The universe of "The Third Story" is a collapsing one. The ecological organism Bitov describes is on its way from life to death. In "The Third Story," Bitov implies that when we move away from our images of life to life itself, we lose the ability to live. We become empty shells of our real selves. Experience saps vitality. The use of the title *The Role* now becomes clear. Bitov says that as one gains experience in life, one plays the role of a real person. We are no longer ourselves, but doubles or twins of real, feeling people. To support this pessimistic reading, we can cite the epigraph to *The Lover* that Bitov affixed to the English translation. The quotation, from Revelation, is: "But I have this against you, that you have abandoned the love you had at first."[20]

Bitov plots the movement of life toward death. In "The Third Story," he uses the image of a record whose rotations produce more and more cracked versions of themselves. The record, a

wheel of sorts, brings to mind the final entries of "The Wheel,"
where Bitov spoke of the inability to escape the wheel of fate/
death. "The Last Bear" concerns a bear who repeats bear
actions, but who has lost the capacity of being a bear. These
works were written at approximately the same time. In each,
Bitov examines the path toward death. "The Wheel" emphasizes abstract, philosophical issues. "The Last Bear" addresses
societal-cultural and biological issues. "The Third Story" concentrates on the process of emotional dying within one individual's life.

At the end of "The Third Story," Monakhov's mother tells
him that his wife has given birth to a "little boy" ("mal'chik")
(p. 99). The entrance into the world of a boy reinforces, in the
reader's mind, the continuity of life. The boy ("mal'chik") of
"The Door" has grown up and has become the father of a boy.
Bitov emphasizes something different, though. He underscores
Monakhov's lack of feeling: "Monakhov looked in horror" (p.
99). His cheek, which he withdraws from his mother's kiss, is
described as "unfeeling" (p. 99). Monakhov the monk withdraws from the world of feeling. In so doing, he abandons the life
he had at first and moves closer to death.

"THE FOREST"

"The Forest" ("Les"), (1965, 1972)[21] depicts Monakhov,
already middle aged, divorced, remarried, and an established
Moscow engineer, as he visits his parents and a former mistress in
Tashkent while on a business trip. Monakhov is the person
anaesthetized to life whom we observed in "The Third Story."
In "The Forest," we read another offprint of the same story.
The pattern is the same – a deceived spouse (this time, Monakhov deceives his wife); a younger man in love with an older
woman who is interested in another man. The "older woman" is
Natalia, in her early twenties, who is worshipped by Lenechka,
four years her junior. She, in turn, is interested in Monakhov.
Monakhov's thoughts, as these people are gathered together,
guide the reader to make the connections to Monakhov's earlier
infatuation with Asya. Monakhov declares that Lenechka now
plays the role that he, Monakhov, once played vis-à-vis Asya.

Bitov infuses this story with parallels to his other works. The epigraph ties the story to *Days of Man*, in which it appears, for the epigraph is the Biblical quotation "The days of man are like grass; he flourishes like a flower in the field" ("Dni cheloveka, kak trava,/Kak tsvet polevoi, tak on tsvetet") (p. 100). This quotation from the Book of Psalms Bitov also referred to in "Life in Windy Weather."

The young Lenechka shares many characteristics with the younger Monakhov of "The Door" and "The Garden."[22] We see the same Lobyshev-type automaton existence in the Monakhov of "The Forest" as we had seen in the Monakhov of "The Garden" and "The Third Story." We see the link between the end of "The Third Story" (Monakhov becomes the father of a son) and the beginning of "The Forest" (Monakhov is son to his parents; he feels he could be Lenechka's father). We see Monakhov hugging his mother "... like a piece of fluff ..." (p. 100). This is the image Bitov uses in "Life in Windy Weather" to describe Sergei's feelings of the interconnectedness of all present (including his wife, baby son, and a woman with whom he is momentarily infatuated).[23] We read a brief reference to Monakhov's aunt, who had died a year before, and we can think of "The Doctor's Funeral," about the death of the narrator's aunt. We read about Monakhov feeling the way he used to feel, in the past, after dances when he would be on an expedition, and we can visualize the scene of the dance in *Such a Long Childhood*. Tashkent, the setting of "The Forest," is the scene of some of Bitov's early travelogues. We read about the Monakhov-like youth, Lenechka, who brings flowers to Natalia and whose eyes are like the clear blue sky, and we think of the early works in which Bitov spoke of his young hero finding a sense of harmony with the grass and the sky. The poetry Lenechka recites, "The Dawn" ("Rassvet"), reminds Monakhov of the fresh early morning day he discovers when he leaves the birthday party for Natalia which they have all been attending. Lenechka's face seems to live and breathe, Monakhov observes; this links Lenechka to many of Bitov's previous heroes who found a sense of vitality in their lives.

In "The Forest," as in "The Third Story," Bitov describes a dying organism. Monakhov is in Tashkent to investigate the accidental death of two workmen. While visiting his parents, he realizes that they are aging quickly. He especially notices his father's weakening state. When he visits Natalia, she describes Monakhov as being dead, and he describes himself as dead as he thinks of his life. Several times, he thinks of a morgue as he is with Natalia and Lenechka. As he is on the airplane, about to depart, a young man who reminds Monakhov of Lenechka is killed by the airplane's propeller as he runs in order to board the airplane. When Monakhov arrives home, anxiety about his father's impending death overwhelms him.

The forest image is introduced into the story within the first few pages. Monakhov's father is telling his son about a television program he has seen. A forest, he explains, is made up not merely of separate trees. It is a unit. The trees, he says, "... are all connected by their roots, ... and they represent a unified system" (p. 106). Monakhov Senior explains that when one tree dies, it immediately dries up, for the remaining trees suck up its juices. The forest, he says, is a "... collective, a society... ." (p. 106).

At the end of the story, Monakhov, terrorized by thoughts of his father's death, understands that his father had been speaking about people's interdependence and, more specifically, about his own death. Monakhov undergoes a mystical experience in which, lying in bed with his wife, he feels a jolt of vital energy pass from his dying father to himself. In that instant, he perceives the interrelationship of all souls and feels that a "... particle of death has passed through ..." him "... in order to prolong the life of his father outside his son" (p. 176).

"The Forest" has been interpreted as containing Christian symbols. Hagen writes persuasively of Monakhov's father (in a reversal of the Christian father/son imagery) representing Christ as he sacrifices himself for another. He writes of the religious (Christian, Zen, and Slavophile) messages that can be gleaned from "The Forest."[24] Ronald Meyer includes, in his analysis, the theme of the continuity of generations in "The Forest" and in the Psalm affixed to it.[25]

These two readings of "The Forest" are plausible. The ambiguity of the ending of the story, and the substance of this work and its context within *The Role*, suggest another interpretation as well. It seems to me that the one tree that is dying is Monakhov, and that bulk of the story points to the dying of this particular organism. We know from the beginning, and the point is reinforced, that Monakhov is spiritually dead. The young Lenechka (who himself is already displaying signs of growing into a latter-day Monakhov – he lies and tells Monakhov that someone else's poetry is his own)[26] reads a poem whose message rings true for Monakhov. One line speaks of a "precipice" existing in the garden.

Here, the author reverses the positive message of "The Garden." The garden of Monakhov's life has not blossomed. Instead, spiritual death has set in. He dreams that he cannot penetrate a wall. He loses all feeling in his body. There is suddenly a "... dark bag ..." ("... tëmnyi meshok") (p. 149), an image reminiscent of the "black bag" ("chërnyi meshok") in which the dying Ivan Ilich in Tolstoy's "The Death of Ivan Ilich" ("Smert' Ivana Il'icha") feels trapped. There are other parallels between the two works. Monakhov and Ivan Ilich are middle aged. Both live lives of hypocrisy and lies. Both are spiritually dead. Ivan Ilich finds a spiritual awakening, a light, when he begins to think of other people, at the end of his life. Monakhov sees a light and experiences an awakening of sorts from death at the end of "The Forest" as he realizes the interrelatedness of all people.

In "The Forest," we are in a world that, as in "The Third Story," is caving in upon itself. During Monakhov's encounter with Natalia and Lenechka, events are described as going "... in reverse order, as if the film of that day were being spun backwards" (p. 137).

Life, too, is going "in reverse order" – away from life, toward death. In the past, Bitov had connected bird imagery with artistic and divine inspiration. In "The Forest," the author uses bird imagery to clip the wings that try to soar. Lenechka's face is described as being in flight, flying over Monakhov. The reader's introduction to Lenechka is to "... someone with the rustle of a bird ..." (p. 136). He is described as a "duckling" (p. 125).

Death imagery is associated with birds: as the propeller hits the vital young man who resembles Lenechka, ". . . he soared up, like a bird" (p. 162). He then falls under the airplane's wing. The airplane becomes a mechanical bird, a bird that kills a duckling. Just as the mechanical bird killed the young bird, Monakhov, living a life of mechanized responses, kills the feelings of innocence, vitality, soaring, and inspiration within himself.

Another character, Ziablikov, one who, explains Monakhov, plays the role of Monakhov (older man rival of Lenechka for Natalia's affection) when Monakhov is not there, is named after a bird. "Ziablik" is the Russian word for "finch."[27] Ziablikov writes children's books about nature. At the airport, Monakhov buys a book of his, about penguins; Bitov refers here to a bird that does not fly. Ziablikov spends most of the time asleep, in a drunken stupor, on a rug made of a dead animal's skin, in a scene with Lenechka, Monakhov, and Natalia. He is as dead as is Monakhov.

Bitov's original title for "The Forest" had been "The Departing/Flying Away/Vanishing Monakhov." In Russian, the word for flying away can also mean vanishing. Monakhov is flying away from Tashkent. He is also flying away from life. If the offprints of the mechanized human being, devoid of human emotion, keep repeating themselves, what we get is a person ever vanishing, until nothing is left but the palest version of all, a person who is dead to life.

When Monakhov's father describes the forest as an interdependent system, the dead tree is seen as an integral part of the forest's "unified system." To me, the final episode of "The Forest" – Monakhov's emotional experiencing of the interconnectedness of the branches of his family tree – does not ring true merely as the dying father's gift of life to his son. Rather, since Monakhov has been identified as an aging lifeless being throughout the story, it seems to me that the symbol of the dead tree in the forest means something else, too.

In "The Garden," Bitov had concluded that an understanding of "non-love" was important to an understanding of love. In "The Forest," Bitov accepts death as part of the cycle of life. A tree dies, and its juices are sucked up by the rest of the trees in the interrelated system of the forest. A dead individual is part of the "unified system" of life. All people, for Bitov, are part of the interdependent forest of life.

It is significant, in "The Forest," that Bitov uses a biological model, the ecology of the forest, as the key image that ties the story's individual parts into a "unified system." For the first time, he uses the metaphor of an ecological system within his fiction. We know, though, that this is the model according to which he has been writing his works from the beginning of his career.

"INFANTIEV" IN *DAYS OF MAN*

The editor's placement of "Infantiev" as the last story of *The Role* in *Days of Man* is not altogether illogical, although it changes the final taste left in the reader's mouth. With "Infantiev" as the fifth story, the novel ends on a positive note. A Monakhov-like man is spiritually awakened by the life he discovers after the death of his wife, Natalia. (Natalia is the name, as we know, of Monakhov's Tashkent mistress in "The Forest.") The ever-increasing numbness of Monakhov in "The Third Story" and in "The Forest" is vitiated by the resurrection the man undergoes in "Infantiev." "Infantiev," an adult with a name designating an infant, rediscovers the child-like spontaneity that Monakhov has lost. In the *Days of Man* version of "Infantiev," the old woman whom Infantiev meets at the cemetery speaks about the origin of various names, including Monakhov, which she says must come from an actor. Monakhov, as we know, has been playing the role of a live human being whilst being, in fact, spiritually dead. The old woman and Infantiev, at the cemetery mourning the loss of their spouses, are extraordinarily vital.

The story, although not intended by Bitov as an ending of *The Role*, can serve as a fitting close to the novel. Bitov's fictional world is an ecological unified system, a forest, in which all the parts are interrelated. However, the placing of one particular tree next to another can change the way the viewer sees the forest. Let us now turn to the story that Bitov intended as the final section of *The Role*.

"THE TASTE"

The skeletal outline of the plot of "The Taste" ("Vkus"), (1966, 1976, 1979),[28] concerns Monakhov as he deals with three instances of death. As he is on a train, he sees the double of Asya, whose name, he finds out when he meets her, is Svetochka. He betrays his second wife when Svetochka visits him at Peredelkino. (The place is never named, but the reader knows, for Monakhov says he lives opposite the poet's grave and quotes, without attribution, two poems from the Zhivago cycle of poems.)[29] Svetochka urges Monakhov to show her the grave. On their way back, they run into Putilin, a schoolmate of Monakhov's whom he has not seen for years. In the course of Putilin's visit with Monakhov and Svetochka, he tells Monakhov that Asya died of cancer – breast cancer and cancer of the reproductive organs. Monakhov receives a telephone call from his wife and learns of the death of her grandmother. He makes the arrangements for the burial and then goes to the cemetery.

In the course of the narrative, Monakhov speculates about coincidence. He discusses the idea of "remote likeness" ("otdalennoe skhodstvo") (p. 67) when, through the law of probability, seemingly unrelated objects, people, and phenomena acquire a resemblance. He interprets his meeting with Asya's double as evidence that "... his life had described a circle" ("zhizn' ego opisala krug") (p. 68). He explains his concept of "rhyme" ("rifma") (p. 72). If one day, for some reason, he ends up in a section of the city in which he has never been, he is sure that he will end up in the same place again that day and then never again. Twice, in the same day, he saw a rare sight: a fallen horse on a street in two different parts of the city, as if, he muses, the same horse had been dragged from one end of the city to the other just so that he would notice it.[30] He explains such occurrences of "rhyme" as being reminders that life exists independently of a person. If one fails to react to life, it reminds one of its existence through an instance of "rhyme." Seeing something now that reminds him of something in his past is the only way for Monakhov to acknowledge life as a moving, living reality (pp. 73–4).

In Bitov's earlier works, things that did not "rhyme," the disconnected fragments of life, had been brought together into an "accidental symmetry." Life had been an expanding entity. Boundaries among seemingly disparate realms had vanished as the protagonist had discovered the way in which those realms were connected. One circle became another circle, as, for example, in *The Big Balloon* ("bol'shoi shar" – "big sphere/world"), where the earthly circle became linked to the celestial circle. "The Wheel" had described the path of many interconnected circles. In these cases, it was as if Bitov were describing an upward spiral ⅜ in which circles could be connected to other circles, but the increase in the numbers of interconnecting circles always led toward an opening up to new spheres of life.

In "The Taste," Bitov adds to the circles described in other works, the circles from which there is no escape. Monakhov feels that his life has described a circle. Bitov repeats the theme, enunciated in "The Third Story," of the patterns of Monakhov's repetitive circles ending up as offprints, paler versions of the previous circles that his life had described. In "The Taste," circles interconnect to form a downward spiral toward death.

The circles of "The Taste" "rhyme" with other works of literature. The English version of "The Taste" contains an epigraph, "And onward I continued –/And fear enveloped me ...," which Bitov identifies only by its author, Pushkin.[31] The source of the quoted phrase is an 1832 poem whose first line, "I dale my poshli – i strakh obnial menia,"[32] forms Bitov's epigraph. The poem, part of a two-poem cycle, deals with Dante's *Inferno*, with his descent into the circles of hell. The direction Pushkin traces is downward along the circles. We have circles within circles. Pushkin, one poet, speaks about a poem in which another poet, Virgil, is guiding Dante. Pushkin's emphasis is only upon the part of Dante's *The Divine Comedy, Inferno*, that details the descent toward hell. He does not deal with the later part of Dante's upward spiral toward paradise. In his poems, Pushkin describes a bad odor, the smell of rotten eggs. Bitov, several times, refers to a bad taste in Monakhov's mouth. Pushkin uses the word "iadro" ("ball," as in cannonball) (a circle, by the way, whose purpose is to cause death). A schoolmate of Monakhov's whom Putilin recalls is named Iadroshnikov.[33]

Pushkin ends his second poem with a line that includes the word "confusion" ("smushcheniem").[34] The third sentence of Bitov's story contains the word "confusion" ("smushchenie") (p. 57).

Dante wrote "La Vita Nuova," a work inspired by his love for Beatrice. He speaks of a man's love for a woman as the path toward divine love. The Dante work includes Beatrice's death, the presence of another loving woman to help console him, and the reaffirmation of his love for the dead Beatrice. Bitov uses the phrase "vita nuova" in "The Taste" as he explains that Monakhov's renting a room at Peredelkino could not be thought of as a "vita nuova" (p. 69). Svetochka is an empathic woman who is with Monakhov when he hears about the death of his first, only, real love, Asya.

In *The Divine Comedy*, Beatrice, representative of Dante's love and faith, is Dante's guide through paradise. In the second canto of *Inferno*, the compassionate Lucia (whose name is derived from "lux," the Latin word for light) is introduced. In "The Taste," Svetochka, whose name is derived from "svet," the Russian word for light, is Monakhov's guide to Pasternak's grave. After emphasizing the fact that they had been going around in circles, Bitov writes that Monakhov was struck by her qualities of immortality. Monakhov is tired of going along the path, which resembles, according to Bitov, ". . . a coiled snail . . ." (p. 77). (It is important, given my further discussion of "The Taste," to note the shape, the spiral, that Bitov emphasizes here.) Monakhov finds himself in a dead end at the end of the spiral path, and it is Svetochka who points out Pasternak's grave. He notices that the gravestone is done ". . . with taste . . ." (". . . s[o] . . vkusom . . .") (p. 78). He feels comfortable and notices that there is no fence around the grave. (Here, we see the absence of boundaries.) He senses the dignity, nobility, and modesty of the surroundings. This scene takes place near the beginning of "The Taste."

At the beginning of the story, Bitov describes, in Svetochka and in Pasternak's gravesite, symbols of love and faith in the positive qualities of life. Unlike the path followed by *The Divine*

Comedy, downward toward hell and then upward, toward paradise, the circles created by Bitov go downward toward hell and remain there. After the scene at Pasternak's grave, Monakhov learns of Asya's death. His schoolmate and he get drunk, and Putilin uses vulgar language as he reads Svetochka's palm.

In the final death scene, the burial of Monakhov's wife's grandmother, the chief gravedigger is described as looking like Lucifer, "god of death ...," "... king of darkness" (pp. 96, 97). Monakhov realizes that he has seen evil, as he observes this gravedigger who appears, at first, to be armless, who then spreads his wings (the flaps of his coat). He makes it clear to Monakhov that a bribe is expected. The grandmother had wanted to be buried with a small clump of earth (from her native Pskov region) which she had saved in a little pre-revolutionary toothpowder box. What Monakhov sees all around him, in the graveyard ruled by the king of darkness, repulses him. The tiny clump of earth in the grandmother's coffin seems to him to be the only bit of life in this evil kingdom of clay and bribes. Monakhov thinks of the contrast between this scene and the scene at the Peredelkino cemetery. This is the land of evil and death. The first line from one of Pasternak's Zhivago poems, "The Wind," is quoted: "I died, but you are alive ..." ("Ia konchilsia, a ty zhiva ..."),[35] referring to Zhivago's death and Lara's living on. Bitov's next line, the last of the story, negates the possibility of life after death: "'She died ...,' he [Monakhov – E.C.] thought" ("'Umerla ...' – podumal on [Monakhov – E.C.]") (p. 98).

Thinking of Bitov's "rhyme" with Dante, we can conclude that Monakhov realizes that Asya, his Beatrice, the hope of love, spiritual fulfillment, and faith, has died.[36] Death concludes Monakhov's journey along the circles.

Another circle of death that "rhymes" with Dante's and with Bitov's circles is that of Solzhenitsyn's *First Circle* (*V kruge pervom*), which had been circulating in samizdat in the Soviet Union since the mid 1960s. The graveyard scene at the end of "The Taste" includes references to the gravediggers as possible prisoners. Solzhenitsyn's novel, whose title recalls Dante's *Inferno*, speaks of the prisoncamp inmates who lived in the corrupt, evil world of Stalin's Soviet Union. Bitov's "king of darkness" ruling over a lifeless kingdom of clay could refer, obliquely, to the evils that Stalin had spewed forth upon the Soviet Union.

Another set of Bitov's "rhymes" with another work of art concerns the relationship of "The Taste" to Pasternak's *Doctor Zhivago*. One of the guiding principles of that novel is its focus, thematically and structurally, on the role of coincidence in life. Thus, Zhivago's poem, "A Winter Night" ("Zimniaia noch'") was inspired by his having seen a candle burning in a window. It turns out, as one of the many coincidences in the novel, that at the time Lara had been in that room with Antipov during his student days. The room is the same one in which Zhivago lives at the end of his life, without suspecting the past history of these living quarters. It is the same room in which Lara, without realizing that Zhivago had lived there, finds his dead body. In the poem, Zhivago writes that the snowstorm had formed "circles" ("kruzhki") on the windowpane.

In creating his interconnecting circles and coincidences, Pasternak, like Dante, traces a trajectory from death to life. Zhivago dies, but his poetry continues to live. Lara dies, but the life-affirming force that she represents lives on in Zhivago's poetry. Her daughter lives on. The permanence of poetry and spirituality conquers physical death. The path in the Zhivago poem cycle moves from the time of the Orthodox holy week and Christ's suffering and crucifixion to the resurrection.

As with *The Divine Comedy*, Bitov "rhymes" his story with the Pasternak novel, but shifts the message from death-to-life to life-to-death. The Pasternak novel begins with the burial of Mar'ia; the Bitov story ends with the burial of Mariia. *Doctor Zhivago* ends with the final poem proclaiming Christ's resurrection and an escape from darkness. "The Taste" begins with Monakhov and Svetochka, the symbol of light, together. It ends in the kingdom of darkness, where he undercuts the positive tones of Zhivago's poem, "The Wind," and affirms Asya's death. Lara's purpose was to give birth; Asya dies of cancer of the breast and of the reproductive organs.

One of the lines of Zhivago's "Winter Night," a delicate tribute to love, is "A candle was glowing on the table" ("Svecha gorela na stole");[37] one of the lines of Bitov's story is "A little candle was flickering in his hand" ("Svechka drozhala v ego ruke") (p. 92). The "rhyming" Bitov line refers to Monakhov as he is attending the church service for the dead grandmother. He has been chewing gum up to the point at which he enters the church. He feels the pangs of a guilty conscience and feels that he is sinful. He had told his wife that he would have to stay with the dead body all night in the church. Instead, he visits a school-friend and spends the night with Svetochka. Beautiful, pure love is described in the Pasternak poem. In the Bitov story, the tasteful situation has been reduced to references to a gum-chewing man.

In *Doctor Zhivago*, a straw hat is worn by the old Swiss governess, Mlle. Fleury, who survives Doctor Zhivago during the scene in which he dies. She continues walking along beside the trolley car in which Zhivago suffers his fatal attack. The wearer of the straw hat in Pasternak's novel is associated with life. Her name derives from "fleur," the French word for flower. Her physical life continues; Zhivago's spiritual life continues. In Bitov's story, a straw hat is the only thing, besides the clump of earth, that the grandmother has saved from the past. By the end of the story, she is physically dead, and Monakhov remains spiritually dead. Mlle. Fleury is from Switzerland. The straw hat of Bitov's grandmother-in-law is from Paris. Mlle. Fleury's documents are wrapped with a "little ribbon" ("lentochkoi"). Within a page of the point at which Bitov mentions the straw hat, he uses the word "ribbon" ("lentoi") (pp. 89–90), which he must fetch for the old woman's funeral.[38]

Bitov quotes another passage from Pasternak's poem, "The Wind," as Monakhov and Svetochka are returning from their visit to the poet's grave. In addition to the line quoted at the end of "The Taste," Monakhov quotes the poem's next two lines, about the crying wind shaking the forest and dacha. It is significant that in the next two lines, describing the wind rocking the trees, he remembers the line, "Not each pine tree separately" ("Ne kazhduiu sosnu otdel'no,"), but forgets the word "poln-ost'iu" ("completely," "fully") in the following line, "But all the trees completely" (Bitov: "A ... *ta-ta-ta-* ... vse dereva ..."),[39] Pasternak: "A *polnost'iu* vse dereva" [italics mine – E.C.]).[40] Part of Monakhov's problem, in many stories in *The Role*, stems from his inability to get close to another person. He is separate, not one tree content to live at peace with other trees in the forest. The only point at which he thinks about the interrelationships of all the trees in the forest is when he considers the effect of a dead tree upon the forest as a whole.

Another Zhivago poem partially quoted in the Bitov text, without title or attribution, is "August" ("Avgust"), a poem about Iurii's death, about the August religious holiday of the Transfiguration, and about the affirmation of the poet's life, in his words, after death. Bitov again turns a life-affirming message into a death knell. Bitov quotes the poem twice (pp. 71, 72). One of his references contains a positive statement about Pasternak's poem, for Monakhov senses that a church described in "August" glows as forcefully in real life as in the poetry. However, a couple of pages before, Monakhov has declared that when he looks at the Peredelkino landscape, he feels that it has already been drunk: "Someone had used it up, had drunk up this nature, so that none was left for Monakhov" (p. 70). Resentfully, he determines that the poet (Pasternak) was responsible for using up this landscape. In the same passage, Monakhov admits to himself that Pasternak is not as good a poet as was Pushkin.

In the past, Bitov had emphasized the positive features of being in a place where a poet had been. In "Life in Windy Weather," he referred to the same Pasternak poem, "The Wind," to demonstrate the life-affirming qualities of "accidental symmetries" in life. In "Armenia Lessons," he was positive about tying one's perception of the landscape to the perception of that same place, captured years ago in a work of art. The contrast with that attitude is striking in "The Taste." The circles of Bitov's downward spiral continue as he declares dead for him the landscape that a great poet's gaze has touched.

Wherever the reader gazes, Bitov clutters his landscape with "rhymes" of death. The title of the story, "The Taste," suggests a "rhyme" with Tolstoy's "The Death of Ivan Ilich," a story that focuses on a man's spiritual awakening in the face of death. The path there is from a state of feeling that he is caught in a black constricting bag (darkness) to his sense, at the end of the story, that there was "light" ("svet") instead of death.

When Ivan Ilich first falls ill, he notices the "strange taste" ("strannyi vkus") in his mouth.[41] Monakhov, spiritually ill, notices a taste in his mouth at several points during "The Taste." Once, it is even described as a "strange taste" ("strannyi vkus") (p. 93). The expression is a common one, so that Bitov's use of it would not suggest the "rhyme" with Tolstoy's story if other telling pieces of evidence were not visible. Bitov, in "The Forest," in describing Monakhov's sensations of death, had spoken of him feeling as if he were in a black bag. As we have seen, in each of Bitov's "rhymes" with other works, he reverses the direction of a darkness/death–light/life pattern. I believe, then, that there is a convincing case for including Tolstoy in Bitov's rhyme scheme.

Two additional "rhymes" with literary works also duplicate Bitov's theme in "The Taste." The portions quoted from the two final lines of Lermontov's poem, "I Go Out Alone On the Road" ("Vykhozhu odin ia na dorogu"), speak of the persona's wish for consolation. Bitov omits words about eternal life – about an eternally greening tree.[42] The Lermontov poem conveys the poet's loneliness, pain, and disillusionment with life. The poet longs for consolation. The tone of the poem is gloomy.

Bitov's authorial digression on the word "suddenly" ("vdrug") brings to mind a passage in another masterpiece of Russian literature, Andrei Bely's *Petersburg (Peterburg)*.[43] In the Bely novel, the passage is located in a section that speaks about Lippanchenko, a double agent. We know that Monakhov leads a deceptive life, deceiving himself and others. Bely's "suddenly" section immediately follows a section entitled "Our Role" ("Nasha rol'"), which, of course, "rhymes" with the title, *The Role*, of the novel in which "The Taste" appears.[44] The circles keep twirling, for Bitov inserts into his "'vdrug" section the word "circle" ("krug"), which, in Russian, literally rhymes with "vdrug" (p. 68). The Bely novel has as one of its principal structural and thematic images the shape of a circle.[45] It, too, distorts Russian literature of the past, by bringing into its structure many parodies of literature. It, too, describes a path of death and destruction.

Another rhyme is provided by Nabokov's *Pale Fire*. In that novel, Shade's poem includes a line about a "richly rhymed life." Nabokov plays with the idea of resemblances and coincidence (we realize, for example, that Zembla even "rhymes" with "resemblance") throughout his novel.[46]

Why all the "rhymes," circles, and downward spirals in "The Taste?" Bitov's message of death "rhymes" with death passages of other things he was writing at approximately the same time. What we have come to, says Monakhov, at the end of "The Taste," is clear. These pessimistic thoughts provide a commentary on society. As in "The Last Bear," "Secluded Street," and "The Doctor's Funeral," Bitov shows the distortions, corruptions, and bribes wrought upon Soviet society by Stalin, represented by the Lucifer-like chief gravedigger, "warden" of the prisoner-gravediggers in the clay cemetery.

The narrator reports, as Monakhov is thinking that his life had described a circle, "The theoretical spiral did not console him" (p. 68). A footnote accompanying this statement in Priscilla Meyer's translation of "The Taste" into English states that the spiral serves as the Marxist model for explaining the dialectics of history.[47] Marxist dialectical materialism offers the model of an upward spiral for socialist development. Bitov, in "The Taste," plots the downward spiral of Soviet society caused by Stalin and his legacy.

Bitov's "rhymes" are part of a rhyme pattern that he repeats ad nauseam (when Monakhov hears about Asya's death, he vomits), in order to form his downward spiral toward death. Monakhov cannot escape the circle of "rhymes" in his life. Bitov cannot escape the circle of "rhymes" in his works. Their circles repeat themselves and finally close in upon themselves.

Bitov, in "The Taste," places the phenomenon of circles, downward spirals, and death on an abstract, philosophical plane as he traces death, one of life's processes. He approaches the issue from a macrocosmic and microcosmic perspective. I have traced, within Bitov's works, the way in which he creates an ecological system in which all the parts exist as interdependent organisms/pieces of a larger whole. I have explained the ways in which Bitov plots the growing, flowering, expanding, blossoming elements of that system. He has, as we have seen, been creating an ecology of inspiration.

In "The Taste," Bitov, true to biological nature, shows us the "seamy" side of the circle of life. He constructs an ecology of expiration. In "The Forest," one tree died, but the forest as a whole was rejuvenated. In nature, there comes a point when an ecological system cannot sustain life, and the forest dies. Through his use of ellipses in "The Taste," Bitov makes his own forest disappear. In "The Forest," although he speaks about the death of one tree, he mentions the good health of the forest as a whole. In "The Taste," when he chooses not to quote the Lermontov lines that deal with an eternally greening tree, he eliminates the part of the life cycle that deals with growth. When he chooses to have Monakhov forget the part of the Pasternak poem that emphasizes the interrelatedness of all the trees, Bitov again moves to destroy the healthy aspects of his ecological whole.

Bitov shows us the spiritual death of a society in which a Lucifer is in power. He shows us the spiritual death of Monakhov, who betrays himself and other people. He no longer feels. Although he comes into contact with forces of life – Pasternak, Svetochka, the church, nature – these forces have no lasting impact upon him. Asya, his emblem of light, life, and hope, has died, her ability to create and nurture new life surgically excised. All that is left is Monakhov's sense of physical taste. He is sentenced to a life without feelings. The humanness of Monakhov vanishes. The vanishing Monakhov vanishes, leaving behind only a taste of humanness.

In other works, Bitov has traced the processes of characters who seek integration and integrity. The characters began with a life of fragments. They ended by finding integration and integrity. They felt themselves to be a part of a meaningful universe. In "The Taste," Bitov shows us the reverse process. The narrator declares that he had thought of alternative titles for "The Taste": "The Fragment" ("Otryvok"), "The Shadow" ("Ten'"), and "The Wreath" ("Venok") (p. 68). The fragment is a piece, not a whole; a shadow is a two-dimensional "offprint" of the original; a wreath can be a circle of death.

The very descriptions of characters in "The Taste" emphasize their fragmentary nature. Monakhov's taste is his only living sense. The gravedigger's apparent armlessness is described. The grandmother's dead body and Asya's surgery, the cutting up of a body, are mentioned. The wholeness of an integrated body, the equilibrium of an integrated life, have been lost. The continuity of life has been broken. In "Armenia Lessons," the creative master had been described as the person who takes the clay into his hands and then allows the clay to flutter out of his hands. The association had been with creative inspiration. In "The Taste," the ruler of the clay cemetery is described as an armless, evil man. The clay devours people. The only living organism in the burial scene is the tiny bit of her native earth that the grandmother had saved in the toothpowder box, a taste of living land in a kingdom of clay.

In plotting the movements along a downward spiral toward death, Bitov has not strayed from capturing life in motion. Along each circle/loop of the spiral, when you feel you have come full circle, you begin to go along another loop. 🌀 At each circle, you know that you have moved. This is an important aspect of Bitov's definition of "rhyme." The "rhymes" are like the original, but are not exactly the same because you have moved in life, and the circle you are moving along takes place in another part of your life. We see the "movement of life" in Bitov's story, even if that movement is toward death. His description of the downward spiral is still the description of an interdependent system, for the circles are all part of the spiral, one circle being only one "rhyme" in the overall spiral "rhyme" pattern. In looking at the ecological system of Bitov's works, we can see that he is expanding the treatment of ecology by including, within the system, the phenomenon of death.

The ideas and structural patterns in "The Taste" "rhyme" with another life process, with the reproduction of life itself. In concentrating on this aspect of life, Bitov shifts his attention from creating a macrocosm of ecological interdependencies and interconnections to creating a microcosm of the life processes within molecular biology. Watson and Crick were involved with questions about how life reproduces itself. When they constructed their molecular model, they envisioned the model, the double helix, as two intertwined spirals, each a mirror image of the other. Cells divide and reproduce when the two strands separate, and each strand, containing the code of life, reproduces a mirror image of itself. In one scene of "The Taste," Monakhov sees a fire extinguisher on which there is a man holding a fire extinguisher on which there is a man holding a fire extinguisher, and so on. Developmental biology books often speak of life as a circle in which the embryo becomes an adult who then produces an embryo who then becomes an adult who then produces an embryo, etc. Death is programmed into the very code of life along the spirals of the DNA. Part of the program is to die.[48] Bitov has already referred, in passing, to death as a part of life, when he speaks of the obstetrician as someone who brings a person closer to death. In "The Forest," Bitov demonstrated his acceptance of death into the cycle of life when he related the fate of the dead tree to the forest. The tree dies; the species as a whole lives on – until the point of the extinction of the species, an issue Bitov does not address in "The Forest." Life contains death. In fact, cancer results from the life process gone awry. Many cells in our bodies stop reproducing, and this is part of the normal life process. Cancer cells do not stop reproducing. They keep reproducing themselves and thereby take over live, healthy cells. In like fashion, Bitov in "The Taste" (and in *The Role* as a whole) keeps reproducing himself, the old patterns of his previous stories, or "cells." Monakhov cannot stop reproducing Asyas, each one a paler version of the one before. Bitov is describing and producing/reproducing stories of the reproductive capabilities gone awry. At some point, the cells of a healthy organism would stop reproducing copies/offprints of themselves. Monakhov cannot stop himself. Bitov produces the life of Monakhov as offprints, each one paler than the one before. He should have stopped reproducing the patterns, but the cancer cells of death take over. Significant in this respect is the fact that Asya died of cancer, and specifically of cancer of the reproductive organs. Bitov has created a woman who cannot reproduce life because her cells are reproducing themselves.

Bitov's narrator explains, in a digression, that in his former works he had refrained from killing his characters (the narrator of "Armenia Lessons" had declared that he never kills his characters). Now, he says, he must kill them because they cannot keep living forever. He then creates another dizzying circle when he imagines that characters in books would then write worse versions of the authors, and so on and so on. This brings us back to the downward spiral, the paler-version-of-offprints phenomenon, and the authorial, literary creative process gone awry. In showing life as a spiral process, Bitov reproduces, in his literature, the spirals of life in actual life.

Bitov's conclusion in "The Taste," as in "The Forest," is that death is an inevitable part of life, whether we look at it from the ecological perspective or from the perspective of the individual organism. For Monakhov, Pasternak is not Pushkin. Svetochka is not Asya. Beatrice is killed off. Lara is killed off. Life is clay instead of earth; taste, instead of feeling. As Bitov writes, "Everything curves round, closing into a ring ..." ("Vsë zakrugliaetsia, zamykaias' v kol'tso ...") (p. 85).

THE ROLE – CONCLUSION

The Role traces the loss of Monakhov's love, the loss of his capacity to feel. A nameless "boy" ("mal'chik") in the first story/chapter of the novel, he becomes Aleksei, then Aleksei Monakhov. By the last story, he is Monakhov, having lost his first name,[49] having lost his humanness. Even his name is not presented as an integrated entity in "The Taste."

Gabriadze declares that Bitov's protagonist is akin to the heroes of Russian psychological novels.[50] Indeed, the name Alesha/Aleksei Monakhov brings to mind Alesha/Aleksei, the monk, in Dostoevsky's *Brothers Karamazov* (*Brat'ia Karamazovy*). In a key episode in the Dostoevsky novel, Alesha is spiritually rescued by Grushenka. Her last name, Svetlova, provides another Bitov rhyme, for Aleksei Monakhov is led to the place of dignity, Pasternak's grave, by Svetochka. There he notices the calming effect of blossoming nature upon him. In *The Brothers Karamazov*, the reader is left with the idea that everything is connected to everything, that the ability to love is the great life-affirming force that will cause the family of man to blossom. The biological seed planted by Dostoevsky in his Biblical epigraph ("Verily, verily, I say unto you, except a corn of wheat fall into the ground and die, it abideth alone: but if it die it bringeth forth much fruit")[51] bears fruit by the end of the novel. Alesha, through his ability to love, plants seeds of love in other people. The final scene (Bitov's, too, is a burial scene) attests to the capacity of religious love to transform the world.

Dostoevsky, author of *The Double* (*Dvoinik*), often, as is well known, used doubles as a structural principle within his works. Bitov, as we recall, had thought of *The Double* as an alternative title for his novel. His "double" of Dostoevsky's character is hardly a double. Rather, he is the downward spiral/mirror image of Dostoevsky's upward-spiral Aleksei. Alesha Karamazov is spiritually alive; Aleksei Monakhov is spiritually dead. Alesha is honest; Aleksei is not. Alesha compassionately interrelates with other people. Aleksei remains entrapped in a circle of isolation. Monakhov is more a double of the intellectual superfluous man Ivan Karamazov.

But even this is not a totally accurate assessment, for Monakhov, unlike Ivan, does not ask the big questions about the meaning of life. Unlike Ivan, even his distaste for the status quo does not lead him to profound questions about God's universe or the meaning of life. Monakhov is merely playing a role. He plays the role of a figure in a Dostoevsky novel. He is a mere offprint.

Gabriadze writes that *The Role* is a novel about love, about a hero who has lost his capacity to love. Emphasizing the "... hopeless spiritual dead-end"[52] in which Monakhov finds himself, Gabriadze says that a person who sinks to the bottom can then attain rebirth.[53]

The beginning of *The Role*, the first sentence of "The Door," describes a little boy freezing under an arch (i.e., a part of a circular structure). The last line of "The Taste" announces Asya's death. The reader has completed the final circle of death. It remains to be seen whether, in his other writings, Bitov will be able to get beyond the circles ever collapsing into themselves.

"BIRDS"

"Birds, or New Information about Man" ("Ptitsy, ili Novye svedeniia o cheloveke"), 1971, 1975, the final piece in *Days of Man*,[54] is one of Bitov's most unusual works. It is a quasi-travelogue, quasi-story, quasi-meditation. More than anything else, it is a philosophical essay about the state of man in the world. Of the sparse critical literature on "Birds," most of it mentions its philosophical bent.[55]

The pretext for Bitov's thoughts about man as a species is his visit to a biological research station, Fringilla, in a remote place along Lithuania's Baltic coast. The biologists there are studying bird migration patterns. They catch birds, ring them, and then release them. Part of Bitov's piece centers on his conversations with "the doctor," a scientist doing research at Fringilla, and part of it focuses on his own ruminations and experiences.

On one level, "Birds" can be read as a response to "The Taste." We had seen what happened when the phenomenon of "rhyming" went beserk. It was then impossible, we read, to escape the downward spiral toward death. One implication is that if everything is always like everything else, then it is impossible to appreciate, to know, what one individual's true self – that part of one which is unique – is. In "Birds," Bitov addresses the issue of the relationship of the individual species, man, to the ecological system of nature as a whole. It is fitting that this essay would end *Days of Man*, for it both addresses the issue of the *ecology* of the "forest of man," so much a part of "The Forest," and takes into account the question of an *individual* entity of life, so much the focus of "The Taste." (An unpublished article by Priscilla Meyer sees "Birds" as an essay that helps us understand *The Role*. Her interpretation emphasizes the duality of the physical and spiritual worlds. Monakhov – twin, lover, double – cannot, she writes, reconcile these two twin/double realms of his life.)[56]

Bitov's emphasis, in "Birds," is upon relationships, in the most abstract sense of that term. *The Role* had considered the concrete, specific relationship of one man and one woman over the course of twenty years. "Birds" concerns the relationship of a genera-lized "I" (humanity) and "the other" (other forms of life) in the world. He first discusses two spheres of life. He likens our life on earth among houses and trees to crabs' life among shells and algae on the bottom of the sea. "Birds," writes Bitov, "are the fish of our ocean" (p. 285). Here Bitov "rhymes" the two spheres of air and ocean, emphasizing, as he often does, the similarity of one realm of life to another.

Much of the rest of "Birds" takes another approach toward man's impulse to find similarities to himself in nature. The doctor declares that he resents the writers of animal fables because they ascribe human characteristics to creatures that are different from people. One of the major points of "Birds" is the necessity of respecting a species, a being, that is different from oneself. The doctor praises fable writer Ivan Krylov for alerting people to the dangers of "... anthropomorphic transfer" (p. 307). The fables he refers to, without mentioning titles, are "The Quartet" ("Kvartet") and "The Swan, The Pike, and the Crab" ("Lebed', shchuka i rak"). "The String Quartet" features a foursome of animals who keep rearranging their seating in order to structure themselves into a quartet. Krylov's moral is that it does not matter how you arrange your seating, if you are not a musician, you are not a musician. The second Krylov fable alluded to by the doctor concerns a swan, a fish, and a crab who, together, attempt to move a loaded cart. The cart remains in place, immobile, for the animals cannot agree upon how to move the cart. Each sees things only from its particular perspective. The swan wants to fly, the crab wants to move backwards, and the pike wants to move the cart into the water.[57]

The point is, says the narrator in a quatrain he quotes from Pushkin, that each being lives according to its own natural laws, which belong uniquely to it. The quotation, whose title Bitov omits, is from the section called "Laws of Nature" ("Zakony prirody") in Pushkin's "Edifying Quatrains" ("Nravouchitel'-nye chetverostishiia").[58] Pushkin describes a wolf and a violet, each living in accordance with the laws of its own nature.

To try to impose a human perspective upon another species is not right, according to Bitov. The narrator condemns the behavior of doves. Despite the doves' reputation as a symbol of peace, the species murders members of its own species. The doctor upbraids the narrator for applying human moral standards to the doves.

In the course of the discussions, the doctor brings up the work of Konrad Lorenz, Nobel Prize-winning ethologist. The doctor

speaks of a 1935 article Lorenz wrote on morals in animals.[59]
The point of the article is that animals – such as lions, wolves,
and ravens – with more strongly developed defense systems
never use their lethal weapons against members of their own
species. Animals with weaker defense systems – such as rabbits
and doves – do not hesitate to kill their own kind.

The narrator wants to apply the situation to human behavior.
He says that according to this law, strongly armed countries,
with the capacity to annihilate mankind, will not declare war on
one another. The doctor insists that the narrator is wrong to
attempt to draw a biological analogy, for atom bombs are made
by human beings. They are not, he says, a product of nature. He
claims that another biological law is at work, the law that
governs the regulation of numbers in a species. The lesson,
therefore, is that one should not try, too quickly, to apply the
laws governing one species to another species. One should not
erase the boundaries between/among different entities.

Much of the discussion in "Birds" has to do with the author's
philosophical speculations upon the meaning of a border, or
boundary. From the title, "Birds, or New Information about
Man," we could surmise, incorrectly, that Bitov would focus, as
he has so often, upon erasing the boundaries between birds and
human beings. Instead, he concentrates upon the positive
features of having a well-defined boundary and upon the
negative features of not having a boundary. First of all, there is
the argument, already mentioned, that animals with highly
developed armor – a strong border defense system – do not kill
members of their own species whereas those with weak armor do.
Secondly, he argues that people are tense and live in conflict
because they live on the boundary between the sky and the
water. Fish and birds are different, he explains, because they live
happily within one homogeneous sphere. Man does not quite
know where he belongs. This state worries Bitov, for he wonders
whether, without fully knowing himself, man can be precise in
his definition of any "other" (p. 309).

The limitations of failing to be sensitive to an "other" are
repeatedly emphasized. Bitov writes, "The spiritual significance
of a scientific discovery is not in the expansion of the sphere of

knowledge, but in surmounting its [the sphere's – E.C.] limitation" (p. 302). One experiment at the research station tests, for purposes of understanding certain migration patterns, the birds' response to a night sky. For the captured birds to experience both light and darkness, a researcher carries their cages up or down the stairs to light or dark rooms. Bitov wonders whether, unbeknownst to the researchers, what is really being tested is the effect upon the birds of being carried in cages from the first floor to the second floor. This incident points out the limitations of human experience when people are not aware of their own limited perspectives and the biases they bring to the subjects they study. They inflict their own perspective upon the world. They are not able to respect the boundary between their individual species and another species. The implication is that man cannot keep his own ego contained within his own border. He keeps projecting it upon the entire world.

The solution, Bitov finds, is to learn to understand the "otherness" of an "other". "Reality," he writes, "is division into one" (p. 332). We discover what is different about ourselves and about others. We can therefore learn to respect the boundary between ourselves and others.

Ultimately, "Birds" teaches us about the necessity of respecting the borders of man's ego. It teaches us about the necessity of considering man as a part of an interdependent ecological whole. It teaches us that by ignoring the fact that we, like the rest of nature, are biological beings who belong to a biological ecological system, we can easily upset the balance of that ecological entity.

As the narrator and the doctor stroll along the dunes, the narrator notices that the imprints of their feet destroy the rippled pattern that the wind had drawn upon the sand. He notices that birds' delicate steps had not destroyed nature's patterns. Bitov implies that human beings do not respect their environment and that they destroy nature.

The narrator describes a blade of grass which, in the wind, makes an arc on the sand, describing a perfect circle and itself taking root in the center. The blade of grass' "private domain" (". . . chastnoe vladenie") is ". . . touching . . ." (". . . trogatel'no

...") (p. 308), writes Bitov. The blade of grass is very much its own being, a blade of grass, yet it lives in harmony with its surroundings. The bird's feet respect the sand. Each part of this balanced whole is what it is, yet each part lives in harmony and equilibrium with other parts of the ecological system. Blades of grass can live in peace with the wind and sand. The East can live in harmony with the West, implies Bitov, for he has a scene in which, from the research station, he observes both the Eastern and the Western seas. He senses the difference, for one reflects sky in water, and the other absorbs water into sky. They are different, yet each he finds deep and infinite.

Bitov's plea, in "Birds," is for an increased sensitivity to an entity's individuality and to its function as a part of a larger whole called life on earth.

THE DAYS OF MAN – CONCLUSION

"The Door," the first story in *The Role* and *The Days of Man*, plots the adventures of a little boy who did not understand the true nature of the older woman upon whom he had a crush. The final paragraphs of "Birds," the final piece in *The Days of Man*, describe a story made up by Julia, a first grader: "'Yesterday a foreigner came to our school. He told us a lot of funny stories, but we didn't understand him. Luckily, an interpreter was with him. He explained to us that the foreigner was talking about ravens and magpies. It turns out that these birds, so alike, do not understand each other very well at all. In the morning, when I came home, I thought, "How strange! We did not understand him well at all, and that's exactly what he was telling us about ...""'[60] A little girl is telling the story, but the narrator informs us that she changed her story so that it would be told in a first-person male voice.[61]

Why would Bitov add this detail? The substance of Julia's story makes sense in the light of the thematic threads Bitov weaves in "Birds." The change to the male voice makes sense if we think about this essay in terms of *The Days of Man* as a whole. "Birds," such a different species from the rest of *Days*, can live in harmony with the rest of the book in the larger ecological whole that comprises *The Days of Man*. There is a lack of understanding between the magpie and the raven, but they are both birds. The philosophical essay is different from a novel, but they are, nevertheless, tied together. Bitov highlights this point by having a little boy's consciousness begin the end *The Days of Man*. (There is also the irony that a little girl is different from a little boy, that by writing in a male voice, she is attempting to be what she is not – and that is what Bitov condemns in "Birds." One entity should not attempt to erase the boundaries between it and another entity, yet he/she should try to understand the "otherness" of the "other.")

The book *The Days of Man*, is a unit that contains very different sorts of writings – a novel, a part of another novel, and a philosophical essay. In his very choice of material for *The Days of Man*, Bitov demonstrates the variety and unity of life. Different genuses, species, live in harmony here. Connections can be drawn between one work and another. Boundaries can be erased between one work and another. These works form one larger ecological whole. Questions about the nature of the relationship between the individual and the larger environment arise. In the themes Bitov addresses in *The Days of Man*, in the way he puts the book together, he asserts the integrity of the individual *qua* individual and the infinite variety and interdependence of the individual pieces of life. Indeed, the multiple connections, interrelationships, and lack of connections among the units of life, human and animal, constantly fill the days of man.

CHAPTER 9

"Metropol": Bitov's stories about life and death

In *Seven Journeys*, a brief section, "The Last Bear" ("Poslednii medved'"), inserted into the penultimate entry of "The Wheel,"[1] seems, at first glance, irrelevant to the theme of the wheel.[2] "The Last Bear" does not appear in the *Image of Life* version of "The Wheel." Neither does the section "The Fifth Corner" ("Piatyi ugol"), a set of paragraphs also inserted into *Seven Journeys* in the penultimate entry of "The Wheel."[3] "The Fifth Corner" relates to the theme of "The Wheel," however, for it includes discussion of a motorcycle.

Structurally, "The Last Bear" fits into a pattern Bitov weaves in his ruminations about life in "The Wheel," for "The Fifth Corner;" "The Flying Dutchman" ("Letuchii gollandets"), a section of the second-to-last entry present in both the *Image of Life* and the *Seven Journeys* versions of "The Wheel;"[4] and "The Last Bear" are all prefaced by the epigraph "To the Memory of . . ." three men who had died. The common message of the three sections, when placed in the context of "The Wheel" as a whole, is that one cannot escape death.

The epigraph to "The Last Bear" in *Seven Journeys* is affixed, instead, to a section, "Fate" ("Sud'ba"), one of the other two stories that appeared together with "The Last Bear" when it was next printed, as the first of a set of three Bitov stories to be published in the important literary almanac called *Metropol* (*Metropol'*).[5]

Edited by Vasily Aksenov, Victor Erofeev, Fazil Iskander, Bitov, and Evgeny Popov, *Metropol* represented, in 1979, during the last years of the Brezhnev era, principles that became known as "glasnost'," or "openness," the centerpiece of the official

Soviet policy toward the arts during Gorbachev's regime. The foreword to *Metropol* bemoaned the fact that many deserving manuscripts outside narrow conformist categories were being rejected by Soviet publishing houses. The goal of *Metropol*, write the editors, is to attempt to gain increased artistic freedom for writers who wish to publish their works officially in the Soviet Union. Most *Metropol* contributions, say the editors, consist of literary works that the authors had been trying, unsuccessfully, to get published in official Soviet publications.[6]

Some of the more than twenty *Metropol* contributors were among the most prominent Soviet mainstream writers, members in good standing of the Writers' Union with records of success and popularity – among them, contemporary poets Bella Akhmadulina and Andrei Voznesensky; and Vasily Aksenov, father of the "Young Prose" movement of the 1950s and 1960s. Vladimir Vysotsky, unofficial balladeer, and Taganka actor, contributed several poems and songs. Some were people who had, over the years, enjoyed the privileges of the elite. Aksenov had been allowed to travel to the West as an officially sanctioned representative of Soviet writers at international meetings with Western writers, and had been one of the writers who met with Western writers when they visited the Soviet Union. Voznesensky often gave poetry readings in the West. Vysotsky, although his songs did not appear in print in the Soviet Union until after his death,[7] enjoyed great popularity as a singer and was often allowed to travel to France with his French actress wife Marina Vlady.

The reaction of the Moscow Writers' Union to *Metropol* was swift and hostile. Two of the youngest, least established contributors, Victor Erofeev and Evgeny Popov, were ousted from the Writers' Union. Vasily Aksenov resigned from the Writers' Union in protest. Although Erofeev and Popov were later reinstated, Aksenov decided to emigrate. In 1980, he settled down in the United States. Other contributors to the literary anthology suffered varying degrees of difficulties because of their connection with *Metropol*. Some were able, eventually, to resume publishing in official publications.[8]

As a result of his participation in *Metropol* (and, presumably, because of the 1978 publication of *Pushkin House*, in Russian, in the United States), Bitov experienced difficulties for a time. One book of his, *Sunday (Voskresnyi den')*, came out in 1980, but his name, previously listed quite frequently in articles about excellent contemporary Soviet writers, was rarely discussed in print. An occasional article by him would appear in the press, but his next book, *Georgian Album (Gruzinskii al'bom)*, came out – not in Leningrad or in Moscow, but in Tbilisi – only in 1985.

What the *Metropol* writers advocated in 1979 – greater diversity, less inertia, and less stringent censorship restrictions in the arts – became a hallmark of the Gorbachev regime's official policy toward culture. And the fate of prominent *Metropol* contributors? They have been allowed to make extended visits to the West. Voznesensky has been involved in plans to create a Marc Chagall museum in the Soviet Union and was instrumental in successfully pushing for the full publication of Pasternak's *Doctor Zhivago* there. He is on the official commission to explore the possibilities of publishing the works of fellow *Metropol* contributor Vladimir Vysotsky. In April, 1987, Bitov was permitted, for the first time, to travel to the United States to the Wheatland Foundation's International Writers' Conference in Washington, D.C. He was one of the two official USSR writers (the other was poet Oleg Chukhontsev) to participate on a panel, entitled "Literature of Russia," together with émigrés Joseph Brodsky, Efim Ėtkind, Andrei Siniavsky, and Thomas Venclova. This was the first time that an official panel had consisted of Soviet and émigré writers.[9]

In 1979, the writer Feliks Kuznetsov, as first secretary of the Moscow branch of the Writers' Union, had sent a letter to five American writers (Edward Albee, Arthur Miller, William Styron, John Updike, and Kurt Vonnegut Jr.)[10] who had protested the union's retaliation against *Metropol*. He upbraided them for rallying around *Metropol* and defended the Writers' Union decision to reject publication of the anthology on the grounds of inferior literary quality.[11] In a final piece of irony, it was Feliks Kuznetsov, who, at a news conference in 1987, announced the upcoming publication in the Soviet Union of the long-suppressed anti-utopian novel of the 1920s, Evgeny Zamiatin's *We (My)*.[12]

The publication history of the Bitov story, "The Last Bear," provides a unique opportunity to see Soviet publishing in action. A comparison of the uncensored *Metropol* text of the story and the *Seven Journeys* version demonstrates that the *Seven Journeys* version, while largely the same as the *Metropol* text, lacks some of the bite of the latter because of minor changes and omissions. An epigraph concerning a World War II battle for the Kaliningrad zoo in which a Soviet lieutenant and his platoon had killed and captured "Hitlerites" is missing in the *Seven Journeys* version, as is the major protagonist's description of himself and his daughter as corpses. Other exclusions are the narrator's comment that he would not drink if he could order sunshine for a half hour; a description of birds in the zoo as black; of the sparrow as a free bird; of the sparrow as the tsar of beasts. A passage explaining that, in its inhibitions, the chimpanzee is like a human being, eliminates the reference to inhibitions and transforms the chimpanzee/human-being likeness to a lack of similarity between the two species.

It is essential to set forth one final piece of background information. There is a subsequent, highly significant chapter to our account of the publication history of "The Last Bear." In 1985, in Bitov's *Georgian Album*, the story appeared in print, in a Soviet publication, nestled in the text of "Choice of Location," which, as we are well aware, had also been published in *Seven Journeys* in 1976.

The *Georgian Album* version of "The Last Bear" reproduces, almost word for word, the *Metropol* text. The only cuts that are not restored are a reference to a joke about a Jew and a reference to Christian love. In the *Georgian Album* text, the joke is told about a generic someone, and the love is not qualified by an adjective. The chimpanzee, in the 1985 version, remains unlike the human being. In all other respects, the text is a replay of the *Metropol* version.

The circulation figure for *Seven Journeys* had been 100,000. The *Georgian Album* edition came out with a circulation of 40,000 copies. A year later, in 1986, "The Last Bear," again located in "Choice of Location," was published in Moscow in Bitov's *Book of Journeys* (*Kniga puteshestvii*), with a circulation figure of 270,000. The 1970–1 text that had been mutilated in the last

years of Brezhnev's regime, which had been restored to its
original state in an unofficial literary anthology that had caused
consternation among the authorities and difficulties for so many
of its contributors, in the liberalized cultural environment under
Gorbachev was now made widely available to Soviet readers in
an official Soviet publication.

"THE LAST BEAR"

That Soviet authorities might have had reservations about
publishing the full text of "The Last Bear" becomes clear as we
analyze the *Metropol* story. Although Bitov repeats the technique
of bridging animal and human worlds, his treatment of the
theme much more readily lends itself to an interpretation of
political/social commentary than does his blending of animate
and inanimate worlds in "The Sun" and "The Wheel." "The
Last Bear" can be read as a political allegory that condemns the
Stalinist legacy. One might substitute the word "person" for
"bear" (often used as a symbol for Russia) who, entrapped in the
zoo (read "prison" or "Stalinist society"), loses a sense of
"bearness" (read "humanness").

The epigraph, about the World War II Soviet troops who, in
1944, captured and killed Hitlerites in a battle for the zoo, brings
to mind both Hitler and Stalin and the prisons they created in
society and of society. The association is set up between caged
human beings – in human prisons – and caged animals – in zoos.
Bitov's narrative continues along this path as he describes a
narrator's and his young daughter's visit to the zoo.

As the narrator and his daughter are on their way to the zoo,
the narrator describes them smiling to themselves "... like dead
people" ("... kak mertvetsy").[13] In an image that sends reverberations to this one, he later describes the caged bear as
continuing his external existence although the bear seemed to
know that the bearness in him was no longer alive. In a haunting
scene, Bitov describes the insane bear, oblivious to itself, its
surroundings, and the pieces of candy being thrown at it, as it
keeps eating the candy without opening the wrappers. The
narrator, upon entering the zoo, declares that observing the
elephant-keeper is instructive. Thus, he watches people as well

as animals when he visits the zoo. He again links animals and people in his statement that the chimpanzee, in his inhibitions, is like a person.

The Soviet authorities may have been especially wary of printing this story because of its similarity in setting to a key scene in Aleksandr Solzhenitsyn's *Cancer Ward* (*Rakovyi korpus*).[14] Bitov's story was written in 1970. Copies of the manuscript of Solzhenitsyn's novel, not published in the Soviet Union, had been circulating among members of the Soviet intelligentsia since 1966.[15]

It seems likely to me that the episode in which Oleg Kostoglotov goes to the Tashkent zoo is a hidden subtext to the Bitov story.[16] The number of parallel images in the two scenes is striking. Both major protagonists go to the zoo on a sunny day. Many of the same animals are mentioned – a goat, birds, bears, an elephant, monkeys, a chimpanzee, predatory animals, horses. Of course, one could argue that a visit to a zoo on a sunny day described by two writers could, coincidentally and naturally, focus on some of the same animals. Other parallels are present, too. Both authors mention the griffin, an animal that one would not ordinarily think of in connection with a contemporary visit to a zoo. (The griffin is a mythical animal with, significantly, the wings of an eagle, the eagle, of course, being the symbol of tsarist Russia.) Both authors use the word "tsar" or "tsardom" (Solzhenitsyn: "a tsardom of kids" ["tsarstvo detvory"];[17] Bitov: "tsar of the birds" ["tsar' ptits"]) (p. 2). Both describe one of the animals as sad (Solzhenitsyn: "sad elephant" ["pechal'nogo slona"];[18] Bitov: "... the chimpanzee ... is sad" ["shimpanze pechalen"]) (p. 2). Solzhenitsyn describes a tormented bear pacing back and forth. Some children discuss the idea of throwing stones at it because, they say, the bear will think that the stones are candies. Kostoglotov thinks to himself that he is one of the animals and, writes Solzhenitsyn, he "... didn't see himself".[19] Bitov's bear scene includes the image cluster of a bear, candies thrown at the bear, and the bear unaware of itself, the bear that had lost its bearness. This is reminiscent of Kostoglotov who, in feeling himself like an animal, has lost his humanness.

The monkeys, in Solzhenitsyn's scene, remind Kostoglotov of

some of his fellow camp prisoners. Bitov compares the chimpanzee, in its inhibitions, to a human being. Both authors refer to
guilt. Both refer to the animals' eyes. Both speak of blindness.
Solzhenitsyn's moving scene describes an empty cage, vacated
by the monkey that had been blinded by a malicious man. Bitov
speaks of the bear's insane blank stare that could at first be
mistaken for blindness.

Two animals central to Solzhenitsyn's zoo scene are missing
from Bitov's menagerie. Near the beginning of Kostoglotov's
stroll through the zoo, he comes upon a squirrel in a wheel (". . .
belka v kolese").[20] It was impossible, writes Solzhenitsyn, to stop
the wheel or to save the squirrel from death. Later in the scene,
Kostoglotov sees a yellow-eyed tiger in whose whiskers, he
notices, ". . . was concentrated his expression of rapacious-
ness."[21] Literary critics have discerned a veiled allusion to Stalin
in the description of the rapacious-looking tiger with the
whiskers and the yellow eyes.[22] *Cancer Ward* as a whole has been
read as a condemnation of Stalinist society.[23]

Bitov inserts into "The Last Bear" some of his own veiled
allusions – to the Solzhenitsyn text and to the Solzhenitsyn
theme of anti-Stalinism. Knowledge of the subtext in Bitov's
story enables us to understand that the placement of "The Last
Bear" in "The Wheel" was not as random as one would have
thought from looking at the episode exclusively in the context of
"The Wheel." A Solzhenitsyn animal episode that Bitov leaves
out of "The Last Bear" is the one about the squirrel in the wheel.
Moreover, in that scene, within one paragraph, Solzhenitsyn
repeats the word "wheel" ("koleso") five times. In addition, in
Cancer Ward the action that immediately follows Kostoglotov's
visit to the zoo is his attempt to visit Vega. She is not at home, but
as Kostoglotov stands there, a man with a motorcycle leaves the
communal apartment. If one reads "The Last Bear" in the light
of its subtext, it makes sense to see why it can fit into the text of
"The Wheel." The images that are not a part of Bitov's text –
Solzhenitsyn's squirrel in the wheel and the motorcycle –
together with a theme of "The Last Bear," the inability to escape
death, provide the reader with the interlocking pieces to complete the difficult jigsaw puzzle of the epicycle of Bitov's "The
Wheel."

Why would Bitov use Solzhenitsyn's *Cancer Ward* as a subtext for "The Last Bear?" He has, I believe, chosen his text carefully, for the story can be read as a bitter indictment of Stalin. The presence of the theme in Bitov's story is underscored by the presence of that theme as a major component in *Cancer Ward* and by the presence of the image of the hateful Stalin in the zoo scene of Solzhenitsyn's novel. Bitov says that under Stalin, people lost their humanness, and reality became a papier-mâché reality.

In *Metropol*, Bitov groups his three stories under the title, "Days of Farewell (from the book *Recollections of Reality*)" ("Proshchal'nye den'ki [iz knigi 'Vospominaniia o real'nosti']") (p. 1).[24] According to Bitov in "The Last Bear," reality under Stalin existed only in people's memories. Stalin deprived people of their human qualities. Like the insane bear described in the story, people ceased to be themselves. In *Pushkin House*, which Bitov finished writing a year after "The Last Bear," he documents the devastation that Stalin wrought on people's lives.

One must acknowledge the political aspects of interpreting this story about the caged insane bear whose actions are automatic because he has lost the sense of being a bear. It is equally important to consider more universal dimensions of the story. (Of course, both interpretations can be intertwined. Bitov might be arguing that when living beings are not free, they die.) Bitov pursues familiar themes. He constructs a living organism. The ecology of that system includes dying. In "The Last Bear," he focuses his attention on the extinction of life. As he observes the bear in the zoo, the narrator realizes that he is looking at the last representative of a species, at the last specimen of bear.

Bitov writes,

And really, if among wild animal instincts that have not yet diverged, by comparison with a human being, from the logic of Creation and the Creator, there has not been lost the precise feeling of impending death, when an animal hides, crawls off, etc., then why can't it experience death more globally as well – the death of a species, of a genus, of life itself? ... Here there no longer remained the pure and the impure – they were all the last ones, blue, in a haze of farewell. I wanted to run back to the elephant, in order to manage to see them all with these eyes opened all of a sudden, to look into their last dear eyes, experiencing guilt and brotherhood, the brotherhood of all living things on earth in the face of death. (p. 4)

At the end of "The Last Bear," Bitov merges two worlds, the animate/animal world and the inanimate/make-believe world of toys. The narrator, in the light of his newly found knowledge, observes that the animals seemed to fuse with the plywood, the hawkers' stands, the fences, and cages. They were, he writes, like their ". . . tin-plate . . . colleagues from the shooting gallery" (p. 4). He notices a pony that he cannot distinguish from a papier-mâché merry-go-round pony. The narrator muses that today there are more artificially made than real animals. Real animals, he realizes, are fast becoming mere ". . . object[s – E.C.] of mythology" (p. 4) and, like dragons and griffins, make-believe (p. 4). "The Last Bear" ends as the narrator is horror-struck that ". . . all our toys and fairy tales are merely the relic of another . . . era, when . . . it was thought that through such games and pastimes, there would be planted in a child's soul the first seed of Christian love for one's neighbor" (p. 4).

"The Last Bear" is gloomier than most of Bitov's previous writings. The technique of merging one world with another leads him not to an acknowledgement of a world of interconnections and interdependencies, but to a statement about dying. The species of bear is becoming extinct, and the bear is unaware of it. The author writes that we make more and more animals out of rubber, plastic, and cotton and do not even know why (p. 4). Bitov implies that real aspects of culture are dying and that no one is aware of it. It is also plausible to assign a cultural interpretation to his ruminations on the extinction of a species. The dating of the story, May, 1970,[25] corresponds to the time-frame when Bitov was thinking about questions of culture. The years 1967–9 marked the time of his writing of "Armenia Lessons," and the years 1971–3, "Choice of Location." *Pushkin House*, his tour de force about Russian and Soviet culture written from 1964–71, contains memorable discussions about the death of Russian culture.

It would be possible to read many Bitov comments about Armenian and Georgian culture as allegories about the death of Russian culture.[26] When he speaks, in "Armenia Lessons," about the old sections of Erevan that will soon die out, he might also have in mind the disappearance of old Russian culture in today's Soviet world that has been wounded by its past. When he wanders through the streets of Tbilisi and is saddened by the thought that the old parts of the city will not survive, Bitov may have in mind thoughts about a similar situation in Soviet culture.

While Bitov might, in "The Last Bear," be making a statement about a specific culture, that of Stalinist Russia, he is also, I believe, making a more universal statement about life. Animals die. People die. Species die. In the past, the trajectory that Bitov had often traced was one from death to life. He had often focused on characters who, spiritually dead, had then spiritually awakened.

It is instructive to investigate the connection between "The Big Balloon" and "The Last Bear," for both deal with a father and his little girl as the two major protagonists. The earlier story, told from a young girl's perspective, is positive. Tonia's faith in the existence of beauty is rewarded with the appearance of the balloon. Tonia's mother, after her death, continues to live. Bitov emphasizes life-affirming qualities.

The point of view shifts, in "The Last Bear," from the daughter's to the father's. The difference between the adult's and the child's perspective is underscored by the varied reactions of the father and the daughter to the pony. The father sees it as a sign of the end of life. The pony, indistinguishable for him from the papier-mâché ponies on the carousel, leads him to think of the extinction of species. In contrast, in the only life-affirming passage in the story, the daughter is struck by the pony's vitality and reality. We might surmise that the adult here, himself closer to death than is his daughter, feels death's approach without being aware of it. The child, more alive than dead, is more attuned to living than to dying. An emphasis upon the continuity of life is an isolated phenomenon in "The Last Bear." (Bitov could have emphasized, in the scene with the pony, the dying out of one species, person, being, and the contrasting bursting into life of another. He chooses not to. In a scene in which he sees a pregnant woman – who, of course, could represent the continuity of life – his thought is one of abhorrence that pregnant women should be brought to zoos.)

Bitov, in many works, demonstrates that individual fragments of life, when brought together in a creative way, breathe more life and form greater wholes, ever moving and expanding. "The Last Bear" is an exception, yet its emphasis, on life's destructive phenomena, is not new for the author. "The Sun" depicts life's creative and destructive forces. Some of his earlier protagonists – Lobyshev, the idler, Alesha in "The Garden" – act in self-destructive patterns. Unaware of what they are doing, they spiritually extinguish their own lives.

That Bitov's ecosystem contains movements toward life and death is made clear by the epigraph to Bitov's second *Metropol* story, an excerpt from the first paragraph of *Time, Cells, and Aging*, a book on the cell biology of aging by American biologist Bernard Strehler:

Among the evolved characters which frequently occur in the self-replicating systems we call living organisms is the termination of the individual. This "natural death" of the living units which carry for a time the unbroken line of descent from the first primordial origin of life is of little consequence to the vast majority of living things, for the places of those that die are soon occupied by other individuals.[27]

"SECLUDED STREET"

"Secluded Street" ("Glukhaia ulitsa")[28] continues Bitov's indictment of Stalin. While "The Last Bear" criticizes Stalin for imprisoning society as a whole and for robbing people of their humane qualities, "Secluded Street" concentrates on several other aspects of Stalinism. Most importantly, it deals with the peasants, with collectivization, and with questions of what constitutes the proper attitude toward the past.

On the surface, the story recounts the thoughts and actions of a first-person urban narrator, a writer, as he is on his way, in the countryside spot to which he returns every year, to do some errands. In the story's first subsection, "The Peasant" ("Muzhik"), the narrator's contemplations center on abstract notions of what reality is. He decides that he would like to write an autobiography that would deal with "only that which was," with "only the real moments of existence" (p. 8), and not with society's conventional notions of reality. So far, the discussion is abstract and philosophical.

The next subsection, "Thirty-Three Years," erases the boundaries between the abstract, philosophical; the personal; and the political aspects of the story. The first words are, "So where is the peasant?" (p. 8). This comment, no doubt, refers to the omission of a peasant in the first subsection, which, after all, had been entitled "The Peasant." Although the remark is playful, it also leads to the anti-Stalinist political commentary which lies at the heart of "Secluded Street." The narrator had said, in abstract terms, that he would like to write about reality as it really existed.

Reality as it had existed in Stalin's Soviet Union of the 1930s, had included the existence of the kulaks, the peasants who had suffered terribly as Stalin collectivized agriculture.

It is this reality to which Bitov turns as he, first of all, establishes the theme of "thirty-three years." Although Bitov writes that his protagonist is thirty-three years old, I believe that given the set of circumstances that occurs in the story, the use of the number "thirty-three" has political significance, too, as a reference to 1933, the year that marked the beginning of Stalin's second Five-Year Plan. The narrator meets a peasant who works in a pumping station with machines, but who had also built a tiled stove for the narrator. The peasant, who is never named in Bitov's story, represents a class that had once been involved with tasks associated with rural life, such as the building of a tiled stove, but was now working at a job associated with industry, the running of machines at the pumping station.

The narrator and the peasant get drunk together and discuss a number of topics. The peasant asks why good books cannot be printed and why only the bad ones are published. The narrator, a writer, is surprised to hear that the peasant is complaining about Semen Babaevskii's *Cavalier of the Golden Star* (*Kavaler zolotoi zvezdy*).[29] The peasant had read Babaevskii's book in a handwritten copy, although, the narrator points out, it had been published and had even won the Stalin Prize. The narrator is happy that at least if good books do not get published, neither does Babaevskii's novel get reprinted. The peasant says that he liked the book, for, he explains, it dealt with the life of the kulak. The peasant then asks why the kulak was treated so unfairly, merely for working diligently (p. 12).[30]

To add to his indictment of Stalin's policy toward the kulaks, Bitov delineates the virtues of a peasant's cultivation of a private plot of land. If we remember the narrator's earlier declaration that he wanted to depict reality as it was, the implications of Bitov's larger statement in "Secluded Street" become clear. Babaevsky represented a literature that lied, in accordance with the contentions demanded by the society of the time, about the effect of Stalin's policies in the countryside.

Bitov tells a different story. He admires the peasant's ability to build a tiled stove for an individual house. He praises a proprietor for her cow, and for her struggle to feed herself and cultivate her land (p. 15).[31] The narrator praises the proprietor for diligence and self-sufficiency.

Bitov links this aspect of life, so mutilated by Stalin, to the theme of his previous story, Stalin's imprisonment of society. The author writes, "... I would have liked it if ... there would have been more cow than bear" (p. 15). He recalls that he had not remembered when an old kulak woman he had known as a child had died.[32] He writes, "Milk was flowing along my fingers in the night of the crazed bear; not to forget to tell ... Whom? what? not to forget ..." (p. 16).

Bitov has arrived at the question referred to in "That is the Question" (p. 11),[33] the title of the story's subsection that deals with Babaevsky, the kulaks, and the cow. The question tormenting the narrator is: to forget or to remember the Stalinist past? The question, for him, is paradoxical. His musings return us to the realm of philosophical speculation that was characteristic of his earlier thoughts about writing about reality as it is. The paradox is this – if one remembers the past, one is not living in the present. On the other hand, if one forgets, the last one who remembers dies. The narrator ponders, "Not to remember, in order to live, without noticing death or to remember in order to be afraid to die and in order not to live ...?" (p. 16).

The segment ends as the narrator, drunk, rolls a wheel off the road. (At the outset, he had met the peasant as the drunken peasant was rolling the wheel.) The last words are, "To forget or to remember? Hamlet – mumblet ..." ("Zabyt' ili pomnit'? Gamlet – miamlet ...") (p. 16).[34] The introduction of the wheel image into "Secluded Street" sets up reverberations to the wheel of life and death theme in "The Wheel" and to the emphasis upon the wheel of death/fate theme that emerged from reading "The Last Bear" in the context of "The Wheel."

Indeed, "Fate" ("Sud'ba") is what the final brief segment of "Secluded Street" is called (p. 16). The episode is dedicated to N. Rubtsov, a Soviet poet who died in 1971 in his mid-30s.[35] It is significant that Bitov would choose Nikolai Rubtsov as the person to whom he dedicates a section of "Secluded Street." First of all, it was rumored that he, like many of the peasants of a previous generation about whom Bitov had been speaking, had been murdered. Secondly, his poetry eulogized Russia of the countryside, the beauties of nature, and old Russia.[36] A famous line from one of his most well-known poems appears on his gravestone in the cemetery of his native Vologda: "Russia, Rus! Preserve yourself, preserve!" ("Rossiia, Rus'! Khrani sebia, khrani!").[37]

The major setting of Bitov's "Fate" is a mysterious house, separated from other houses near the narrator's dacha. The house is an isolated piece of the past, writes Bitov, with its own plot of land, its own life of generations of family members and family tragedies, murders, its own wide-open gate, its own fence, its own self-sufficient, isolated existence. These people are a piece of leftover fate of another era. Bitov's conclusion is that one's past, imperfect as it may have been, is part of one's fate; it is all one has.

By the end of "Secluded Street," he answers the agonizing question – to remember or to forget? One must remember, the implication is, for the past is part of one's fate. The fate of a people is to include recognition of the past in present-day life. This idea appears, in embryo form, in Bitov's past writings. "Journey to a Childhood Friend" treats the same theme, but more indirectly. Genrikh was a larger-than-life "positive hero" like positive heroes depicted in Socialist Realist novels (such as Babaevsky's). The protagonist of "Journey" realized that he, rather than Genrikh, was the true positive hero in that he succeeded in living his ordinary, everyday life with its ordinary everyday incidents. As in "Secluded Street," Bitov punches holes in the "perfection" of the Stalinist myth of reality. Just as in the later work, he concludes that one must face one's past in order to live a real life in the present.

The ending of "Secluded Street" deals with a section of the street – the mysterious house and the constellations of activities and people that are an integral part of that household – which is but a remnant of a bygone era. It is dying out. Bitov, one might surmise, is speaking about a specific era of Soviet history and about a specific event of that era, the fate of the kulaks.[38] At the same time, though, the ending, in its discussion of a "species" that is dying out, returns us to the story's epigraph, the natural biological law by which individual organisms die and are replaced by others. We are brought back to Bitov's thoughts about the extinction of a species in "The Last Bear." We are brought back to "The Wheel," where we read that the horse dies out and the motorcycle replaces it in function. In "Secluded Street," the kulak dies out, and others take his place. The peasant worked the land and his own plot; now he works in a pumping station with machines.

"Secluded Street" condemns Stalin, yet the message is also a universal one: no matter what biological organism exists, it will die, and others will take its place.

"THE DOCTOR'S FUNERAL"

Bitov's third and final contribution to *Metropol* is "The Doctor's Funeral" ("Pokhorony doktora").[39] The story is dedicated to E. Ral'be. In his book of essays, *Articles from a Novel*, Bitov explains that Elena Samsonovna Ral'be was his "first reader" ("pervyi chitatel'"), his ideal reader.[40] She was an elderly woman with whom he had corresponded for almost a decade. He describes her literary taste as greatly superior to his own. He treasured their special friendship and was deeply saddened by her death. He writes that no one can replace her.[41] Elena Ral'be died in 1977,[42] two years before the appearance of the *Metropol* anthology where "The Doctor's Funeral" was published.

"The Doctor's Funeral" stars a woman of the same generation as Elena Ral'be's. "Auntie" ("tëtka") (pp. 19ff),[43] the narrator's aunt by marriage, is approximately eighty years old. She is a great doctor whose qualities, according to the narrator, no longer exist: human decency, caring, empathy. Bitov describes Auntie while the warm, vital energy that has always been her hallmark struggles in her with the counterforce of physical decline.

Bitov uses the occasion of her funeral to describe the hypocrisy of people interested only in status, without genuine feelings of compassion. Generals come to the funeral and make meaningless speeches. Others observe the important people at the funeral and, for this reason alone, are eager to be part of the mourning throng. The narrator observes that none of these people respected the qualities of empathy and sensitivity that had set Auntie apart.

In "The Doctor's Funeral," Bitov's final *Metropol* glimpse of the consequences of Stalinism for society, the author fixes his lens on the relationship of individual human beings toward one another. He speaks of the extinction of certain forms of human behavior that characterized people of Auntie's generation, a generation, one can infer, that had experienced life before the Stalin era. Auntie, he declares, had acted according to the dictates of her heart. She had trusted people. She had been a good, pure, kind human being, he writes. The highly placed bureaucrats and careerists who perfunctorily gave their funeral speeches and then zoomed off in large, ostentatious cars were dead in terms of human kindness. The narrator, too, feels that he is not as noble a person as she had been.

The idea in the passage from Strehler's book, the notion that individual organisms die and are replaced by other different organisms, applies to "The Doctor's Funeral." The aunties of the world are dying out, we can conclude from our reading of these stories, and they are not being replaced. Bitov, in this story, documents the damage done by Stalin in the realm of human interaction. On one level, the story is about the erosion of empathy that Stalin caused. Bitov treats this theme, in greater depth, in *Pushkin House*.

On another level, like "Secluded Street," this story highlights one segment of Soviet society that was particularly damaged by Stalin. The very title, "The Doctor's Funeral," alludes, I believe, to the so-called doctors' plot, the incident in January, 1953, when nine doctors were falsely accused of plotting the assassination of certain Soviet officials.[44] The accusations signaled what seemed to be the beginning of another purge of intellectuals. The target of Stalin's doctors' plot persecutions were often Jewish doctors. Only Stalin's death, shortly thereafter in March, 1953, brought his rule of naked terrorism to a close. What is important for our purposes, in this respect, is that Auntie is a doctor and that she is Jewish, a point Bitov emphasizes throughout the text.

By the end of his trilogy on Stalin, Bitov has focused (1) on society as a whole, (2) on the peasants, and (3) on the intelligentsia. By the end of "The Doctor's Funeral," we have come to understand the heading under which the stories appear. The "Farewell Days" refers to the farewell to humanness, in general, that was inflicted upon a society in jail. The farewell days refer to a farewell to the peasant class. They refer to a farewell to an old generation uncorrupted by Stalin's lies. As a whole, the story cycle constitutes Bitov's "Recollections of Reality," the reality of the Stalinist past.

CHAPTER 10

"Sunday": more "I-lands" and journeys

Bitov's next book, *Sunday. Stories, Tales, Journeys* (*Voskresnyi den'.
Rasskazy, povesti, puteshestviia*)[1] contained, almost exclusively,
works that had come out at least once in other collections of his.
The first section, "Island" ("Ostrov"), reproduces most of the
stories in *Apothecary Island*: "The Big Balloon," "Apothecary
Island," "The Idler," "Penelope," and "Infantiev." The one
change, in "Island," in that cluster of stories, is the insertion of
"Life in Windy Weather." Taken as a group, the "Island"
stories document the growing-up process, in Leningrad, of
people at different stages of life. A little girl's fulfilled dreams
and a little boy's crushed dreams; an immature young man's
lack of responsibility at work and at play; a young man's and an
older man's discovery of spirituality – these are the pairings of
stories that Bitov gives us in his 1980 book.

The second section of *Sunday*, "The Ark" ("Kovcheg"), pairs
"The Forest" with the only Bitov work not previously antholo-
gized, a "film tale," "The Wildlife Preserve" ("Zapovednik").
Noah's ark had taken animals away from centrally populated
areas. Bitov's "ark" presumably refers, indirectly, to the fact
that each of these two stories concerns a man visiting a place that
is far away from the Soviet Union's urban centers.

The third and final section of *Sunday*, "Choice of Location,"
contains "Armenia Lessons" and "The Gamble," two Bitov
accounts of travel to the Soviet Union's non-Russian republics.
Sunday takes us on a spatial and temporal journey to Leningrad
and to distant places while simultaneously taking us on a journey
toward an increased awareness of values and of self-knowledge.

CHAPTER II

"Pushkin House": the riddles of life and literature

The consequences of the Stalin cult are condemned and debunked; however, the terror that it nailed into our flesh and blood still binds and paralyzes people's consciousness. And wherever there is terror, there can be no truth.[1]

Dmitrii Likhachev, "From Repentance – To Action"
("Ot pokaianiia – k deistviiu")

The circle is ... symbolic of a consciousness locked in upon itself. How can one break out of it? People run along the circle and cannot reach reality.[2]

Andrei Bitov, "Breaking Out of the Circle"
("Prorvat' krug")

... the task ... is: to debunk all false concepts, to remain with nothing and *suddenly* to grasp the *secret* ... At this point a revolution in consciousness takes place – and the earth is saved.[3]

Andrei Bitov, *Pushkin House* (*Pushkinskii dom*)

Bitov began writing *Pushkin House* in 1964 and completed it in 1971. The fate of *Pushkin House* in print has been a curious one. During the 1970s, fragments from it appeared in official Soviet publications as separate short stories or essays. Most of the second section, "A Hero of our Time," was included, as "The Young Odoevtsev, Hero of a Novel," in Bitov's *Days of Man*, in 1976.[4]

Bitov submitted the completed novel to the Soviet publisher, "Soviet Writer" ("Sovetskii pisatel'"), but the author was unsuccessful in his efforts at having the entire text of the novel accepted for publication in the USSR. It came out, in full, in Russian, in the United States in 1978.[5]

Critical literature addressing itself to the fragments and/or to the novel as a whole appeared in the Soviet Union throughout the 1970s.[6] An appendix to the novel, with commentary keyed to the relevant page numbers of the Ardis edition of the novel, existed only in manuscript form for several years.[7] The English translation, *Pushkin House*, came out in the United States in 1987.[8] Under the liberalized conditions for the arts that marked the Gorbachev years, *Pushkin House* was published in the prestigious Soviet literary magazine *Novyi mir*.[9] It came out in book form in the USSR in 1989. A short excerpt from the novel, about the return from the Stalinist camps of a member of the intelligentsia, came out in *Literaturnaia gazeta* in 1987. Another excerpt, from the beginning of the novel, was featured in the popular Soviet journal *Ogonëk* in October, 1987.[10] A couple of segments from *Pushkin House* were also reprinted, with supplementary material, in Bitov's 1986 *Articles from a Novel*.[11]

The connections of *Pushkin House* to Bitov's other writings are as involved as are the details of the novel's publication history. Moreover, the years during which he was working on *Pushkin House* correspond to the years during which he was also writing other compositions. It is not surprising, then, that the works overlap one another. *Pushkin House*'s brilliant, eccentric grandfather, Modest Platonovich, whose comments alert his audience to the environmental dangers facing the planet Earth, shares characteristics with another wise, eccentric old man, the artist in "Armenia Lessons." He, too, could step away from immediate, everyday concerns and offer a far-sighted global perspective on issues.

Aleksei Monakhov, the young man whose life Bitov had been documenting since the late 1950s, shares many behavioral traits with Leva Odoevtsev, the major protagonist of *Pushkin House*. The fact that they can be viewed as the same person is suggested, for the author places a section of *Pushkin House* in the English collection, *Life in Windy Weather*. In that work, Bitov includes "The Soldier (From the Memoirs of the Monakhov Family)," and throughout "The Soldier," instead of using the name Leva Odoevtsev, Bitov calls the hero Alexei Monakhov.[12] In *Pushkin House*, Leva, like Alexei Monakhov, is deceitful. He is easy prey to Faina, an unfaithful Asya-like woman. He, like Monakhov, lies. He, like Monakhov, realizes that his images of life, the idealized versions he held of life, do not correspond to reality.

A key theme of "Life in Windy Weather" and of *Pushkin House* is the importance, for a person, of breaking away from old structures in order to live and write creatively. A key structural trait of "The Wheel," "The Taste," and *Pushkin House* is the omnipresence of the shape of a circle. In these works, the use of circle imagery is interwoven with the substantive issues these writings tackle. The *Metropol* stories and "The Taste" share with *Pushkin House* powerful descriptions of a society and people that feel the dislocations of life that have issued from Stalin's regime of terror. "Armenia Lessons," like *Pushkin House*, cries out for the importance of preserving culture. The two works forge connecting links between culture and values, between genuine art and a personal life lived with integrity.

Pushkin House is the story of Leva, a graduate student in Russian literature in Pushkin House, the Academy of Science's Institute of Russian Literature in Leningrad. The novel is divided into three parts, each highlighting an incident from his life, all three episodes from the same time period. The first deals with his past. Leva's grandfather, a distinguished literary scholar, had been arrested and sent to the camps during Stalin's reign. The grandfather Leva had thought was dead is suddenly resurrected. The second section introduces Leva to the pains of involvement with a woman who does not love him. The third section spotlights the duel, literal and figurative, between Leva and his professional and personal rival, Mitishatiev, personification of evil. Appended to each section, the reader discovers commentary, under the rubric "The Italics Are Mine – A.B.;" "Versions and Variants," alternative versions of each section; and "appendices," writings by some of the main characters – two short stories by Leva's surrogate grandfather, Uncle Dickens; pieces by Leva's real grandfather, Modest Platonovich; and Leva's article analyzing three poems.

The novel begins with a prologue, "What Is to Be Done?" ("Chto delat'?"). Bitov plays with well-known titles in the rest of the book, too. Each of the three sections refers to a famous nineteenth-century masterpiece of Russian literature: *Fathers and Sons* (*Ottsy i deti*); *A Hero of Our Time* (*Geroi nashego vremeni*); and "The Poor Horseman" ("Bednyi vsadnik"). One chapter of this final section the author playfully dubs "Bronze People" ("Mednye liudi"), thus intertwining Pushkin's "Bronze Horseman" ("Mednyi vsadnik") and Dostoevsky's *Poor Folk* (*Bednye liudi*).

Near the beginning of *Pushkin House*, Bitov writes that until a certain point in the 1960s, the life of the novel's major protagonist, Leva Nikolaevich Odoevtsev, resembled a "divine thread" that flowed evenly, continuously, and uninterruptedly. After that time, declares the narrator at another point in the novel, the thread began to form rings, one on top of the other, all piled on top of the first ring (p. 12). In investigating *Pushkin House*, we must follow a divine thread in order to unravel the myriad complexities of this extraordinarily difficult, powerful, important novel. In following that thread, we, like Bitov, see that Leva's life "... curls up into rings: forming ... rope coils or a sleeping snake" ("svertyvaetsia kol'tsami: obrazuia ... bukhtu kanata ili spiashchuiu zmeiu") (p. 160).

The ring is, indeed, the central image, the image that provides the key to unlock the major message of the book. Stylistically, too, Bitov places "O"s and rings throughout his novel. The chief protagonist's last name, Odoevtsev, begins with the letter "o." The first word, "Table of Contents" ("Oglavlenie") begins with "o;" the novel's last word, "anew" ("zanovo") ends with "o" (pp. 9,412). The first word of the first section, "Fathers and Sons" ("Ottsy i deti") begins with an "o." The first five out of seven subsections have titles that begin with an "o": "Father" ("Otets"); "Separately about Dickens" ("Otdel'no o Dikkense"); "Father (Continued)" ("Otets [prodolzhenie]"); "Father's Father" ("Otets ottsa"); and "Father's Father (Continued)" ("Otets ottsa [prodolzhenie]") (p. 7). The final word of the table of contents, "Odoevtsev," begins with an "o."

The lives of Leva, Faina, and Mitishatiev form a circle from which there is no escape, writes Bitov's narrator. Rings recur throughout the novel. Leva and Faina both mouth the sound "o" when they meet; they are introduced to one another by

Mitishatiev. All three are at a party at which people sit in a circle in order to play "Spin the Bottle." The bottle goes round and round (forming rings). Leva steals Faina's wedding ring (she is married, but neither to Leva nor to Mitishatiev) from her pocketbook.

Near the end of the first section, Leva notices, on his way to visit his grandfather, a "trolley car ring." ("tramvainoe kol'tso"). We know that the visit ends disastrously for Leva. The ring formed by Mitishatiev, Faina, and Leva also ends badly for Leva. Near the end of the novel's second section, when the narrator alerts us to the importance of the ring, a significant scene, repeated later, takes place at a "trolley car stop" ("tramvainoi ostanovke"). The final epilogue of the third section of *Pushkin House* concludes with a reference to Leva and to the author and to the readers – "... on his little trolley car ..." ("... na svoem tramvaichike ...") (p. 396). Everything keeps forming rings.

The scholarly article that Leva writes repeats, with scholarly apparatus, the events of his life as recorded in the rest of *Pushkin House*. Leva is twenty-seven years old at the time we observe him. Each of the three poets – Pushkin, Lermontov, and Tiutchev – whose poems he analyzes, was twenty-seven at the time he wrote the poem on which Leva concentrates. Leva's article underscores this fact. When we look at other details, we see that at twenty-seven, Leva reads a piece his grandfather had written when *he* was twenty-seven. The date Bitov writes at the end of his novel is the twenty-seventh day of the month. Bitov was born on May 27, and he began writing *Pushkin House* when he was 27.

The beginning and end of Bitov's novel form a ring. We see Leva's body, with a pistol in his hand and a burning cigarette butt (another circle) sticking out of the end of the pistol (another circle). Mitishatiev, who had taught Leva to smoke, had placed it there. The linkage of cigarettes and revolvers appears in another work of Russian literature which Bitov does not acknowledge but which, I believe, forms still another circle of repetition. In Nabokov's *The Gift* (*Dar*), there is a writer who composes a literary biography of Chernyshevsky, the title of whose novel *What Is to Be Done?* has started Bitov's own ring.

Nabokov's fictional author, Fyodor, writes a "... biography in the shape of a ring ..." ("... zhizneopisanie v vide kol'tsa ...").[13] Fyodor's fiancée, Zina, upon reading the book within the book, notices that a "circle" ("krug") was being formed.[14] Nabokov's main character kills off his hero, only to bring him to life again; Bitov's narrator uses this technique.

Still more rings appear in Bitov's novel, for he refers, a few times, to the legend that scorpions commit suicide by turning in on themselves and stinging themselves. "... The narration," he writes, "will commit suicide, like a scorpion, for a scorpion forms a circle in ... its final moment" ("... povestvovanie pokonchit s soboi, kak skorpion, ibo i skorpion obrazuet kol'tso v ... svoi poslednii moment ...") (p. 255). The appendix containing Leva's article echoes the thought: "Embodied experience stings itself, like a scorpion, and goes to the bottom. And if you have already had the misfortune to acquire it (experience ...), don't embody it, because you won't repeat it – it'll repeat you!" (pp. 283–4). The final appendix, "Achilles and the Tortoise" ("Akhilles i cherepakha"), includes these words: "... the beginning repeated the end and closed, like a scorpion, into a ring" ("... nachalo povtorilo konets i somknulos', kak skorpion, v kol'tso") (p. 408).

Leva falls in love with Faina, who is attracted to Mitishatiev. Both Mitishatiev and Leva spend time with another woman, Liubasha. Albina is in love with Leva, but he does not care for her. At one point they all end up at the same place, in the youth café, Café Molecule. The episode takes place at approximately the center of the novel. On a napkin, Leva draws a diagram that shows the complex relationship of each of these people to all of the others. Their relationships, he decides, are structured according to the principles of organic chemistry: "Chains. Cycles. Each element is bonded with another by one or two connections/bonds, and all of them together are connected ..." ("'Tsepi. Tsikly. Kazhdyi èlement sviazan s drugim odnim ili dvumia sviaziami, a vse vmeste – sviazany ...'") (p. 250).

After making several diagrams, Leva declares, "A molecule ... A real molecule! Not one of us represents a chemically independent unit. We are unified as a whole." Liubasha, he declares, ". . . is, for us, like [CH] or [OH] and unites us" (". . . nam kak [CH] ili [OH], vsekh nas soediniaet") (p. 251). In the copy of the novel in my possession, Bitov crossed out the words "ONA" and "ON" in the original text, "A Liubasha nam kak ONA ili ON . . ." and substituted "[CH]" and "[OH]." He has thus transformed the pronouns into chemical compounds. He also plays with the Latin and Russian alphabets, for "ON" ("HE") in Russian script, would be equal to [OH], the compound, in Latin script, that represents alcohol.

The whole novel *Pushkin House* is, I believe, structured according to the principles of organic chemistry.[15] In the episode at the Café Molecule, Leva's drawings, although Bitov does not identify them as such, are of carbon molecules. Ordinarily, carbon is arranged in a tetrahedron with angles of 109.5°. These molecules, in carbon chemistry, would be described as being "constrained molecules." When the angles become 60°, as they are in the relationships Leva describes in his drawings, the molecules are under a great deal of strain. This kind of structure is known, in organic chemistry, as a "strained ring," or, in Russian, "kol'tso."[16]

These "unhealthy" rings form the basis of what *Pushkin House* is all about – the unhappy, unhealthy relationships to which Leva is constantly drawn. [CH_4] is methane gas, the primordial gas that bubbles out of the earth. [OH] is alcohol or, of course, "ON" ("HE"). Leva's grandfather and Uncle Dickens are alcoholics. Leva drinks heavily in a couple of key scenes, once when he is visiting his grandfather, and once when he is with Mitishatiev. Leva cannot escape the corrosive powers of alcohol, Mitishatiev, and Faina. He inflicts upon himself endless humiliation, like the scorpion that, forming a ring, closes in on itself, "stings itself, and dies."

The "OH" ("HE") that "unites us all" is a hidden reference to the key cause of all of Leva's miseries: Stalin. Stalin is never once mentioned by name, yet the entire novel is a tragic rendering of the endless humiliation perpetrated by Stalin on Soviet society. The entire novel is a deep, bitter, brilliant rendering of that first ring[17] (Stalin), which caused all the other rings to be rotten, to be strained, to be self-destructive. The entire novel is a tragic, brilliant, sensitive rendering of the generation – Leva's generation, Bitov's generation (Leva was born in 1937, as was Bitov) – that grew up in the atmosphere of lies and deceit that strangled Soviet society for so many years. Bitov considered *Betrayal* (*Obman*) and *The Lie* (*Lozh'*) as alternative titles for *Pushkin House*.

Throughout his writing career, as we have seen, Bitov had emphasized the interconnectedness of various aspects of life. His model, as we know, had been that of the life science of ecology – in the way he structured his works, as well as in the fundamental principles that drove his subject matter. In "The Taste," we followed Bitov along a spiral of the life science of molecular biology. Approaching "The Taste" according to a model of molecular biology illuminated the inner workings of Bitov's imaginative powers.

In many previous works, Bitov had spoken about everything's being connected. In *Pushkin House*, he concentrates his attention on the phenomenon of the *connectors* themselves, on the phenomenon of the nature of the relationships, the nature of the chemical bonding process of the dependencies and interdependencies in our lives. In an absolutely fundamental way, at its most basic level, *Pushkin House* is modelled according to the principles of organic chemistry, for that science studies the *bonds* that connect atom to atom. It is the science that studies *connections*.

Pushkin House is extraordinarily complex and extraordinarily powerful. Bitov takes on questions of history, philosophy, literary history, literary theory, science, individual human integrity, artistic integrity, psychology, and the psychology of the creative process.

In at least one copy of *Pushkin House*, the author has added a subtitle, in parentheses: ("A Novel about Endless Humiliation") ("roman o beskonechnom unizhenii").[18] *Pushkin House* documents the devastating psychological toll that the Stalin era took on the generation born during his reign. Bitov's point is that if the first ring is forged out of lies, all those that lie on top of it will also be lies. The ring that caused Leva's life to go awry is the Stalin era. Because of that, everything, in all realms of his

9 Newspaper clipping.

personal, creative, and professional life, ended up in additional rings of endless humiliation. His relationship to that era is what causes his psychological fragmentation, his vulnerability in life.

The central fact of life, according to Bitov, is everyone's connection/relationship/bond to Stalin. "Fathers and Sons," the first section of the novel, tackles Leva's relationship to his past. The second section, "A Hero of Our Time," takes on his relationship to the present. The third and final section, "Bronze People," grapples with his relationship to his creative gifts.

Bitov begins his preoccupation with connections in the prologue, where he incorporates a scrap of newspaper into the text. He explains that he would like the reader to be able to place this torn piece of newspaper anywhere in the novel, ". . . serving as a natural continuation and in no way breaking the narration" (p. 15). I include a reproduction of the newspaper clipping in Bitov's text (p. 15) (Figure 9).[19]

Although Bitov does not identify the source, the scrap of newspaper is from a June, 1970 real article, entitled, significantly, "The Connection of the Times' ("Sviaz' vremen").[20] It appeared in the newspaper *Literary Gazette* (*Literaturnaia gazeta*), a publication that Pushkin helped to establish.[21] The continuity of the present time with that of Pushkin is established, through this hidden reference to the *Literary Gazette*. The connection is also broken, for the reader does not know what the article is. The reader knows, however, that the word "Pushkin" does not once appear in full in the section of the newspaper clipping that Bitov uses in *Pushkin House*.[22]

The original article explores the unity of literature in an epoch. It treats of the unity of themes in distant eras. It poses a question about the relationship of Pushkin's "Bronze Horseman" to contemporary realist Avar poetry. Its final line, "A big and useful book might be formed out of all these questions and answers" (see above for Russian text), I believe we should apply to *Pushkin House*. The three sets of concerns in the 1970 article duplicate, broadly, the major themes set forth in the three sections of Bitov's novel – the relationship to the past; the relationship to the present; and the relationship to past literature, in large part to Pushkin. The fact that we see a chopped-up version of the "Connection of the Times" is crucial to Bitov's message throughout the book. The fact that he suggests placing this scrap of torn newspaper – a product of contemporary life – on any page of the novel as a natural continuation of the novel underscores Bitov's major message, the fragmentation in contemporary life that has resulted from the rupture in life that was caused by Stalin. If the line of continuity is broken, we get endless rings of humiliation.

The section following Bitov's prologue, "Fathers and Sons," is subtitled "A Leningrad Novel" ("Leningradskii roman") and begins with an epigraph from Turgenev's *Fathers and Sons*. The passage, not identified in Bitov's text, describes Bazarov's parents as they mourn their dead rebellious son. An association between this 1860s dead son and Bitov's 1960s protagonist is set up. Bazarov and Leva are both dead. In the prologue, Bitov writes, "... on scattered pages, lifelessly ... [with – E.C.] his left arm *under* him, *lay* a man. A body" ("... *na* rassypannykh stranitsakh, bezzhiznenno ... *pod* sebia levuiu ruku, *lezhal* chelovek. Telo") (p. 13). Turgenev's words, as quoted by Bitov, are "... they look *at* the mute stone *under* which their son *lies*" ("... oni ... smotriat *na* nemoi kamen', *pod* kotorym *lezhit* ikh syn ...") (p. 17).

The first section of *Pushkin House* focuses on formative experiences during the youth of Leva, a Leningrad "son" (Bitov writes, in a hidden reference to the non-life of the Stalin era, that his protagonist, unlike the hero of Tolstoy's *Childhood, Boyhood, Youth*, had had no boyhood) (pp. 27–8).

The point is that lie breeds lie, humiliation spawns humiliation. Acts of destruction and self-destruction are locked into each other because the "father," Stalin, had terrorized his "children." At one point in "Fathers and Sons," Bitov writes, "Father was the time itself. Father, papa, cult – what other synonyms are there?" (p. 56). All levels of society – fathers and children – have, according to Bitov, been deeply traumatized. Leva's father, a metaphysically "dark" figure often described by Bitov as being physically in a shadow, had betrayed his own father. After his father, a noted scholar, had been arrested and sent to Siberia, he had built his reputation by criticizing his father's theories.

Leva's parents had created a domestic atmosphere of lies, for they had never told him that his grandfather was alive. After Stalin's death, Modest Platonovich is rehabilitated and returns to Leningrad. When Leva hears that his grandfather is not dead, his reaction is to rebel against his father, even denying that his father is his father. Rotten ring begets rotten ring. Leva calls his father a dictator-father. He expects to develop a close bond with a loving, gentle, dignified grandfather. Instead, he finds a victim of the Stalin era, psychologically broken, a bitter, nasty alcoholic who lashes out at Leva.

Modest Platonovich lives in a small, filthy apartment. His roommate Koptelov is his former prison guard, a man whom Modest Platonovich likes because "... twice he didn't kill me ..." (p. 69). Human relationships have become distorted. Human being associates with human being because "... twice he didn't kill me ..." Relationships are no longer based on family ties or on love.

In some of the most powerful, painful episodes of the book, Modest Platonovich examines his fall from self-esteem. He explains that what finally broke him was not being sent to Siberia. Serving time in the camps, he explains, was justifiable. Had he been that regime, he confesses, he, too, would have imprisoned someone like him.[23] He disintegrated, he asserts, when he was rehabilitated. He could not bear rehabilitation, for that meant that he had served his time in the gulag in vain, that the last thirty years of his life had been meaningless. Examining his psychological disintegration, he draws an analogy between his becoming an alcoholic and a woman's being raped. He chose, he says, to destroy himself in order to preserve some measure of individuality, just as a person about to be raped will, of her own free will, undress herself in front of the rapist in order to preserve some measure of individuality.

In his speech, although he is drunk, dirty, and nasty, he shows the insight into life that had characterized his former brilliant breadth of vision. He tells Leva that he, Leva, belongs to the Soviet system, even if he fights against it. Everyone, he says, is Soviet, whether he is for or against the system. People are not free, he says, because their lives are "... only in relation to the system" (p. 81).[24] If you were to go abroad, he tells Leva, you would ask to return: "If you were untied, you yourself would ask to be tied up again, for your neck would freeze without the collar" (p. 82). Modest Platonovich says that he sees deeply into the efficacy of the Soviet educational system that has succeeded in preventing Leva from seeing reality. Modest Platonovich remarks that Leva cannot stand him because he does not fit his preconceived notion of grandfatherhood. Rather than dealing with reality, Leva rejects it. In this, says Modest Platonovich (and we can make analogies to the lies perpetrated by a society that refused to admit the truth about its Stalinist legacy), the schools succeeded brilliantly.

In an impassioned defense of culture, Modest Platonovich cries that social inequality is necessary for human potential to be fulfilled. Culture, he says, can only be born on a base of wealth, and wealth presupposes inequality. Culture cannot exist without an aristocracy which, after all, supported Haydn, Bach, Michelangelo, and Raphael. Nature, he explains, is not interested in equality; rather, it is interested in "expediency" and "perfection" (p. 77). He attacks technological progress for having raped the earth, for overpowering the earth with brute force. He cries out that it will be too late by the time mankind realizes that it has destroyed nature. He accuses man of a myopic view; he will do nothing to sacrifice today's pleasures in exchange for tomorrow's life. He declares that this is happening not on the surface social level of life, but "... in the invisible depths..." (p. 79) of life's processes. The great task, he says, is to "... debunk all false concepts, remain with nothing and *suddenly* grasp the *secret* ... At this point, a revolution in consciousness takes place – and the earth is saved" (p. 79).

This process, this secret force, this "spiritual revolution" (p. 79), explains Modest Platonovich, is in a race with progress. If progress wins, he says, the "ovaries" of Earth are doomed to "cosmic frost" (p. 79). The same forces Modest Platonovich sees at work in culture. He declares that the 1917 revolution did not destroy Russian culture. To the contrary, Russian culture from Derzhavin to Blok is in place, he says, precisely because there was no continuity. With the rupture brought about by Stalin, there was no possibility for the pure, true words of the prerevolutionary era to be distorted into "false concepts," for there was no continuity. "... Russia," he says, "remained a sanctuary country" (p. 80). Words that seem true to you now, he tells Leva, in a decade or so will seem false, for the concept of progress has entered into culture – "... a consumer and not a creative relationship to spiritual ideas and values ..." (p. 80).

The important thing is to observe, he says. He still retains, he explains, his capacity to be surprised by the world. This, he says, is healthy and nourishing. What is driving him crazy, though, he continues, is that people consider normal and natural what he knows is not. Modest Platonovich declares that the cultural freedoms that are given to those who consider themselves free are the same as the material products that are given to people whose only concerns are material. The authorities, he says, throw cultural "freedoms," like bones, to people. Your "independence," he says, is given to you only in relation to what is permitted by the system. "The thought about your dependence is inaccessible to you" (p. 86). Modest Platonovich is distressed by people's impulse to deny reality. In tragic tones, he admits, "... my soul is literally sinking because of the dexterity, the sweet expediency of the human world-structure ..." (p. 86).

Modest Platonovich curses the authorities for exacting the insulting, cruel fate of rehabilitation upon him. He deplores, he says, the humiliation which forces him to deny the last twenty-seven years of his life. He resents Leva for expecting him to be as he was before his imprisonment, saying that Leva had lived all those years, whereas he, Modest Platonovich, had become a different person. All that is left, he says in a rage, is this, as he fumbles for his penis. His roommate and another friend stop him, and Leva feels the acute pain of the disintegration and humiliation of a person.

Modest Platonovich's wandering drunken monologue contains bursts of genius. The tragedy of his present situation is made more poignant by the flashes of originality that suggest the sheer power and brilliance of his pre-arrest thoughts.

His grandfather's anger, attacks, and viciousness overwhelm Leva. He gets drunk. In a taxi on the way home, he vomits.

When he arrives home, his parents anxiously await news of the visit. Leva repeats the cruelty that his grandfather had inflicted upon him. He knows that his parents want to hear about his visit, and he says nothing. Retreating to his room, he thinks that that day, he "became worse" (p. 102).

Historically, the crimes Stalin committed, the incarceration of many of the most creative members of the intelligentsia, are reflected in the broken spirit of Modest Platonovich. The fear of confronting the truth and the practice of setting family member against family member are reflected in the behavior of Leva's father toward his father (making his professional reputation by going against his father's ideas) and toward his son (for decades, not telling his son that Modest Platonovich was alive). The cruelty engendered by Stalin's policies Modest Platonovich then bestows upon Leva during their brief meeting. Historical connections are broken (Leva's lack of knowledge of his grandfather's past and Leva's family's secretiveness). The original ring formed by Stalin has engendered ring upon ring of lies, deception, cruelty, and humiliation, in personal lives and in the lives of families. Leva, in "becoming worse," is inheriting a tradition, a "ring" of Stalinism to which he is tightly bonded.

Another Stalin victim whose fate Bitov describes is Dmitrii Ivanovich Iuvashev, "Uncle Dickens", or "Uncle Mitia." Uncle Dickens, a former neighbor of the Odoevtsevs, is an elderly aristocratic bachelor who, after being in the camps for many years, is given a room by Leva's parents. The man is utterly his own person, dressing elegantly in clothes that are out of fashion but never out of style. He has strong opinions (mostly the epithet "shit" ["govno"]) about a variety of topics. He spends his days tidying himself, his room, and his belongings; and reading from his extensive library containing many Russian and Western classics. He studies Dal''s dictionary and wants to find precise, concise definitions for words. Every evening, he, a representative of the Westernized pre-revolutionary aristocracy, goes, appropriately, to Leningrad's "European" ("Evropeiskaia") Hotel. He gets drunk and then returns to the Odoevtsevs.

They welcome him, for, as Leva realizes, he serves as a

surrogate, to the whole family, for the real father/grandfather Modest Platonovich. After Uncle Dickens moves in, for the first time that Leva can remember, his parents laugh and show some feeling. They sit around, drink tea, and talk. Leva likes to spend time with his surrogate grandfather. He fantasizes that Uncle Mitia is his father. The set-up Bitov describes underscores the fact of the break-up of normal everyday family life which was a result of Stalin's viciousness.

Uncle Mitia, like Modest Platonovich, paid an enormous price in terms of his own life. The camp experience had turned him into a psychologically broken alcoholic whose entire life-force was aimed at holding himself together and maintaining self-respect. Bitov's narrator, in describing him, repeats the word "humiliated" ("unizhennyi") to characterize this pathetic old man who no longer has the strength to give emotional energy to anyone else. At one point, for example, Leva desperately needs emotional support. He turns to Uncle Dickens, who, because of his own wounds, cannot allow anyone to touch him emotionally, for, as Bitov explains, the old man would crumble. Decent, fighting for his individuality, humiliated, Uncle Dickens, in his demise, is another of the circles of humiliation drawn by the evil dictator.

The second section of *Pushkin House* is a "version and variant of the first part" (p. 149). In "The Italics are Mine," his introductory remarks to this section, Bitov speaks about the contemporary practice, in newspapers, of using previous titles that have been slightly altered, but not changed enough to eliminate the purposeful "connection of times" ("sviaz' vremen") (p. 152) that they elicit. The lines present distorted versions of the past, but they do, nevertheless, provide links with the past. This idea provides a link with Bitov's own Part One, for the "Italics Are Mine" section there had offered the torn-up newspaper article, entitled "The Connection of the Times," where the very name Pushkin had been distorted in the scrap of newspaper included in Bitov's text. In his own title, "The Italics Are Mine," Bitov underscores the device of italicization whereby authors literally change the original, past text by italicizing its words. Thus, the text is distorted, but its link with the past remains.

Thematically, Bitov continues his thoughts in "The Italics Are Mine" section of Part Two by explaining that the title of his novel is stolen, for Pushkin House is an institution. He explains that *Pushkin House* is an excursion through the novel-museum (p. 154).

The title of Part Two, "A Hero of Our Time," like Bitov's other chapter titles, is part of his excursion through past Russian literature. Lermontov, in his book by that name, had declared that he was writing about the vices of his generation. Bitov turns his readers' attention to the preface of Lermontov's novel, where he links his "hero" Pechorin to the negative societal values of his times and declares that he is drawing a portrait of a contemporary man. The portrayal of a "hero" of *his* time is the task that Bitov sets himself.[25]

He continues, in Part Two of *Pushkin House*, to show the malformations of personality that poison Leva's (and Bitov's) generation because of the links with a Stalinist past. In Part One, Bitov had documented the twisted family relationships that had resulted from Stalin's actions. The historical links (grandfather/father/son) were broken – normal connections were broken – and the rotten rings kept repeating themselves.

In Part Two, Bitov depicts a Leva who runs from one version and variant to another (p. 246) and who repeats the distorted behaviors that have issued from the Stalinist legacy to his generation. Here, he is locked into unhealthy relationships with his peers. Bitov describes the way in which Leva, Faina, and Mitishatiev, the parts of a love triangle, are interlocked with others in what the reader can see as the complicated bonds of their personal chemistry, of their personal chemical interactions. Thus, explains Bitov, there was a chain reaction whereby if one person treated another person badly, that person would then treat someone else badly. Faina would act cruelly toward Leva, the person who loved her, and he would then reproduce that nasty behavior in his treatment of Albina, who loved him.

This chain reaction and the vicious circle of peer relationships duplicate the chain reaction and the vicious circles that operated in the historical arena spotlighted in Part One, where the political "father" Stalin had poisoned his "children" (Modest

Platonovich and Leva's father), who, in turn, then poisoned their children. In Part Two, Bitov describes this type of behavior as being equivalent to the mechanism by which those who have once been poisoned by carbon dioxide remain weakened, and their organisms are for ever after more susceptible to future poisonings (pp. 161–2).

In this atmosphere of distortions, everyone lies. In a restaurant, Faina lies to the waitress, telling her that she and Leva are married. Everything false is substituted for everything genuine. Faina's gold ring is not really gold. At the Café Molecule, where Leva, Faina, Mitishatiev, and company meet, Bitov tells the reader that everyone was there as a substitute for someone else. The great actor Smoktunovsky was supposed to be there. Someone else was supposed to come in his place, and still a third party came in place of that substitute. Instead of the showing of a great film, one of Fellini's or Hitchcock's, something inferior was shown. The poem that was read on the occasion was about that very theme in poetry: "the substitution of something false for something real" ("podmen") (p. 248).

The theme resonates with that of the "rhyming" deadening patterns of Monakhov's life in *The Role*, and particularly in its last story, "The Taste." That these works belong together becomes clear when we note, in Bitov's 1976 collection *Days of Man*, the placement of most of Part Two of *Pushkin House* in a position immediately following *The Role*.[26]

The theme anticipates Part Three of *Pushkin House*, where a drunken Leva on the statue of a lion is substituted for Pushkin's Evgenii, who is a stand-in for the bronze horseman; where Pushkin's title, "Bronze Horseman," is contorted into "Poor Horseman"; and where Dostoevsky's title "Poor People" is twisted into "Bronze People." Moreover, the theme returns us to the "Italics Are Mine" section at the beginning of Part Two, where the titles were distorted versions of the originals. The theme also ties in with a part of Modest Platonovich's speech in Part One, where he had spoken of the present perverted "progressive" relationship to spiritual ideas and values, that is, a consumer attitude toward culture rather than a creative relationship to it (p. 80).

The discussion also brings us to a part of *Pushkin House* that ties together the three major divisions of the book: the appendix to Section Two, entitled "The Hero's Profession" ("Professiia geroia"). This appendix contains the article Leva wrote as a graduate student at Pushkin House: "Three Prophets" ("Tri proroka"), about the three nineteenth-century Russian poets, Pushkin, Lermontov, and Tiutchev.

The article actually appeared, in separate form, under Bitov's name, with his introductory note explaining that his hero had written it, in the Soviet Union's most prestigious literary theory journal, *Questions of Literature (Voprosy literatury)*.[27] The ideas in the article provoked a lively debate among scholars and writers such as Tiutchev scholar K. Piragev, literary theorist Lidiia Ginzburg, and poet Aleksandr Kushner, on the pages of *Questions of Literature*.[28] One of the objections made was that Bitov had not acknowledged the original source of one of Leva's ideas – the relationship between Tiutchev's and Pushkin's poetry – as formalist critic Iurii Tynianov's idea.[29] We know, from reading the novel, that Leva had not read Tynianov's works, which, since 1929, had not been reissued until the early 1960s. This point, and the narrator emphasizes this point, fits into Bitov's overall framework in *Pushkin House*. Because of the societal disfigurements caused by Stalin, one's entire life is tainted. Now, we see the fruits of that legacy in the cultural arena: Leva had not read certain works that had been forbidden to be printed under Stalin. We can also conclude, from Leva's gap in knowledge, that those afflicted by the wounds of the Stalin era cannot be original. Thus, the titles are distortions of the originals, Leva's ideas are not original, and Bitov's themes are recycled versions of nineteenth-century novels. Bitov admits, in "The Italics Are Mine" section of Part Two, that in his chapter and section titles he is following the schools' syllabus (p. 154).

The gist of Leva's article is that Pushkin, Lermontov, and Tiutchev represent three different types of people. Pushkin, like Mozart, was a genius, a god, who was totally free, who did not look to authorities for his artistic inspiration. He created freely and independently. Leva extracts portions of Pushkin's poem,

"The Prophet," whose theme is the divine nature of the poet. Leva contrasts Pushkin to Lermontov, who, like Beethoven, was an adolescent crying out, in rebellion, to be noticed. Pushkin (a god) has surrendered his "I" and sees the world as whole; Lermontov (a human being) cannot let go of his ego and therefore sees only fragments of the world. Lermontov's poem "The Prophet" Leva reads as bitter whining at his fate. Tiutchev, who, for Leva, represents the devil, he characterizes as carrying on a hidden duel with Pushkin. Tiutchev resents Pushkin, he wants to "murder" him, and, to Tiutchev's great annoyance, Pushkin does not even notice. To prove his case, Leva places Tiutchev's poem "Insanity" ("Bezumie") alongside Pushkin's "The Prophet." Tiutchev, claims Leva, deeply resented Pushkin, for Pushkin had that quality for which Tiutchev so desperately longed. He envied the fact that Pushkin had come first. Leva, writes Bitov, worshipped Pushkin; saw features of his own adolescent behavior in Lermontov; and in Tiutchev, hated someone. Bitov explains that the article was ". . . not about Pushkin, not about Lermontov, and . . . not about Tiutchev, but about . . . Leva . . ." and his experience (p. 267). Leva's idea, he continues, is that each person, irrespective of the historical epoch in which he lives, contains three stages of life: ". . . God, man, and death" (p. 269).[30] Each person, he goes on, can choose any of the three paths. Pushkin chose God. Lermontov chose the spiritual death of constant repetition. The reader can surmise that this is the human being, constantly bemoaning the fact that he is not God. The third path, the demonic path of death, the reader presumes is that chosen by Tiutchev.

After reading Leva's article, we can make new connections to the parts of *Pushkin House* that relate to Leva's experiences. We can draw an analogy between Pushkin and Modest Platonovich. Like Pushkin's poems, Modest Platonovich's writings are brilliant, original, and prophetic. One of them is even called "God Is." Also analogous are the Lermontov of Leva's article and Leva himself. He is often the helpless, passive agent who lets himself come under the sway of other people. The Tiutchev in Leva's life is Mitishatiev, who engages Leva in a hidden duel. In a conversation in Part Three, Mitishatiev plays the role of

Tiutchev to Leva's Pushkin as he tells Leva that he resents him because he is a prince with the aristocratic name Odoevtsev, whereas he, Mitishatiev, has no place. He resents, he says, the fact that Leva ignores him. He wants to destroy him.

The verbal duel brings up the historical question of the masses' attitude toward the aristocracy in Russia. It relates, in broader terms, to psychological attitudes of the non-aristocrats to the aristocrats, of the masses to the elite, of popular culture to elite culture in any country.[31] The Tiutchev/Mitishatiev duel can also be seen as Stalin's duel with the elite, as Stalin's duel with the representatives of the elite culture that had grown out of Peter the Great's prerevolutionary Petersburg and Lenin's Soviet Union. Stalin is rebelling against the whole of Russian and Soviet culture that had preceded him.

There are other crucial ways in which the themes of Leva's article directly relate to Part Three of *Pushkin House* and to the meaning of the book as a whole. The most straightforward is in terms of plot. In a final cruel degradation of Leva, during an alcohol-infused conversation in the literary institute Pushkin House, the jealous Mitishatiev makes anti-Semitic remarks to Blank, an elderly Pushkin House colleague of Leva's. Leva and Blank had always respected one another. In this instance, Leva fails to defend Blank, and therefore, according to Bitov's narrator, sinks to his lowest circle of humiliation. Afterwards, Leva and his rival Mitishatiev literally duel over Faina. Using the pistols that had been used in Pushkin's duel, Mitishatiev shoots his hated classmate. The description of Leva's lifeless body, sprawled on the floor with a pistol in his hand, repeats the historic real duel scene in which Pushkin, the man, was killed by d'Anthès in a duel over the love of a woman. It repeats the theme from Leva's article, in which Tiutchev, out of envy, took aim at Pushkin, the poet, in his own artistic duel with him. The scene repeats, literally, the opening pages of *Pushkin House*, which had begun with this death scene.[32] Like the scorpion that turns on itself, stings itself, and dies, Leva, made vulnerable by the noxious atmosphere of Stalinist Russia, submits himself over and over again to the endless rings of humiliation. In a final bit of humiliation, Mitishatiev places a "North" ("Sever") cigarette, the kind he has been smoking and offering to Leva throughout the novel, in the barrel of the gun. "Sever" cigarettes, È. Khappenenn explains in the appendix to *Pushkin House*, were a type of cheap cigarette identified with the lower social classes, that were popular during the 1960s.[33] Mitishatiev's final touch, then, is to brand the already felled aristocrat Leva Odoevtsev with a sign of the masses. The shape of the burning "Sever" cigarette is, of course, circular.

In addition to connecting with the actual events of Part Three of *Pushkin House*, the themes of Leva's article relate in a more complex way to the meaning of the book as a whole. At one point, the narrator writes that LO (Leva Odoevtsev) is equivalent to AB (Andrei Bitov, we can surmise). I believe that throughout the novel, Bitov the writer wages a hidden duel with Pushkin and with Russian literature. Born in 1937, at the height of Stalin's purges, Bitov, like Leva, has been wounded by the Stalin era. The 1973 version of "The Hero's Profession," in Bitov's book of essays, *Articles from a Novel*, is slightly expanded. Its introductory section includes this sentence:

I was curious to study the way in which personal experience was embodied in impersonal material precisely in that instance when the person writing did not at all intend to betray his secrets, and perhaps even sought to hide them, choosing for the reflection of his ideas topics that were infinitely removed from him both in time and in space.[34]

Bitov's comments about his Russian literature scholar, Leva, vis-à-vis his article about Russian literature apply, I believe, equally well to Bitov vis-à-vis his novel about Russian literature. Just as Tiutchev wages a secret battle with Pushkin, Bitov carries on a secret duel with Russian literature. He, Bitov, feels that he has come too late just as Tiutchev, in Leva's article, resented the fact that he had come too late. And we should recall the title of another article by Leva, "Latecomer Geniuses" ("Opozdavshie genii") (pp. 276, 404). In a footnote to Leva's article, the narrator declares that Bunin, like Tiutchev, envied people whose talents had been acknowledged. Outliving them all, writes Leva, Bunin spent the rest of his life moving away from most of his contemporaries (with the exception of Chekhov) and toward Tolstoy (p. 276).

This sounds like Bitov in *Pushkin House*, where he calls his hero Lev Nikolaevich, in honor of Tolstoy. Odoevtsev is an old Russian aristocratic name, a point Bitov underscores by having Mitishatiev constantly refer to Leva as "Prince" and bring up Leva's origins. The name Odoevtsev calls to mind the nineteenth-century aristocratic Russian writers, Prince Aleksandr Ivanovich Odoevsky (1802–39) and his cousin, Prince Vladimir Fedorovich Odoevsky (1803 or 1804–69). In his recent biography of Vladimir Odoevsky, Neil Cornwell observes that the family traced its lineage all the way back to Riurik and that during the nineteenth century, Odoevsky was considered to be Russia's most ancient aristocratic name.[35] In *Articles from a Novel*, Bitov describes Vladimir Odoevsky as a "writer-aristocrat" ("pisatel'-aristokrat").[36]

Modest Odoevtsev, Leva's grandfather, shares his first name with the patronymic of Vladimir Odoevsky's Irenei Modestovich Gomozeiko, the wise narrator of *Motley Stories* (*Pëstrye rasskazy*). Gomozeiko believes in the importance of transcendent human values and the larger, synthesizing characteristics of human knowledge rather than in narrow specialization and the material aspects of life.[37]

In *War and Peace*, Tolstoy shapes his view of the world according to a scientific (mechanistic) principle whereby people's interactions are described as interdependent parts of a machine. In *Pushkin House*, Bitov shapes his view of the world according to a scientific (organic chemistry) principle whereby people's interactions are described as interdependent parts of chemical compounds.

As we have seen, Bitov writes about the malformations of old titles in contemporary newspapers. He shows us the distortions in people's personalities resulting from the Soviet Union's historical conditions. He shows us that rings of humiliation keep repeating themselves. In the same way, he himself distorts and repeats previous works of Russian literature.

For example, the name Odoevsky becomes Odoevtsev. Aleksandr Odoevsky, a poet and member of the Decembrist uprising, had been, like Modest Platonovich Odoevtsev, exiled to Siberia. The Odoevtsev "family heritage" is that of rebellion.

Aleksandr Odoevsky wrote a poem in response to Pushkin's 1827 poem in which Pushkin urges the Decembrist rebels not to lose heart. Pushkin's sympathies, as is well known, were with the rebel Decembrists. Like Modest Platonovich Odoevtsev and Aleksandr Odoevsky, he, too, spent time as a political exile. Odoevsky's reply to Pushkin's poem served as a testament to rebellion.

Bitov's naming his hero Odoevtsev relates directly to the theme of revolt in *Pushkin House*. Falconet's statue, "The Bronze Horseman," so central to Bitov's plot, stands on Decembrist Square in Leningrad. The flood about which Pushkin wrote in his "Petersburg poem," "The Bronze Horseman," took place on November 7, 1824, the same day of the month as the post-revolutionary anniversary of the November 7, 1917 revolution. Pushkin's "Bronze Horseman" can be interpreted as a poem about rebellion against political authority. The main events in *Pushkin House* transpire in Pushkin House as Leva is acting as guard during the November 7th anniversary celebrations, i.e., during celebrations in honor of rebellion. Leva, like Evgenii in Pushkin's "Bronze Horseman," mounts the lion statue as Peter the Great is mounted on the horse. Geographically, the lion statue is located on Admiralty Prospect[38] in Leningrad, which is the street that directly touches one side of Decembrist Square.

Vladimir Odoevsky was an extraordinarily learned member of the nineteenth-century Russian intelligentsia. As Deputy Director of St. Petersburg's Public Library and as Director of the Rumiantsev Museum, he preserved culture. As a music and literary critic, as journal editor, writer of philosophical essays and prose, he tackled questions about the place of the creative artist in society and about the artist's calling.

The themes that Aleksandr and Vladimir Odoevsky represent in their lives and works – rebellion, the preservation of culture, and the role of the artist – "rhyme" with some of the central concerns of Bitov's *Pushkin House*. It makes sense, therefore, that he would give his hero the name Odoevtsev.

Bitov's repetitions of Russian literature in *Pushkin House* are everywhere. From the title of the novel to the section headings with their nineteenth-century Russian-literature titles, to the

epigraphs, all are taken from Russian literary works. All are
carefully selected to remain within the repeating circles of
Bitov's themes.

There are rhymes, too, with Western European literature.
Bitov's repetition of other literature is as well chosen as are his
examples from the Russian tradition. Bitov's narrator writes
that Uncle Dickens read Charles Dickens' *Bleak House*. Bitov's
novel, like Dickens', uses the word "house" in its title. In each
novel, a house of the past is deemed to be psychically unhealthy
for present-day inhabitants. Dickens' first pages contain a scene
in which the external world is described as having been drawn
with ink. Compare Dickens' and Bitov's passages: Dickens –
"The view from my Lady Dedlock's own windows is ... a view in
Indian ink;"[39] Bitov – "... as if these houses had been written in
dilute ink" (p. 11). In each novel, ink, the instrument a writer
uses, is spoken of as tracing the movements of life, embodied, in
each instance, in the weather conditions of a gloomy November
day. In each novel, an important parental figure, thought to be
dead, is resurrected (Esther's mother, in *Bleak House*; Leva's
grandfather, in *Pushkin House*). In each novel, a benign parental
figure steps in to help the protagonist – Jarndyce, in Dickens'
book, and, appropriately, Uncle Dickens in *Pushkin House*.

Another Western European work whose influence is felt in
Pushkin House is Proust's *Swann in Love*, a book Bitov admits he
had read before he wrote the Faina and Albina chapters of
Pushkin House.[40] The plot, that of Swann's jealousy of Odette and
the lies bred by betrayals in love, is familiar to the reader of
Pushkin House.[41] The destructive love triangle that shapes the
action in *Swann in Love* prefigures the love triangle carved out by
Leva, Mitishatiev, and Faina.

The initial scene of the novel, where we are introduced to the
body (Leva's) lying on the floor – after the duel, we discover at
the end of the novel – takes place in Pushkin House. Pushkin, we
know, died in a duel over Natalia Goncharova. Leva and
Mitishatiev fight their duel over Faina. The conversation in
Pushkin House when Mitishatiev, Leva, and the others are
drinking heavily, contains a section about Natalia Goncharova.
A duel takes place in Pushkin's "The Shot" ("Vystrel"), quoted

in an epigraph to the chapter "The Duel" ("Duel'"), in which Mitishatiev shoots Leva. The two combatants were wearing copies of Pushkin's death masks (we find out later that Pushkin House had stacks of imitations of the masks) and are, we know, using the pistols that had been fired in Pushkin's final duel. The next Bitov chapter, to which is affixed another epigraph from Pushkin's "The Shot," is called "The Shot." Pushkin's *Eugene Onegin* contains a duel scene in which Onegin and Lensky fight over a woman. Lermontov's *A Hero of Our Time*, the title of Part Two of Bitov's novel, contains a duel scene in which Pechorin and Grushnitsky wage a duel over Princess Mary. Turgenev's *Fathers and Sons*, the title of Bitov's section one, contains a duel between antagonists Bazarov, a "son," and Pavel Kirsanov, a member of the generation of the fathers.

A variant of Pushkin's "Tales of Belkin" ("Povesti Belkina") begins *Pushkin House* as its initial epigraph, declaring that we will no longer be (p. 9).[42] In addition to "The Shot," another Belkin Tale, "The Blizzard" ("Metel'"), is referred to as "The Little Blizzard" ("Metel'nitsa"), a story written by Uncle Dickens that recounts the basic plot of Pushkin's story.[43]

"The Bronze Horseman," Pushkin's "Petersburg Tale," is referred to in *Pushkin House*, where "A Leningrad Novel" is the subtitle to the section "Fathers and Sons." The presence of Pushkin's "Bronze Horseman" is felt in other ways in *Pushkin House*. Both works speak of windows as connectors. Pushkin says that Petersburg is the window through which Russia looks at Western Europe. Bitov's use of windows fits into his theme of the importance of connectors/bonds/relationships in making life what it is. I shall turn, in greater detail, to the importance of connections, in a later part of my discussion of the novel.

The initial action in "The Bronze Horseman" and *Pushkin House* takes place along the banks of the Neva during a blustery, unpleasant November day. The rain beats at the window in "The Bronze Horseman," and in Bitov's novel it goes into the broken window in Pushkin House. In "The Bronze Horseman," children throw rocks at Evgenii. A child with a toy pistol shoots at Leva (the duel theme again) at the end of *Pushkin House* as he is showing a visiting American novelist[44] around Leningrad. A house is repeatedly mentioned in "The Bronze Horseman," and it, by the end, is empty and destroyed, just as, by the end, Evgenii is dead, his body lying at the entrance to the house. Leva's fate is similar, and he, too, lies, a lifeless body in a Pushkin house, in Bitov's *Pushkin House*.

A theme in many of the Pushkin works Bitov cites is rebellion. A duel, literal or figurative, takes place between antagonists. Envy, another prominent theme in *Pushkin House*, is the subject of other works to which Bitov refers. "Mozart and Salieri" is a work noted in passing as Leva discusses his Pushkin/Tiutchev duel theory. Of course, the relationship Leva sets up between Tiutchev and Pushkin is the one that forms the central driving force of Pushkin's "Mozart and Salieri." The competent, plodding composer, Salieri, envies the genius Mozart. Mitishatiev's behavior toward Leva, and Stalin's toward Modest Platonovich, reproduce this Pushkin plot.

Rings form another repeating plot line as Bitov keeps quoting – as in "The Taste," he himself cannot escape the ring of ever-repeating repetitions of Russian literature – works of literature that contain scenes with rings. Lermontov's *A Hero of Our Time*, repeatedly quoted in Bitov's epigraphs to his section entitled "A Hero of Our Time," recounts the story of Princess Mary, who gave Grushnitsky a ring.[45] Leva steals Faina's ring and then returns it to her.

I have already mentioned some of the parallels, in this respect, with Nabokov's *The Gift*. In that novel, the name of Nabokov's Cherdyntsev is derived from the name Chernyshevsky; Bitov makes the same kind of transition of names when he switches Odoevsky to Odoevtsev. His character's book, explains Nabokov, is a spiral within a sonnet. The circles in Leva's life, explains Bitov, keep piling up, one on top of another. Nabokov's novel contains a scene in which he describes a triangle inscribed in a circle as the proper way to explain the relationship between Iasha, Rudolf, and Olia. Leva sees his relationship with Faina and Mitishatiev as triangular, also as triangles within other geometric shapes. Bitov, in *Pushkin House*, like Nabokov in *The Gift*, plays with previous works of Russian literature. As does Pushkin in *Eugene Onegin*, Nabokov bids farewell to his book at the end of *The Gift*. Nabokov describes the revolver being passed around from Rudolf to Iasha to Olia like a "ring" ("kol'tso")[46] in a game. Mitishatiev, Leva, and Faina, sitting in a circle, play a game of spin the bottle. Nabokov, as Bitov later does, mentions Pushkin's "Blizzard." Nabokov claims, in *The Gift*, that Russian literature is the hero of his book. Bitov follows Nabokov's practice of mentioning writers of nineteenth- and early twentieth-century Russian literature. Nabokov includes Dostoevsky's use, in *Brothers Karamazov*, of the detail of a "circular" ("kruglyi") imprint left by a wine glass on the table.[47] As in the later *Pushkin House*, Nabokov gives us two versions of a death. Nabokov, as Bitov later does, mentions Pushkin's "Prophet." Bitov, like Nabokov and Pushkin, speaks of windows. Nabokov writes that he will see a Russian autumn through a window. There is a joke in *The Gift* about a mock duel fought with sticks. The themes, in Nabokov's novel, are shown to be describing a circle.

The parallels of *Pushkin House* with *The Gift* are not surprising, given the fact that Bitov read Nabokov's *Gift* and *Invitation to a Beheading* (*Priglashenie na kazn'*) while working on *Pushkin House*.[48] Here, too, we see repetition, as the first scene of that Nabokov novel proclaims the death sentence of Cincinnatus and speaks of the approach of the end. *Pushkin House* opens with a death scene. Ring imagery is repeated in *Invitation to a Beheading*, and the major protagonist, like Bitov's later hero, cannot escape, cannot break away from his connections to certain people.

The theme of fathers and sons is touched upon by many writers whose works Bitov brings into the framework of his novel about fathers and sons. Turgenev's *Fathers and Sons* focused on a generation of nihilistic "sons" of the 1860s, represented by Bazarov, who rebelled against their fathers, men of the 1840s. Bitov's "hero" is a member of the generation of the 1960s who is rebelling against his "father," Stalin, of the 1930s and 1940s. Dostoevsky's *Devils* (*Besy*), mentioned in *Pushkin House*, is another novel about ideological sons pitted against their fathers. It shows the damage done to a society twisted by the terrorist tactics of a Nechaev-like leader and traces, historically, the issuance of these terrorist "devils" ("besy") from one generation

to another. Dostoevsky bases his novel on historical facts connected with Sergei Nechaev, his secret political terrorist group,
its tactics, publications, and actions. Bitov follows Dostoevsky's
example in tracing the issuance of his "devils" from the original
"devil," Stalin, to later generations. Bitov has said that he
wanted to finish *Pushkin House* in time for the hundredth
anniversary of the publication of Dostoevsky's *Devils*, which
came out in 1871.[49] Bitov marks the date of completion of *Pushkin
House* as 1971.

One chapter of *Pushkin House*, "Devils Invisible to the Eye"
("Nevidimye glazom besy"), begins with three quotations from
works with "devils" ("besy"), each of which relates to the one
before. Thus, Dostoevsky's *Devils* begins with an epigraph from
Pushkin's 1830 poem "The Devils" ("Besy"), talking about the
fact that demons are everywhere. Bitov quotes Dostoevsky's
Devils and the same Pushkin poem that Dostoevsky quotes. He
quotes the two lines of Pushkin's poem that precede the final four
lines quoted by Dostoevsky. (The first four lines of Dostoevsky's
Pushkin excerpt speak of a devil that "circles" ["'kruzhit'"].)[50]
Bitov's excerpt from the Pushkin poem has relevance for his own
themes in *Pushkin House*, for he speaks of devils circling as if they
were leaves in November: "'Diverse devils began to go round,/
As if they were November leaves ...'" ("'Zakruzhilis' besy
razny,/Budto list'ia v noiabre ...'").[51] Bitov's "devils" whirling
like leaves in November are his revolutionary sons, Leva and
Mitishatiev, going around in circles, physically located in the
house of Pushkin and in the time of a celebration of another
November revolution. Pushkin's poem contains, in the second
line, a form of the word "invisible being" ("nevidimkoiu"),[52]
whose adjectival form Bitov has used in his chapter title.
Pushkin's poem keeps repeating some of the same lines. Bitov's
novel keeps repeating the same themes and images. Dostoevsky's
novel, taking off from the Pushkin poem, speaks of devils
reproducing devils. As we have seen, this is one of the major
themes of Bitov's book.

Bitov's final epigraph to this chapter comes from Sologub's
Petty Demon (*Melkii bes*), itself a parody of Dostoevsky's *Devils*.[53]

Ronald Meyer and others speak of Mitishatiev as a "devil," and we can readily see his similarity to Dostoevsky's devils in his novel by that name.[54]

It seems to me that there is another Dostoevskian dimension to Mitishatiev, for he can also be seen as akin to Ivan Karamazov's devil in a novel that also deals with the destructive influence of a father upon his children. In the chapter "The Devil. Ivan Fedorovich's Nightmare" ("Chert. Koshmar Ivan Fedorovicha"), Ivan tells his devil,

You are a lie, you are my illness, you are a phantom ... You are my hallucination. You are the embodiment of me myself, but only one side of me ... of my thoughts and feelings, but only of my most repulsive and stupid ones.

(Ty lozh', ty bolezn' moia, ty prizrak ... Ty moia galliutsinatsiia. Ty voploshchenie menia samogo, tol'ko odnoi, vprochem, moei storony ... moikh myslei i chuvstv, tol'ko samykh gadkikh i glupykh.)[55]

Leva tells Mitishatiev, "You are my nightmare" ("Ty moi koshmar") (p. 355).

Ivan Karamazov's devil appears to him because of his lack of faith in God. His mind generates a double, a devil. In Dostoevsky's novel, Ivan's illness stems from a lack of belief in God. Leva's "nightmare," "devil" Mitishatiev, holds sway over him because Leva allows him to exert power over him. Everything in life, according to Bitov, depends on our connections and relationships to other people. If we hand over the power to them, we alone, by that act, endow them with that power. The power of the devil in *Pushkin House* is psychologically motivated, whereas in *Brothers Karamazov* it is religiously motivated.

The novels *The Devils*, *Brothers Karamazov* and *Pushkin House* deal with violence against one's fathers and/or children. Although Bitov states that he got the name Mitishatiev out of the telephone book,[56] the name might be construed as having certain literary resonances – especially with Goethe's Mephistopheles. Ronald Meyer sees Mitishatiev's name as possibly derivative of Shatov's in Dostoevsky's *Devils*.[57] The latter conjecture does not seem to make sense since Shatov is a good

character whereas Mitishatiev is clearly diabolical and more
akin to Peter Verkhovensky, the petty terrorist who knows only
how to destroy, whose ideas represent nobler ideas that have
been reduced to the level of sheer terror.

For Dostoevsky, in *The Devils*, the demons run, untamed,
through the social fabric of the countryside. For Dostoevsky, the
vacuum represented by Stavrogin (neither hot nor cold) and
representative of a Westernized Russia (Stavrogin is the pupil of
Stepan Verkhovensky, man of the liberal Westernized ideas of
the 1840s) sprouting demon after demon, is ideological, societal.
For Bitov, the demons, originally created by the major demon
Stalin, create demon after demon. For Bitov, the demons are
created by a person's attitude; had Leva not allowed Mitishatiev
to exert power over him, his demonic personality would not have
affected Leva.

Not only previous Russian literature but the study of Russian
literature in the nineteenth and twentieth centuries is something
with which Bitov is carrying on his duel. Spiritual "children" of
Chernyshevsky, in Bitov's novel, want, like Chernyshevsky, to
see political, ideological meaning in art. In the final section of
Pushkin House, Bitov singles out these people for attack. The
Formalists are also criticized, for Bitov insists that Leva, in his
article "Three Prophets," wants to speak about the *meaning*
rather than about the form of the poems. This impulse to
emphasize meaning, adds the narrator ironically, is not at
present considered a scientific study of literature.

Bakhtin, too, plays a role in the novel. In the Khappenenn
appendix to the novel, Bitov writes that Bakhtin, the man,
served as one of the models for his portrait of Modest Platonovich. Here was a man who had spent many years in disfavor after
his arrest under Stalin; a man whose ideas, like Modest Platonovich's, had begun to be resurrected in the Soviet Union of the
early 1960s.[58]

Bakhtin was important in *Pushkin House* only in terms of his
personal biography, Bitov insists.[59] Ronald Meyer devotes some
attention to the presence, in *Pushkin House*, of certain of Bakhtin's ideas. For instance, he speaks of the relevance to a study of

the Bitov novel of Bakhtin's notion of the polyphonic novel, whereby individual characters speak dialogically in their own individual voices with their own individual points of view without the author's monologic viewpoint.[60]

I believe that the Bitov/Bakhtin connections are much more complex. I believe that Bitov was waging his battle with literary authorities with Bakhtin, as well as with other schools of literary interpretation. Paradoxically, the fact that he is carrying on a dialogue with Bakhtin means that Bitov is thereby writing according to the formula of dialogue highlighted by Bakhtin in his Dostoevsky book. In that book, reprinted in the Soviet Union in 1963, one year before Bitov began to write *Pushkin House*, Bakhtin spoke about the author, in a Dostoevsky book, as existing in the interstices between the antagonistic, dialogic voices of various *characters*.[61] Bitov, in the structure of *Pushkin House*, takes issue with Bakhtin, for Bitov claims that the author's relationship to the hero is different from the one suggested by Bakhtin. What Bitov says is that the *author* lives in the interstices between life and the written word. Bakhtin had spoken about the life of a book as existing in the spaces between the voices of the *characters* in that book. Bitov turns the discussion around and thinks about the writer's place in life rather than about the author's place in the book. For Bitov, the writer, in life, lives in the connecting space, in what he calls the "middle of the contrast." We will return to this idea, in another context, later on in the discussion of *Pushkin House*.

Formalist critic Tynianov's ideas play a complex role in *Pushkin House*. Leva's article "Three Prophets" reproduces an idea of Tynianov's, and the narrator draws the reader's attention to this fact. I believe that Bitov weaves Tynianov into the novel in more complicated ways as well. In *Archaists and Innovators (Arkhaisty i novatory)*, Tynianov speaks about literary history as comprising a battle of the literary "sons" with their "fathers" and returning to the methods of their literary "grandfathers." This theme is familiar to the readers of *Pushkin House*, who see that Leva is doing battle with his father and returning to the ideas of his grandfather. Bitov "rhymes" his *Pushkin House* with

many other works of Russian literature. Tynianov had written
about parody as imitation of the original in, for example, his
famous article about Dostoevsky and Gogol.

Tynianov had always taught the importance of relationships
for the study of literature. He claimed that one must see the way
in which the meaning of one word changes, depending on its
relationship to other words that surround it in the text. He spoke
of dynamic relationships within a text. He spoke of the way in
which one part of the text dominates and sets the tone for the
highly complex relationship that is a literary text. He urged the
critic to place a text in the context of other texts written at the
time. He emphasized the necessity of taking the historical
context into account when studying a work of literature.[62]

It seems to me that what Bitov does in *Pushkin House* is to take
Tynianov's ideas concerning the study of a literary text, and to
apply them to the "real world" life that he, as author, creates in
Pushkin House. Bitov is therefore saying, obliquely, that he agrees
with Tynianov's idea about the importance of relationships, but
that relationships/connections/bonds are important not only in
the study of a literary text, but in the examination of life itself.
The dominating element in Bitov's novel is Stalin, who set the
tone for the entire system of Soviet life.

Bitov thus breaks down the barrier between life and literature,
for he applies the literary-theory ideas of a literary critic to the
"actual" life of his characters, and he constructs his novel about
the lives of these characters according to the principles of
Tynianov's ideas about literature.

Rebellion, rivalry, revolution. Duels, devils, duplicity. Why
does Bitov keep repeating the theme and reproducing other
works of Russian literature that share the same territory? Bitov
has shown the level of degradation to which contemporary
culture, contaminated by the demonic Stalin, had sunk. In one
scene in *Pushkin House*, people do not even read *Anna Karenina* or
War and Peace anymore. They have merely seen the movies. Bitov
draws a portrayal of a modern-day Natasha and Anna who are
petty reproductions of the past noble heroines of Tolstoy's
novels. Leva is a "pale offprint" of his nineteenth-century
counterparts. Throughout the novel, Bitov shows the cultural

distortions that have taken shape because of the historical conditions that have shaped Soviet society. He documents the crudeness, coarseness, and degradation of Mitishatiev's ugly remarks to Blank, the uncontained hatred that non-aristocratic Mitishatiev hurls at Leva. Mitishatiev wants to destroy Russian literature. He brings an informer into Pushkin House, is writing a dissertation on the detective element (intimations of crimes) in Russian literature, physically ruins a Pushkin House room, scattering papers all over, is responsible for the fight that leads to a broken window in Pushkin House (a symbolic breaking of the window about which Pushkin talked in his "Bronze Horseman"); shoots Leva, who has been writing about Pushkin; and, significantly, hurls the inkwell (a tool for writing) of a nineteenth-century Russian, writer, Dmitry Grigorovich, out of the window of Pushkin House. Interestingly, it was Grigorovich who introduced Dostoevsky to Nekrasov in 1845, thereby facilitating the beginning of Dostoevsky's writing career, for it was Nekrasov who had been so enthusiastic about Dostoevsky's *Poor People*. (The reader should remember that this incident of Mitishatiev's throwing Grigorovich's inkwell out the window takes place in Bitov's Part Three, "Poor Horseman," a distorted version, together with one of its epilogues, of the title of that Dostoevsky novel.) Grigorovich died in 1899, one hundred years after the birth of Pushkin in 1799, thus providing another link in Russian literature. By throwing away Grigorovich's inkwell, Mitishatiev is, symbolically, breaking the continuity of Russian literature. Academician Leva Odoevtsev's 1999 "commentary" to the jubilee edition of *Pushkin House* is affixed to Bitov's novel, providing still another link in the chain of Russian literature that had begun with Pushkin's birth.

The violence Mitishatiev brings into Pushkin House, the repository of Russian culture, is symbolically equivalent to the destruction that Stalin caused to Russian literature and to the intelligentsia who were the preservers and continuators of that culture. And it is this scene that ends the novel proper.

Three epilogues and an appendix follow, and the ideas advanced in these portions of *Pushkin House* help resolve the mystery of Bitov's duel with Russian literature. Why would he rebel against Russian literature of the past? And what does his distortion of previous Russian literature signify?

Another author, another Andrei – Bely – had also parodied many works of previous Russian literature in *Petersburg*, his novel about the same city about which Bitov is writing. For Bely, in *Petersburg*, as for the anthroposophists and theosophists who were so important to his thinking, historical revolution (again, sons versus fathers) was necessary in order for people to be able to transcend historical time, and, through symbols, to attain a transcendent, non-linear world. Thus, Bely destroys/distorts the previous works of Russian literature that he parodies throughout his novel, just as on the temporal, linear plane the revolution is destroying the continuity of history. Bitov's novel, like Bely's, moves in a circular direction. Bitov, like Bely, ends his novel with a symbol of an ancient dead culture – a sphinx. In *Petersburg*, Nikolai Apollonovich is in Cairo, sitting in front of the sphinx. In Bitov's novel, Modest Platonovich is sitting in front of the sphinx statue in Leningrad. Bitov claims, however, not to have read *Petersburg* before he had finished writing *Pushkin House*.[63]

With the last section of *Pushkin House*, the appendix, the political/personal rings of Leva's fate vis-à-vis Stalin and his grandfather begin to merge with the artistic/personal rings of his fate vis-à-vis Mitishatiev and his own writing. And these themes begin to fit neatly together with the theme of Bitov's own duel with Russian literature.

The appendix is entitled "Achilles and the Tortoise" ("Akhilles i cherepakha") and relates to the ancient Greek philosopher Zeno's paradox about Achilles and the tortoise. What Zeno said was that Achilles, running a race with the tortoise in which the tortoise had a head start, would never catch up with the tortoise because the tortoise would always be taking steps ahead of Achilles. Zeno's paradox advances the idea that motion is impossible. There would always be, said Zeno, distance between Achilles and the tortoise.

What the reader of Bitov's novel can gather is that this predicament parallels the predicament described by Leva in his article "Latecomer Geniuses," i.e., that Tiutchev could never catch up with Pushkin because Pushkin had come first. The situation also parallels that of Leva, from the aristocracy, and Mitishatiev, from the masses. Mitishatiev would never be able to catch up with Leva because Leva had come first. This situation also describes the position of Bitov vis-à-vis Pushkin and all of Russian literature through Nabokov because they had come first. All of the "latecomers" could never catch up with those who had preceded them.

This state of affairs would hold true forever, as long as the "rivals" (Achilles, Tiutchev, Mitishatiev, Bitov) remained in the race, as long as they continued to lock themselves into a "duel" with the objects of their envy. However, there is a way to solve Zeno's paradox. *Only* as long as one remains in the race, competing with the rival, does one "lose." If one steps out of the framework set up as a competitive situation, the same conditions do not prevail. The Zeno paradox remains a paradox only as long as you accept its preassumptions. If you step out of the system, it is no longer a paradox. Thus, it was only when Leva *let* himself come under Mitishatiev's power that he was "poisoned." It was only when Bitov was conscious of previous literature and did not break away from it that he started getting caught in the endless rings of repetitions and distortions of previous literature. When Pushkin created freely, as in "The Prophet," where only divine inspiration – and no other influence – moved him to write, he bowed to no authority, envied no one, and did not feel that he was a latecomer because he was not in the degrading position of comparing himself to anyone.

Bitov, in *Pushkin House*, plots the process whereby he, as a writer, is breaking away from the authorities of previous literature that, through Bitov's own consciousness of their superiority, must have a deleterious effect upon his own individual creative, original gifts. He must solve Zeno's paradox by refusing to be in the race. *Pushkin House* is the story of his revolution, his rebellion against his "fathers," and his ultimate stepping away from that rebellion.

Within the final pages of *Pushkin House*, the author resurrects the dead Leva. Both Uncle Dickens, also resurrected from the dead, and his friend Albina, help him fix up the mess that he and

Mitishatiev had caused in Pushkin House. One of the details described is the replacement, with Uncle Dickens' and Albina's help, of a new window in Pushkin House. Russia's past culture, in the emblematic form of a window (the window between two cultures, according to Pushkin's "Bronze Horseman" notion), is restored by Leva and his friends who respect past culture. Albina, who works there, gives a guided tour through the museum part of the Academy of Sciences' literary institute. During her tour, she speaks of "Count" Lev Tolstoy, thus preserving, in her comments, the knowledge of Russia's nineteenth-century aristocratic past.

The author visits Leva in Pushkin House. Leva, as part of Bitov's finished and therefore dead/past book, remains in Pushkin House (we must recall that Bitov has called his *Pushkin House* a novel-museum) in the museum of dead/past literature. Bitov steps out of Pushkin House. We can only make sense of the name of Leva's new article, "The Middle of the Contrast" ("Seredina kontrasta") – about Pushkin's "Bronze Horseman" – when we read the last few pages of the novel.

To be original, implies Bitov, one must not be caught in the house of dead literature. One must go outside the house. One must break with the past. Yet as we have seen, this presents a paradox, for Stalin, by insisting on breaking the continuity with the past, caused physical, psychic, and creative death.

This paradox, too, is addressed in the novel's final brilliant pages. As the author is about to take leave of Leva and step out of Pushkin House, Leva hands him a few pages that his grandfather, Modest Platonovich Odoevtsev, had written. He tells the author that he may take these pages with him, and the author leaves Pushkin House, these pages in hand. The pages, "The Sphinx," allegedly from the elder Odoevtsev's composition, "God Is", are highly significant in tying up the loose threads of the novel.

"The Sphinx" recounts what seem to be the final events and thoughts before Modest Platonovich's arrest. These pages are proof of his personal, political, and artistic integrity and are his declaration of independence from authorities, from the stifling interdependencies/bonds/connections in his life. Grandfather

Odoevtsev goes to the statue of the sphinx along the Neva.[64] He
has just acted with great personal courage and integrity, for he
has told the truth at the deliberations of a commission. A non-
courageous person, one through whose weakness and lies the
rings of Stalin's humiliation were allowed to take such a tight
grip on Soviet society,[65] has told Modest Platonovich that he
should have lied at the meeting. If, says I-lev, he had said that
Ecclesiastes was a materialist, he would have gone free. Modest
Platonovich, however, had not distorted the truth. We can
surmise that this was the reason for which he was sent to
Siberia.

Modest Platonovich looks up at the sky and concludes that
had he not told the truth, he might not have looked up at the sky
and would not have known that he was a free person. Echoing
Dostoevsky in *Crime and Punishment*, Bitov says that freedom is an
internal state. This thought links up to a major theme of the
novel, for Leva/Bitov can be truly free only when they step out of
the Achilles/tortoise duel framework and act in accordance with
the principles of integrity.

Modest Platonovich quotes, without attribution of the poem,
an excerpt from Blok's 1921 poem, "Pushkin House" ("Pushkinskii Dom"), which the poet wrote in honor of a Pushkin
celebration at Pushkin House. The lines he quotes contain the
words "secret freedom" ("'tainuiu svobodu'")[66] in a verse that
asks for Pushkin's help, during a time of bad weather, in a silent
battle (p. 411). Modest Platonvich says that I-lev would probably interpret the lines as containing a dangerous hidden political
meaning because of the words "secret freedom," "foul weather,"
and "silent battle" (p. 411). Odoevtsev says that the real
meaning of the poem is Blok's call for true cultural and creative
freedom.

It is time, declares Modest Platonovich, to remain silent
rather than to corrupt the meanings of words. He says, "The
connections are broken ... The secret is born!" (p. 409). The
reader gathers that there is a great paradox in what Modest
Platonovich has realized, here, and in his speech to Leva earlier
in the book. What he is implying is that by remaining silent
rather than distorting culture, he will not be continuing Russian

culture. The fate of Russian culture, with Stalin's blows to it, is that the connection/links/bonds to it were broken. The "connections of the times," as exemplified in the torn-up fragmented newspaper clipping at the beginning of the novel, were broken, and this was devastating to Modest Platonovich's creativity and to his life. He remained silent, and he suffered a great deal. The rings of endless humiliation kept repeating themselves. However, at the same time, a paradox was born, for, as Modest Platonovich himself had told Leva, this meant that prerevolutionary literature would, like a nature sanctuary, be preserved forever. Like the sphinx, monument from another age, it will remain intact, its mystery preserved forever. The fact that there was a break in culture was devastating, yet that same break in continuity was precisely the thing that would save past culture forever. The death of culture resulted in its continuing to live.

There is another paradox, for Modest Platonovich says that silence is necessary in order for him to remain true to himself and true to the word. The implication is that in order to be truly creative, one must step away from the past into dangerous territory. In other words, to use the words of the title of Leva's article, one must step into "the middle of the contrast" in order to pronounce the word anew. A true artist must step away from the old framework and look up at the sky. A true artist must not distort words. A true artist must step into the silence, into the middle of the contrast, in order to pronounce the word anew.

The secret freedom, the internal state of freedom, cannot be found, we can infer, by looking for time-bound meanings of words/life/culture. True meaning can only be found by following the dictates of one's conscience and by following the calling of one's higher creative potential. Thus, while I-lev is myopically looking for the political, temporally bound meanings of Blok's words, the reader, along with Modest Platonovich, can discover the true meaning of the silent, secret freedom. Modest Platonovich gives us the words of Blok's "Pushkin House" poem. He speaks about words having lost their "function" ("naznachenie") (p. 411). What he remains silent about (this is part of the internal, secret freedom) is a fact that a careful reader, sensitive to Modest Platonovich's silence, can discover. What is important for us to realize, although Bitov's text is silent about this, is that when Blok wrote "Pushkin House," he also wrote a speech in honor of Pushkin. The title of that speech, "On a Poet's Function" ("O naznachenii poèta"), includes the same word, "function" ("naznachenie"), that Modest Platonovich uses several paragraphs before and after he quotes the Blok poem.

The Blok speech is about the divine function of the poet, about the harmony that the true poet, whose calling is dictated by an inner state, must give form to, no matter what the external political pressures are upon him.[67] Blok's cry is for that same untrammeled elemental secret freedom about which Modest Platonovich is speaking in "The Sphinx." These words, Modest Platonovich's, Blok's, and Pushkin's, live on. They continue to live because they were courageous and authentic words that had not lost their meaning. The most important thing in the world, writes Modest Platonovich, is to fulfill one's calling. This is what Pushkin did, the reader can recall, in "The Prophet," where God tells the poet to burn people's hearts with his word. Modest Platonovich's last words are a call to strive always toward the sky, toward the new, toward what we can assume him to mean, toward the "middle of the contrast." The elder Odoevtsev writes, "But even if the word is pronounced accurately and can live through its own muteness right up to the resurrection of Phoenix-meaning, does this then mean that people will look for it in the paper dust, that they will begin, in general, to search for it in its former, even if genuine, meaning, and will not simply pronounce it anew?" (p. 412).

One of Bitov's recurrent images in *Pushkin House* is that of the scorpion that forms a circle, stings itself, and dies in a ring of fire. The image of the Phoenix Bitov uses in his final words of the book, the passage just quoted. Like the scorpion, the mythological Phoenix died in a fire. Out of the ashes, a new glorious phoenix, mythological symbol of immortality, would come to life.

Pushkin was dead. Russian literature was dead. Nabokov was dead. Modest Platonovich's voice was silenced. Leva remained in Pushkin House, making sure that the words of Pushkin and of Modest Platonovich would continue to live.

Those words – the words in "The Sphinx," a part of "God Is," a composition whose title affirms the existence of eternal life – guarantee the continuity of life as they create the bonds between the courageous statements of Modest Platonovich, Blok, and Pushkin. And we should keep in mind that Odoevtsev creates the links as he sits in front of the sphinx, a living monument to another dead culture. Paradoxically, only those people who dare to exercise true creative freedom – that is, again paradoxically, to rebel against their "fathers" by refusing to be a part of the system; by, paradoxically, simultaneously refusing to rebel; by stepping away from the old Achilles/tortoise framework; by stepping into the "middle of the contrast" – only those people will create the genuine works of art that will provide links to other genuine works (the sphinx, Pushkin, Blok, "The Sphinx") and will last forever.

And again, paradoxically, only those people who have sacrificed a part of themselves in life can, according to Bitov, produce works of art that will last. This requirement of the necessity of death for genuine life, with decided religious overtones about the divine nature of the artist, becomes clear as we approach Bitov's ideas, in *Pushkin House*, about the relationship of the author to his hero. The writer, according to Bitov, occupies a space between life and the word. This idea of Bitov's thus imparts to the expression, the "middle of the contrast," another meaning. Modest Platonovich, in "The Sphinx," had said that he lives between life and the word, between the earth and the sky. In *Articles from a Novel*, in "The Tortoise and Achilles" ("Cherepakha i Akhilles"), an essay that has definite resonances with *Pushkin House*, Bitov speaks of the poet as living between life and the word.[68] In several philosophical ruminations on the nature of time that are scattered throughout *Pushkin House*, the writer speaks of the nature of the present. The present, he reflects, is, paradoxically, at once this precise undivided moment and, at the same time, memory, the capacity of stepping away from this particular moment. The writer's function, we can conclude from Bitov's thoughts, is to live this particular moment less fully. In order to preserve the present, the writer must move away from it so as to capture it in the form of a moment/monument that can be preserved. The fate of the writer is to preserve life by sacrificing a part of his own present life, yet – once again, paradoxically – the act of dying to this life ensures that this life will be preserved in the future. The writer lives in the connections/bonds between life and the word. The act of the writer's serving as a connection between life and culture ensures his serving as a connector, a window, a bond to future generations. Death, on one level, for Bitov, results in life. Russian culture died and therefore continues to live. The writer does not live fully so that his works may live. On the other hand, for Bitov, death results in death, too, for the death sentence that Stalin pronounced upon Soviet society and culture was one that resulted in Leva's upbringing, with its atmosphere of death-like silence about the truth.

By the end of the book, we have read that we must live in order to live, die in order to live, live in order to die, and die in order to die. By the end of the book, breaks in continuity are shown to be good and bad. Rebellions are shown to be bad and good. Confusing? Yes. But then, that is the nature of the riddle of the sphinx, which, after all, is the section of *Pushkin House* that Bitov chooses to end his book with. The riddle of the ancient Egyptian sphinx was a question she posed about the cycles of human life. According to Greek legend, when Oedipus answered her riddle, she died. The monument and the riddle have continued to live. *Pushkin House*, in the final analysis, is a tribute to the riddle of life and death – a paradox, a puzzle, as mysterious as life itself.

The final scene of Bitov's novel takes place in Leningrad, as Modest Platonovich is sitting near the sphinx statues along the bank of the Neva. The statues, monuments of a past culture, are directly across the Neva from "The Bronze Horseman," another monument to a past culture, itself immortalized in a literary monument written by Pushkin. Odoevtsev is quoting the Blok poem "Pushkin House," which Blok had written for Pushkin House in 1921, the year of Blok's death, the year of celebration of the living poetry of the dead poet Pushkin. At the time that Blok wrote the poem, Pushkin House was located in a building (the present-day main building of the Leningrad Academy of Sciences) along the same Neva embankment as the sphinxes and across the river from Falconet's "Bronze Horseman" statue. That building, the Leningrad Academy of Sciences and former Pushkin House, is situated at the corner of the University Embankment and of a street called Mendeleev Line.

The Blok poem Modest Platonovich quotes at the very end of *Pushkin House* is the same one (although Bitov does not mention this) from which Bitov has quoted another excerpt, its first stanza, in the second of his opening two epigraphs to the novel. The gist of this epigraph is that Pushkin House (Russian culture, we can conclude) lives on. The first epigraph, from a Pushkin variant to "The Tales of Belkin," declares that we will not be in the future. The end of the novel brings us full circle to its beginning, for we are again brought into the circle of the sphinx's riddle. Pushkin is talking about death, about the break in continuity, and Blok, in hailing Pushkin House, is speaking about the continuation of Pushkin's art into the present.

Modest Platonovich is sitting by the sphinxes, not far from Pushkin House, the Academy of Sciences institute, and not far from a monument immortalized in a literary monument by the immortal poet Pushkin. As he sits there, he looks up at the sky and then later writes about the experience in a composition entitled "The Sphinx," which is from "God Is." It is important that Modest Platonovich is, by name, "son of Platon," or "son of Plato." Plato, it is thought, spent some time in Egypt. He founded an Academy to carry forth his teachings. He believed in the existence of the divinely inspired poet. He believed in absolute truth, in the importance of the quest for the absolute truth. Like his "father," Plato, Modest Platonovich, son of Plato, looks to the sky, toward the absolute. Like his "father," he, like Pushkin, knows intuitively that all things in the universe are connected.

All of the pieces of this highly complex novel are interconnected, interdependent. The fact that the 1921 Pushkin House was located on the corner of what is now Mendeleev Line, the name of the famous chemist who constructed the Periodic Table that shows the interrelationships of chemical elements, brings us to another important theme of the book, the theme of the interconnections themselves. We return to the organizing principle of the book, to the principle of organic chemistry. Organic chemistry, the science that studies connections, bonds of elements, has guided us to the major connecting principle holding together Bitov's *Pushkin House*.

In the Khappenenn "Appendix" to *Pushkin House*, we read that the novel is all about relationships: "It [the novel – E.C.] is about the fruits of a relationship ..." ("On [roman – E.C.] – o plodakh otnosheniia ...").[69] What Bitov's novel says, finally, about the riddle of life is that life is made up of the connections/bonds that connect us to other people, to our history, to our culture. The nature of the bonds/connectors themselves, according to Bitov, is of crucial importance in the way in which we conduct ourselves. If the bonds are healthy, the result will be healthy and life-affirming. If the bonds are not, the results will be rings that spawn new rings, constrained rings, rings of alcohol and poison, rings of endless humiliation. The same elements, the elements of life – such as oxygen, hydrogen, carbon – can be bonded and can result in compounds that are harmful to life. The important thing in life, though, we learn from reading Bitov's novel, is the relationship – the thing that connects a person to life. In the final analysis, as Bitov has amply demonstrated in his unusual novel, the important thing in leading a life of personal and artistic integrity is the ability to step into the creative connection, the "middle of the contrast," the silence, the bond that connects life to freedom.

CHAPTER 12

Bitov's post-"Pushkin House" prose, or life in the images of life

> My space chums say they're learning so much about us
> ... They said to me, "Trudy, the human mind is so-o-o
> strange." ... They find it hard to grasp some things that
> come easy to us, because they simply don't have our
> frame of reference. I show 'em this can of Campbell's
> tomato soup. I say, "This is soup." Then I show 'em a
> picture of Andy Warhol's painting of a can of Campbell's
> tomato soup. I say, "This is art." "This is soup." "And
> this is art." Then I shuffle the two behind my back. Now
> what is this? No, *this* is soup and *this is art!*[1]
>
> Lily Tomlin in Jane Wagner
> *The Search for Signs of Intelligent Life in the Universe*

The narrator's commentary to the article by Leva Odoevtsev, of
Pushkin House, revealed that Leva's article about Pushkin,
Lermontov, and Tiutchev told us more about Leva than about
those poets. The commentator's commentary on Leva's commentary on the nineteenth-century poets can be read as a signal
to look at Leva's article as commentary on his past works and on
Pushkin House. Each person, Leva had written, contains within
himself God (Pushkin, Mozart), man (Lermontov, Beethoven),
and the devil/death (Tiutchev). The Pushkin/Mozart part
of Bitov can be seen in his "Life in Windy Weather" and
"Armenia Lessons," as he describes the harmony and divine
inspiration of coming into contact with authentic life, art, and
culture. His Lermontov/Beethoven side comes out in the portrayals of adolescent or adolescent-like characters such as the
idler, "Penelope"'s Lobyshev, and Aleksei Monakhov. His
Tiutchev characteristics come out full-blown in *Pushkin House* in

246

the character of Mitishatiev. The Pushkin and Lermontov traits are, as we have seen, also prominently displayed in *Pushkin House*. Modest Platonovich could step into the middle of the contrast. The end of that novel describes the ability to break away from authorities and, concomitantly, to accept/continue and to break away from one's past. It describes Bitov's acceptance of and break from his literary "fathers." Bitov is describing the psychology of the creative process. Stepping into the middle of the contrast can mean living between the past and the present. The middle of the contrast represents that point at which the past ends and the present begins. The present, the middle of the contrast, contains within it both the past and the immediate moment.

Bitov's creative path, since *Pushkin House*, has followed his old directions and has carved out new territory. There is continuity and a break in continuity.

Georgian Album (1985) contains mostly works from previous collections, although Bitov chops them up, adds to them, and rearranges them in the new collection.[2] Most of them relate to Georgia. The Mozart/Pushkin side is emphasized first, for the collection begins with the "Phenomenon of the Norm" essay, part of "Choice of Location," which speaks of the divine norm of creation. The major theme of "Choice of Location" had been the interrelationship of art and life, and this remains the primary focus of *Georgian Album*. Bitov links culture to culture in *Georgian Album* as he takes what was the end of "Armenia Lessons," a section about the narrator's travels to the geographical boundary of Armenia and Georgia, and places that section of his Armenia travelogue near the beginning of his book about Georgia. It is this passage, "Recollection of Agartsina," that describes the harmony that comes from being attentive to divine inspiration, to the "reflection of God's face in his own creation."

The ability to be authentic had, in "Armenia Lessons," been linked to the ability to accept a nation's history. In *Georgian Album*, the piece to follow the "Recollection of Agartsina" passage is "The Last Bear," one of his stories dealing with the Soviet Union's past. It is appropriate that this story would be included in a volume devoted to Georgia, for Stalin was born and grew up in Georgia. Bitov intersperses his other Stalin stories throughout *Georgian Album*.[3]

In a key passage in *Georgian Album*, the "P.S." to a section entitled "Direct Inspiration" ("Priamoe vdokhnovenie"), Bitov explains his methodology. The book, he says, is conceived as and constructed like the ruins of a temple that he had spent many years building.[4] The reader begins to understand why Bitov has chopped up his stories to put them into *Georgian Album*. He is dealing, as he had in *Pushkin House*, with a book about the destruction of another house, with chopping up and destroying his own artistic past. He himself destroys the temple, but, given our knowledge of *Pushkin House*, we might ask whether this destructive tendency has been caused by Stalin.

In this same *Georgian Album* passage, Bitov asks whether the temple had a "cupola" and answers that perhaps it had not, but that in the reconstruction, someone might build a cupola. When Leva, in *Pushkin House*, writes his article, "The Middle of the Contrast," he suddenly sees what he calls the "cupola" when he understands Modest Platonovich's ideas and his own inspiration.[5] Leva stops working at that point, is distracted by his conversation with a Pushkin House employee, and then falls asleep. His sleep is interrupted by the shrill ring of the telephone that brings with it Mitishatiev's announcement that he will visit Leva. The continuity of Leva's thoughts and of his flash of insight into the connection between Pushkin and Modest Platonovich is broken. The "cupola" is not built. The house is destroyed by Mitishatiev, the surrogate Stalin.

The point, for Bitov, in "P.S.," is that culture cannot be interrupted, just as life cannot be interrupted.[6] Bitov declares that the image of the "cupola" existed before the unbuilt temple because the thought of it existed. The reconstruction will therefore include the cupola.

These points he emphasizes as he keeps intermeshing, as he has before, life with art. For example, he had described a photograph in "Choice of Location," as the narrator, while visiting Georgia, thumbs through a photography album – i.e., a "Georgian album." The photographs described are remarkably similar to the real photographs that are reproduced on the front and inside covers of Bitov's *Georgian Album*.

In spite of impulses to the contrary, Bitov, in *Georgian Album*, still attempts to integrate parts into wholes, to fuse fragments and chopped up pieces of life and art into transcendent cupolas. The final sections of the book attest to this fact. The penultimate essay, "Diffuse Light" ("Rasseiannyi svet"), returns the narrator to his childhood and to his childhood room. He contemplates a ray of sun and the diffuse light that sunlight gives off. He understands that light is whole, that any light particle is a part of the whole.[7] He grasps, momentarily, this insight about life and, we can see, about Bitov's own creative methods, and then the clarity once again disappears.

Bitov is describing the creative process. At the same time, he is bringing the reader back to the beginning of his creative path, when, in "The Sun," he had dealt with life's creative and destructive forces. He creates his works as tiny sun rays that, when placed together, belong to the larger category, sunlight. The boundaries are erased between Bitov's past and present works, between one particle of light and another.

"Birds" closes *Georgian Album*. It does not relate to Georgia, and its very point is that one species is different from another, that we must respect the boundaries between/among species. Its message is that all sorts of different entities constitute the larger ecological whole. In tearing down his temple in *Georgian Album*, Bitov implicitly acknowledges that the destruction of culture is also part of the ecological system of life. By linking "Diffuse Light" to "Birds," he implicitly shows that the transcendent "cupola" of inspiration links and connects, builds and affirms the integral nature of life.

Bitov's next book, *Book of Journeys* (*Kniga puteshestvii*) (1986) is almost a replay of the 1976 collection of travelogues, *Seven Journeys*. It, too, contains seven journeys; six of the seven had appeared in *Seven Journeys*. He eliminates "Such a Long Childhood" from the new book and includes "Birds" instead. The new order of journeys assumes a logic of its own. First come "One Country" and "Journey to a Childhood Friend," which tell of the necessity of going away in space (to another place) and in time (to one's past) in order to get to know oneself. The next two journeys are "The Wheel," which speaks of similar functions in life of very different activities (riding an animal and a machine), and "Birds," which urges us to respect differences in life. The final three address the issue of finding oneself. "The Gamble" asserts that one must listen to one's inner voice. The "Armenia Lessons" teach us about authenticity in all cultures and times. "Choice of Location," which ends the collection, documents the merging of art and life. All these works direct us to search for values that transcend the mundane everyday pieces of life. They guide us to look for the "cupola."

In *Pushkin House*, we had read about the necessity of being "in the middle of the contrast," in the silence, in the muteness, in order to find one's creative "I." In many later essays, Bitov speaks of "silence" as necessary to the creative process. The silence can be interpreted as a necessary state of existence for the writer of integrity living under the severe pressures of censorship, as was the case with Bitov during the late 1970s and early 1980s. What Bitov is talking about is more than political-societal constraint, though, as he admits in an essay in *Articles from a Novel*, about Pushkin's "creative crisis." Bitov, purportedly speaking about Pushkin, explains that the writer did not publish for a time, not only because of the externally imposed censorship, but more importantly, out of an internal need to find a new direction.

I believe that the statement can be applied to Bitov's silence during the late 1970s and early 1980s.[8] The thoughts in the "Sphinx" chapter of *Pushkin House* indicate a "secret freedom," a break from authorities. Bitov himself seems to follow that same path of breaking with the past in many of his later post-*Pushkin House* creations. There are points of intersection with Bitov's previous works, as I have demonstrated with respect to *Georgian Album* and *Book of Journeys*. There are other points of contact (to which I will alert the reader), but what is important is that in recent works, Bitov breaks away from certain old patterns, themes, and forms.

Monakhov and Leva Odoevtsev fade from the later works. Monakhov is mentioned once, in an oblique reference to "The Taste," in *Articles from a Novel*, and Leva plays a small role in that book. Bitov all but ceases to depict a contemporary man, a focus that had preoccupied him since the inception of his literary career. Much of his career, we know, he had devoted to

10 Bitov, on statue of a tiger, at Princeton University. May, 1987.

describing a person's attempt to get away from the images of life and to get to life itself. In the new stage, represented primarily by *Articles from a Novel* (1986) and three stories published in 1987, Bitov describes life processes that take place within the images of life. He has gone, therefore, from (1) images of life to (2) life to (3) life within the images of life. Take, for example, *Articles from a Novel*. His references, in the title, are to *Doctor Zhivago* and to *Pushkin House*,[9] and indeed, some of the articles, "Achilles and the Tortoise" and "The Hero's Profession," are taken from *Pushkin House*. The last page or so of the last section, "Flight with the Hero" ("Polet s geroem"), contains, without attribution, entire paragraphs from the end of *Pushkin House*. One paragraph is taken from the end of Part Three of the novel, and by the end of the paragraph, Bitov changes the pronoun from "he" (instead of "Leva," in the original) to the first person, "I." He, therefore, stops talking about a fictional character and talks about himself instead.[10] The final paragraph of "Flight with the Hero" is from the final section of *Pushkin House*, the "Sphinx" chapter. Here, Modest Platonovich's words, told in the first person, become Bitov's words, told in the first person (Figure 10).[11]

In these passages, he merges life and art. In other respects, *Articles from a Novel* concerns the same issues Bitov had spoken about with respect to life, but instead, he discusses the issues as they relate to art. For example, as we know, Bitov had often written about the bonds and connections that unite or divide people. In *Articles from a Novel*, he takes on the same subject, but abstractly – the grammatical "conjunction" ("soiuz"), the relationship between the writer and the reader; the writer and the critic. Gone is a focus on the relationship between one person and another in his/her daily life. (Bitov had begun to move in this direction previously, for in *Pushkin House* he addresses the relationship of the author to his character.) The essay, "The Ecology of the Word," is on a subject Bitov has addressed all his writing days, but again, here he speaks of the relationship of the *word* to the text and time rather than about the relationship of the person to life as a whole. At the same time, though, Bitov says that the writer, in order to be able to write, has to know that other people exist. He also emphasizes the necessity of a concern with ethical questions.

When he speaks about the creative process – much of the book is devoted to a series of articles about Pushkin – Bitov uses words that refer to life in order to describe Pushkin's method: "birth" ("rozhdenie"); "body" ("telo"); "breathe" ("dyshat'"); "respiration" ("dykhanie").[12]

The function of literature, Bitov writes, is that it "con-joins" ("so-ediniaet").[13] Only love, he writes, can fill the gap between literature and life, and a book, he says, is love. Before, Bitov had spoken, in his books, about the way to attain love. Now the *book* acquires attributes of life.

The three 1987 stories move farther and farther away from contemporary life. "Pushkin's Photograph (1799–2099)" ("Fotografiia Pushkina [1799–2099])"[14] is a science fiction story about Igor' Odoevtsev, illegitimate grandson of Leva Odoevtsev and Faina. He is asked, on the three hundredth anniversary of Pushkin's birth, to go back to earth (people now live in space) and back in time in order to photograph and tape the great writer, since no photograph or tape of Pushkin exists. The tone is playful. We learn about the Sputnik of the United Nations

("SON") – i.e., "DREAM." There is an unattributed reference to Joseph Brodsky's poetry.[15] Bitov writes "part of speech" ("chast' rechi"), which is the title of a Brodsky poetry collection. By the end of the story, we learn that a person who lives in one time can never understand another time. Igor' cannot live in Pushkin's nineteenth century, just as Leva could not live in Pushkin House, just as Bitov could not live in past literature.

"Man in the Landscape" ("Chelovek v peizazhe")[16] is an abstract discussion about first causes, art and life, and the place of the human being in the universe. Most of the conversation takes place as the narrator and an elderly icon-restorer are drunk. In his own mind, Bitov affixes this quasi-essay to "Birds."[17] In one respect, it is easy to see the links between the two works, for here, as in "Birds," Bitov emphasizes the distinction between human beings and other natural phenomena. As in "Birds," he emphasizes the fact that we can think only from our own individual perspective and that we can never know how, for example, a rock perceives the world.

His major questions here are what a human being is and why. The old man, dispenser of questions and wisdom, is reminiscent of other wise men in Bitov's oeuvre – the elderly artist in "Armenia Lessons" and Modest Platonovich in *Pushkin House*. The old man's conclusion in "Man in a Landscape" is that the image of the world preceded the world and that the image is God. He concludes that God is an artist.[18] The world, he continues, had already been created when man appeared, and man's only contribution has been negative – i.e., spoiling a landscape by, for example, erecting telephone poles. Instead of assigning the wise old philosopher a small part in a large work, as in "Armenia Lessons" and *Pushkin House*, Bitov, in this story, gives him the lead role. The story is more abstract than previous works, with the exception of "Birds." We see, though, that Bitov is again preoccupied, as in *Articles*, with the primacy of images of life over life.

In "The Teacher of Symmetry," Bitov goes completely into the world of images of life; he makes up an author. The story, "The Teacher of Symmetry," claims Bitov in his introductory remarks, is by È. Taird-Boffin, and he, Bitov, gives the reading audience a "free translation from a foreign language."[19] The reader might surmise that "È. Taird-Boffin" is a Russian-sounding English equivalent (or vice versa) for "A Tired Buffoon."[20] In the translator's foreword, Bitov claims that he had read this author long ago, while on geological expeditions, but had never been able to find the book again. He says that he is therefore recording what he remembers. The "book," which he interrupts midway to announce that he hopes to continue the translation next year, is divided into four unrelated episodes/stories. Two of them star eccentric, isolated men who are seers of sorts. One says he comes from the moon, and he is not believed. The other has a photograph of a view of the Troy sky (the Troy of ancient times, he insists, although he lives in the present). Both men are suspected of being mad; both are highly imaginative. Both live totally in their imaginative universes.

"The Teacher of Symmetry" is preceded by a quotation from a letter of Vladimir Odoevsky, who, writes Bitov, is one of his favorite writers. "The Teacher of Symmetry," in a departure from most Bitov works, is reminiscent of Odoevsky's *Russian Nights* (*Russkie nochi*) with their strange mixture of romantic, gifted artistic types. The tone is a combination of Odoevsky and the "magic realism" of contemporary Latin American writers. Bitov has said that he feels a particular affinity for writers like Marquez.[21] The story has a Borges quality about it with its strange blurring of imagination and reality.

The final episode, "Verses from a Coffee Cup," contains a passage about an author who writes a foreign novel – i.e., a made-up novel with non-existing people and in nonexistent space. This, says the narrator, is the best way the author could find to break with his past.[22] The situation sounds remarkably similar to Bitov's.

At this point in his journey of books, Bitov, the Tired Buffoon, has come full circle from the beginning of his writing career when he wrote humorous stories. He has come full circle to the silence and blank pages before the beginning of his writing career, for there is, in this story, a nonexistent author Bitov, nonexistent characters, and nonexistent space. Like his first stories, his latest is reminiscent of Daniil Kharms'. In "Blue

Notebook No. 10" ("Golubaia tetrad' No. 10"), Kharms gives
the reader, by the end of the story, a blank page:

> There was once a red-haired man who had no eyes and no ears. He also
> had no hair ... he didn't have a mouth. He had no nose, either. He
> didn't even have any arms or legs. He also didn't have a stomach, and
> he didn't have a back, and he didn't have a spine ... He didn't have
> anything. So it's hard to understand whom we're talking about. So
> we'd better not talk about him any more.[23]

What will Bitov's next steps be? I, as a literary scholar, write
about a literary work after the author has written it. In studying
the works of a contemporary writer, the scholar's time can never
coincide with the author's time. Chances' Achilles can never
overtake Bitov's tortoise.

It is time for me to stop learning Bitov's Armenia lessons,
Russia lessons, life lessons, and literature lessons and turn to a
different set of lessons about a different kind of tortoise – the
lessons taught by Lewis Carroll in "The Mock Turtle's Story":

> "And how many hours a day did you do lessons?" said Alice ...
>
> "Ten hours the first day," said the Mock Turtle: "nine the next, and
> so on."
>
> "What a curious plan!" exclaimed Alice.
>
> "That's the reason they're called lessons," the Gryphon remarked:
> "because they lessen from day to day."
>
> This was quite a new idea to Alice, and she thought it over a little
> before she made the next remark. "Then the eleventh day must have
> been a holiday?"
>
> "Of course it was," said the Mock Turtle.
>
> "And how did you manage on the twelfth?" Alice went on eagerly.
>
> "That's enough about lessons," the Gryphon interrupted in a very
> decided tone ..."[24]

Notes

1 *Andrei Bitov's ecological prose*

1 Letter to Stephen Hagen, as quoted in Stephen George Sidney Hagen, "The Stories of Andrei Bitov, 1958–1966. A Search for Individual Perception." MA Diss. University of Durham (England), 1980, p. 245.
2 Andrei Bitov, "Ėkologiia slova," in Andrei Bitov, *Stat'i iz romana* (Moscow, 1986), p. 46.
3 Andrei Bitov, "Raznye dni cheloveka," *Literaturnaia gazeta*, July 22, 1987, p. 6.
4 Andrei Bitov, "Les," in Andrei Bitov, *Dni cheloveka. Povesti* (Moscow, 1976), p. 106.
5 Andrei Bitov, "Peizazh," in *Den' poèzii*. Ed. Iurii Kuznetsov (Moscow, 1983), p. 94; Andrei Bitov, "Tri stikhotvoreniia," *Druzhba narodov*, no. 12, 1988, pp. 105–7; Andrei Bitov, "Lestnitsa," in Bitov, *Uletaiushchii Monakhov. Roman-punktir* (Moscow, 1990), pp. 148–50. "Lestnitsa" appeared separately in Andrei Bitov, "Punktir. Okonchanie knigi," *Literaturnaia gazeta*, August 1, 1990, p. 6.
6 Andrei Bitov, *Pushkinskii dom* (Ann Arbor, Michigan: Ardis Publishers, 1978).
7 Precedents for an anthology like *Metropol* had been set in the 1950s and early 1960s with the publication, in the Soviet Union, of anthologies representing artistic openness. See *Literaturnaia Moskva. Literaturno-khudozhestvennyi sbornik Moskovskikh pisatelei* (Moscow, 1956), vols. 1 and 2; and *Tarusskie stranitsy. Literaturno-khudozhestvennyi illiustrirovannyi sbornik* (Kaluga, 1961), the anthology that Konstantin Paustovsky helped to appear.

We must also note that during the late Brezhnev period, Bitov's older brother Oleg (the two are not close) defected to the West and made stridently anti-Soviet comments in the Western press. (He later returned to the USSR and then made anti-Western statements in the Soviet press.)

8 For a discussion of *Metropol* and of Bitov's contributions to the volume, see chapter 9 of my book.

9 Andrei Bitov, *Pushkinskiii dom, Novyi mir*, no. 10, 1987, pp. 3–92; no. 11, 1987, pp. 55–91; no. 12, 1987, pp. 50–110.

10 Andrei Bitov, *Pushkinskii dom. Roman* (Moscow, 1989).

11 See note 66 of this chapter.

12 Andrei Bitov, *Chelovek v peizazhe. Povesti i rasskazy* (Moscow, 1988), Andrei Bitov, *Povesti i rasskazy. Izbrannoe* (Moscow, 1989), and Bitov, *Uletaiushchii Monakhov*. Each collection contains previously published work and work that is published for the first time in book form.

13 Andrei Bitov, *La maison Pouchkine. Roman de l'humiliation infinie*, trans. Philippe Mennecier (Paris: Albin Michel, 1989).

14 See, for example, "Kruglyi stol. Vladimir Nabokov: Mezh dvukh beregov," *Literaturnaia gazeta*, August 17, 1988, p. 5; Andrei Bitov, "Ob otkryvshikhsia vosmozhnostiakh i naidennom puti," *Sovetskii èkran*, no. 7, 1988, pp. 4–5; Andrei Bitov, "V poiskakh real'nosti. Beseda korrespondenta 'LO' Evg. Shklovskogo s Andreem Bitovym," *Literaturnoe obozrenie*, no. 5, 1988, pp. 32–8; Andrei Bitov and A. Znatnov, "Konflikty i kontakty," *V mire knig*, no. 11, 1987, pp. 75–7; Andrei Bitov, "Ustalost' parovoza. Zapiski nachinaiushchego iazvennika," *Nezavisimaia gazeta*, March 30, 1991, p. 7.

15 See, in particular, chapter 5, "The Friends and Foes of Change: Soviet Reformism and Conservatism," in Stephen F. Cohen, *Rethinking the Soviet Experience. Politics and History Since 1917* (New York and Oxford: Oxford University Press, 1986), pp. 128–57.

16 *Ibid.*

17 The 1970s debates about Socialist Realism are a case in point. Socialist Realism as an aesthetic method was declared by some to be an "open system" ("otkrytaia sistema"). Some Soviet critics urged expanding the definition of Socialist Realism to allow for experimentation in style and emphasis upon a writer's subjective apprehension of the world. Some Soviet literary scholars wrote that Socialist Realism is not a rigid concept given once and for all, with no room for development. See L.Ia. Iakimenko, *Na dorogakh veka. Aktual'nye voprosy sovetskoi literatury* (Moscow, 1973), p. 308; D. Markov, "Istoricheski otktrytaia sistema pravdivogo izobrazheniia zhizni (O novykh aspektakh obsuzhdeniia problem sotsialisticheskogo realizma v poslednie gody)," in *Voprosy literatury*, no. 1, 1977, pp. 29 and 37; L.G. Iakimenko, "Èsteticheskaia sistema sotsialisticheskogo realizma i problema khudozhestvennogo myshleniia," in *Sotsialisticheskii realizm segodnia. Problemy i suzhdeniia* (Moscow, 1977), pp. 11 and 42; D. F. Markov, "O teoreticheskikh

osnovakh poètiki sotsialisticheskogo realizma," in *Sotsialisticheskii*, p. 100.

18 For background on Socialist Realism, see Herman Ermolaev, *Soviet Literary Theories 1917–1934. The Genesis of Socialist Realism* (1963; reprint edn., New York: Octagon Books, 1977). For an analysis of the methodology of Socialist Realist novels, see Katerina Clark, *The Soviet Novel. History as Ritual* (Chicago, Illinois: University of Chicago Press, 1981).

19 Examples include literary critics Lev Anninskii, Galina Belaia, Adol'f Urban, Marietta Chudakova, Aleksandr Chudakov, and Lidiia Ginzburg; the literary journals *Druzhba narodov* and *Literaturnoe obozrenie*; writers Aleksandr Kushner and Andrei Voznesensky (his religious poetry, for instance). Village prose writers, neither Socialist Realist nor liberal nor experimental, advocated a return to pre-Soviet values.

20 For more on Bitov's affinity to Olesha, see the notes to my analysis of Bitov's "The Sun" in the next chapter.

21 Chances, conversations with Bitov, May, 1987, Princeton.
   For examples of Goliavkin's writings, see Viktor Goliavkin, *Odin, Dva, Tri ... Povesti* (Leningrad, 1978); Viktor Goliavkin, in Muza Konstantinovna Pavlova, *Chto ia liubliu* (n.p., n.d.), pp. 9–30; Viktor Goliavkin, *Ia zhdu vas vsegda s interesom* (Moscow, 1980); Viktor Goliavkin, *Arfa boks. Roman* (Leningrad, 1969).

22 Chances, conversations with Bitov, May, 1987, Princeton.
   "Liudi, pobrivshiesia v subbotu," in Andrei Bitov, "Chuzhaia sobaka i drugie rasskazy," in *Chast' rechi, Al'manakh literartury i iskusstva*, 2–3 (1981–2), pp. 82–5. The second and third stories he wrote are also in his collection: "Rasskaz," pp. 77–9 and "Strakh," pp. 79–80. Chances, conversations with Bitov, May, 1987, Princeton.
   Two of Bitov's earliest stories came out in Soviet journals in 1987 and 1988. Andrei Bitov, "Avtobus," *Studencheskii meridian*, no. 8, 1988, pp. 31–6. Andrei Bitov, "Liudi, pobrivshiesia v subbotu," *Teatral'naia zhizn'*, no. 16, 1987, p. 23.
   Four of Bitov's mini-stories (three in translation; one, in translation and in Russian) from his unpublished collection, *With Bread in Mouth (S khlebom vo rtu)*, 1959–60, appear in "A. Bitov: from *With Bread in Mouth*," translated by Beckie Barker, in the journal *Cherez* (Department of Slavic Languages and Literatures, University of Texas at Austin), vol. 1, no. 1, 1977, pp. 26–39. The stories are "So There You Are," pp. 27–9; "And On Television ...," pp. 29–33; "The Chinese," p. 33; "Blue Blood," pp. 34–6; and "Golubaia krov'," pp. 37–9.

In her introduction, Barker explains that *With Bread in Mouth* was a samizdat collection written by Bitov. Although she states that Bitov knew the literature of Russian absurdist Oberiu writers, she does not mention Kharms, a major Oberiu writer.

Much later, in 1983, in an article/interview on humor and irony, Bitov mentions Kharms by name. He sees him as an exception to the Russian tradition because of Kharms' "organic eccentricity," the attempt to unite, within himself, eccentricity in life and in literature. Andrei Bitov, "Pokhval'noe slovo chudakam . . .," *Literaturnaia gazeta*, September 7, 1983, p. 5.

23 *Chast' rechi*, pp. 77–9.

24 Daniil Kharms, "Skazka," *Izbrannoe*, ed. George Gibian (Würzburg: Jal-Verlag, 1974), pp. 281–4.

25 Andrei Bitov, Columbia University talk, New York City, April 28, 1987.

26 When he filled out his visa for his 1987 visit to the United States, he designated Georgia as one of his intended stops, not because he wanted to go to America's Georgia, but because he had been to the Soviet Union's Georgia. An essay, "Birds" ("Ptitsy"), contains, in a passage about butterflies, a witty aside to Vladimir Vladimirovich. He has Nabokov in mind (Chances, conversations with Bitov, Moscow, December, 1980), but does not state this outright in the text. At the time he wrote the essay, it would have been difficult to mention Nabokov's name in Soviet publications, yet a careful reader could catch in his/her literary net the oblique reference to Nabokov. *Pushkin House* opens with a scene describing a dead body. The narrator undercuts the tragedy; he tells the reader that he does not know why this death makes him laugh.

27 In conversation, Bitov claims never to have read Bely's *Petersburg*. Chances, conversations with Bitov, May, 1987, Princeton. He is a great admirer of the others. In 1980, he spoke of his love for Pushkin, Gogol, and Zoshchenko. Chances, conversations with Bitov, Moscow, December, 1980.

28 Bitov thinks of himself as belonging to that tradition. See his comments in Ted Ruehl, "Soviet Prose Writer Bitov Discusses Work, Life As Contemporary Artist," *The Daily Princetonian*, May 8, 1987, p. 4.

29 Bitov, as quoted in "Bitov: l'énergie de l'erreur," *Magazine littéraire*, March, 1988, pp. 40–1.

30 Ewa Berard Zarzycka, "Andrei Bitov: 'Ne pas marcher au même pas que l'Histoire, mais rester soi-même'" [Interview with Andrei Bitov], *La quinzaine littéraire*, Feb. 1–15, 1989, p. 7.

31 Bitov states, "I think of myself as being not at all in the avant garde

tradition, but in the classical tradition ... I always look to Pushkin and Gogol ..." Bitov, "Konflikty i kontakty" [Interview with Andrei Bitov], *V mire knig*, no. 11, 1987, p. 76.

32 I am grateful to Robert Maguire and Catharine Nepomnyashchy for their illuminating comments on this aspect of Soviet literature.

33 Andrei Bitov, "The Habit of Fear," *Index on Censorship*, vol. 17, no. 5, May, 1988, p. 11.

34 Bitov, as interviewed in "... I nikto ne znaet, chto delat' s ètoi stranoi ...", in Andrei Karaulov, *Vokrug Kremlia, Kniga politicheskikh dialogov* (Moscow, 1990), p. 20.

35 Bitov, "Konflikty," p. 76.

36 He admits that he has forgotten the specifics of his training. Chances, conversations with Bitov, May, 1987, Princeton.

37 See, for instance, his discussion of geological changes in relation to a story he was thinking of writing. Bitov, "Postskriptum cherez piatnadtsat' let," in "Pastoral' xx veka," in Bitov, *Stat'i iz romana*, pp. 97–8. Also, see his comments on geological and historical changes in Bitov, "Polët s geroem," in Bitov, *Stat'i*, p. 314.

38 I am thankful to Mark von Hagen for his insights on Soviet geology.

39 Ted Ruehl, "Soviet Prose Writer," p. 4.

40 Bitov, "Raznye dni," p. 6.

41 See, for example, "Vybor natury" in Andrei Bitov, *Sem' puteshestvii* (Leningrad, 1976), pp. 523–91.

42 Andrei Bitov, "Draw It and Live in It" ("Narisuem–budem zhit' [Kinopovest']," in Bitov, *Aptekarskii ostrov*, pp. 147–247, and Andrei Bitov, "The Wildlife Preserve" ("Zapovednik"), in Bitov, *Voskresnyi den'*, pp. 202–62. Bitov's scenario, "Zapovednik," served as the basis for the film, "On Thursday and Never Again" ("V chetverg i bol'she nikogda"), 1977, directed by Anatoly Èfros, later to replace Yuri Liubimov as Chief Director of Moscow's Theatre on the Taganka. Music was by composer Dmitry Shostakovich, and one of the actors was the renowned Innokenty Smoktunovsky.
    Bitov's film scenarios repeat his major themes. They are of inferior literary quality. Dialogue and "objective" third-person narration are not Bitov's forte. The author excludes the scenarios from his literary oeuvre, and I agree with his assessment. Chances, conversations with Bitov, Moscow, August, 1988.

43 He asserts that she taught him a tremendous amount. Chances, conversations with Bitov, May, 1987, Princeton.

44 See Tynianov's articles on film in Iu.N. Tynianov, *Poètika. Istoriia literatury. Kino* (Moscow, 1977), pp. 320–48.

45 Lidiia Ginzburg, "Tynianov–literaturoved," in her *O starom i novom. Stat'i i ocherki* (Leningrad, 1982), pp. 302–27.

46 Bitov, *Stat'i*, passim.
47 Lidiia Ginzburg, "Pole napriazheniia." Interview with Lidiia Ginzburg, *Literaturnaia gazeta*, January 5, 1986, p. 7. Ginzburg said, "In the formal sense of that word, I have almost no disciples ... But my contacts with young people have been enormously meaningful in my life. Young writers, perhaps, have learned something from me, not in a direct, didactic sense, but indirectly ... I'll name here only Andrei Bitov, Aleksandr Kushner. One of them has become a genuine prose writer; the other, a genuine poet ..."
48 *Ibid.*, p. 7.
49 Lidiia Ginzburg, *O psikhologicheskoi proze* (Leningrad, 1971); *O literaturnom geroe* (Leningrad, 1979).
50 He agreed that this idea had merit. Chances, conversations with Bitov, May, 1987, Princeton; August, 1988, Moscow; December, 1990, Moscow. Vladimir Lavrov notes this tendency in Bitov's works. Vladimir Lavrov, *Formula tvorchestva. Knigi o zhizni i iskusstve v sovremennoi literature* (Leningrad, 1986), pp. 201–9.
51 Andrei Bitov, "Ekologiia slova," in Bitov, *Stat'i*, pp. 43–8.
52 Andrei Bitov, "Nikanor Ivanych i vedomstva ...' *Literaturnaia gazeta*, March 13, 1965, p. 2.
53 Andrei Bitov, "Izobrazhenie i slovo," *Neva*, no. 8, 1970, p. 12.
54 Andrei Bitov, "Masterstvo–eto garmoniia (Beseda s pisatelem A. Bitovym)." Interviewed by M. Mamatsashvili and V. Khanumian. *Molodezh' Gruzii*, Nov. 19, 1981, p. 4.
55 Bitov comment to Chances, New York City, May 7, 1987.
56 Andrei Bitov, "Prorvat' krug," *Novyi mir*, 12 (1986), p. 249.
57 Bitov, *Stat'i*, p. 222.
58 *Ibid.*, p. 288.
59 *Ibid.*, p. 217.
60 Andrei Bitov, "Portret khudozhnika v smelosti," *Moskovskie novosti*, February 15, 1987, p. 13.
61 Bitov talk, Columbia University, April 28, 1987. In a 1987 interview, quoted in an epigraph to this chapter, he asserts that everything he writes is part of one house. Bitov, "Razyne dni cheloveka," p. 6.
62 See, for example, Lavrov, *Formula*. Gerald Mikkelson argues that "derevenskaia proza" and other tendencies in contemporary Soviet literature are beginning to resemble one another. Question and answer period, panel on Soviet literature, AAASS Annual Convention, New Orleans, Louisiana, November, 1986.
63 A. Bocharov, *Beskonechnost' poiska. Khudozhestvennye poiski sovremennoi sovetskoi prozy* (Moscow, 1982).
64 Vasilii Belov, *Lad. Ocherki o narodnoi estetike* (Moscow, 1982).
65 Andrei Bitov, "Ekologiia slova," in Bitov, *Stat'i*, p. 44. The topic of

ecology has, for the past few years, been widely discussed in Soviet publications. For instance, Dmitrii Likhachev wrote an article, "The Ecology of Culture," calling for the conservation of culture in the same way in which we conserve our natural resources. Dmitrii Likhachev, "Èkologiia kul'tury," in his *Zametki o russkom* (Moscow, 1984), pp. 54–61.

66 Andrei Bitov, "Fotografiia Pushkina," *Znamia*, no. 1, 1987, pp. 98–120; "Chelovek v peizazhe," *Novyi mir*, no. 3, 1987, pp. 64–99; and "È. Taird-Boffin. Prepodavatel' simmetrii. Vol'nyi perevod s inostrannogo Andreia Bitova," *Iunost'*, no. 4, 1987, pp. 12–50.

67 My book was already in press when volume one of Bitov's collected works came out. Andrei Bitov, *Sobranie sochinenii. Povesti i rasskazy*, vol. 1 (Moscow, 1991). In the volume are groups of stories and works that have appeared in other collections. (The two exceptions are the story "The Bus" ["Avtobus"], pp. 45–57, and "Friday, Evening" ["Piatnitsa, vecher"], pp. 23–8.) I discuss the works, except "The Bus" and "Friday, Evening," in the relevant sections of my book.

Bitov's datings of his early works are in appendices to Hagen's *The Stories*, pp. 226–31. The arrangement of works in a collection is Bitov's choice, except where I indicate otherwise.

2 *"The Big Balloon": terrestrial and celestial spheres*

1 Andrei Bitov, "Biography," Appendix, pp. 4–8, in Frederick R. Croen, "A translation of 'The Wheel' of Andrei Bitov," Princeton University Senior Thesis, 1974. The biographical material on pages 18–20 of this chapter is based primarily on the Bitov autobiography in Croen's appendix.
2 *Ibid.*, p. 6.
3 *Ibid.*
4 *Ibid.*
5 D. S. Mirsky, *A History of Russian Literature* (New York: Alfred A. Knopf, 1973), p. 491.
6 Andrei Bitov, "Biography," in Croen, "A Translation."
7 *Ibid.*, p. 7.
8 *Ibid.*
9 Priscilla Meyer, "Andrei Georgievich Bitov," *The Modern Encyclopedia of Russian and Soviet Literature*, ed. Harry B. Weber, vol. 3 (Academic International Press: Gulf Breeze, Florida, 1979), p. 32.
10 A. Bitov, "Masterstvo," p. 4.
11 Bitov, "Biography," in Croen, "A Translation," p. 7.
12 "Bitov," in Wolfgang Kasack, *Lexikon der russischen literatur ab 1917* (Stuttgart: Alfred Kröner, 1976), p. 57.

13 Andrei Bitov, "Odna strana (Puteshestvie Borisa Murashova)," in Andrei Bitov, *Bol'shoi shar* (Moscow, 1963), pp. 5–104. Hereafter in my section on "One Country," I shall place page references to this edition in parentheses immediately following the quotation.

14 Boris becomes Sergei in other editions of "Odna strana." The character's name remains the same in Andrei Bitov, "Odna strana (Puteshestvie Borisa Murashova)," in Andrei Bitov, *Dachnaia mestnost'. Povesti* (Moscow, 1967), pp. 5–69. In later versions of the story, the subtitle is changed, as is the major protagonist's name. The new subtitle is "Puteshestvie molodogo cheloveka." These changes appear in the version of "Odna strana" in Andrei Bitov, *Puteshestvie k drugu detstva* (Leningrad, 1968); *Sem' puteshestvii* (Leningrad, 1976); and *Kniga puteshestvii* (Moscow, 1986).

15 For more on Bitov's childhood memories, see David Remnick, "Andrei Bitov, In Search of the Voice of Memory. The Russian Novelist and the Possibilities of Freedom," *Washington Post*, September 8, 1988, pp. C1, C8.

16 I am thankful to Robert Maguire for suggesting that Bitov might be referring, here, to the way in which literature works.

17 This passage is reminiscent of a section of Icelandic Nobel laureate Halldor Laxness' *The Atom Station*. The Laxness paragraph, in a chapter entitled "Phoning," is:

> I think that was our conversation, as nearly as one can recall a conversation when a girl talks to a man and a man to a girl, for ... the words ... say least of all, ...; what really informs us is the inflection of the voice ..., the breathing, the heart-beat, the muscles round the mouth and eyes, the dilation and contraction of the pupils, ... the chain of mysterious reactions in the nerves and the secretions from hidden glands ...; all that is the essence of a conversation – the words are more or less incidental. (Laxness, *Atom Station*, p. 176)

18 Wolf Schmid, "Verfremdung bei Andrej Bitov," *Wiener Slawistischer Almanach*, vol. 5, 1980, pp. 25–49.

19 Schmid links Bitov's "ostranenie" and "ostrovidenie" to ethics in reference to one scene in Bitov's "Life in Windy Weather" ("Zhizn' v vetrenuiu pogodu"). Schmid, "Verfremdung," p. 47.

20 Bitov, "Biography," in Croen, "A Translation," p. 1.

21 V. Ermilov, "Budem tochnymi," *Literaturnaia gazeta*, April 16, 1964, p. 3.

22 L. Anninskii, "Tochka opory. Èticheskie problemy sovremennoi prozy," *Don*, no. 6, 1968, p. 170; G. A. Belaia, "Rozhdenie novykh stilevykh form kak protsess preodoleniia 'neitral'nogo stilia'," in *Teoriia literaturnykh stilei. Mnogoobrazie stilei sovetskoi literatury. Voprosy tipologii*, ed. N. K. Gei *et al.* (Moscow, 1978), p. 476; V. A.

Apukhtina, *Sovremennaia sovetskaia proza (60-e–nachalo 70-kh godov)* (Moscow, 1977), p. 24; N. A. Kozhevnikova, "O tipakh povestvovaniia v sovetskoi proze," in *Voprosy iazyka sovremennoi russkoi literatury* (Moscow, 1971), pp. 148–9; Wolf Schmid, "Thesen zur innovatorischen Poetik der russischen Gegenwartsprosa," *Wiener Slawistischer Almanach*, vol. 4, 1979, p. 75.

23 V. A. Apukhtina, *Sovremennaia*, p. 23; L. Anninskii, "Tochka," p. 173.

24 L. Anninskii, "Tochka," p. 170; Schmid, "Thesen," p. 75.

25 Sylva Tvrdíková, "Modifikace hrdiny a žánru (Andrej Bitov)," *Bulletin ruského jazyka a literatura*, vol. 20, 1976, p. 53.

26 Bitov, "Biography," in Croen, "A Translation," pp. 4–8.

27 Studies of *La Strada* emphasize, among other things, its episodic, fragmentary nature, its open form, and its ability to confront fundamental issues about the meaning of life. See, for example, Edward Murray, *Fellini the Artist* (New York: Ungar Publishing Company, 1976), chapter 6, "La Strada," pp. 62–83, and Stuart Rosenthal, *The Cinema of Federico Fellini* (South Brunswick, New Jersey and New York: A. S. Barnes and Company, 1976), passim.

28 Chances, conversation with Bitov, December, 1980, Moscow.

29 Mihail Lermontov, *A Hero of Our Time*, trans. Vladimir and Dmitri Nabokov (Garden City, New York: Doubleday and Company, Inc., 1958), vi–ix.

30 Mikhail Lermontov, *Geroi nashego vremeni* in *Izbrannye*, vol. ii, p. 382.

31 Tynianov, "O 'Puteshestvii v Arzrum'," in Iu. N. Tynianov, *Pushkin i ego sovremenniki* (Moscow, 1969), p. 200.

32 Iurii Trifonov, "Sredi knig," *Iunost'*, no. 4, 1964, p. 74.
  The critical response to "One Country" was mixed. Most assessments, whether positive or negative, tackled style, genre, and/ or the place of "One Country" in the literary tradition. One critic, V. Akimov, was distressed by what he termed the "immature" quality of Bitov's first book. Frustrated by the "imperceptible" plot, or lack of plot, he saw "One Country" as a set of scattered pieces of facts yielding no insight into life. V. Akimov, "Osvoenie vremeni," *Zvezda*, no. 4, 1964, p. 211. Another critic deemed the foray into literary experimentation mere monkey tricks. Vsevolod Voevodin, "Otvetstvennost' talanta," *Literaturnaia gazeta*, March 24, 1964, p. 3. A third found the genre boring and eclectic. Vladimir Solov'ev, "Problema talanta," in *Puti k khudozhestvennoi pravde. Stat'i o sovremennoi sovetskoi proze*, ed. A. A. Urban (Leningrad, 1968), p. 264. The anonymous author of one piece claimed that the ideas in "One Country" were good, but that they did not fully come to fruition in the artistic structure. The critic continued, "They [the ideas – E.C.] swim on its [the artistic

structure's] surface, like sparkles of fat in bouillon." "Kogo my berem v druz'ia?" *Detskaia literatura*, no. 3, 1969, p. 12. These negative comments were typical of Stalinist old-guard literary criticism that demanded simplistic plots.

Positive reactions to "One Country" outweighed the negative. Soviet writer Iurii Trifonov complimented his young colleague on his originality. Trifonov used the word "sharp-vision" ("ostrovid-enie") to characterize Bitov's sensitive powers of observation. Iurii Trifonov, "Sredi knig," p. 74. Trifonov's assessment was mostly favorable, although he qualified his praise by faulting Bitov for occasional lapses into a feuilleton-like, instead of humorous, style, and a saccharine, instead of sincere, quality.

33 One of the only people to discuss the story was Iurii Trifonov, who rated it and "A Nothing" ("Fig") as the best stories in *The Big Balloon* because of their simplicity, sincerity, and lack of plot. Iu. Trifonov, "Sredi knig," p. 74. The most extensive discussion of the story, to date, is in Kurt Cony Shaw, "Chasing the Red Balloon: Psychological Separation in the Early Fiction of Andrej Bitov, 1958–1962." Diss. University of Kansas, 1988, pp. 23–40.

34 Bitov, "Babushkina piala," in Bitov, *Bolshoi shar*, p. 112.

35 *Ibid.*, p. 107. Bitov identifies the quotation only by the name of its author, Takuboku. "Babushkina piala," in *My – molodye* (Moscow, 1969), p. 403. The anthology of young writers also included selections written by, among others, Chinghiz Aitmatov, Iurii Kazakov, Vasilii Shukshin, Vasil' Bykov, Vasilii Belov, Evgenii Evtushenko, and Andrei Voznesensky.

A version of the story which predates *The Big Balloon* by three years contains no epigraph. Andrei Bitov, "Babushkina piala," in *Molodoi Leningrad. Al'manakh, 1960* (Leningrad, 1960), p. 245.

Bitov's epigraph is from Part One of "Insolvable Discord," a long poem by Japanese poet Ishikawa Takuboku (1886–1912). The three Takuboku stanzas preceding the one which Bitov uses refer to the narrator's parents' aging. The poem begins with the words, "My father and mother are aged ..." Ishikawa Takuboku, "Insolvable Discord," in *A Handful of Sand*, trans. Shio Sakanishi (Westport, Connecticut: Greenwood Press Publishers, 1976), p. 28. For a discussion of Takuboku, see Makoto Ueda, *Modern Japanese Poets and the Nature of Literature* (Stanford, California: Stanford University Press, 1983), pp. 95–136.

36 Bitov's explorations of a child's psychology in "A Nothing" and other stories about children are called "psychological études" by one critic. S. Sergeev, "Sredi knig i zhurnalov," *Don*, no. 2, 1969, p. 174.

37 Andrei Bitov, "Fig," in Bitov, *Bol'shoi shar*, p. 116. Hereafter in my

section on "A Nothing," I shall place page references to this edition in parentheses immediately following the quotation.

38 See Shaw, "Chasing," pp. 126, 161.

39 Andrei Bitov, "Solntse," in Bitov, *Bol'shoi shar*, pp. 124–9. Hereafter in my section on "The Sun," I shall place page references to this edition in parentheses immediately following the quotation.

40 Schmid, "Verfremdung," pp. 37–9. Hagen, *The Stories*, pp. 27–9; Shaw, "Chasing," pp. 56–69.
    Other analyses of "The Sun" miss the mark. One article criticizes the lack of poetic quality of the story when compared to other works in *The Big Balloon*. V. Ermilov, "Budem tochnymi," p. 3. Another evaluation features the characters' behavior and the plotlessness as key factors in the story. E. A. Shubin, *Sovremennyi russkii rasskaz. Voprosy poètiki zhanra* (Leningrad, 1974), p. 119.

41 In the Soviet Union, the expression "blue screen" ("goluboi èkran") refers to television.

42 This sentence is like a sentence, near the beginning of Olesha's *Envy* (*Zavist'*), which uses the same descriptive method: "The blue and pink world of the room moves around in the mother-of-pearl lens of the button" ("Goluboi i rozovyi mir komnaty khodit krugom v perlamutrovom ob"ektive pugovitsy"). Iurii Olesha, *Zavist'*, in Iurii Olesha, *Izbrannoe* (Moscow, 1974), p. 14.
    Wolf Schmid draws parallels between Bitov's style and Olesha's experimental prose (see Schmid's "Verfremdung"). I. Motiashov, "Otvetstvennost' khudozhnika (Zametki kritiki)," in *Voprosy literatury*, no. 12, 1968, p. 17, sees a parallel between Bitov's "Journey to a Childhood Friend" ("Puteshestvie k drugu detstva") and *Envy*. Priscilla Meyer suggests an Olesha influence in "Life in Windy Weather," but says that Bitov denies the influence. Priscilla Meyer, "Andrei Georgievich Bitov," p. 32. I. Grinberg writes of a similarity between Olesha's and Bitov's, "acute sensation of colors, sounds and scents." I. Grinberg, "'A rasti emu–v nebo ...','" *Literaturnaia gazeta*, January, 1965, p. 3.

43 Andrei Bitov, "Inostrannyi iazyk," in Bitov, *Bol'shoi shar*, p. 139.

44 As quoted in V. Geideko, "Ot opisanii k osmysleniiu (Zametki o sovremennom rasskaze)," *Sibirskie ogni*, no. 3, 1965, p. 174.

45 For more on this approach to the superfluous man, see Ellen Chances, *Conformity's Children: An Approach to the Superfluous Man in Russian Literature* (Columbus, Ohio: Slavica Publishers, Inc., 1978).

46 Andrei Bitov, "Strashnaia sila," in Bitov, *Bol'shoi shar*, p. 150. Hereafter in my section on "A Terrible Force," I shall place page references to this edition in parentheses immediately following the quotation.

47 Shaw highlights the isolated Vitia's psychological mechanism of withdrawal from reality as a response to the cruelty of the collective. Shaw, "Chasing," pp. 126–42.

48 Andrei Bitov, "Dver'," in Bitov, *Bol'shoi shar*, p. 181.

49 V. Geideko, "Ot opisanii," *Sibirskie ogni*, p. 177.

50 Olga Hassanoff Bakich, "A New Type of Character in the Soviet Literature of the 1960s: The Early Works of Andrei Bitov," *Canadian Slavonic Papers*, vol. 23, no. 2, June, 1981, p. 127.

51 One could also argue that the child's keen imagination, demonstrated by his creating an ox out of a crack on the wall, could invent the would-be lover's betrayal. This viewpoint would favor Geideko's argument.

52 Shaw interprets the story this way. "Chasing," p. 110.

53 In another context, Swiss psychoanalyst Alice Miller describes the mechanism whereby society/adults/authority figures, because of their own unresolved conflicts with their parents, insist that the child's view of the world is wrong when, in fact, the adults were the ones distorting reality. Miller writes that it is incorrect to assume that the child is imagining an incident of abuse. She claims that the incident did take place and that the adults, whether consciously or unconsciously, sometimes do not want children to become aware of the truth. Alice Miller, *Thou Shalt Not Be Aware. Society's Betrayal of the Child*, trans. Hildegarde and Hunter Hannum (New York: Farrar, Straus and Giroux, 1984).

54 Alla Marchenko also attributes symbolic significance to the door. For her, the boy cannot open the door because he is a child, and the woman is an adult. Alla Marchenko, "Sredi knig," *Iunost'*, no. 8, 1969, p. 76.

55 Bitov, "Dver'," p. 175.

56 N. Bazhin unjustly takes Bitov to task for failing to talk about the "result" ("itog") of Boris Karlovich's life. N. Bazhin, "Nash drug," *Neva*, no. 1, 1965, p. 191. The same attack could be levelled at Chekhov with respect to "A Boring Story." Bitov, like Chekhov, was concerned with other issues.

57 Andrei Bitov, "Bol'shoi shar," in Bitov, *Bol'shoi shar*, p. 208. Hereafter in my section on "The Big Balloon," I shall place page references to this edition in parentheses immediately following the quotation.

58 The film received a "spontaneous ovation" (Gene Moskowitz, *Variety*, May 16, 1956, p. 6) and won a special award at the 1956 Cannes Film Festival (Bosley Crowther, review of "The Red Balloon," *New York Times*, March 12, 1957, p. 38).

59 Chances, conversation with Bitov, Moscow, August, 1988.

60 See the discussion of Lamorisse (pp. 185–91) in a 1958 article, "Novaia shkola frantsuzskogo korotkometrazhnogo fil'ma," reproduced in S.I. Iutkevich's *Frantsiia–kadr za kadrom. O liudiakh, fil'makh, spektakliakh, knigakh* (Moscow, 1970), pp. 139–93.

61 Another fact to keep in mind is Latvian director G. Frank's prizewinning 1961 film, "Belye kolokol'chiki" ("White Bluebells"), which has been described by Soviet film historians as a "... remenistsentsi[a] na temu 'Krasnogo shara' Lamorissa...," *Istoriia sovetskogo kino*,ed. S. Ginzburg *et al.* (Moscow, 1978), vol. 4, p. 279. In this film, a small girl wanders through the city looking for a bouquet of white flowers that she had dropped. *Ibid.*, p. 279.

62 Albert Lamorisse, *The Red Balloon* (Garden City, New York: Doubleday and Company, Inc., 1956), n.p.

63 *Ibid.*, n.p.

64 *Ibid.*

65 French film director François Truffaut found the film "Le Ballon Rouge" objectionable because "... out of fear of being dismissed simply as an 'enchanter,' Lamorisse shifts the focus and pretends to raise his fantasy to the level of tragedy." François Truffaut, "Albert Lamorisse, 'Le Ballon Rouge'," in *The Films in My Life*, trans. Leonard Mayhew (New York: Simon and Schuster, 1978), p. 221.

3 *"Such a Long Childhood"*: growing pains

1 Andrei Bitov, *Takoe dolgoe detstvo* (Leningrad, 1965), pp. 179–80. Hereafter in my section on *Such a Long Childhood*, I shall place page references to this edition in parentheses immediately following the quotation.

2 Bitov, "A Twentieth-Century Pastoral," in "Introduction," Grant Matevosian, *The Orange Herd* (Moscow: Progress Publishers, 1976), trans. Fainna Glagoleva, p. 9. A Russian version, "Pastoral', XX vek," appears in Bitov, *Stat'i*, p. 88.

3 A failure to understand this method has caused critics to misinterpret *Such a Long Childhood*. Vladimir Solov'ev complains about the work's lack of wholeness. Pointing to the inconsistency between the first and second halves of the book, he writes disparagingly of the fact that the reader does not grasp the meaning until halfway through the book. Vladimir Solov'ev, "Problema talanta," *Puti k khudozhestvennoi pravde. Stat'i o sovremennoi sovetskoi proze*, ed. A. A. Urban (Leningrad, 1968), p. 23.

4 L. Anninskii, "Tochka opory," p. 170. The dates are 1960 for "One Country" and 1959–61, for *Such a Long Childhood*. In *Seven Journeys* (*Sem' puteshestvii*), a 1976 collection of his travel literature, Bitov

places *Such a Long Childhood* first and "One Country" immediately afterwards. Andrei Bitov, "Takoe dolgoe detstvo (Prizyvnik)," pp. 5–134 and "Odna strana (Puteshestvie molodogo cheloveka)," pp. 135–200 in *Sem' puteshestvii* (Leningrad, 1976).

5 The *Sem'puteshestvii* version includes the specific detail, "68°37'". Bitov, *Sem'*, p. 10. The *Takoe* version does not include this information. Bitov, *Takoe*, p. 10.

6 Solov'ev, "Problema," p. 271; Genrikh Mitin, "Proshchanie s detstvom," *Smena*, no. 12, 1965, p. 19.

7 Mikael Klefter, "Rejsemotivet hos Andrej Bitov," *Slavica othiniensia* (Odense [Denmark]), *Universitets Slaviske Institut*, vol. 4, 1981, p. 31.

8 Schmid, "Verfremdung," p. 28.

9 O. H. Bakich speaks of Kirill's search for identity and values and of the ". . . intense focus on the inner life and thought processes . . ." of the heroes in Bitov's early works. Bakich, "A New Type," pp. 125, 127. She writes of the same types of searches in the prose of V. Aksenov, A. Gladilin, and A. Kuznetsov.

10 Deming Brown, "Narrative Devices in the Contemporary Soviet Russian Short Story: Intimacy and Irony," in *American Contributions to the Seventh International Congress of Slavists*, Warsaw, August 21–7, 1973, vol. II, *Folklore and Literature*, ed. Victor Terras (The Hague: Mouton, 1973), p. 56. Brown's valuable article (*Ibid.*, pp. 53–74) provides a very useful analysis of this and other devices used by a number of contemporary writers (Vasilii Aksenov, Bitov, Anatolii Gladilin, I. Grekova, Fazil' Iskander, Vladimir Voinovich, and Il'ia Zverev) in order to achieve a sense of immediacy and intimacy in their works.

N. A. Kozhevnikova discusses the common practice among some Soviet writers (Aksenov, Bitov, Rasputin, Trifonov, Shukshin, Zalygin) of the 1960s and 1970s of filtering the world through a protagonist's consciousness. "O sootnoshenii rechi avtora i personazha," in *Iazykovye protsessy sovremennoi russkoi khudozhestvennoi literatury. Proza*, ed. A. I. Gorshkov and A. D. Grigor'eva (Moscow, 1977), p. 13.

Schmid emphasizes the perceiving consciousness of Bitov's travelers, as they filter the outside world through their subjective vision in order to achieve self-definition. Schmid, "Thesen," p. 62.

11 Adol'f Urban, writing about the jogging scene, emphasizes Kirill's propensity to observe himself. Bitov's heroes, he explains, engage in intense self-examination. "V razmyshlenii i deistvii," *Zvezda*, no. 12, 1971, pp. 190, 191.

12 Some analyses criticize Bitov for not subjecting the immature Kirill to moral scrutiny. G. Brovman, *Problemy i geroi sovremennoi prozy*.

Kriticheskoe obozrenie (Moscow, 1966), p. 246. N. Klado objects that in *Such a Long Childhood*, Bitov does not offer wisdom about life's meaning. " 'Osoboe sostoianie' geroia," *Literaturnaia Rossiia*, Feb. 5, 1965, p. 10. Avgusta Anan'eva also misses the point when she attacks Bitov (and Aksenov) for their "... immature vision and comprehension of the world ..." "Preuvelichenie chuvstv," *Sibirskie ogni*, no. 2, 1966, p. 172.

The point of Bitov's book is to show Kirill's movement toward an ethical, "harmonious," intelligent view of life. Klefter, "Rejsemotivet;" Mitin, "Proshchanie;" Schmid, "Verfremdung;" and A. A. Terpelova, "Geroi i zhanr (O nekotorykh osobennostiakh povesti 50–60k gg.)," *Russkaia literatura XX veka. Sovetskaia literatura. Moskovskii gosudarstvennyi pedagogicheskii institut. Uchënye zapiski*, 456 (1971), pp. 244–57, all understand the importance to *Such a Long Childhood* of this search for essential truths.

As in the rest of his interesting dissertation on Bitov's early fiction, Shaw, in his chapter on *Such a Long Childhood*, emphasizes "psychological separations" within Kirill's personality that keep him alienated from reality. Shaw sees this work as different from the bulk of Bitov's early fiction because Kirill finally steps away from his isolation. Shaw, "Chasing," pp. 199–239.

13 V. I. Gusev makes this assessment, but does not substantiate his claims. *V predchuvstvii novogo. O nekotorykh chertakh literatury shestidesiatykh godov* (Moscow, 1974), p. 154.

4 *Dacha District: Automatic-pilot living and creative living*

1 Andrei Bitov, *Dachnaia mestnost'. Povesti* (Moscow, 1967).
2 Igor' Zolotusskii correctly views "Journey to a Childhood Friend" as primarily an investigation of a person's inner life. Bitov, writes Zolotusskii, uses the external world more and more as a pretext for delving into a human being's internal world. Igor' Zolotusskii, "Ostriëm vnutr'," in his *Teplo dobra* (Moscow, 1970), p. 194.
3 Mikael Klefter mentions the past/future contrast of "Journey to a Childhood Friend" and *Such A Long Childhood*. Klefter, "Rejsemotivet," p. 32.
4 T. Khmel'nitskaia writes, "The ... parodying of newspaper and essay stock phrases and their recurring juxtaposition with 'life as it is' ... form its ["Journey's" – E.C.] base." T. Khmel'nitskaia, "Mezhdu pomyslom i postupkom. O psikhologicheskoi proze," in *V seredine semidesiatikh. Literatura nashikh dnei*, compiler I. S. Èventov (Leningrad, 1977), p. 207.
5 Andrei Bitov, "Puteshestvie k drugu detstva," *Dachnaia mestnost'*, p.

74. Hereafter in my section on "Journey to a Childhood Friend," I shall place page references to this edition in parentheses immediately following the quotation.

6 This exchange is, perhaps, Bitov's tongue-in-cheek response to those critics who had upbraided him for not depicting positive hero types. Precisely this type of criticism can be found in a later anonymous review of "Journey to a Childhood Friend." The author rebukes Bitov for his attack on the positive hero. "Kogo my berëm v druz'ia?" *Detskaia literatura*, no. 3, 1969, p. 14.

7 Tvrdíková claims that the narrator builds the model of a hero while, at the same time, not believing in the existence of such a type. The hero of "Journey to a Childhood Friend," according to this view, is the narrator. Tvrdíková, "Modifikace," p. 55.

8 Lev Anninskii speaks of Bitov's peeling away, like an onion, the layers from the legend of Genrikh to reveal the total emptiness within him. L. Anninskii, "Tochka," p. 173.

9 Bakich's approach to "Journey" is that Bitov implicitly condemns both Genrikh and the "indecisive" narrator. Bakich, "A New Type," p. 133.

10 Bakich, "A New Type," p. 132.

11 Anatolii Lanshchikov believes that the device of inserting newspaper articles into the text detracts from Bitov's "journey". He praises the author's psychological depictions and his sensitivity to details. Anatolii Lanshchikov, "Ot literaturnykh fiktsii k literature deistvitel'nosti," *Moskva*, no. 3, 1969, p. 214.

12 Khmel'nitskaia, "Mezhdu," p. 207.

13 *Ibid.*, p. 208. Khmel'nitskaia borrows the term "autopsychological" heroes from Lidiia Ginzburg, who, explains Khmel'nitskaia, characterizes such heroes as those in whom an author invests his or her own thoughts. Often the narration is in the third person, although the tone is first person. The boundary between author and character is erased. L.Ia. Ginzberg, *O psikhologicheskoi proze*, as referred to in Khmel'nitskaia, *Ibid.*, p. 204. Khmel'nitskaia points out what we have observed: this type of narration is typical of Bitov's style. Khmel'nitskaia, "Mezhdu," pp. 204–5.

14 Khmel'nitskaia, "Mezhdu," p. 208.

15 Bitov does not identify the chapter source of the passage; it is from chapter 11, "Nightgown," *Moby Dick*. Herman Melville, *Moby-Dick or, The Whale* (Indianapolis, Indiana: The Bobbs-Merrill Company, Inc., 1964), pp. 86–7.

16 Melville, *Moby Dick*, p. 86. Bitov, "Sad," in Bitov, *Dachnaia mestnost'*, p. 174.

17 Melville, *Moby Dick*, p. 87. Bitov, "Sad," p. 175.

18 Bitov, "Sad," p. 184.
19 The "strange" book Aleksei is reading is the Bible, a fact that we
   can determine by reading the final section of Bitov's 1990 *Vanishing
   Monakhov*, whose second section is "The Garden" and whose final
   pages, "The Staircase," include an epigraph (identified only as
   "From the book found by Aleksei") from Revelation: "But I have
   this against you, that you have abandoned the love you had at
   first." Bitov, "Lestnitsa," in *Uletaiushchii Monakhov*, p. 148.
      In 1986, Bitov uses the second part of this quotation, in English,
   with attribution to Revelation, as an epigraph to *The Lover*, the
   section of his translated collection of works, *Life in Windy Weather*,
   that contains "The Garden." Bitov, epigraph to *The Lover*, in *Life in
   Windy Weather*, p. 187.
20 Priscilla Meyer, "Andrei Georgievich Bitov," p. 33.
21 *Ibid.*
22 Meyer, "Introduction," in Andrei Bitov, *Life in Windy Weather.
   Short Stories*, ed. Priscilla Meyer (Ann Arbor, Michigan: Ardis
   Publishers, 1986), p. 8.
23 *Ibid.*
24 V. Gusev, "Sovest' i dni cheloveka," in Andrei Bitov, *Dni cheloveka.
   Povesti* (Moscow, 1976), p. 349.
25 V. Oskotskii, "Aleksei Monakhov na randevu," *Literaturnoe obozrenie*, no. 1, 1977, p. 55.
26 Urban, "V razmyshlenii," pp. 190–1.
27 *Ibid.*, p. 190. This Russian folk melody can be heard on the record,
   Lidiia Ruslanova, *Rasskaz o zhizni, Otvety telezriteliam. Pesni* (Melodiia Records M60-42349–50, 1980), Side Two.
28 Urban, "V razmyshlenii," p. 190.
29 Bitov, "Notes from the Corner," in Bitov, *Life in Windy Weather*, p.
   180; Bitov, "Zapiski iz-za ugla," *Novyi mir*, no. 2, 1990, pp. 162–3.
30 Sergei is the protagonist's name in Bitov, *Dachnaia mestnost'*. pp.
   187–222. His name is Alexei in the Ardis translation. (He is Alexei
   in the Ardis volume, *Contemporary Russian Prose*, where the English
   translation in the 1986 Ardis Bitov volume originally appeared:
   "Life in Windy Weather," trans. Carol Luplow and Richard
   Luplow, ed. Priscilla Meyer, in *Contemporary Russian Prose*, ed. Carl
   and Ellendea Proffer [Ann Arbor, Michigan: Ardis Publishers,
   1982], pp. 305–33). He is Sergei when the story appears in Andrei
   Bitov, *Obraz zhizni. Povesti* (Leningrad, 1972), pp. 71–105, and in
   Andrei Bitov, *Voskresnyi den'. Rasskazy, povesti, puteshestviia* (Moscow, 1980), pp. 75–108.
      Bitov changed the character's name to Alexei in the Ardis
   volume of Bitov works so that many of the short stories become

explicitly linked by their focus on the same person at various points in his life.

31 Priscilla Meyer, Afterword, "Autobiography and Truth: Bitov's *A Country Place*," in Bitov, *Life in Windy Weather. Short Stories*, ed. Priscilla Meyer, pp. 365–6. "Notes from around the Corner" appeared for the first time in any language in the Ardis collection, pp. 145–85.

32 *Ibid.*, p. 370.

33 Priscilla Meyer, "Interview with Vasily Pavlovich Aksenov," *Russian Literature Triquarterly*, no. 6, 1973, p. 571.

34 Deming Brown, *Soviet Russian Literature Since Stalin* (Cambridge, England: Cambridge University Press, 1978), p. 196.

35 *Ibid.*, p. 196.

36 Anninskii, "Tochka opory," p. 181.

37 Viacheslav Ivashchenko, "Sredi knig," *Iunost'*, no. 5, 1968, p. 96.

38 V. Kamianov, "Poèticheskii mir prozy," *Literaturnaia Rossiia*, August 9, 1968, p. 20.

39 A. Bocharov, "Krugi khudozhestvennogo konflikta (Razdum'ia nad tekushchei prozoi)," *Voprosy literatury*, no. 5, 1974, p. 61.

40 Urban, "V razmyshlenii," p. 193.

41 V. Sakharov, "Novye geroi Bitova," *Iunost'*, no. 6, 1973, p. 74.

42 A. A. Terpelova, "Geroi i zhanr (O nekotorykh osobennostiakh povesti 50–60-kh gg.)," in *Russkaia literatura XX veka. Sovetskaia literatura. Moskovskii gosudarstvennyi pedagogicheskii institut. Uchënye zapiski*, vol. 456, 1971, p. 252.

43 George Gibian, "The Urban Theme in Recent Soviet Russian Prose: Notes Toward a Typology," *Slavic Review*, vol. 37, no. 1 (1978), p. 46.

44 Igor' Zolotusskii, *Teplo dobra* (Moscow, 1970), pp. 196–7.

45 Schmid, "Verfremdung", p. 40.

46 *Ibid.*, pp. 41–2.

47 *Ibid.*, p. 46.

48 *Ibid.*, pp. 46–7.

49 Priscilla Meyer, "Autobiography and Truth," p. 365.

50 *Ibid.*, p. 366.

51 *Ibid.*, p. 367.

52 *Ibid.*, p. 368.

53 *Ibid.*

54 *Ibid.*, p. 369.

55 *Ibid.*

56 *Ibid.*, p. 371.

57 Ronald Meyer, "Andrej Bitov's *Puškinskij Dom*," Diss. Indiana University, 1986, pp. 28–43.

58 *Ibid.*, pp. 32–3.
59 Hagen, *The Stories*, p. 127. See pp. 127–46 for his discussion of "Life in Windy Weather."
60 *Ibid.*, p. 139.
61 *Ibid.*, p. 128.
62 *Ibid.*
63 *Ibid.*, p. 131.
64 *Ibid.*, p. 128.
65 *Ibid.*, p. 137.
66 *Ibid.*, pp. 137–8.
67 Bitov letter as quoted by Hagen, *The Stories* p. 245. The letter is reproduced in Stephen Hagen, "An Unpublished Letter by Andrei Bitov," *Scottish Slavonic Review*, no. 5, 1985, pp. 108–18.
68 Hagen, *The Stories*, p. 137.
69 *Ibid.*, p. 133.
70 *Ibid.*, p. 132.
71 *Ibid.*, p. 137.
72 Andrei Bitov, "Zhizn' v vetrenuiu pogodu (Dachnaia mestnost')," in Bitov, *Dachnaia mestnost'*, p. 214. Hereafter in my section on "Life in Windy Weather," I shall place page references to this edition in parentheses immediately following the quotation.
73 Bitov, letter to Croen, in Croen, "A Translation," Appendix, p. 1.
74 Hagen, *The Stories*, p. 128 and Priscilla Meyer, "Autobiography and Truth," p. 366.
75 Priscilla Meyer writes that the description of the dacha matches that of Bitov's in-laws' dacha in Toksovo, near Leningrad. Priscilla Meyer, "Autobiography and Truth," p. 365.
76 Priscilla Meyer, "Autobiography and Truth," pp. 367–8.
77 Boris Pasternak, *Stikhotvoreniia i poèmy*. Intro. A. D. Siniavskii (Moscow–Leningrad, 1965), p. 432; English translation by Vladimir Markov and Merrill Sparks, *Modern Russian Poetry* (Indianapolis, Indiana: The Bobbs-Merrill Company, Inc., 1967), p. 605.
78 Ronald Meyer quotes a section of È. Khappenenn's "Commentary," where Khappenenn explains that Bitov had wanted to name the entire collection in which the story appears *Life in Windy Weather* (*Zhizn' v vetrenuiu pogodu*). (Ronald Meyer says that the story came out under the title "Dacha District" ["Dachnaia mestnost'"] in 1967. This is not true. The *book* in which the story "Life in Windy Weather" appeared in 1967, is called *Dacha District* [*Dachnaia mestnost'*]. The story appears there as "Life in Windy Weather" with a subtitle "Dacha District.") Khappenenn writes, "In general it's dangerous [to write about – E.C.] the weather ... They didn't let me call the book *Life in Windy Weather*: What kind of

climate, where is the weather? where is the wind blowing from?" È. Khappenenn, ed., "Kommentarii," unpublished manuscript, p. 47, as quoted by Ronald Meyer, *Andrej*, p. 28; p. 42.

79 Andrei Bitov, "Vkus," in *Literaturnaia Gruziia*, no. 1, 1983, pp. 80–1; Andrei Bitov, "The Taste," in Andrei Bitov, *Life in Windy Weather*, p. 351.

80 Bitov, "The Taste," p. 351; Bitov, "Vkus," p. 81.

81 Ronald Meyer, *Andrej*, p. 60.

82 *Ibid.*, pp. 65–6.

83 Boris Pasternak, "Veter (Chetyre otryvka o Bloke)," in Boris Pasternak, *Stikhotvoreniia i poèmy*, p. 464.

84 Pasternak, "Veter (Chetyre)," in *Stikhotvoreniia i poèmy*, p. 465.

85 Boris Pasternak, *Doctor Zhivago*, trans. Max Hayward and Manya Harari (New York: Pantheon Books, Inc., 1958), p. 75; Boris Pasternak, *Doktor Zhivago* (Moscow, 1989), pp. 85–6.

86 The Book of Psalms, as quoted in Andrei Bitov, "The Forest," in Andrei Bitov, *Life in Windy Weather*, p. 269; the Book of Psalms, as quoted in Bitov, "Les," in Bitov, *Dni cheloveka*, p. 100. These lines, from Psalm 103, in the standard English version of the Bible and from Psalm 102 in the Russian version, are rendered, "As for man, his days are like grass; he flourishes like a flower of the field;" *The Holy Bible* (New York: Thomas Nelson and Sons, 1953), p. 631.

87 Ronald Meyer explains that the novel *Dni cheloveka* appears as a unified novel for the first time as the volume entitled *Life in Windy Weather* in English. Ronald Meyer, *Andrej*, p. 44, p. 74.

88 The Holy Bible, Psalm 103, p. 631; *Bibliia, ili Knigi sviashchennogo pisaniia vetkhogo i novogo zaveta*, v russkom perevode (Moscow, 1956), Psalm 102, p. 572. I quote from this edition of the Russian Bible because the prerevolutionary Bible's rendering of the "days of man" verse does not match Bitov's quotation from the Book of Psalms, in "The Forest" or in the title of his 1976 collection of short stories. The prerevolutionary version is: "Chelovek, – kak trava, dni ego" ("Man – like grass are his days"), *Sviashchennye knigi vetkhogo i novogo zaveta* (Vienna: British and Foreign Bible Society, 1912), p. 577.

89 *Bibliia*, p. 573.

90 *Ibid.*

91 Hagen, *The Stories*, p. 142. Hagen speaks of the relevance of the song to the wind theme and to Sergei's confused feelings after his experiences of harmonious clarity. Hagen sees the woman as a symbol of the wind (life-force), churning up man's (the island's) ordinary life. Hagen, *The Stories*, p. 142.

92 Hagen, *The Stories*, pp. 134, 136, 137, 141, and passim.

93 Pasternak, *Doktor Zhivago*, p. 501.
94 Priscilla Meyer, "Introduction," in Bitov, *Life in Windy Weather*, p. 7.
95 Ronald Meyer, *Andrej*, pp. 39, 40.
96 Pasternak, "Pakhota," in Pasternak, *Stikhotvoreniia i poèmy*, p. 483.

5 *"Apothecary Island": "I-lands" of existence*

1 "Aptekarskii ostrov," in *Aptekarskii ostrov* (Leningrad, 1968), pp. 24–42. Hereafter in my section on "Apothecary Island," I shall place page references to this edition in parentheses immediately following the quotation. In 1966, the story was published with the title "Pobeda" in *Sem'ia i shkola*, 3 (1966), pp. 26–9. The story reappeared as "Aptekarskii ostrov (No-ga)" in a later collection of Bitov's works, *Voskresnyi den'. Rasskazy, povesti, puteshestviia* (Moscow, 1980), pp. 22–34.
2 Bitov, "Biography," in Croen, "A Translation", Appendix, p. 4.
3 In *Aptekarskii ostrov*, "The Big Balloon" is the first story, followed by "Apothecary Island." In *Voskresnyi den'*, "The Big Balloon" opens the collection (pp. 9–21), and "Apothecary Island. Fo-ot" comes next.
4 Bitov, letter to Steven Hagen, August 12, 1978, as quoted in Hagen, *The Stories*, p. 91 and p. 245.
5 Bitov, "Bezdel'nik," in Bitov, *Aptekarskii ostrov*, pp. 51–85. Hereafter in my section on "The Idler," I shall place page references to this edition in parentheses immediately following the quotation.
6 Schmid, "Verfremdung," p. 30, p. 48.
7 Wolfgang Kasack refers to Bitov's use of the Western European stream-of-consciousness technique. Wolfgang Kasack, "Bitov," in *Lexicon*, p. 57.
8 Hagen compares him to Holden Caulfield, J. D. Salinger's hero in *Catcher in the Rye*, which was popular in the Soviet Union in the 1960s. Hagen, *The Stories*, pp. 82–3, pp. 87–8. Hagen writes that Vera Panova's introduction to the Russian translation of Salinger's novel characterizes Caulfield as an "idler" ("bezdel'nik"). Hagen, *The Stories*, p. 82.
   Catcher in the Rye (*Nad propasti'iu vo rzhi*), translated by R. Rait-Kovaleva, appeared in *Inostrannaia literatura*, no. 11, 1960, pp. 28–137. Vera Panova's "bezdel'nik" comment, in her afterword, "O romane Dzh. D. Selindzhera" (pp. 138–41), is on page 138.
9 Priscilla Meyer, "Andrei Georgievich Bitov," p. 33.
10 Priscilla Meyer, "Introduction," in Bitov, *Life in Windy Weather*, p. 7.

11 *Ibid.*
12 See Hagen, *The Stories*, p. 85 and B. Bursov, "Vechernie dumy. Polemicheskie zametki," in *Zvezda*, no. 8, 1968, p. 206. George Gibian associates many Bitov protagonists with Dostoevsky's "... Underground Man crossed with his dreamer." Gibian, "The Urban Theme," p. 46.
13 Bursov, "Vechernie," p. 206.
14 Fedor M. Dostoevskii, *Prestuplenie i nakazanie* in *Polnoe sobranie sochinenii*, vol. 6 (Leningrad, 1973), pp. 46–59, passim; Bitov, "Bezdel'nik," pp. 76–8, passim.
15 A discussion of this point and the betrayal motif characterize Priscilla Meyer's approach to "Penelope." Priscilla Meyer, "Introduction," in Bitov, *Life in Windy Weather*, p. 9.
16 On Kozhinov's role in helping Bakhtin's works appear in print and in helping Bakhtin and his wife in their daily life, see Katerina Clark and Michael Holquist, *Mikhail Bakhtin* (Cambridge, Massachusetts: Harvard University Press, 1984), pp. 332–40.
17 V. Kozhinov, "Sovremennost' iskusstva i otvetstvennost' cheloveka," *Moskovskii komsomolets*, May 7, 1966, p. 2.
18 *Ibid.*, p. 3.
19 Bakich, "A New Type of Character," p. 127. For her extended discussion of Lobyshev, see pp. 128–32.
20 S. Sergeev, "Sredi knig," *Don*, no. 2, 1969, p. 175.
21 Anninskii, "Tochka opory," p. 175.
22 *Ibid.*, p. 176.
23 Hagen, *The Stories*, p. 94.
24 *Ibid.*, pp. 99–102.
25 Evaluating models of the short story genre, Bitov said that he had recently been reading Gogol's "Nevsky Prospect." Andrei Bitov, "Kharakter podrobnyi ili èskiznyi? Kak uchit'sia u velikikh?" *Literaturnaia Rossiia*, September 25, 1964, p. 19.
26 Bitov, "Infant'ev," in Bitov, *Aptekarskii ostrov*, pp. 127–46. Hereafter in my section on "Infantiev," I shall place page references to this edition in parentheses immediately following the quotation.
27 *Aptekarskii ostrov; Life in Windy Weather*, pp. 81–92.
28 Hagen conjectures that the word "love" ("liubov'") was added by the editor of *Voskresnyi den'* in response to "Infantiev"'s more imprecise ending in the *Aptekarskii ostrov* version: "... what's this all about? This turns out to be what it is." Bitov, "Infant'ev," in *Aptekarskii ostrov*, p. 146.
29 Hagen, *The Stories*, pp. 147, 158.
30 See "Infant'ev," pp. 188–9 in Bitov, *Dni cheloveka*, pp. 120–1 in *Voskresnyi den'*, and "Infantiev," pp. 90–1 in *Life in Windy Weather*.

31 Bitov, "Infant'ev," in *Dni cheloveka*, p. 188.
32 *Ibid.*, p. 189.
33 *Ibid.*, p. 188.
34 Hagen, *The Stories*, pp. 147–59.
35 A. Marchenko, "Sredi knig," p. 76.
36 Priscilla Meyer, "Introduction," p. 11.
37 *Ibid.*
38 Hagen, *The Stories*, p. 148.
39 Priscilla Meyer, "Introduction," pp. 10–11.
40 Hagen, *The Stories*, p. 147.
41 *Ibid.*, p. 148.
42 *Ibid.*, p. 154.
43 *Ibid.*, p. 157.
44 *Ibid.*, p. 156.
45 *Ibid.*, p. 155.
46 *Ibid.*, p. 154.
47 Priscilla Meyer, "Introduction," p. 11.

6 *"Image of Life": life and images of life*

1 Andrei Bitov, *Obraz zhizni. Povesti* (Moscow, 1972).
2 Andrei Bitov, "Koleso," in Bitov, *Obraz*, pp. 107–63. Hereafter in my section on "The Wheel," I shall place page references to this edition in parentheses immediately following the quotation.
3 Andrei Bitov, "Uroki Armenii," in Bitov, *Obraz*, pp. 165–285.
4 "Obraz zhizni" also means "way of life" in Russian. I use the definition of "obraz" that means "image" because Bitov's works often juxtapose our *images* of life to life itself.
5 Bitov, "Dver' (prolog)" in "Sad," in Bitov, *Obraz*, p. 5.
6 There are minor differences between the texts of "The Garden" in the two editions. Bitov, in the later version, leaves out many dashes and commas to make the text read more smoothly.
7 Andrei Bitov, "Granitsy zhanra," *Voprosy literatury*, no. 7, 1969, pp. 72–6.
8 *Ibid.*, p. 74.
9 *Ibid.*, p. 76.
10 Schmid, "Verfremdung," p. 38.
11 Gibian, "The Urban Theme," pp. 47, 42.
12 George Gibian, "New Aspects of Soviet Russian Literature," in *The Soviet Union Since Stalin*, ed. Stephen F. Cohen, Alexander Rabinowitch and Robert Sharlet (Bloomington, Indiana: Indiana University Press, 1980), p. 260.
13 T. Khmel'nitskaia, "Mezhdu pomyslom," p. 206.

14 N. A. Kozhevnikova, "O sootnoshenii," p. 30.

15 Sylva Tvrdíková, "Modifikace," p. 53.

16 Mikael Klefter, "Rejsemotivet," p. 36.

17 Introduction to Andrei Bitov, "Tri puteshestviia," ("Uroki Armenii," "Vybor natury," "Koleso"), in A. Bitov, I. Ziedonis and V. Korotich, *Ne schitai shagi, putnik!* (Moscow, 1974), n.p.

18 Timur Pulatov, "Razvedka boem," *Literaturnaia gazeta*, October 25, 1972, p. 5.

19 V. Turbin, "Listopad po vesne," *Novyi mir*, no. 4, 1972, pp. 259–64.

20 Vladimir Kantorovich, "Khudozhestvennaia publitsistika (èsse)," in his *Zametki pisatelia o sovremennom ocherke*, pp. 130, 131.

21 Vsevolod Sakharov, "Alkhimiia prozy," *Literaturnaia gazeta*, October 3, 1973, p. 5.

22 For an examination of the circle in Western writings from the Renaissance to the twentieth century, see Georges Poulet, *The Metamorphoses of the Circle*, trans. Carley Dawson and Elliott Coleman in collaboration with the author (Baltimore, Maryland: The Johns Hopkins Press, 1966).

23 "Letka-enka" is an upbeat Finnish dance melody that was popular in the Soviet Union in the 1960s. It is available on the record "V novogodniuiu noch'. Tantsy" on the Soviet recording label Melodiia.

24 Although he does not refer more precisely to the Goethe text, Bitov quotes from Part Two, Naples, March 17, 1787. In that section, Goethe has just marveled that the world reveals itself to him more and more. Goethe's words, in the Auden translation of the passage quoted by Bitov, are "Certainly the world is only a simple wheel and every point on its circumference is equidistant from its centre. It only looks so strange to us because we ourselves are revolving with it." J. W. Goethe, *Italian Journey*, trans. W. H. Auden and Elizabeth Mayer (New York: Pantheon Books, 1962), p. 201.

25 I. F. Burns, "Cosmogony and Cosmology (Greek) in *Encyclopaedia of Religion and Ethics*, ed. James Hastings *et al.* (New York: Charles Scribner's Sons, 1912). vol. 4, p. 148; Michael Revon, "Cosmogony and Cosmology (Japanese)," *Ibid.*, p. 163.

26 See, for instance, L. A. Waddell's "The Buddhist Pictorial Wheel of Fate," *Journal of the Asiatic Society of Bengal*, vol. 61, no. 1, 1892, pp. 133–55; "Wheel," in Benjamin Walker, *The Hindu World. An Encyclopedic Survey of Hinduism*, vol. 2 (New York: Frederick A. Praeger), pp. 597–9.

27 Robert M. Pirsig, *Zen and the Art of Motorcycle Maintenance. An Inquiry into Values* (Toronto: Bantam Books, 1984). The original version appeared in April, 1974, two months before the only

English translation of "The Wheel" was made accessible to the public: Frederick R. Croen, "A Translation of 'The Wheel' by Andrei Bitov," Princeton University senior thesis, 1974. Pirsig did not know about Croen's translation or about Bitov's "The Wheel." However, like Bitov, he claims that Fellini's film *La Strada* profoundly affected him. Robert Pirsig, letter to Ellen Chances, September, 1986. On the Bitov-Pirsig connection, see Ellen Chances, "Soviet and American Motorcycle Wheels: Wheels of Life in Andrei Bitov's 'The Wheel' and Robert Pirsig's *Zen and the Art of Motorcycle Maintenance*," forthcoming.

28 Andrei Bitov, *Uroki Armenii* (Erevan, 1978), p. 175.
29 Lewis Carroll, *Alice's Adventures in Wonderland and Through the Looking Glass* (New York: A. L. Burt Company n.d.), p. 15.
30 Andrei Bitov, *Uroki Armenii* (Erevan, 1978), p. 35.
31 One exception is Sven Spieker's "Andrei Bitov's Bookish Landscapes: Travelling through the Texts in 'Uroki Armenii,'" *Wiener Slawistischer Almanach*, no. 24, 1989, pp. 171–85.
32 Genrikh Mitin, "Narodnoe i lichnoe," *Literaturnaia Armeniia*, no. 10, 1973, p. 102.
33 Georgii Kubat'ian, "Nauka puteshestvii i nauka liubvi," *Literaturnaia Armeniia*, no. 6, 1970, p. 87.
34 The editors, "S raznykh tochek zreniia," *Literaturnoe obozrenie*, no. 10, 1973, p. 45.
35 Igor' Zolotusskii, "Poznanie nastoiashchego," *Voprosy literatury*, no. 10, 1975, p. 24.
36 Bitov, "Uroki Armenii," in Bitov, *Obraz zhizni*, p. 167–285. In my discussion, I also refer to "After the Lessons," a final short section of the work, not included in *Obraz zhizni*, but contained in later publications of "Uroki Armenii": Bitov, "Uroki Armenii (Puteshestvie v nebol'shuiu stranu)" in Andrei Bitov, *Sem' puteshestvii*, pp. 390–8; Bitov, *Uroki Armenii* (Erevan, 1978), pp. 172–83; and Andrei Bitov, *Kniga puteshestvii*, pp. 427–31. The final section of "After the Lessons," "Reminiscences of Agartsina (Three Years Later)," also appears in Bitov's *Georgian Album* (*Gruzinskii al'bom*) (Tbilisi, 1985), pp. 15–19. My page references to *Armenia Lessons* are to the Erevan edition since certain other key sections to the work are not found in the *Obraz zhizni* edition. Hereafter in my section on "Armenia Lessons," I shall place page references to the Erevan edition in parentheses immediately following the quotation.
37 On this point, see G. Trefilova, "Rabochii moment," *Literaturnoe obozrenie*, no. 10, 1973, p. 40.
38 Osip Mandel'shtam, "Puteshestvie v Armeniiu," *Zvezda*, no. 5,

1933, pp. 103–25; *Literaturnaia Armeniia*, no. 3, 1967, pp. 83–99, with material added to and omitted from the *Zvezda* version. Also see O. Mandel'shtam, "Zapisnye knizhki. Zametki," *Voprosy literatury*, no. 4, 1968, pp. 180–204. Much of this material relates to *Puteshestvie v Armeniiu*.

The publication history appears in Jane Gary Harris' commentary, affixed to the translation of Mandelstam's prose. Osip E. Mandelstam, *The Complete Critical Prose and Letters*, ed. Jane Gary Harris, trans. Jane Gary Harris and Constance Link (Ann Arbor, Michigan: Ardis, 1979), p. 669. For more on Mandelstam's travelogue, see Jane Gary Harris, "The 'Latin Gerundive' as Autobiographical Imperative: A Reading of Mandel'shtam's *Journey to Armenia*," *Slavic Review*, 45 (1986), Spring, pp. 1–19; Carol Avins, *Border Crossings. The West and Russian Identity in Soviet Literature 1917–1934* (Berkeley, California: University of California Press, 1983), chapter 12, "Narrowed Borders. Osip Mandelstam, 'Journey to Armenia' (1933)," pp. 148–56; and Nancy Pollak, "The Obscure Way to Mandel'shtam's Armenia," PhD dissertation, Yale University, 1983.

39 In the final version of Pushkin's travelogue, the quotation remains the same until the word "kirpichakh." After that, it reads, "... slavoliubivymi puteshestvennikam." The next two sentences are in the final version. See A. S. Pushkin, "Puteshestvie v Arzrum vo vremia pokhoda 1829 goda," in A.S. Pushkin, *Polnoe sobranie sochinenii* (Leningrad, 1948), VIII, Book One, p. 448; (Leningrad, 1940 [*sic*]), VIII, Book Two, p. 1033; A. S. Pushkin, *Polnoe sobranie sochinenii v desiati tomakh* (Moscow, 1964), VI, p. 647 and p. 744. Pushkin's drafts named the count: "graf Pushkin."

40 Bitov does not explain this phrase, but knowledge about Mesrop-Mashtotz, venerated as a saint by the Armenian church, clarifies his statement. Mesrop-Mashtotz, a member of the Christian Church, invented an alphabet (ca 404 or 406 A.D.) for the dual purpose of spreading Christianity (bringing God's *word* to the people) and of giving Armenians a sense of national identity. For more on Mesrop and the Armenian alphabet, see David Marshall Lang, *Armenia. Cradle of Civilization* (London: George Allen & Unwin Ltd., 1970), pp. 264–7. In its very origins, then, the language Bitov is describing contains a spiritual dimension.

41 The book which Bitov cites as *Genotsid armian v Osmanskoi imperii* (*Sbornik dokumentov i materialov*) (Erevan, 1966) (Bitov, *Uroki*, p. 36) was edited by M. G. Nersisian. Although he does not cite the Nersisian page numbers, the sections Bitov quotes are: Bitov, *Uroki*, p. 36/Nersisian, p. 91; *Uroki*, p. 38/Nersisian, p. 95, p. 91, pp. 97–8;

Bitov, *Uroki*, pp. 38–9/Nersisian, p. 484; Bitov, *Uroki*, p. 40/
Nersisian, p. 285; Bitov, *Uroki*, pp. 40–1/Nersisian, pp. 185–6.

42 Georgii Kubat'ian writes that Bitov cites Mandelstam's cycle of
Armenian poems three times. Georgii Kubat'ian, "Nauka," p. 88.

43 Bitov, *Uroki*, p. 66. On this point, see Kubat'ian, "Nauka," p. 86.

44 O. Mandelstam, "Journey to Armenia," in Mandelstam, *The
Complete Critical Prose*, p. 350; O. Mandel'shtam, "Puteshestvie v
Armeniiu," in *Literaturnaia Armeniia*, p. 87.

45 The poem is called "Oh, Nothing Do I See, And My Poor Ear Has
Gone Deaf" ("Akh, nichego ia ne vizhu, i bednoe ukho oglokhlo.")
O. Mandel'shtam, "Armeniia," no. III, "Akh, nichego ia ne vizhu, i
bednoe ukho oglokhlo," in O. Mandel'shtam, *Sobranie sochinenii*,
vol. I (Washington: Inter-Language Literary Associates, 1964),
pp. 137–8.

46 Martiros Sar'ian (1880–1972). Illustrations of and information
about him can be found in *Al'bom Sar'ian*, intro. and compiled by
Aleksandr Abramovich Kamenskii (Moscow, 1968) and *Martiros
Saryan*, intro. and compiled by Sh. Khachatrian (Leningrad,
1975).

   Genrikh Mitin was the first to confirm, in print, that the painter
Bitov describes is Saryan. Mitin, "Narodnoe," pp. 103–4.

47 Bitov often uses the words "accuracy" ("tochnost'") and "accurate" ("tochen") in "Armenia Lessons." These words are common
Bitov words in other works, too, but they appear more frequently
here.

48 This comment repeats almost word for word Bitov's statements, in
letters, about his own writing process.

49 A. S. Pushkin, "Puteshestvie, v Arzrum," as quoted in Bitov, *Uroki*,
p. 3.

50 Bitov's citation of Turgenev does not include the source, "Russkii
iazyk." In that work, Turgenev speaks about the Russian language
as his support and as having been given to a great people. I. S.
Turgenev, "Russkii iazyk," in I. S. Turgenev, *Polnoe sobranie
sochinenii i pisem v dvadtsati vos'mi tomakh* (Moscow–Leningrad,
1967), vol. 13, p. 198.

51 Vsevolod Sakharov writes of Bitov's repeated references to Mandelstam's "Journey to Armenia." He does not elaborate. Vsevolod
Sakharov, "Alkhimiia prozy," *Literaturnaia gazeta*, October 3, 1973,
p. 5.

52 Hagen, *The Stories*, Appendix IV, p. 231. The first published version
of "Uroki Armenii," in *Druzhba narodov*, no. 9, 1969 (pp. 161–227),
bore the subtitle, "A Sentimental Journey" ("Sentimental'noe

puteshestvie"), p. 161. The *Sem' puteshestvii* version was subtitled "Journey to a Small Country" (*"Puteshestvie v nebol'shuiu stranu"*), p. 261.

53 Osip E. Mandelstam, "Journey to Armenia," in Mandelstam, *The Complete Critical Prose*, p. 349; O. Mandel'shtam, "Puteshestvie v Armeniiu," *Literaturnaia Armeniia*, p. 87.

54 Mandelstam, "Journey," p. 350; Mandel'shtam, "Puteshestvie," p. 87.

55 Mandelstam, "Journey," p. 358; Mandel'shtam, "Puteshestvie," p. 90.

56 Mandelstam, "Journey," p. 374; Mandel'shtam, "Puteshestvie," p. 97.

57 Mandelstam, "Journey," p. 372; Mandel'shtam, "Puteshestvie," p. 96.

58 O. Mandel'shtam, "Armeniia," no. XIII, "Koliuchaia rech' araratskoi doliny –," in Osip Mandel'shtam, *Sobranie sochinenii*, vol. I (Washington: Inter-Language Literary Associates, 1964), p. 142 and no. xv, "Dikaia koshka–armianskaia rech'–," pp. 142–3.

59 In this connection, French actor Jean-Louis Barrault, in *La Langage du corps*, writes, "Like the flower, human speech is part of the flesh of the human body. If the deep soul of a people is contained in speech, it is speech that is above all the most subtle emanation of its body ..." I am thankful to Troup Mathews for bringing this passage to my attention.

60 Quoted in Bitov, *Uroki*, p. 66. O. Mandel'shtam, "Armeniia," no. III, "Akh, nichego ia ne vizhu, i bednoe ukho oglokhlo," in O. Mandel'shtam, *Sobranie sochinenii*, vol. I, pp. 137–8.

61 O. Mandel'shtam, "Armeniia," no. XI, "Ia tebia nikogda ne uvizhu," in O. Mandel'shtam, *Sobranie sochinenii*, vol. I, p. 141.

62 Quoted in Bitov, *Uroki*, p. 154. O. Mandel'shtam, "Armeniia," no. III, "Akh, nichego ia ne vizhu, i bednoe ukho oglokhlo," in Mandel'shtam, *Sobranie sochinenii*, vol. I, p. 138.

63 O. Mandel'shtam, "Kamen'," in Mandel'shtam, *Sobranie sochinenii*, vol. I, pp. 1–51.

64 O. Mandel'shtam, "Obraz tvoi, muchitel'nyi i zybkii," in O. Mandel'shtam, *Sobranie sochinenii*, vol. I, p. 18.

65 A. S. Pushkin, "Prorok," in A. S. Pushkin, *Sobranie sochinenii v desiati tomakh* (Moscow, 1959), vol. II, p. 149.

66 *Ibid.*, p. 150.

67 Vsevolod Sakharov, "Alkhimiia prozy," p. 5.

68 Igor' Zolotusskii, "Poznanie nastoiashchego," in *Voprosy literatury*, no. 10, 1975, p. 24.

69 V. Sakharov, "Novye geroi Bitova," *Iunost'*, no. 6, 1973, p. 74.
70 V. Gusev, "Iskusstvo, analiz, poisk," *Druzhba narodov*, no. 5, 1973, p. 278.
71 Bitov, *Uroki*, p. 183.

7 *"Seven Journeys": Journeys to the other and journeys to the self*

1 Andrei Bitov, *Sem' puteshestvii* (Moscow, 1976).
2 Schmid, "Verfremdung," pp. 25–53.
3 Klefter, "Rejsemotivet," pp. 27–37. See, in particular, pp. 33, 34.
4 Anonymous editor, *Ne schitai shagi, putnik!*, pp. 5, 6.
5 Andrei Bitov, "Azart (Iznanka puteshestviia)," in Andrei Bitov, *Sem' puteshestvii*, pp. 469–522. Hereafter in my section on "The Gamble," I shall place page references to this edition in parentheses immediately following the quotation.
6 Avicenna, "Book of Salvation," as quoted in Bitov, "Azart," in Bitov, *Sem' puteshestvii*, p. 470.
7 "The Book of Salvation," or "Al-Najāt," "The Salvation (from Error)," is in three parts, Logic, Natural Science, and Metaphysics. Bitov's quotation is from a chapter on the eternal and the created, which is a part of Avicenna's Metaphysics section. See Ibn Sīnā (Avicenna), *Al-Najāt*, ed. M. S. Al-Kurdi (Cairo, 1938), p. 218. I am thankful to Basim Musallam of Cambridge University for his help with the Arabic text.
8 Andrei Bitov, "Vybor natury (Tri gruzina)" in Bitov, *Sem' puteshestvii*, pp. 523–91. Hereafter in my section on "Choice of Location," I shall place page references to this edition in parentheses immediately following the quotation. The work had appeared, flanked on one side by "Armenia Lessons" and, on the other, by "The Wheel," under the rubric "Three Journeys" ("Tri puteshestviia,") in the collection, *Ne schitai shagi, putnik!*, pp. 152–218. The other contributors to this collection were Imant Ziedonis and Vitaly Korotich. Korotich, as editor of the Soviet magazine *Ogonëk*, later gained prominence as an outspoken proponent of glasnost under the regime of Mikhail Gorbachev.
    Bitov's *Tri puteshestviia*, with the introductory essay that accompanied it in the 1974 Moscow edition, is reproduced in Andrei Bitov, *Tri puteshestviia* (New York: Orfei, 1986).
9 M. Lermontov, *Geroi nashego vremeni* in M. Iu. Lermontov, *Izbrannye proizvedeniia v dvukh tomakh*, vol. II (Moscow, 1963), p. 362; as quoted in Bitov, "Vybor natury (Tri gruzina)," in Bitov, *Sem' puteshestvii*, p. 524.
10 Lermontov, *Geroi*, as quoted in Bitov, "Vybor," p. 524.

11 The title, epigraph, introductory, and concluding sections of the essay merge the two realms. The remaining sections, whose titles focus on art or life, include links to the other category as well.

12 Bitov's text identifies the Pirandello work as "Kuvshin." The English translation would be "Jug." Pirandello's "La giara" is known, in English, as "The Jar."

Parts of Claude Tillier's "My Uncle Benjamin" ("Mon Oncle Benjamin") were made into the 1969 Soviet film, "Don't Grieve!," directed by Georgian director Georgi Daneliya. See Jay Leyda, *Kino. A History of the Russian and Soviet Film* (Princeton, New Jersey: Princeton University Press, 3rd edition, 1983), Appendix 5, p. 466, and Yuri Vorontsov and Igor Rachuk, *The Phenomenon of the Soviet Cinema* (Moscow, 1980), p. 398.

13 Èrlom Akhvlediani, "Vano i Niko. Sovremennaia skazka," trans. Aida Abuashvili, *Druzhba narodov*, No. 10, 1969, pp. 126–33. The stories are narrated in a direct way with a child-like simplicity of logic. Thus, one story, "Vano and Niko, Niko and Vano" ("Vano i Niko, Niko i Vano") begins this way: "Formerly, Niko was Vano, and Vano was Niko. Then Niko became Vano, and Vano became Niko. And near the end, both of them became Vano." Akhvlediani, "Vano i Niko," p. 132.

14 A reproduction of the 1906 Pirosmanashvili painting, "Drinking Bout of the Five Princes" ("Kutezh piati kniazei"), is found in Sh. Amiranashvili, *Al'bom 'Pirosmanashvili'* (Moscow, 1967), Plate 55. Amiranashvili uses the title, "Feast of Five Princes."

15 Chances, conversation with Bitov, May 5, 1987, Princeton.

8 *"The Days of Man": roles and rhymes*

1 Andrei Bitov, *Dni cheloveka. Povesti* (Moscow, 1976).

2 "Tretii rasskaz" was published as "Obraz" ("The Image") in *Zvezda*, no. 12, 1973, pp. 135–51, and "Les" was published as "Uletaiushchii Monakhov" ("Vanishing Monakhov") in *Zvezda*, no. 8, 1976, pp. 3–48.

3 Priscilla Meyer, "Bitov's 'roman-punktir': Whose Lover? Whose Twin? Whose Double?" unpublished paper (AAASS Annual Conference, November 22, 1986, New Orleans, Louisiana), p. 1.

4 Revaz Gabriadze, "O rasskaze 'Vkus' i o romane 'Uletaiushchii Monakhov,'" *Literaturnaia Gruziia*, no. 1, 1983, pp. 58–61.

5 Bitov, Columbia University, New York City, April 28, 1987.

6 Andrei Bitov, *Uletaiushchii Monakhov. Roman-punktir* (Moscow, 1990).

7 Hagen, *The Stories*, p. 161. Chances, conversation with Bitov,

Moscow, August, 1988. "Vkus" appears as the last part of the novel *Uletaiuschii Monakhov. Roman-punktir* in Bitov, *Povesti i rasskazy*, pp. 401–34. It is the first selection in Bitov, *Chelovek v peizazhe*, pp. 5–38. In *Uletaiushchii Monakhov*, "Vkus" is on pp. 123–47.

8 Bitov, "Vkus," *Literaturnaia Gruziia*, no. 1, 1983, pp. 57–98. Gabriadze, "O rasskaze."
9 Priscilla Meyer, "Introduction," in Bitov, *Life in Windy Weather*, p. 8.
10 *Ibid.*, p. 9.
11 Hagen, *The Stories*, p. 160.
12 *Ibid.*, p. 182.
13 Ronald Meyer, "Bitov's *Puškinskij Dom*," pp. 54–7.
14 Gabriadze, "O rasskaze," p. 59.
15 Bitov, "Preface," in Bitov, *Life in Windy Weather*, p. 15.
16 Priscilla Meyer speaks of the similarity, in their automaton-like existence, of Alesha in "The Garden," who steals, and Lobyshev in "Penelope," who treats his new acquaintance badly. She groups "The Idler" and "The Garden" together as both concerning adolescence. "Introduction," in Bitov, *Life in Windy Weather*, pp. 8–9. Hagen finds that the major protagonist of "The Third Story" shares the trait of role-playing with Lobyshev. Hagen, *The Stories*, p. 180.
17 Hagen points out scenes in "The Third Story" that repeat scenes in "The Door." As Monakhov is waiting for Asya in the stairwell, both Monakhov and the boy want to smoke, and both hear the same sounds. Hagen, *The Stories*, p. 184.
18 Bitov, "Tretii rasskaz," in Bitov, *Dni*, p. 88. Hereafter in my section on "The Third Story," I shall place citations to this edition in parentheses immediately following the quotation.
19 Hagen writes that Bitov added this passage to the story in the *Dni cheloveka* version. Hagen, *The Stories*, p. 187.
20 Bitov, *The Lover*, in Bitov, *Life in Windy Weather*, p. 187. Also, see note 19 to my section on "The Garden," page 272.
21 Bitov, "Les," in Bitov, *Dni cheloveka*, pp. 100–76. Hereafter in my section on "The Forest," I shall place citations to this edition in parentheses immediately following the quotation.
22 Hagen mentions this and draws parallels between the situations of "The Garden" and "The Forest." He describes parallels between "The Third Story" and "The Forest." For his discussion of "The Forest," see Hagen, *The Stories*, pp. 189–207.

Ronald Meyer also describes links between "The Forest" and Bitov's "Life in Windy Weather," "The Garden," and "The Door." For his analysis of "The Forest," see Ronald Meyer, "Bitov's *Puškinskij Dom*," pp. 59–63.

23 Priscilla Meyer mentions the "Forest"–"Life in Windy Weather" parallel of the "piece of fluff" in another context. Priscilla Meyer, "Bitov's 'roman-punktir'," pp. 8–9.

24 Hagen, *The Stories*, pp. 202–7. Hagen also speaks of the story's pessimism.

25 Ronald Meyer, "Bitov's *Puškinskij Dom*," p. 63.

26 This incident parallels an event in Bitov's life. He was accepted into a literary circle by submitting, as his own, the poems written by his brother. See chapter 2.

27 Priscilla Meyer speaks of Bitov's finch imagery in *Days of Man*. Priscilla Meyer, "Bitov's 'roman-punktir'," p. 6.

28 Bitov, "Vkus," *Literaturnaia Gruziia*, no. 1, 1983, pp. 57–98. Hereafter in my section on "The Taste," I shall place citations to this edition in parentheses immediately following the quotation. Bitov, "The Taste," in Andrei Bitov, *Life in Windy Weather*, pp. 335–64. A section of the story appeared in *Ogonek*. Andrei Bitov, "Vkus," *Ogonek*, no. 17, 1987, pp. 22–5.

29 Pasternak's name appears in the English version of "Vkus," in Bitov, "The Taste," *Life in Windy Weather*, pp. 342, 344.

30 Bitov is describing what Jung referred to as synchronicity, the "... simultaneous occurrence of two meaningful but not causally connected events ..., ... a coincidence in time of two or more causally unrelated events which have the same or a similar meaning ..." Carl G. Jung, *Synchronicity. An Acausal Connecting Principle*, trans. R.F.C. Hull (Princeton, New Jersey: Princeton University Press, 1973), p. 25.

31 Alexander Pushkin, as quoted in Bitov, "The Taste," in Bitov, *Life in Windy Weather*, p. 335.

32 Aleksandr Pushkin, "I dale my poshli – i strakh obnial menia," in A. Pushkin, *Polnoe sobranie sochinenii* (Leningrad, 1948), III, 281–2.

33 The English version of "The Taste" repeatedly misspells Iadroshnikov's name, leaving out the "d."

34 Pushkin, "Togda ia demonov uvidel chernyi roi," in A. S. Pushkin, *Polnoe*, III, p. 282.

35 Pasternak, "Veter," in Pasternak, *Doktor Zhivago*, p. 509.

36 Ronald Meyer interprets the final line of the Bitov story as an ambiguous reference to Asya's and the grandmother's deaths.

37 Pasternak, *Doktor Zhivago*, p. 518.

38 Pasternak, *Doktor Zhivago*, pp. 474–5.

39 Pasternak, "Veter," as quoted in Bitov, "Vkus," *Literaturnaia Gruziia*, pp. 80–1.

40 Pasternak, "Veter," in *Doktor Zhivago*, p. 508.

41 L. N. Tolstoi, "Smert' Ivana Il'icha," in *Polnoe sobranie sochinenii* (Moscow, 1936), XXVI, p. 82.

42 Bitov: "'nado mnoi sklonialsia i shumel'" ("Vkus," p. 78); Lermontov: "Nado mnoi chtob, vechno zeleneia,/Tëmnyi dub sklonialsia i shumel." Lermontov, "Vykhozhu odin ia na dorogu," in M. Iu. Lermontov, *Izbrannye proizvedeniia* (Moscow, 1963), I, p. 316.

43 Ronald Meyer mentions Bitov's reference to Bely's *Petersburg* in the use of the word "vdrug." Ronald Meyer, Bitov's "*Puškinskij Dom*," p. 73.

44 Andrei Belyi, *Peterburg* (Moscow, 1978), pp. 45, 46–50.

45 On Bely's use of the circle and spiral in *Petersburg*, see the brilliant analysis of Robert A. Maguire and John E. Malmstad in their "Petersburg," in John E. Malmstad, ed., *Andrey Bely. Spirit of Symbolism* (Ithaca and London: Cornell University Press, 1987), pp. 96–144.

46 Vladimir Nabokov, *Pale Fire* (New York: Berkeley Books, 1985), p. 41 and passim. Bitov read all of Nabokov in English and in Russian. For more on the Bitov–Nabokov connection, see my chapter on *Pushkin House*.

47 Bitov, "The Taste," in *Life in Windy Weather*, p. 342.

48 I am thankful to Lee Silver of Princeton University's Department of Biology for his discussions of molecular biology.

49 Revaz Gabriadze, "O rasskaze," p. 58.

50 *Ibid.*, p. 59.

51 F. M. Dostoevskii, *Brat'ia Karamazovy* in *Polnoe sobranie sochinenii v tridtsati tomakh* (Leningrad, 1976), XIV, 5.

52 Gabriadze, "O rasskaze," pp. 60–1.

53 *Ibid.*, p. 61.

54 Andrei Bitov, "Ptitsy, ili Novye svedeniia o cheloveke," in Bitov, *Dni cheloveka*, pp. 283–346. Hereafter in my section on "Birds," I shall place citations to this edition in parentheses immediately following the quotation. "Ptitsy" has since appeared in Andrei Bitov, *Gruzinskii al'bom*, pp. 173–223, in Bitov, *Kniga puteshestvii*, pp. 187–249, and in Bitov, *Chelovek v peizazhe*, pp. 194–251.

55 V. Kamianov writes of its lyrical-philosophical quality, which, he says, places it in a category of works such as Vasilii Belov's *Privychnoe delo* in contemporary Soviet prose. V. Kamianov, "Vzamen tragedii," *Voprosy literatury*, no. 11, 1978, pp. 18–19. Adol'f Urban characterizes Bitov's writing in *Days of Man* as standing on the boundary between philosophy and literature, between science and morality. Adol'f Urban, "Filosofichnost' khudozhestvennoi prozy," *Zvezda*, no. 9, 1978, pp. 218–19. L. Anninskii's description of "Birds" is of a "philosophical monologue ... (or dialogue)." Lev Anninskii, "Strannyi strannik," afterword in Bitov, *Kniga puteshestvii*, p. 604.

56 Priscilla Meyer, "Bitov's 'roman-punktir': Whose Lover? Whose Twin? Whose Double?" paper delivered at AAASS Annual Conference, New Orleans, Louisiana, Nov. 22, 1986.

57 I. A. Krylov, "Kvartet" and "Lebed', shuchka i rak," in I. A. Krylov, *Stikhotvoreniia* (Leningrad, 1954), pp. 170, 176.

58 A. S. Pushkin, "Nravouchitel'nye chetverostishiia," *Stikhotvoreniia* in *Polnoe sobranie sochinenii v desiati tomakh* (Moscow, 1963), II, pp. 366–8.

59 The English-speaking reader can find a discussion of the topic in chapter 12, "Morals and Weapons," in Konrad Lorenz, *King Solomon's Ring. New Light on Animal Ways* (New York: Thomas Y. Crowell, Publishers, 1952), trans. Marjorie Kerr Wilson, pp. 181–99.

60 Bitov, "Ptitsy," in Bitov, *Dni*, p. 346.

61 *Ibid.*

9 *"Metropol"*: Bitov's stories about life and death

1 Andrei Bitov, "Poslednii medved'," in "Koleso," in Bitov, *Sem' puteshestvii*, pp. 462–8.

2 Bitov confirms that the story does not belong in "The Wheel." Chances, conversation with Bitov, May, 1987, Princeton, New Jersey.

3 Andrei Bitov, "Piatyi ugol,"in Bitov, *Sem' puteshestvii*, pp. 458–9.

4 Andrei Bitov,"Letuchii gollandets," in Bitov, *Obraz zhizni*, pp. 160–3; *Sem' puteshestvii*, pp. 459–62.

5 Andrei Bitov, "The Last Bear," in *Metropol. Literary Almanac*, ed. Vasily Aksenov, Viktor Yerofeyev, Fazil Iskander, Andrei Bitov and Yevgeny Popov (New York: W. W. Norton & Company, 1982), pp. 273–8; "Poslednii medved'," in *Metropol'. Literaturnyi al'manakh* (Moscow, 1979), facsimile edition (Ann Arbor, Michigan: Ardis Publishers, 1979), pp. 1–4, which are also pp. 54 1/2 to 55. The story also appeared in Andrei Bitov, "Poslednii medved'," *Studencheskii meridian*, no. 2, 1975, pp. 26–7.

The pagination of the Ardis edition presents difficulties. Each author numbered the pages of his/her manuscript separately, and another pagination, numbered for the entire collection, is erratic. Thus, pages 1, 2, 3, and 4 of Bitov's "Poslednii medved'" fall between pages 54 and 55, as do pages 3, 4, and 5 of the *Metropol* contribution preceding Bitov's, several poems by Semyon Lipkin.

6 *Metropol*, pp. XIX, XX; *Metropol'*, n.p. (before Table of Contents).

7 He died in 1980. Seven Melodiia records with some of his blander songs appeared in the USSR, and a collection of his poems, *Nerv*, was published in Moscow in 1981. Additional records have since

come out in the Soviet Union. Before glasnost, Vysotsky's songs were often considered unofficial and were scorned by the authorities.

8 For more on *Metropol*, see Kevin Close, "Foreword," in *Metropol* (W. W. Norton), pp. XI–XVII; "Soviet Café's Cleaning Day Thwarts Writers' Gathering," *New York Times*, January 24, 1979, p. A7; Kevin Close, "Moscow Journal Challenges Tight Control of Arts," *Washington Post*, January 24, 1979, pp. A1, A18; Craig R. Whitney, "Soviet Rebuffs Top Authors Seeking to Get Censored Works Printed," *New York Times*, January 28, 1979, p. 14; Kevin Close, "Moscow Harasses Top Writers Over Unofficial Journal," *Washington Post*, February 4, 1979, p. A25; "U.S. Authors Protest Suppression of Soviet Writers," *New York Times*, August 12, 1979, p. 5; Feliks Kuznetsov, "O chem shum?" *Literaturnaia gazeta*, Sept. 19, 1979, p. 9; Craig R. Whitney, "Writers Say Soviet Yields in a Dispute," *New York Times*, October 24, 1979, p. 9; Anthony Austin, "The Metropol Affair," *New York Times Book Review*, March 2, 1980, pp. 3, 19; "Two Leading Soviet Writers Plan to Emigrate to the West," *New York Times*, April 17, 1980, p. A10; Helen von Ssachno, "Metropol feiert Premiere," *Süddeutsche Zeitung* Munich, August 8, 1979, p. 8; Helen von Ssachno, "Tauziehen hinter den Kulissen," *Süddeutsche Zeitung* Munich, March 7, 1980, p. 35.

References to much of this information can be found in Ellen Chances, "The Reds and *Ragtime*: The Soviet Reception of E. L. Doctorow," in *E. L. Doctorow. Essays and Conversations*, ed. Richard Trenner (Princeton, New Jersey: Ontario Review Press, 1983), p. 156.

9 For information on the Wheatland Conference, see Charles True-heart, "The Den of the Literary Lions," *Washington Post*, April 25, 1987, pp. B1, B5; Irvin Molotsky, "Writers Joust Orally At Literary Conference," *New York Times*, April 27, 1987, p. C11; Raymond M. Lane, "Tough Talk from the Literati," *Boston Globe*, April 28, 1987, pp. 25–6.

10 Updike contributed a section of his novel, *The Coup*, in English and in Aksenov's translation into Russian, to *Metropol'*. Dzhon Apdaik, "Otryvok iz novogo eshche neopublikovannogo romana 'Pere-vorot'," *Metropol'* (Ardis), pp. 103, 104/pp. 1, 2, 3, 2, 3, 4, 5, 4, 5, [*sic*].

11 A condensed version of Kuznetsov's letter was printed in the *New York Times*. Feliks Kuznetsov, "A Soviet Reply to 5 U.S. Writers," *New York Times*, September 8, 1979, p. 21.

12 "Soviet to Publish 'We'," *New York Times*, June 25, 1987, p. C25.

13 Bitov, "Poslednii medved'," in *Metropol'* (Ardis), p. 1. Hereafter in my section on "The Last Bear," I shall place citations to this edition

in parentheses immediately following the quotation.

14 I am grateful to Caryl Emerson for suggesting to me the *Cancer Ward* zoo episode as a possible parallel to Bitov's zoo story.

15 Michael Scammell, *Solzhenitsyn. A Biography* (New York: W. W. Norton & Company, 1984), pp. 571–2.

16 Aleksandr Solzhenitsyn, *Rakovyi korpus* (Frankfurt/Main, West Germany: Posev, 1968), Part two, pp. 222–9.

17 *Ibid.*, p. 222.

18 Solzhenitsyn, *Rakovyi*, p. 226.

19 Solzhenitsyn, *Rakovyi*, p. 225.

20 *Ibid.*, p. 223.

21 *Ibid.* p. 228.

22 See, for example, Scammell, *Solzhenitsyn*, p. 577. Robert Tucker, prominent political scientist and specialist on Stalin, confirms that the reference to Stalin is unmistakable. Conversation, July 2, 1987.

23 Scammell, *Solzhenitsyn*, p. 565.

24 The book Bitov thought would be "Vospominaniia o real'nosti" turned out to be *Gruzinskii al'bom*. Chances, conversation with Bitov, Moscow, August, 1988.

25 The date is affixed only to the *Georgian Album* version of the story. Bitov, *Gruzinskii al'bom*, p. 25.

26 In like fashion, Tenzig Abuladze's suppressed film "Repentance," released in the more relaxed cultural atmosphere of the Gorbachev era, allegedly about a Georgian tyrant mayor, is obviously about Stalin. For Bitov's review of "Repentance," see his "Portret khudozhnika v smelosti," *Moskovskie novosti*, no. 7, February 15, 1987, p. 13.

27 Bernard L. Strehler, *Time, Cells, and Aging* (San Francisco: Academic Press, 1977), p. 1. As quoted, without publication and pagination reference, in Andrei Bitov, "Nowhere Street," *Metropol* (W. W. Norton), pp. 278–9. Bitov quotes the passage in Russian in "Glukhaia ulitsa," *Metropol'* (Ardis), p. 5.

28 Andrei Bitov, "Nowhere Street," *Metropol* (W. W. Norton), pp. 278–300; "Glukhaia ulitsa," *Metropol'* (Ardis), pp. 5–18. Hereafter in my section on "Secluded Street," I shall place citations to the Ardis edition in parentheses immediately following the quotation.

29 This book is a typical Socialist Realist novel whose peasant protagonist turned Party member, Sergei, becomes involved in harnessing the collective will to the implementation of collective farm tasks. Babaevskii won the 1948 Stalin Prize for the novel. Semen Babaevskii, *Kavaler zolotoi zvezdy* (Moscow, 1949). For more on Babaevskii, see Gleb Struve, *Russian Literature under Lenin and Stalin 1917–1953* (Norman, Oklahoma: University of Oklahoma Press, 1971), pp. 383–4 and Vera S. Dunham, *In Stalin's Time*.

Middleclass Values in Soviet Fiction (Cambridge, England: Cambridge University Press, 1979), p. 272, n. 3. Dunham's section, "Rural Quilt," pp. 225–8, on post-World War II Soviet literature's depictions of peasants, collective farms, and agriculture provides excellent background for Bitov's discussion, as does that whole chapter, "Populist Pressure," pp. 225–40. Extremely valuable are Edward Brown's remarks on Babaevskii, on Stalinist literature, and on post-Stalinist literature that deals with the countryside. See, especially, pp. 14, 181–2, and 299 of Brown's highly intelligent book. Edward J. Brown, *Russian Literature Since the Revolution* (Cambridge, Mass.: Harvard University Press, 1982).

30 When "Glukhaia ulitsa" was republished, as part of "Vybor natury," in *Gruzinskii al'bom* and in *Kniga puteshestvii*, the word "kulak" did not appear in this passage. In *Gruzinskii al'bom*, Bitov substitutes "collective farm workers" ("kolkhoznikov") and "proprietor" ("khoziainu"), p. 43. The *Kniga puteshestvii* version, p. 469, contains the words "proprietor" ("khoziaina," "khoziainu") in both places. The word "prize" remains in these two editions, but "Stalin" is deleted. *Gruzinskii al'bom*, p. 43; *Kniga*, p. 469.

31 The reference to the cow's owner ("khoziaki korovy") stands unchanged in *Gruzinskii al'bom*, p. 47; *Kniga*, p. 474.

32 Official Soviet publications of "Glukhaia ulitsa" retain Bitov's word "kulachka" to describe the old woman. *Gruzinskii al'bom*, p. 48; *Kniga*, p. 474.

33 These words are, of course, the end of Hamlet's famous "To be or not to be" soliloquy, rendered into Russian as "Byt' ili ne byt', vot v chem vopros."

34 The word "miamlet" comes from the verb "miamlit'," "to mumble, vacillate, procrastinate." The word play does not quite come off in English. In Russian, there is a rhyming quality about all four words with their "-yt'," "-it'," "-et," "-et" endings. In addition, the proximity of the Russian word for Hamlet to the Russian word for vacillate is not duplicated in the English. George Saunders, translator of the Bitov stories into English in *Metropol* (W. W. Norton), renders the phrase, "Hamlet rambles ..." Bitov, "Nowhere Street," in *Metropol* (W. W. Norton), p. 296.

35 He was born in 1936.

36 See Nikolai Rubtsov, *Izbrannoe* (Moscow, 1982). On Rubtsov, see Vadim Kozhinov, *Nikolai Rubtsov* (Moscow, 1976) and his "Nikolai Rubtsov," in Kozhinov, *Stat'i o sovremennoi literature* (Moscow, 1982), pp. 161–90.

37 Nikolai Rubtsov, "Videniia na kholme," in his *Izbrannoe*, p. 39. For a picture of the gravestone, see photograph opposite p. 17 in *Vospominaniia o Rubtsove* (Arkhangel'sk), 1983).

38 It is no coincidence, I believe, that Bitov included the story "Glukhaia ulitsa," in *Gruzinskii al'bom* and in *Kniga puteshestvii*, in "Vybor natury," his travelogue about Georgia, the birthplace of Stalin.

39 Andrei Bitov, "Pokhorony doktora," in *Metropol'* (Ardis), pp. 19–29. It has appeared in Bitov, *Chelovek v peizazhe*, pp. 107–23. Hereafter in my section on "The Doctor's Funeral," I shall place citations to the Ardis edition in parentheses immediately following the quotation.

40 Andrei Bitov, "Pisatel' i chitatel'," in *Stat'i*, p. 8.

41 *Ibid.*

42 In conversation, Bitov said that her death was one of three significant deaths in his life in the year 1977. (The other two were his father's and Nabokov's.) Bitov explained that he speaks about her at the end of "The Wheel," when he describes someone showing him a passage from Goethe's *Italian Journey*. Chances, conversation with Bitov, May, 1987, Princeton.

43 George Saunders' translation of "tëtka" as "Auntie" is a good one; I use it in my discussion of the story. Bitov, "The Doctor's Funeral," *Metropol* (W. W. Norton), pp. 300 and ff.

44 Bitov states that he had not had this incident in mind when he wrote "The Doctor's Funeral." Chances, conversation with Bitov, Moscow, August 1988.

10 *"Sunday": more "I-lands" and journeys*

1 Andrei Bitov, *Voskresnyi den'. Rasskazy, povesti, puteshestviia* (Moscow, 1980).

11 *"Puskin House": the riddles of life and literature*

1 Dmitrii S. Likhachev, "Ot pokaianiia – k deistviiu," Interview with Dmitrii Likhachev, *Literaturnaia gazeta*, Sept. 9, 1987, p. 2.

2 Andrei Bitov, "Prorvat' krug," *Novyi mir*, no. 12, 1986, p. 249.

3 Andrei Bitov, *Pushkinskii dom* (Ardis), p. 79.

4 "Soldat. Iz vospominanii o semeistve Odoevtsevykh," *Zvezda*, no. 7, 1973, pp. 24–40; "Chto bylo, chto est', chto budet ... Istoriia odnoliuba. Povest'," *Avrora*, no. 1, 1975, pp. 25–44; "Akhilles i cherepakha," *Literaturnaia gazeta*, Jan. 22, 1975, p. 6; "Pod znakom Al'biny. Iz khroniki semeistva Odoevtsevykh," *Druzhba narodov*, no. 7, 1975, pp. 89–99; "Tri proroka," *Voprosy literatury*, no. 7, 1976, pp. 145–74. For a listing of these facts, see Wolf Schmid, "Materialen zu einer Bitov-Bibliographie," *Wiener Slawistischer Almanach*, vol. 4, 1979, pp. 483, 484.

An English version of "Pod znakom Al'biny" appeared, with the title, "Under the Sign of Albina. From the Odoyevtsev Family Chronicle," in the Soviet Union's English-language journal *Soviet Literature*, no. 10, 1976, pp. 39–53.

5 Andrei Bitov, *Pushkinskii dom* (Ann Arbor, Michigan: Ardis Publishers, 1978). Hereafter in my section on *Pushkin House*, I shall place page references to the Ardis edition in parentheses immediately following the quotation.

Bitov jokes that it was comforting to see that even his typographical errors were preserved in the Ardis version of *Pushkin House*. Bitov talk, Columbia University, New York City, April 28, 1987.

For a detailed account of the publication history of *Pushkin House*, see Ronald Meyer, "Bitov's *Puškinskij Dom*," chapter 3, "The Phantom Novel: The Pre-Publication History of *Puškinskij Dom*," pp. 76–93.

6 See, especially, Ronald Meyer, "Bitov's *Puškinskij Dom*," and È. Khappenenn, "Roman-prizrak 1964–1977. Opyt bibliografii neizdannoi knigi," *Wiener Slawistischer Almanach*, vol. 9, 1982, pp. 431–75.

7 È, Khappenenn, "Prilozhenie k romanu Andreia Bitova 'Pushkinskii dom,'" 1978. I am grateful to Ronald Meyer for making this text available to me. It has now appeared, as "Commentary" ("Kommentarii"), in the 1989 Soviet book, Andrei Bitov, *Pushkinskii dom* (Moscow, 1989), pp. 355–99; in "Blizkoe retro, ili kommentarii k obshcheizvestnomu," *Novyi mir*, no. 4, 1989, pp. 135–64; and as "Commentary to the Anniversary Edition of the Novel (1999) (Compiled by Academician L. N. Odoevtsev)," in Andrei Bitov, *Pushkin House*, trans. Susan Brownsberger (Ann Arbor, Michigan: Ardis Publishers, 1990), pp. 373–414.

8 Andrei Bitov, *Pushkin House*, trans. Susan Brownsberger (New York: Farrar, Straus and Giroux, 1987).

9 *Novyi mir*, nos, 10, 11, 12, 1987.

10 Andrei Bitov, "Otets ottsa," *Literaturnaia gazeta*, September 16, 1987, p. 6. Andrei Bitov, *"Pushkinskii dom"* (excerpt), in *Ogonëk*, no. 41, October 1987, pp. 20–4. The *Ogonëk* excerpts are from the prologue and the first chapter, "Otets," in Andrei Bitov, *Pushkinskii dom*, pp. 11–38.

11 "Akhilles i cherepakha" and "Professiia geroia,"in Andrei Bitov, *Stat'i iz romana* (Moscow, 1986), pp. 148–55 and pp. 175–209.

12 Bitov, "The Soldier (From the Memoirs of the Monakhov Family)," in Bitov, *Life in Windy Weather*, pp. 93–113.

13 Vladimir Nabokov, *The Gift*, trans. Michael Scammell with the collaboration of the author (New York: Capricorn Books, 1963),

p. 216; Vladimir Nabokov, *Dar* (New York: Izdatel'stvo imeni Chekhova, 1952), p. 230.

14 *Ibid.*, p. 217; p. 230.

15 That Bitov is familiar with organic chemistry makes sense since geologists' training at the Mining Institute includes organic chemistry as a subject of study.

Two other recent novels whose structural and thematic concerns depend upon scientific principles are Italo Calvino's *Mr. Palomar*, trans. William Weaver (San Diego, California: Harcourt Brace Jovanovich, 1985) and Primo Levi's *The Periodic Table*, trans. Raymond Rosenthal (New York: Schocken Books, 1984).

16 I am thankful to Maitland Jones and Joseph LaPrade of Princeton University's Department of Chemistry for their discussions of organic chemistry.

17 Bitov's image of the first "ring," "kol'tso," is, I believe, reminiscent of the title of Solzhenitsyn's *First Circle* (*V kruge pervom*), which itself hails back to Dante's *Inferno*.

18 The copy of the novel in which this handwritten addendum appears is in my possession. The French translation includes the subtitle. Andrei Bitov, *La maison Pouchkine. Roman de l'humiliation infinie.*

19 Bitov, *Pushkin House* (Farrar, Straus), p. 6.

20 Nikolai Uvarov, "Sviaz' vremen," *Literaturnaia gazeta*, June 10, 1970, p. 3.

21 In the Khappenenn Appendix, Bitov mentions this fact. He explains that he found the piece of newspaper in August, 1970, but did not use it "for its purpose," a playful reference to the use, in the Soviet Union, of torn pieces of newspaper for toilet paper. Khappenenn, "Prilozhenie," p. 6.

22 Bitov remarked upon this device in a conversation with me, May, 1987, Princeton.

23 Bitov makes the same point, in his own words, in "... I nikto ne znaet, chto delat' s ètoi stranoi ... (Dialog s Andreem Bitovym)," in Andrei Karaulov, *Vokrug Kremlia. Kniga politicheskikh dialogov* (Moscow, 1990), p. 19.

24 I summarize Modest Platonovich's important speech, Bitov, *Pushkin House*, pp. 75–90, on pages 213–5 of this chapter.

25 G. Mondri, "Roman Andreia Bitova 'Pushkinskii Dom' (k voprosu o zhanre)," *Slavic Symposium 1982*, Proceedings of the First Symposium on Slavic Culture, University of Witwatersrand (Johannesburg, South Africa), Department of Russian Studies, 23–24 September, 1982. Ed. Irene Masing-Delic, p. 183.

26 The title, in *Days of Man*, of the excerpts from *Pushkin House* was

"The Young Odoevtsev, Hero of a Novel" ("Molodoi Odoevtsev, geroi romana"). Bitov's original title, "A Hero of Our Time," had been changed by the censors (Khappenenn, "Prilozhenie k romanu Andreia Bitova 'Pushkinskii dom,'" p. 48), who were therefore guilty of substituting something false for something real.

27 Andrei Bitov, "Tri 'Proroka'," *Voprosy literatury*, no. 7, 1976, pp. 145–74.

28 "Nuzhny li v literaturovedenii gipotezy?" *Voprosy literatury*, no. 2, 1977, pp. 82–112.

29 *Ibid.*

30 For the *Voprosy literatury* version of the article, Bitov substituted "spirit" and "life" ("dukh," "zhizn'") for God and man. Bitov, "Tri 'Proroka,'" *Voprosy literatury*, p. 148. He restored the words God, man, and the devil/death in the "Hero's Profession" version in Bitov, *Stat'i*, p. 180. In that version, Bitov calls Leva's article "Tiutchev's Duel" ("Duèl' Tiutcheva"). Bitov, *Stat'i*, p. 178.

31 It also relates to present Soviet historical circumstances. In 1989, Bitov stated, "Mitishatiev is a potential leader of a nationalist party, of Pamiat', for example." Bitov, "Andrei Bitov: 'Ne pas marcher,'" p. 7.

32 The second paragraph on pages 365 through the third full paragraph on page 367 reproduces, word for word, the second paragraph on pages 11 through the third paragraph on page 13. Bitov, *Pushkinskii dom* (Ardis).

33 Khappenenn, "Prilozhenie," p. 4.

34 Bitov, "Professiia geroia," in *Stat'i*, p. 176.

35 Neil Cornwell, *The Life, Times and Milieu of V. F. Odoyevsky 1804–1869* (London: The Athlone Press, 1986), p. 3. In a playful footnote in the Khappenenn appendix to *Pushkin House*, the author insists that his class origins are not aristocratic, that they are bourgeois, like Mikhail Zoshchenko's protagonist Michel Siniagin's, in his "Mishel' Siniagin," Khappenenn, "Prilozhenie," p. 25. The passage Khappenenn quotes, not quite accurately, from "Mishel' Siniagin," is "Mat' ego byla dvorianka, a otets pochetnyi grazhdanin." Mikhail Zoshchenko, "Mishel' Siniagin," in Mikhail Zoshchenko, *Izbrannye proizvedeniia*, vol. 1 (Leningrad, 1968), p. 401. In his footnote, the author "rhymes" his life with that of a literary character from early Soviet literature.

   In fact, Bitov's mother, O. A. Kedrova (to whom he dedicated *Such a Long Childhood*) was a jurist by occupation. His father was an architect. Chances, conversation with Bitov, May, 1987, Princeton.

36 Bitov, *Stat'i*, p. 213.

37 On this, see Simon Karlinsky, "A Hollow Shape: The Philosophi-

cal Tales of Prince Vladimir Odoevsky," *Studies in Romanticism*, vol.
5, Spring 1966, no. 3, pp. 172–3.

38 *Literaturnye pamiatnye mesta Leningrada*, ed. A. M. Dokusov (Leningrad, 1968), p. 190.

39 Charles Dickens, *Bleak House* (New York: George Routledge and Sons, n.d.), vol. 1, p. 5. In 1981, Bitov, in response to a question about how he first came to literature, acknowledged the enormous impression Dickens' *Pickwick Papers* had made upon him as a teenager. Bitov, "Masterstvo – èto garmoniia," p. 4.

40 Khappenenn, "Prilozhenie," p. 49.

41 The question of influence is complicated, as Bitov admits. For example, he comments that while "The Garden" is "reminiscent" of *Swann in Love*, he had not yet read Proust when he wrote "The Garden." Khappenenn, "Prilozhenie," p. 49.

42 Pushkin's words are: "[A vot] to budet, chto i nas ne budet," "poslovitsa Sv.[iatogorskogo] Igu[mena]," from "Proekt èpigrafa," "Povesti Belkina. Varianty avtografa," in A. S. Pushkin, *Polnoe sobranie sochinenii* (Leningrad, 1940), vol. 8, Part II, pp. 580–1.

43 Ronald Meyer points out the similarity of plot in "The Little Blizzard" and "The Blizzard." Ronald Meyer, "Bitov's *Puškinskij Dom*," pp. 185–6.

44 Bitov asserts that he had Erskine Caldwell in mind here. The incident is vaguely autobiographical in that Caldwell visited the USSR, and Bitov met him. Chances, conversation with Bitov, May, 1987, Princeton.

45 Ronald Meyer refers to this Lermontov scene which is repeated in Bitov's novel. Ronald Meyer, "Bitov's *Puškinskij Dom*," pp. 126–7, 165.

46 Nabokov, *Dar*, p. 54.

47 *Ibid.*, p. 84.

48 Khappenenn, "Prilozhenie," p. 51; Bitov talk at Columbia University, April 28, 1987.

49 Khappenenn, "Prilozhenie," p. 44.

50 A. S. Pushkin, "Besy," as quoted in F. M. Dostoevskii, *Besy*, in F. M. Dostoevskii, *Polnoe sobranie sochinenii* (Leningrad, 1974), vol. 10, p. 5.

51 A. S. Pushkin, "Besy," as quoted in Bitov, *Pushkinskii dom* (Ardis), p. 311.

52 A. S. Pushkin, "Besy," in A. S. Pushkin, *Polnoe sobranie sochinenii* (Leningrad, 1948), vol. 3, p. 226.

53 Ronald Meyer correctly traces a progression – or we might call it a retrogression – from Bitov's first epigraph, to the chapter, "Duel," of Part Three, where the duelling scenes described have some

stature, through Dostoevsky's Gaganov/Stavrogin encounter, to Sologub's demons, where the demons have been reduced to petty, parodistic dimensions. Meyer shows that the drunken brawl that Bitov describes in this section is itself utterly petty. Meyer, "Bitov's *Puškinskij Dom*," pp. 153–4.

54 *Ibid.*, pp. 133, 166; Iu. Karabchievskii, "Tochka boli. O romane Andreia Bitova, 'Pushkinskii Dom,'" *Grani*, vol. 106, 1977, p. 171 and Sasha Sokolov, "Untitled," Ardis archive, as quoted in Ronald Meyer, "Bitov's *Puškinskij Dom*," p. 230.
55 F. M. Dostoevskii, *Brat'ia Karamazovy*, in *Polnoe sobranie v tridtsati tomakh* (Leningrad, 1976), vol. 15, pp. 69, 72.
56 Chances, conversations with Bitov, May, 1987, Princeton.
57 Ronald Meyer, "Bitov's *Puškinskij Dom*," p. 198.
58 Khappenenn, "Prilozhenie," p. 20.
59 Chances, conversations with Bitov, May, 1987, Princeton.
60 Ronald Meyer, "Bitov's *Puškinskij Dom*," 176–7. Meyer also notes an earlier commentator on the connections between Bakhtin's ideas on the polyphonic novel and Bitov's *Pushkin House*. A. Gimein, in a short piece on *Pushkin House*, states that Bitov's novel incorporates a dialogic relationship between author and hero. A. Gimein, "Nulevoj čas," *Kontinent*, no. 20, 1979, p. 363; as quoted in Ronald Meyer, "Bitov's *Puškinskij Dom*," pp. 176, 203.
61 Mikhail Bakhtin, *Problemy poètiki Dostoevskogo* (Moscow, 1963).
62 For a thorough examination of Tynianov's ideas consult Sandra Gayle Freels Rosengrant, "The Theoretical Criticism of Ju. N. Tynjanov," PhD dissertation, Stanford University, 1976.
63 Chances, conversations with Bitov, May, 1987, Princeton.
64 The statue is on the University Embankment (Universitetskaia naberezhnaia) on the Neva, in front of the Academy of Arts. For a description, see Y. Doroshinskaya and V. Kruchina-Bogdanov, *Leningrad and Its Environs. A Guide* (Moscow, 1979), pp. 100–1.
65 Tengiz Abuladze's film "Repentance" ("Pokaianie") concentrates on characters such as these, who kept the lies alive in Soviet society. For more on *Pushkin House* and "Repentance," see Ellen Chances, "Keeping the Lies Alive: Case Studies of the Psychology of Stalinism in Contemporary Soviet Literature and Film," *The Harriman Institute Forum*, vol. 4, no. 4, 1991, pp. 1–8.
66 Aleksandr Blok, as quoted in Bitov, *Pushkinskii dom* (Ardis), p. 410.
67 Aleksandr Blok, "O naznachenii poèta," in Aleksandr Blok, *Sobranie sochinenii* (Moscow–Leningrad, 1962), vol. 6, pp. 160–8.
68 Bitov, "Cherepakha i Akhilles ("Vtorichnye zametki)," in Bitov, *Stat'i iz romana*, p. 174.
69 Khappenenn, "Prilozhenie," p. 45.

12. *Bitov's post-"Pushkin House" prose, or life in the images of life*

1 Lily Tomlin as Trudy, the Bag Lady, in Jane Wagner, *The Search for Signs of Intelligent Life in the Universe* (New York: Harper & Row, Publishers, 1986), pp. 26, 29.
2 The new sections are "Pal'ma pervenstva," pp. 60–78; "Vopros Ivanova," pp. 89–99; "Rodina, ili mogila," pp. 141–59; and "Rasseianyi svet," pp. 159–70.
3 "The Doctor's Funeral" was supposed to be here instead of the "Battle" section that comprises pages 124–41 of *Georgian Album*. Chances, conversations with Bitov, May, 1987, Princeton.
4 Bitov, *Gruzinskii al'bom*, p. 98.
5 Bitov, *Pushkinskii dom* (Ardis), pp. 294–5.
6 Bitov, *Gruzinskii al'bom*, p. 99.
7 Bitov, "Rasseiannyi svet," in *Gruzinskii al'bom*, p. 169.
8 Bitov concurs with this interpretation. Chances, conversation with Bitov, April, 1988, Wesleyan University, Middletown, Connecticut.
9 Bitov, Columbia University talk, April 28, 1987.
10 Bitov, *Pushkinskii dom* (Ardis), pp. 395–6; Bitov, *Stat'i*, pp. 317–18.
11 Bitov, *Pushkinskii dom*, p. 409; Bitov, *Stat'i*, p. 318.
12 Bitov, *Stat'i*, pp. 74, 78, 84.
13 *Ibid.*, p. 165.
14 Andrei Bitov, "Fotografiia Pushkina (1799–2099)," *Znamia*, no. 1, 1987, pp. 98–120.
15 *Ibid.*, p. 98.
16 Andrei Bitov, "Chelovek v peizazhe," *Novyi mir*, no. 3, 1987, pp. 64–99. "Chelovek v peizazhe" was issued as a booklet in the *Ogonëk* series. Andrei Bitov, *Posledniaia povest'. "Chelovek v peizazhe,"* (Moscow: Biblioteka "Ogonek," no. 15, 1988). It has appeared in Bitov, *Chelovek v peizazhe*, pp. 252–306.
17 Chances, conversations with Bitov, May, 1987, Princeton.
18 Bitov, "Chelovek," p. 77.
19 È. Taird-Boffin, "'Prepodavatel' simmetrii,' (vol'nyi perevod s inostrannogo Andreia Bitova)," *Iunost'*, no. 4, 1987, pp. 12–150. It has since appeared in Bitov, *Chelovek v peizazhe*, pp. 309–458.
20 Bitov says that the name is an anagram for Andrei Bitov (the "v" of Bitov being replaced by "ff"). Chances, conversations with Bitov, Moscow, August, 1988.
21 Chances, conversation with Bitov, Washington, D.C., April 25, 1987.
22 Bitov, "Prepodavatel' simmetrii," p. 50.
23 Daniil Kharms, "Blue Notebook No. 10," in *Russia's Lost Literature*

of the Absurd. A Literary Discovery. Selected Works of Daniil Kharms and Alexander Vvedensky, trans. and ed. George Gibian (New York: W. W. Norton and Company, Inc., 1974), p. 53; Daniil Kharms, *Izbrannoe*, p. 47.

24 Lewis Carroll, *Alice's Adventures in Wonderland* (New York: A. L. Burt Company, n.d.), pp. 130–1.

Bibliography

WORKS BY ANDREI BITOV

Bitov, Andrei. "Akhilles i cherepakha." *Literaturnaia gazeta,* January 22, 1975, p. 6.

Analysis of Mikhail Popov, "Baloven' sud'by. Povest'." *Literaturnaia ucheba,* 6 (1983), 37–8.

"Andrei Bitov: In Search of Lost Meaning." [Interview with Andrei Bitov.] *Books and Art in the USSR,* no. 3/58 (1988), pp. 34–5.

"Andrei Bitov: 'Ne pas marcher au même pas que l'Histoire, mais rester soi-même.'" [Interview with Andrei Bitov.] *La Quinzaine littéraire,* no. 525, Feb. 1–15, 1989, p. 7.

Aptekarskii ostrov. Leningrad, 1968.

"A Twentieth-Century Pastoral" [English translation of Andrei Bitov, "Pastoral' XX vek"], Introduction, Grant Matevosian, *The Orange Herd.* Moscow, 1976, pp. 7–11.

"Avtobus." *Studencheskii meridian,* 8 (1988), 31–6.

"Babushkina piala." *My–molodye.* (Moscow, 1969), pp. 403–6.

"Bitov: l'energie de l'erreur." [Interview with Andrei Bitov.] *Magazine littéraire,* March, 1989, pp. 39–41.

"Blizkoe retro, ili kommentarii k obshcheizvestnomu." *Novyi mir,* 4 (1989), 135–64.

Bol'shoi shar. Moscow, 1963.

"Chelovek v peizazhe." *Novyi mir,* 3 (1987), 64–99.

Chelovek v peizazhe. Povesti i rasskazy. Moscow, 1988.

"Chto bylo, chto est', chto budet ... Istoriia odnoliuba. Povest'." *Avrora,* 1 (1975), 25–44.

"Chuvstvo Doma." *Nedelia,* 22 (1987), 8–9.

"Chuzhaia sobaka i drugie rasskazy." *Chast' rechi. Al'manakh literatury i iskusstva,* 2–3 (1981–2), 76–94.

Dachnaia mestnost'. Povesti. Moscow, 1967.

"Days of Leavetaking (from the book, *Remembrances of Reality*) ["The Last Bear," "Nowhere Street," "The Doctor's Funeral"]. Trans. George Saunders. *Metropol. Literary Almanac.* Ed. Vasily Aksyonov, Viktor Yerofeyev, Fazil Iskander, Andrei Bitov and Yevgeny Popov. New York: W. W. Norton & Company, 1982, 273–315.

"Dlia kogo pishet kritik?" *Voprosy literatury*, 3 (1976), 76–82.

Dni cheloveka. Povesti. Moscow, 1976.

"Dom poèta. Iz Gruzinskogo al'boma." *Literaturnaia gazeta*, September 12, 1984, p. 7.

"The Door." *Soviet Literature*, 4 (1990), 80–8.

"'Dospekh tiazhël, kak pered boem' (Razmyshlenie na granitse poèzii i prozy)." *Voprosy literatury*, 7 (1983), 194–203.

"Fotografiia Pushkina (1799–2099)." *Znamia*, 1 (1987), 98–120.

"From *With Bread in Mouth*." Trans. Beckie Barker. *Cherez*, Spring, 1977, 26–39.

"Genial'nyi shkoliar." *Literaturnaia Rossiia*, January 6, 1989, p. 17.

"Gorizontali i vertikali slova." *Druzhba narodov*, 9 (1972), 260–1.

"Granitsa i kozha." [Interview with Andrei Bitov.] *Literaturnyi Azerbaidzhan*, 5 (1988), 109–15.

"Granitsy zhanra." *Voprosy literatury*, 7 (1969), 72–6.

"Gruppovaia fotografiia." *Literaturnaia gazeta*, August 18, 1964, pp. 2–3.

Gruzinskii al'bom. Tbilisi, 1985.

"Gruzinskii al'bom. Rodina poèta. Dom poèta. Rasseiannyi svet. Mogila poèta." *Literaturnaia Gruziia*, 2 (1985), 162–96.

"The Habit of Fear." [Interview with Andrei Bitov.] *Index on Censorship*, 17, no. 5 (1988), 11.

"Iasnost' bessmertiia (Vospominaniia nepredstavlennogo)," Introduction, Vladimir Nabokov, *Krug*. Leningrad, 1990, pp. 3–20.

"'... I nikto ne znaet, chto delat' s ètoi stranoi ...' (Dialog s Andreem Bitovym)." *Vokrug Kremlia. Kniga politicheskikh dialogov.* Andrei Karaulov. Moscow, 1990, 17–25.

Intro. to V. Narbikova, "Ravnovesie sveta dnevnykh i nochnykh zvezd." *Iunost'*. 8 (1988), 15.

"Izobrazhenie i slovo." *Neva*, 8 (1970), 186–8.

"Iz sbornika 'S khlebom vo rtu.'" in *The Blue Lagoon Anthology of Modern Russian Poetry*. Ed. Konstantin Kuzminsky and Gregory L. Kovalev. Newtonville, Mass.: Oriental Research Partners, 1983. vol. IIa, 191–9.

"Iz tsikla 'Pogrebenie zazhivo.'" *Sintaksis*, 24 (1988), 132–52.

"Kharakter: podrobnyi ili èskiznyi? Kak uchit'sia u velikikh?" *Literaturnaia Rossiia*, September 25, 1964, pp. 18–19.

Kniga puteshestvii. Moscow, 1986.

"Kommentarii k obshcheizvestnomu." *Literaturnaia gazeta*, Apr. 12, 1989, p. 6.

La maison Pouchkine. Roman de l'humiliation infinie. Trans. Philippe Mennecier. Paris: Albin Michel, 1989.

Life in Windy Weather. Short Stories. Ed. Priscilla Meyer. Trans. Priscilla Meyer *et al.* Ann Arbor, Michigan: Ardis Publishers, 1986.

"Life in Windy Weather." Ed. Priscilla Meyer. Trans. Carol and Richard Luplow, in *Contemporary Russian Prose.* Ed. Carl and Ellendea Proffer. Ann Arbor, Michigan: Ardis Publishers, 1982, pp. 305–33.

"The Little Devil." *Soviet Literature*, 4 (1990), 88–92.

"Liudi, pobrivshiesia v subbotu." *Teatral'naia zhizn'*, 16 (1987), 23.

"Masterstvo – èto garmoniia (Beseda s pisatelem A. Bitovym)." Interviewed by M. Mamatsashvili and V. Khanumian. *Molodezh' Gruzii*, Nov. 19, 1981, p. 4.

"Mogila poèta." *Studencheskii meridian*, 8 (1988), 36–7.

"Naedine so vsemi. Anketa." *Literaturnoe obozrenie*, 10 (1977), 96–7.

"Nekrolog." *Sintaksis*, 21 (1988), 60–3.

"Net! Nikogda ia zavisti ne znal ...." *Literaturnaia gazeta*, July 7, 1982, p. 3.

"Nikanor Ivanych i vedomstva...." *Literaturnaia gazeta*, March 13, 1965, p. 2.

"Novyi Robinzon (k 125-letiiu vykhoda v svet 'Zapisok iz Mertvogo doma')." *Znamia*, 12 (1987), 221–7.

"Ob otkryvshikhsia vozmozhnostiakh i naidennom puti." Material prepared by Tat'iana Moskvina. *Sovietskii èkran*, 7 (1988), 4–5.

"Obraz." *Zvezda*, 12 (1973), 135–51.

Obraz zhizni. Povesti. Moscow, 1972.

"Obshchaia sud'ba," *Novyi mir*, 9 (1987), 251–4.

"Odnoklassniki." *Novyi mir*, 5 (1990), 224–42.

"Okonchanie knigi." *Literaturnaia gazeta*, August 1, 1990, p. 6.

"On voshël v nashu zhizn'." [Bitov's answer to questionnaire about Pushkin.] *Nauka i zhizn'*, 3 (1987), 24–6.

"Ot 'a' do 'ia.'" *Literaturnaia gazeta*, Nov. 25, 1981, p. 6.

"Otets ottsa." *Literaturnaia gazeta*, September 16, 1987, p. 6.

"Pastoral', XX vek." *Literaturnaia gazeta*, June 28, 1967, p. 6.

"Peizazh." *Den' poèzii.* Ed. Iurii Kuznetsov. Moscow, 1983, p. 94.

"Pervyi dom." *Literaturnaia gazeta*, February 19, 1986, p. 6.

"Pisatel' pishet smyslami ...'" *Literaturnaia gazeta*, August 3, 1983, p. 5.

"Pobeda (rasskaz)." *Sem'ia i shkola*, 3 (1966), 26–9.

"Pochemu ia nichego ne smysliu v balete ..." *Novoe russkoe slovo*, April 26, 1988, p. 8.

"Pod znakom Al'biny. Iz khroniki semeistva Odoevtsevykh." *Druzhba narodov*, 7 (1975), 88–99.

"Poèziia i proza kooperativnoi èpokhi." *Literaturnaia gazeta*, May 2, 1990, p. 4.

"Pokhval'noe slovo chudakam …" *Literaturnaia gazeta*, September 7, 1983, p. 5.

"Polët s geroem." *Literaturnaia Rossiia*, November 15, 1985, pp. 18–19.

"Portret khudozhnika v smelosti." *Moskovskie novosti*, Feb. 15, 1987, p. 13.

Posledniaia povest'. *"Chelovek v peizazhe."* Biblioteka "Ogonëk," Moscow, no. 15, 1988.

"Poslednii medved'." *Studencheskii meridian*, 2 (1975), 26–7.

"Poslednii tekst." *Literaturnaia gazeta*, June 3, 1981, p. 6.

"Postskriptum cherez piatnadtsat' let." *Literaturnaia Armeniia*, 3 (1983), 102–6.

Povesti i rasskazy. Izbrannoe. Moscow, 1989.

"Prazdnik." *Moskovskii komsomolets*, July 28, 1967, p. 4.

"Predpolozhenie zhit'." *Zvezda*, 1 (1986), 153–76.

"Priamoe vdokhnoven'e. Pamiati Iuriia Kazakova." *Voprosy literatury*, 7 (1984), 174–81.

"Prorvat' krug." *Novyi mir*, 12 (1986), 245–51.

"Proshchal'nye den'ki (iz knigi 'Vospominaniia o real'nosti')" ["Poslednii medved'," "Glukhaia ulitsa," "Pokhorony doktora"]. *Metropol'*. Ed. V. Aksenov, A. Bitov, V. Erofeev, F. Iskander and E. Popov. Moscow, 1979, facsimile edition. Ann Arbor. Michigan: Ardis Publishers, 1979, 1–29.

Pushkin House. Trans. Susan Brownsberger. Ann Arbor, Michigan: Ardis Publishers, 1990.

Pushkin House. Trans. Susan Brownsberger. New York: Farrar, Straus and Giroux, 1987.

Pushkinskii dom. Ann Arbor, Michigan: Ardis Publishers, 1978.

Pushkinskii dom. Novyi mir, 10 (1987), 3–92; 11 (1987), 55–91; 12 (1987), 50–110.

"Pushkinskii dom," (Excerpts), *Ogonëk*, no. 41, October, 1987, pp. 20–4.

Pushkinskii dom. Roman. Moscow, 1989.

"Pushkin's Photograph (1799–2099)." Trans. Priscilla Meyer. *The New Soviet Fiction. Sixteen Short Stories.* Compiled by Sergei Zalygin. Ed. Jacqueline Decter. New York: Abbeville Press Publishers, 1989.

Puteshestvie k drugu detstva. Leningrad, 1968.

"Quia nominor Leo ... Retrospektiva." *Literaturnaia Armeniia*, 1 (1987), 16–31; 2 (1987), 18–36.

Rannii Bitov. vols. 1, 2, Leningrad (manuscript), 1960.

"Razgovor idet o rasskaze." *Literaturnaia Rossiia*, Aug. 2, 1964, pp. 6–7.

"Raznye dni cheloveka." [Interview with Andrei Bitov.] *Literaturnaia gazeta,* July 22, 1987, p. 6.

"Revaz Gabriadze." *Panorama iskusstv,* 8 (1985), 367–74.

"Roman – postupok zhizni," 156–9 in "Na perednem krae literatury. (Obsuzhdaiutsia problemy romana)." *Literaturnaia Gruziia*, 7 (1982), 145–75.

"Romantizm i opyt." *Druzhba narodov*, 3 (1982), 256–60.

Sem' puteshestvii. Leningrad, 1976.

Sobranie sochinenii. Povesti i rasskazy. vol. 1. Moscow, 1991.

"Soldat. Iz vospominanii o semeistve Odoevtsevykh." *Zvezda,* 7 (1973), 24–40.

"Soobrazhenie prozaika o muze." *Den' poèzii.* Ed. V. S. Fogel'son. Moscow, 1981, pp. 234–6.

"Soprotivlenie kul'tury (Akltual'noe interv'iu)." Interviewed by Aleksandr Nikolaev. *Knizhnoe obozrenie*, April 27, 1990, pp. 8–9.

Stat'i iz romana. Moscow, 1986.

"Svobodu Pushkinu!" *Sintaksis*, 27 (1990), 167–75.

Takoe dolgoe detstvo. Leningrad, 1965.

"Tridtsatogo dekabria (otryvok iz povesti 'Sad')." *Moskovskii komsomolets,* June 8, 1966, p. 4.

"Tri 'Proroka'." *Voprosy literatury*, 7 (1976), 145–74.

"Tri puteshestviia. (Uroki Armenii, Vybor natury, Koleso)," in *Ne schitai shagi, putnik!,* Moscow, 1974, pp. 13–281.

"*Tri puteshestviia (Uroki Armenii, Vybor natury, Koleso).* Reprint of Bitov, "Tri puteshestviia" (Moscow, 1974). New York: Orfei, 1986.

"Tri stikhotvoreniia." *Druzhba narodov,* 12 (1988), 105–7.

"'Ty odin mne podderzhka i opora...'" *Sintaksis*, 23 (1988), 176–7.

"Uletaiushchii Monakhov." *Zvezda,* 8 (1976), 3–48.

Uletaiushchii Monakhov. Roman–punktir. Moscow, 1990.

"Under the Sign of Albina. From the Odoyevtsev Family Chronicle." *Soviet Literature*, 10 (1976), 39–53.

"Uroki Armenii." *Druzhba narodov*, 9 (1969), 161–227.

Uroki Armenii. Erevan, 1978.

"Ustalost' parovoza. Zapiski nachinaiushchego iazvennika." *Nezavisimaia gazeta,* March 30, 1991, p. 7.

"Vkus." *Literaturnaia Gruziia*, 1 (1983), 57–98.

"Vkus." *Ogonëk*, 17 (1987), 22–5.

Voskresnyi den'. Rasskazy, povesti, puteshestviia. Moscow, 1980.

"Vospominanie ob Argartsine. Rasskaz." *Literaturnaia Armeniia*, 10 (1984), 70–4.

"Vospominanie o Pushkine." *Znamia*, 12 (1985), 195–226.

"V poiskakh real'nosti. Beseda korrespondenta 'LO' Evg. Shklovskogo s Andreem Bitovym." *Literaturnoe obozrenie*, 5 (1988), 32–8.

"The Wheel." Trans. Frederick R. Croen. Croen, "A Translation of 'The Wheel' of Andrei Bitov," Princeton University Senior Thesis, 1974.

"Zapiski iz-za ugla." *Novyi mir*, 2 (1990), 142–65.

"Zapovednik. Kinomelodrama." *Iskusstvo kino*, 8 (1977), 159–91.

Bitov, Andrei and others. "Kruglyi stol. Andrei Platonov segodnia." *Literaturnaia gazeta*, September 23, 1987, p. 3.

"Kruglyi stol. Vladimir Nabokov: Mezh dvukh beregov." *Literaturnaia gazeta*, August 17, 1988, p. 5.

Bitov, Andrei and Pulatov, Timur. "Dialog. Iazyk naroda i iazyk iskusstva." *Literaturnaia gazeta*, April 30, 1986, p. 3.

Bitov, Andrei and Znatnov, A. "Konflikty i kontakty." [Interview with Andrei Bitov.] *V mire knig*, 11 (1987), 75–7.

Khappenenn, È. [Bitov]. "Prilozhenie k romanu Andreia Bitova 'Pushkinskii dom.'" Unpublished manuscript, 1978.

"Roman-prizrak 1964–1977. Opyt bibliografii neizdannoi knigi." *Wiener Slawistischer Almanach*, 9 (1982), 431–75.

Taird-Boffin, È. [Bitov]. "'Prepodavatel' simmetrii.' Vol'nyi perevod s inostrannogo Andreia Bitova." *Iunost'*, 4 (1987), 12–50.

GENERAL BIBLIOGRAPHY

Akhvlediani, Èrlom. "Vano i Niko. Sovremennaia skazka." Trans. Aida Abuashvili. *Druzhba narodov*, 10 (1969), 126–33.

Akimov, V. "Chto otkryvaet 'putevaia proza'?" *V nachale semidesiatykh. Literatura nashikh dnei.* Compiler I. S. Eventov. Leningrad, 1973, 129–53.

"Mir v kaple rasskaza ... Zametki o rasskaze v Leningradskikh zhurnalakh." *Avrora*, 4 (1975), 59–62.

"Osvoenie vremeni." *Zvezda*, 4 (1964), 209–17.

Al'bom Sar'ian. Intro. and compiled by Aleksandr Abramovich Kamenskii. Moscow, 1968.

Alenina, N. "... Ne bez dobrykh liudei." *Iskusstvo kino*, 9 (1967), 48–9.

Amiranashvili, Sh. *Al'bom 'Pirosmanashvili'.* Moscow, 1967.

Anan'eva, Avgusta. "Preuvelichenie chuvstv." *Sibirskie ogni*, 2 (1966), 169–76.

Anashenkov, B. "'Vyedennoe iaitso. Seredina. Sedina ...'." *Literaturnoe obozrenie*, 1 (1977), 59–61.

Anninskii, Lev. "Slozhnost' mirooshchushcheniia ..." *Literaturnaia gazeta*, April 17, 1968, p. 5.

"Strannyi strannik." Afterword in Andrei Bitov, *Kniga puteshestvii*. Moscow, 1986, pp. 598–606.

"Strannyi strannik." *Literaturnaia Armeniia*, 10 (1985), 63–70.

"Tochka opory. Èticheskie problemy sovremennoi prozy." *Don*, 6 (1968), 168–81.

Tridtsatye – semidesiatye. Literaturno-kriticheskie stat'i. Moscow, 1977.

Antopol'skii, L. "Nuzhnoe slovo (Nravstvenno-filosofskie poiski sovremennoi prozy)." *Voprosy literatury*, 10 (1975), 73–102.

Apukhtina, V. A. *Sovremennaia sovetskaia proza (60-e–nachalo 70-kh godov).* Moscow, 1977.

Arieti, Silvano. *Creativity. The Major Synthesis.* New York: Basic Books, Inc., 1976.

Austin, Anthony. "The Metropol Affair." *New York Times Book Review*, March 2, 1980, pp. 3, 19.

Austin, Paul. Review of *Pushkinskii Dom. Canadian Slavonic Papers*, vol. 21, no. 3, (1979), 409–10.

Avins, Carol. *Border Crossings. The West and Russian Identity in Soviet Literature 1917–1934.* Berkeley, California: University of California Press, 1983.

Babaevskii, Semen. *Kavaler zolotoi zvezdy.* Moscow, 1949.

Bakhtin, Mikhail. *Problemy poètiki Dostoevskogo.* Moscow, 1963.

Bakich, Olga Hassanoff. "A New Type of Character in the Soviet Literature of the 1960s: The Early Works of Andrei Bitov." *Canadian Slavonic Papers*, 23, no. 2 (1981), 125–33.

Bayley, John. "Riding the Bronze Horse." (Review of *Pushkin House* and Leonid Borodin's *Partings*). *New York Review of Books*, vol. 34, no. 16 (October 22, 1987), 9–10.

Bazhin, N. "Nash drug." *Neva*, 1 (1965), 188–94.

Belaia, G. A. "Rozhdenie novykh stilevykh form kak protsess preodoleniia 'neitral'nogo stilia'." *Teoriia literaturnykh stilei. Mnogoobrazie stilei sovetskoi literatury. Voprosy tipologii.* Ed. N. K. Gei et al. Moscow, 1978, 460–85.

"Sviaz' chuvstv s deistviiami ...," *Zvezda*, 5 (1974), 201–11.

Zatonuvshaia Atlantida. Biblioteka "Ogonëk," Moscow, no. 14, 1991.

Belov, Vasilii. *Lad. Ocherki o narodnoi èstetike.* Moscow, 1982.

"Bitov." *Roshia. Soren o shiru jiten (A Dictionary to Know Called Encyclopedia of Russia and the Soviet Union).* Tokyo: Heibonsha, 1989, 478.

Blok, Aleksandr. *Sobranie sochinenii.* vol. VI, Moscow–Leningrad, 1962.

Bocharov, A. *Beskonechnost' poiska. Khudozhestvennye poiski sovremennoi sovetskoi prozy.* Moscow, 1982.
"Krugi khudozhestvennogo konflikta (Razdum'ia nad tekushchei prozoi)." *Voprosy literatury,* 5 (1974), 41–71.
"Puti tvorcheskogo voobrazheniia." *Druzhba narodov,* 12 (1978), 238–47.
Trebovatel'skaia liubov'. Kontseptsiia lichnosti v sovremennoi sovetskoi proze. Moscow, 1977.
Brovman, G. *Problemy i geroi sovremennoi prozy. Kriticheskoe obozrenie.* Moscow, 1966.
Brown, Clarence. Review, "*The New Soviet Fiction: Sixteen Short Stories,* compiled by Sergei Zalygin." [Includes Bitov's "Pushkin's Photograph."] *The New Republic,* October 2, 1989, pp. 40–1.
Brown, Deming. "Czechoslovak and Polish Influence on Soviet Literature." *The Influence of East Europe and the Soviet West on the USSR.* Ed. Roman Szporluk. New York: Praeger Books, 1975, 117–46.
"Narrative Devices in the Contemporary Soviet Russian Short Story: Intimacy and Irony." *American Contributions to the Seventh International Congress of Slavists. Warsaw, August 21–27, 1973. Vol. II: Literature and Folklore.* Ed. Victor Terras. The Hague: Mouton and Co., 1973, 53–74.
Soviet Russian Literature Since Stalin. Cambridge, England: Cambridge University Press, 1978.
Brown, Edward J. Review, "*Pushkin House* by Andrei Bitov. Trans. Susan Brownsberger." *The Nation.* 246, March 12, 1988, 346–7.
Russian Literature Since the Revolution. Cambridge, Massachusetts: Harvard University Press, 1982.
Burns, I. F. "Cosmogony and Cosmology (Greek)." *Encyclopaedia of Religion and Ethics.* Ed. James Hastings *et al.* New York: Charles Scribner's Sons, 1912. IV, 141–51.
Bursov, B. "Vechernie dumy. Polemicheskie zametki." *Zvezda,* 8 (1968), 198–214.
Bushnell, Scott M. "Life in Windy Weather. Andrei Bitov and the Russian Literary Dialogue." *Wesleyan,* Vol. LXXXI, no. 3, Fall, 1988, 16–17.
Calvino, Italo. *Mr. Palomar.* Trans. William Weaver. San Diego, California: Harcourt Brace Jovanovich, 1985.
Chances, Ellen. "Andrei Bitov's 'Armenia Lessons': Culture and Values," *Armenian Review.* 41, nos. 3–163 (1988), 41–52.
"Andrei Bitov's 'Zhizn' v vetrenuiu pogodu': The Creative Process in Life and Literature." *Slavic Review,* 50, no. 2 (1991), 400–9.
"Andrei Bitov: The Attenuated Boundary Between Art and Life." *Slavic and East European Arts,* 6, no. 2 (1990), 148–58.

"Authenticity as the Tie that Binds: Andrej Bitov's 'Armenia Lessons.'" *Russian Literature*, 28 (1990), 1–9.

Conformity's Children: An Approach to the Superfluous Man in Russian Literature. Columbus, Ohio: Slavica Publishers, Inc., 1978.

"Keeping the Lies Alive: Case Studies of the Psychology of Stalinism in Contemporary Soviet Literature and Film." *The Harriman Institute Forum*, 4, no. 4 (1991), 1–8.

"The Reds and *Ragtime*: The Soviet Reception of E. L. Doctorow." *E. L. Doctorow. Essays and Conversations.* Ed. Richard Trenner. Princeton, New Jersey: Ontario Review Press, 1983, pp. 151–7.

"Sunny Side Up: Creativity in Andrei Bitov's 'Sun.'" *Festschrift for Thomas G. Winner, (Canadian–American Slavic Studies)*, 22, nos. 1–4 (1988), 329–36.

Chudakova, M. and Chudakov, A. "I togda prikhodit povest'." *Literaturnaia gazeta*. August 29, 1973, p. 6.

Chudakova, M. O. *Poètika Mikhaila Zoshchenko*. Moscow, 1979.

Chudnovskaia, È. È. "Za ramkami ocherka (O proze A. Bitova)." *Tashkent. Gosudarstvennyi pedagogicheskii institut. Uchënye zapiski*, 196 (1977), 89–100.

Clark, Katerina. *The Soviet Novel. History as Ritual.* Chicago, Illinois: University of Chicago Press, 1981.

Clark, Katerina and Holquist, Michael. *Mikhail Bakhtin.* Cambridge, Massachusetts: Harvard University Press, 1984.

Close, Kevin, "Moscow Harasses Top Writers over Unofficial Journal." *Washington Post*, February 4, 1979, p. A25.

"Moscow Journal Challenges Tight Control of Arts." *Washington Post*, January 24, 1979, pp. A1, A18.

Cohen, Stephen F. *Rethinking the Soviet Experience. Politics and History Since 1917.* New York and Oxford: Oxford University Press, 1986.

and vanden Heuvel, Katrina. *Voices of Glasnost. Interviews with Gorbachev's Reformers.* New York: W. W. Norton and Company, 1989.

Cornwell, Neil. *The Life, Times and Milieu of V. F. Odoevsky 1804–1869.* London: The Athlone Press, 1986.

Crowther, Bosley. Review of "The Red Balloon," *New York Times*, March 12, 1957, p. 38.

Danow, David K. "Bitov, Andrei Georgievich." *Handbook of Russian Literature.* Ed. Victor Terras. New Haven and London: Yale University Press, 1985, 53–4.

Dedkov, I. "Sladkie, sladkie slezy." *Literaturnoe obozrenie*, 1 (1977), 57–9.

Dickens, Charles. *Bleak House.* New York: George Routledge and Sons, n.d.

310 *Bibliography*

Doroshinskaya, Y. and Kruchina-Bogdanov, V. *Leningrad and Its Environs. A Guide.* Moscow, 1979.
Dostoevskii, F. M. *Polnoe sobranie sochinenii v tridtsati tomakh.* vol. X, Leningrad, 1974; vol. XIV, XV, Leningrad, 1976.
Drozdov, Ivan. "S samoi pristrastnoi liubov'iu." *Ogonëk*, 19 (1969), 24–6.
Dunham, Vera S. *In Stalin's Time. Middleclass Values in Soviet Fiction.* Cambridge, England: Cambridge University Press, 1979.
Èl'chin [*sic*]. "Molla, pomogi mne! Zametki o sovremennom rasskaze." *Druzhba narodov*, 10 (1976), 252–60.
Èligulashvili, Èduard. "Fenomen normy." *Literaturnaia Gruziia*, 11 (1986), 196–200.
Èl'sberg, Ia. "Kul'tura perezhivaniia mira." *Literaturnoe obozrenie*, 10 (1973), 40–4.
"'Mechta o motore' i 'schastlivaia tishina'." *Literaturnaia gazeta*, May 24, 1972, pp. 4–5.
Èpshtein, M. "Vremia samopoznaniia." *Druzhba narodov*, 8 (1978), 276–80.
Ermilov, V. "Budem tochnymi." *Literaturnaia gazeta*, April 16, 1964, p. 3.
Ermolaev, Herman. *Soviet Literary Theories 1917–1934. The Genesis of Socialist Realism.* 1963. Reprint. New York: Octagon Books, 1977.
Erokhin, Aleksei. "Preodolenie nemoty." *V mire knig*, 7 (1987), 48–9.
Ershov, L.F. *Iz istorii sovetskoi satiry. M. Zoshchenko i satiricheskaia proza 20–40kh godov.* Leningrad, 1973.
Evans, Richard I. *Konrad Lorenz. The Man and His Ideas.* New York: Harcourt Brace Jovanovich, 1975.
Falileeva, Anna. "Biografiia chuvstv." Review of *Gruzinskii al'bom. Literaturnaia Gruziia*, 7 (1987), 160–2.
Filiushkina, S. "Ispytanie povsednevnost'iu." *Literaturnaia gazeta*, April 10, 1974, p. 4.
Fomichev, Sergei. "O literaturovedenii chistom i nechistom. O zavedomykh gipotezakh i Leve Odoevtseve." *Zvezda*, 4 (1978), 202–12.
Freedman, John. Review, "*Pushkin House* by Andrei Bitov." *American Book Review*, March–April, 1988, p. 14.
Fridman, Dzhon. "Iskrivlenie real'nosti i vremeni v poiske istiny v romanakh 'Pushkinskii dom' i 'Shkola dlia durakov' (Nenauchnyi ocherk)." *Dvadtsat' dva*, 48 (1986), 201–10.
Gabriadze, Revaz. "O rasskaze 'Vkus' i o romane 'Uletaiushchii Monakhov.'" *Literaturnaia Gruziia*, 1 (1983), 58–61.
Gabriadze, Rezo. "Drug malen'kogo teatra." *Teatral'naia zhizn'*, 16 (1987), 22.

Gei, N. K. *et al. Teoriia literaturnykh stilei. Mnogoobrazie stilei sovetskoi literatury. Voprosy tipologii.* Moscow, 1978.

Geideko, V. "Ot opisanii k osmysleniiu (Zametki o sovremennom rasskaze)." *Sibirskie ogni,* 3 (1965), 173–80.

Gibian, George. "New Aspects of Soviet Russian Literature." *The Soviet Union Since Stalin.* Ed. Stephen F. Cohen, Alexander Rabinowitch and Robert Sharlet. Bloomington, Indiana: Indiana University Press, 1980, 252–75.

"The New and the Old: From an Observer's Notebook." *Problems of Communism,* 2 (1967), 57–64.

"The Urban Theme in Recent Soviet Russian Prose: Notes toward a Typology." *Slavic Review,* 37 (1978), 40–50.

Gifford, Henry. "Mandelstam and the *Journey.*" in Osip Mandelstam, *Journey to Armenia.* Trans. Sidney Monas and Henry Gifford. San Francisco, California: George F. Ritchie, 1979, 7–33.

Gimein, A. "Nulevoi chas." *Kontinent,* 20 (1979), 369–73.

Ginzburg, Lidiia. "O dokumental'noi literature i printsipakh postroeniia kharaktera." *Voprosy literatury,* 7 (1970), 62–91.

O literaturnom geroe. Leningrad, 1979.

O psikhologicheskoi proze. Leningrad, 1971.

O starom i novom. Stat'i i ocherki. Leningrad, 1982.

[Interview] "Pole napriazheniia." *Literaturnaia gazeta,* January 5, 1986, p. 7.

Ginzburg, S. *Istoriia sovetskogo kino.* vol. 4, Moscow, 1978.

Girshman, M. M. and Kuzin, S. V. "Osobennosti avtorskoi pozitsii i organizatsiia povestvovaniia v rasskaze A. Bitova 'Soldat'." *Voprosy russkoi literatury: Respublikanskii Mezhv-edomstvennyi nauchnyi sbornik,* vol. 1 (29), 1977, pp. 69–76.

Gladilin, Anatolii. Review of *Pushkinskii Dom. Tret'ia volna. Al'manakh literatury i iskusstva,* 6 (1979), 105–9.

Goethe, Johann Wolfgang von. *Italian Journey.* Trans. W. H. Auden and Elizabeth Mayer. New York: Pantheon Books, 1962.

Goliavkin, Viktor. *Arfa i boks. Roman.* Leningrad, 1969.

Ia zhdu vas vsegda s interesom. Moscow, 1980.

Odin, Dva. Tri . . . Povesti. Leningrad, 1978.

Goodman, Walter. "Soviet Writers Revel in New-Found Freedom." *New York Times,* March 9, 1989, p. C26.

Grinberg, I. "'A rasti emu – v nebo. . .'." *Literaturnaia gazeta,* January 19, 1965, p. 3.

"Bol'shie ozhidaniia." *Voprosy literatury,* 10 (1970), 3–24.

Gulia, Georgii. "Kak zhe byt' s iumorom? Vopros Vsevolodu Voevodinu." *Literaturnaia gazeta,* April 2, 1964, p. 3.

Gusev, V. "Iskusstvo, analiz, poisk." *Druzhba narodov,* 5 (1973), 277–9.

"Sovest' i *Dni cheloveka.*" in Andrei Bitov, *Dni cheloveka.* Moscow, 1976, 347–50.

V predchuvstvii novogo. O nekotorykh chertakh literatury shestidesiatykh godov. Moscow, 1974.

Hagen, Stephen. "An Unpublished Letter by Andrei Bitov," *Scottish Slavonic Review,* no. 5, 1985, pp. 108–118.

Hagen, Stephen George Sidney. "The Stories of Andrei Bitov, 1958–1966. A Search for Individual Perception." M.A. Dissertation. University of Durham (England), 1980.

Harris, Jane Gary. "The 'Latin Gerundive' as Autobiographical Imperative: A Reading of Mandel'shtam's *Journey to Armenia.*" *Slavic Review,* 45 (1986), 1–19.

Hosking, Geoffrey. *Beyond Socialist Realism. Soviet Fiction Since "Ivan Denisovich".* New York: Holmes and Meier Publishers, Inc., 1980.

Iakimenko, L. "Kriterii otsenok. Metodologicheskie problemy sovremennoi literaturnoi kritiki." *Novyi mir,* 7 (1974), 230–49.

Na dorogakh veka. Aktual'nye voprosy sovetskoi literatury. Moscow, 1973; Moscow, 1978.

Ibn Sīnā (Avicenna), Al-najāt. Ed. M. S. Al-Kurdi (Cairo, 1938).

Ignat'ev, Igor'. "Vstrecha v biblioteke kongressa." *Literaturnaia gazeta,* May 13, 1987, p. 9.

Iutkevich, Sergei I. *Frantsiia – kadr za kadrom. O liudiakh, fil'makh, spektakliakh, knigakh.* Moscow, 1970.

Ivanova, Liudmila. "Rasstavanie s detstvom." *Moskva,* 8 (1965), 200–2.

Ivanova, Natal'ia, "Sud'ba i rol'." *Druzhba narodov,* 3 (1988), 244–55.

"Sud'ba i rol' (Andrei Bitov), in Natal'ia Ivanova, *Tochka zreniia. O proze poslednikh let.* Moscow, 1988, 167–201.

Ivashchenko, Viach. "Sredi knig." *Iunost',* 5 (1968), 96.

Jung, Carl G. *Synchronicity. An Acausal Connecting Principle.* Trans. R. F. C. Hull. Princeton, New Jersey: Princeton University Press, 1973.

Kamianov, V. "Evklidu – Evklidovo (Iz zhizni molodoi prozy)." *Voprosy literatury,* 4 (1969), 26–47.

"Poèticheskii mir prozy." *Literaturnaia Rossiia,* August 9, 1968, p. 20.

"Vzamen tragedii." *Voprosy literatury,* 11 (1978), 3–40.

Kanchukov, Evg. "Ochki dlia zreniia seichas." *Literaturnaia Rossiia,* March 11, 1988, p. 6.

Kantorovich, Vladimir. *Zametki pisatelia o sovremennom ocherke.* Moscow, 1973.

Karabchievskii, Iu., "Tochka boli. O romane Andreia Bitova, 'Pushkinskii Dom,'" *Grani* 106 (1977), 141–203.

Kardin, V. "'Vzryv' i volna 'vzryvnaia'. Zametki o dokumental'noi literature." *Druzhba narodov,* 11 (1976), 246–60.

Karlinsky, Simon. "A Hollow Shape: The Philosophical Tales of Prince Vladimir Odoevsky." *Studies in Romanticism*, 5, no. 3 (1966), 169–82.

Kasak, Wolfgang, "Bitov." *Lexikon der russischen literatur ab 1917*. Stuttgart: Alfred Kroner, 1976, 57–8.

Kasper, K. "Entwicklung und Leistung des Genres der Erzählung in der sowjetischen Literatur, 1945–1975." *Zeitschrift für Slawistik*, 6 (1977), 733–9.

"Proza russkikh-sovetskikh poètov – sovest' chelovechestva." *Zeitschrift für Slawistik*, 31 (1986), 333–6.

Kaverin, V. "Uroki i soblazny," *Voprosy literatury*, 4 (1974), 116–21.

Keller, Bill. "Forum for Solzhenitsyn and Other Dissidents." *New York Times*, August 28, 1989, p. A7.

Kermode, Frank. Review, "*Pushkin House* by Andrei Bitov. Trans. Susan Brownsberger." *New York Times Book Review*, January 3, 1988, p. 10.

Khailov, A. "Grani rasskaza." *Zhanrovo-stilevye iskaniia sovremennoi sovetskoi prozy*. Moscow, 1971, 200–31.

Kharms, Daniil. *Izbrannoe*. Ed. George Gibian. Würzburg: Jal-Verlag, 1974.

Khemlin, Margarita. "Pravo na otvet." Review of *Gruzinskii al'bom* and *Stat'i iz romana*. *Oktiabr'*, 5 (1987), 202–4.

Khmel'nitskaia, T. "Mezhdu pomyslom i postupkom. O psikhologicheskoi proze." *V seredine semidesiatykh. Literatura nashikh dnei.* Compiler Isaak Eventov. Leningrad, 1977, 199–224.

"Zapisniki dushi." *Literaturnaia gazeta*, May 19, 1966, p. 3.

Klado, N. "'Osoboe sostoianie' geroia." *Literaturnaia Rossiia*, February 5, 1965, pp. 10–11.

"Piat'sot strok umileniia." *Literaturnaia Rossiia*, Aug. 20, 1965, p. 15.

Klefter, Mikael. "Rejsemotivet hos Andrej Bitov." *Slavica othiniensia* (Odense [Denmark] universitets slaviske institut), 4 (1981), 27–37.

Koehler, Liudmila. Review of *Pushkinskii Dom. Slavic and East European Journal*, vol. 23, no. 2 (1979), 291–3.

"Kogo my berëm v druz'ia?" *Detskaia literatura*, 3 (1969), 11–15.

Kozhevnikova, N. A. "O sootnoshenii rechi avtora i personazha." *Iazykovye protsessy sovremennoi russkoi khudozhestvennoi literatury. Proza.* Ed. A. I. Gorshkov, A. D. Grigor'eva. Moscow, 1977, 7–98.

"O tipakh povestvovaniia v sovetskoi proze." *Voprosy iazyka sovremennoi russkoi literatury.* Moscow, 1971, 97–163.

"Otrazhenie funktsional'nykh stilei v sovetskoi proze." *Voprosy iazyka sovremennoi russkoi literatury.* Moscow, 1971, 220–300.

Kozhinov, Vadim. *Nikolai Rubtsov.* Moscow, 1976.

"Sovremennost' iskusstva i otvetstvennost' cheloveka." *Moskovskii komsomolets*, May 7, 1966, pp. 2–3.

Stat'i o sovremennoi literature. Moscow, 1982.

Krylov, I. A. *Stikhotvoreniia*. Leningrad, 1954.

Ksepma, V. O. [A. M. Peskov]. "'Po tu storonu lobnoi stenki.'" *Literaturnoe obozrenie*, 3 (1989), 24–7.

Kubat'ian, Georgii. "Nauka puteshestvii i nauka liubvi." *Literaturnaia Armeniia*, 6 (1970), 85–9.

Kulavig, Erik. "Pa sporet af en ny sovjetisk socialkarakter – en analyse af to noveller af Andrej Bitov." *Slavica othiniensia* (Odense [Denmark] universitets slaviske institut), 6 (1983), 24–41.

Kuritsyn, Viacheslav. "Legko, radostno i pokoino." *Ogonëk*, no. 18 (1991), 20–1.

Kuz'michev, Igor'. "'V rabote, v poiskakh puti …'" *Neva*, 5 (1987), 165–8.

Kuz'muk, V. A. "Èpichnost' sovremennogo rasskaza." *Russkaia literatura*, 1 (1979), 163–71.

Kuznetsov, Feliks. "O chëm shum?" *Literaturnaia gazeta*, September 19, 1979, p. 9.

Laird, Sally. Review, *"Pushkin House* by Andrei Bitov. Trans. Susan Brownsberger." *Times Literary Supplement*, July 22–28, 1988, p. 801.

Lamorisse, Albert. *The Red Balloon*. Garden City, New York: Doubleday and Company, Inc., 1956.

Lane, Raymond M. "Tough Talk from the Literati." *Boston Globe*, April 28, 1987, pp. 25–6.

Lang, David Marshall. *Armenia. Cradle of Civilization*. London, England: George Allen & Unwin Ltd., 1970.

Lanshchikov, Anatolii. "… ili tol'ko mir oshchushchenii?" *Literaturnaia gazeta*, April 17, 1968, p. 5.

"Ot literaturnykh fiktsii k literature deistvitel'nosti." *Moskva*, 3 (1969), 206–216.

Voprosy i vremia. Moscow, 1978.

Latynina, A. "Duèl' na muzeinykh pistoletakh. Zametki o romane Andreia Bitova 'Pushkinskii dom.'" *Literaturnaia gazeta*, January 27, 1988, p. 4.

Lavrov, V. *Formula tvorchestva. Knigi o zhizni i iskusstve v sovremennoi literature*. Leningrad, 1986.

Laxness, Halldor. *The Atom Station*. Trans. Magnus Magnusson. Sag Harbor, New York: Second Chance Press, 1982.

Lermontov, Mihail. *A Hero of Our Time*. Trans. Vladimir Nabokov. Garden City, New York: Doubleday and Co., Inc., 1958.

Izbrannye proizvedeniia. vols. I and II. Moscow, 1963.

"Letka-enka." on record "V novogodniuiu noch'. Tantsy." Melodiia record.

Levi, Primo, *The Periodic Table*. Trans. Raymond Rosenthal. New York: Schocken Books, 1984.

Leyda, Jay. *Kino. A History of the Russian and Soviet Film*. Princeton, New Jersey: Princeteon University Press, 3rd edn., 1983.

"Life in Windy Weather." *Publishers Weekly*, June 13, 1986, p. 67.

Lifshitz-Losev, L. "Books as Vodka." *New York Review of Books*, May 31, 1979, pp. 29–33.

Likhachev, D. S. "Ot pokaianiia – k deistviiu," Interview with Dmitrii Likhachev. *Literaturnaia gazeta*, September 9, 1987, p. 2.

Zametki o russkom. Moscow, 1984.

Lipkin, Semen. "Obraz i davlenie vremeni. Otkrytoe pis'mo." *Vremia i my. Illiustrirovannyi zhurnal literatury i obshchestvennykh problem*, 47 (1979), 126–33.

Lisitskii, Sergei. "Stydlivaia nevinnost'." *Zhurnalist*, 2 (1969), 58–60.

Literaturnye pamiatnye mesta Leningrada. Ed. A. M. Dokusov. Leningrad, 1968.

Lorenz, Konrad Z. *King Solomon's Ring. New Light on Animal Ways*. Foreword by Julian Huxley. Trans. Marjorie Kerr Wilson. New York: Thomas Y. Crowell, Publishers, 1952.

Lowe, David, "E. Ginzburg's *Krutoi maršrut* and A. [*sic*] Aksenov's *Ožog*: The Magadan Connection." *Slavic and East European Journal*, vol. 27. no. 2 (1983), pp. 200–10.

Maguire, Robert A. Review, "*Life in Windy Weather* by Andrei Bitov, Ed. Priscilla Meyer." *The New York Times Book Review*, September 14, 1986, p. 33.

Maguire, Robert A. and Malmstad, John E. "*Petersburg.*" *Andrey Bely. Spirit of Symbolism*. Ed. John E. Malmstad, Ithaca and London: Cornell University Press, 1987, 96–144.

Mandelstam, Osip E. *The Complete Critical Prose and Letters*. Ed. Jane Gary Harris. Trans. Jane Gary Harris and Constance Link. Ann Arbor, Michigan: Ardis Publishers, 1979.

"Puteshestvie v Armeniiu." *Literaturnaia Armeniia*, 3 (1967), 83–99.

"Puteshestvie v Armeniiu," *Zvezda*, 5 (1933), 103–25.

Sobranie sochinenii. vol. 1. Washington: Inter-Language Literary Associates, 1964.

"Zapisnye knizhki. Zametki." *Voprosy literatury*, 4 (1968), 180–204.

Marchenko, A. "Iz knizhnogo raia...." *Voprosy literatury*, 4 (1969), 48–71.

"'Metallicheskii vkus podlinnosti'...." *Literaturnaia gazeta*, October 3, 1973, p. 5.

"Sredi knig." *Iunost'*, 8 (1969), 76–7.

Markov, D. "Istoricheski otkrytaia sistema pravdivogo izobrazheniia zhizni (O novykh aspektakh obsuzhdeniia problem sotsialisti-cheskogo realizma v poslednie gody)." *Voprosy literatury*, 1 (1977), 26–66.

Martiros Saryan. Intro. and compiled by Sh. Khachatrian. Leningrad, 1975.

Mathewson, Rufus W. *The Positive Hero in Russian Literature.* New York: Columbia University Press, 1958.

McClurg, Jocelyn. "Glastnost [*sic*] Gives Rise to Literary Resurrection." *Hartford Courant*, April 27, 1988, pp. C1, C6.

McMillin, Arnold. "Russian Prose in the 1970s: From Erofeev to Edichka." *Journal of Russian Studies*, 45 (1983), 25–33.

Melville, Herman, *Moby Dick or, The Whale.* Indianapolis, Indiana: The Bobbs-Merrill Company, Inc., 1964.

Meyer, Priscilla. "Afterword. Autobiography and Truth: Bitov's *A Country Place*" in Andrei Bitov, *Life in Windy Weather. Short Stories.* Ed. Priscilla Meyer. Trans. Priscilla Meyer *et al.* Ann Arbor, Michigan: Ardis Publishers, 1986, 365–71.

"Aksenov and Soviet Literature of the 1960's." *Russian Literature Triquarterly*, 6 (1973), 447–60.

"Aksenov and Soviet Prose of the 1950s and 1960s." Diss. Princeton University, 1971.

"Bitov, Andrei Georgievich." *The Modern Encyclopedia of Russian and Soviet Literature.* Ed. Harry B. Weber. Gulf Breeze, Florida: Academic International Press, 1979. vol. III, 32–5.

"Bitov's 'roman-punktir': Whose Lover? Whose Twin? Whose Double?" unpublished paper (presented at AAASS Annual Conference, November 22, 1986, New Orleans, Louisiana).

"Interview with Vasily Pavlovich Aksenov." *Russian Literature Triquarterly*, 6 (1973), 569–74.

Meyer, Ronald, "Andrei Bitov's Memoir of Pushkin." *Studies in Comparative Communism*, 21, no. 3/4 (1988), 379–87.

"Andrej Bitov's *Puškinskij Dom.*" Diss. Indiana University, 1986.

Mikhail Zoshchenko. Stat'i i materialy. Leningrad, 1928.

Milivojevic, Dragan. "*Metropol'.*" *Russian Language Journal*, 35, Nos. 121–122 (1981), 303–8.

Miller, Alice. *Thou Shalt Not Be Aware. Society's Betrayal of the Child.* Trans. Hildegarde and Hunter Hannum. New York: Farrar, Straus and Giroux, 1984.

Mirsky, D. S. *A History of Russian Literature.* Ed. and abr. Francis J. Whitfield, New York: Alfred A. Knopf, 1973.

Mitin, Genrikh. "Narodnoe i lichnoe." *Literaturnaia Armeniia*, 10 (1973), 100–4.

"Proshchanie s detstvom." *Smena*, 12 (1965), 18–19.

Molotsky, Irvin. "Writers Joust Orally at Literary Conference." *New York Times*, April 27, 1987, p. C11.

Mondri, G. "Roman Andreia Bitova 'Pushkinskii Dom' (k voprosu o zhanre)." *Slavic Symposium 1982*, Proceedings of the First Symposium on Slavic Culture, University of Witwatersrand (Johannesburg, South Africa), Department of Russian Studies, 23–24 September, 1982. Ed. Irene Masing-Delic, pp. 178–92.

Motiashov, Igor'. "Glavnaia zapoved'." *Literaturnaia gazeta*, March 19, 1969, p. 6.

"Otvetstvennost' khudozhnika. (Zametki kritika)." *Voprosy literatury*, 12 (1968), 3–32.

Murray, Edward. *Fellini the Artist*. New York: Ungar Publishing Company, 1976.

Nabokov, Vladimir. *Dar*. New York: Izdatel'stvo imeni Chekhova, 1952.

The Gift. Trans. Michael Scammell with the collaboration of the author. New York: Capricorn Books, 1963.

Invitation to a Beheading. New York: G. P. Putnam's Sons, 1959.

Pale Fire. New York: Berkley Books, 1985.

Nakhimovsky, Alice Stone. "Looking Back at Paradise Lost: The Russian Nineteenth Century in Andrei Bitov's *Pushkin House*." *Russian Literature Triquarterly*, 22 (1988), 195–204.

Nersisian, M. G. *Genotsid armian v Osmanskoi imperii (Sbornik dokumentov i materialov)*. Erevan, 1966.

Novello, Adriano Alpago; Jeni, Giulio; Manoukian, Agopik; Pensa, Alberto; Uluhogian, Gabriella; Zekiyan, B. Levon. *The Armenians*. New York: Rizzoli International Pubns., 1986.

Novikov, Vladimir. "Tainaia svoboda." *Znamia*, 3 (1988), 229–31.

"The Short Story: A New Upsurge." *Soviet Literature*, 3 (1988), 3–6.

"Nuzhny li v literaturovedenii gipotezy?" *Voprosy literatury*, 2 (1977), 82–112.

Olesha, Iurii. *Izbrannoe*. Moscow, 1974.

Oskotskii, V. "Aleksei Monakhov na randevu." *Literaturnoe obozrenie*, 1 (1977), 55–7.

"...sushchestvuet–i ni v zub nogoi." *Literaturnaia gazeta*, August 11, 1971, p. 4.

Pankov, A. V. *Proza – 1976. Novoe v zhizni, nauke, tekhnike. Seriia "Literatura"*, no. 9, 1977. Moscow, 1977.

Panova, Vera. "O romane Dzh. D. Selindzhera." *Inostrannaia literatura*, 11 (1960), 138–41.

Pasternak, Boris. *Doctor Zhivago*. Trans. Max Hayward and Manya Harari. New York: Pantheon Books, Inc., 1958.

Doktor Zhivago. Moscow, 1989.

Stikhotvoreniia i poèmy. Intro. A. D. Siniavskii. Moscow–Leningrad, 1965.

Pikach, Anatolii. "Beg trustsoi po labirintu." *Neva*, 4 (1988), 181–4.

Pirsig, Robert M. *Zen and the Art of Motorcycle Maintenance. An Inquiry into Values.* Toronto: Bantam Books, 1984.

Pollak, Nancy. "The Obscure Way to Mandel'shtam's Armenia." Diss. Yale University, 1983.

Poulet, Georges. *The Metamorphoses of the Circle.* Trans. Carley Dawson and Elliott Coleman in collaboration with the author. Baltimore, Maryland: The Johns Hopkins Press, 1966.

Protchenko, V. I. "Povest' 60-kh–nachala 70-kh godov." *Sovremennaia russkaia sovetskaia povest'.*" Ed. N.A. Groznova and V. A. Kovalev. Leningrad, 1975, 161–223.

Proust, Marcel. *Remembrance of Things Past.* Trans. C. K. Scott Moncrieff. New York: Random House, 1934, vol. I.

Pulatov, Timur, "Razvedka boem." *Literaturnaia gazeta*, October 25, 1972, p. 5.

Pushkin, Alexander. *Complete Prose Fiction.* Trans. Paul Debreczeny. Stanford, California: Stanford University Press, 1983.

Polnoe sobranie sochinenii. vol. III (Leningrad, 1948); vol. VIII, Book One (Leningrad, 1948); Book Two (Leningrad, 1940 [*sic*]).

Polnoe sobranie sochinenii v desiati tomakh. vol. II (Moscow, 1963); vol. VI (Moscow, 1964).

Sobranie sochinenii v desiati tomakh. vol. II (Moscow, 1959).

"Ragovor idet o rasskaze." *Literaturnaia Rossiia*, September 25, 1964, p. 14.

Remnick, David. "Andrei Bitov, in Search of the Voice of Memory. The Russian Novelist & the Possibilities of Freedom." *Washington Post*, September 8, 1988, pp. C1, C8.

"The Life and Work of Andrei Bitov." *Los Angeles Times*, Oct. 9, 1988, Part VI, pp. 10–11.

Review of *Pushkin House*, in "Forecasts," *Publishers Weekly*, October 2, 1987, p. 81.

Revon, Michael. "Cosmogony and Cosmology (Japanese)." *Encyclopaedia of Religion and Ethics.* Ed. James Hastings *et al.* New York: Charles Scribner's Sons, 1912. IV, 162–7.

Rodnianskaia, I. B. "Bitov, Andrei Georgievich." *Kratkaia literaturnaia èntsiklopediia.* vol. IX, Moscow, 1978, pp. 130–1.

"Obraz i rol'." *Sever*, 12 (1977), 111–19.

"Obraz i rol' (O proze Andreia Bitova)." *Literatura i sovremennost'. Sbornik 16, Stat'i o literature 1976–1977 godov.* Moscow, 1978, 280–93.

Romenets, M. V. *Problema gumanizma v sovremennom russkom rasskaze.* Khar'kov, 1969.

Rosenberg, Karen. Review, *"Pushkin House."* *New Society*, April 15, 1988, 30–1.

Rosengrant, Sandra Gayle Freels. "The Theoretical Criticism of Ju. N. Tynjanov." Diss. Stanford University, 1976.

Rosenthal, Stuart. *The Cinema of Federico Fellini*. South Brunswick, New Jersey and New York: A. S. Barnes and Company, 1976.

Rougle, Charles. Review, *"Life in Windy Weather* by Andrei Bitov. Ed. Priscilla Meyer," *Slavic and East European Journal*, vol. 31, no. 3 (1987), pp. 450–1.

Rubtsov, Nikolai. *Izbrannoe*. Moscow, 1982.

Poslednii parokhod. Moscow, 1973.

Zelenye tsvety. Moscow, 1971.

Ruehl, Ted. "Soviet Prose Writer Bitov Discusses Work, Life as Contemporary Artist." *The Daily Princetonian*, May 8, 1987, pp. 1, 4, 5.

Ruslanova, Lidiia. *Rasskaz o zhizni. Otvety telezriteliam. Pesni.* (Melodiia Records M60-42349-50, 1980).

Sakharov, V. "Alkhimiia prozy." *Literaturnaia gazeta*, October 3, 1975, p. 5.

"Novye geroi Bitova" *Iunost'*, 6 (1973), 74.

"Vlast' kanona. Zametki o rasskaze." *Nash sovremennik*, 1 (1977), 156–64.

Sapgir, Kira, "Zapazdyvaiushchii poezd." *Grani*, 132 (1984), 312–16.

Scammell, Michael. *Solzhenitsyn. A Biography*. New York: W. W. Norton & Company, 1984.

Schmid, Wolf. "Materialen zu einer Bitov-Bibliographie." *Wiener Slawistischer Almanach*, 4 (1979), 481–95.

"Nachtrag zur Bitov-Bibliographie." *Wiener Slawistischer Almanach*, 5 (1980), 327–34.

"Thesen zur innovatorischen Poetik der russischen Gegenwartsprosa." *Wiener Slawistischer Almanach*, 4 (1979), 55–93.

"Verfremdung bei Andrej Bitov." *Wiener Slawistischer Almanach*, 5 (1980), 25–53.

Selindzher, Dzh. D. "Nad propasti'iu vo rzhi." Trans. R. Rait-Kovaleva. *Inostrannaia literatura*, 11 (1960), 28–137.

Sergeev, S. "Sredi knig i zhurnalov." *Don*, 2 (1969), 172–85.

Shakhidzhanian, V. *Moskovskii komsomolets*, September 25, 1963, p. 3.

Shaw, Kurt Cony. "Chasing the Red Balloon: Psychological Separation in the Fiction of Andrej Bitov, 1958–1962." Diss. University of Kansas, 1988.

Sherel', A. "Na poroge otkrytii." *Komsomol'skaia pravda*, March 17, 1965, p. 3.

Shklovskii, Viktor. *Gamburgskii schet*. Leningrad, 1928.

Shneidman, N. N. "Man, Nature, and the *Roots* in Recent Soviet

Russian Prose." *Studies in Honour of Louis Shein.* Eds. S. D. Cioran, W. Smyrniw and G. Thomas. Hamilton, Ontario: McMaster University Printing Services, 1983, 125–33.

Shubin, È. A. *Sovremennyi russkii rasskaz. Voprosy poètiki zhanra.* Leningrad, 1974.

Sidirov, Evgenii. *"V poiskakh istiny." Stat'i i dialogi o literature.* Alma-Ata, 1983.

Sidorov, E. and Iakimenko, L., compilers. *Sotsialisticheskii realizm segodnia. Problemy i suzhdeniia.* Moscow, 1977.

Slonim, Marc. *Soviet Russian Literature. Writers and Problems 1917–1977.* New York: Oxford University Press, 1977.

Smelkov, Iulii. "Zametki kritika," in *My–molodye.* (Moscow, 1969), pp. 384–8.

Solov'ev, Vladimir. "Problema talanta." *Puti k khudozhestvennoi pravde. Stat'i o sovremennoi sovetskoi proze.* Ed. A. A. Urban. Leningrad, 1968, 262–95.

"Rasskaz i ego metamorfozy." *Neva* 4, (1974), 185–92.

"Soprichastnost' veku. Literaturnaia èvoliutsiia i problemy zhanra." *Novyi mir,* 8 (1974), 235–52.

"Status istiny." *Literaturnaia gazeta,* February 16, 1977, p. 6.

"Sud'ba cheloveka v zhanre rasskaza." *Iunost',* 10 (1974), 70–4.

Solov'eva, Inna. "Varianty sud'by." *Iunost',* 6 (1975), 81–3.

Solzhenitsyn, Aleksandr. *Rakovyi korpus.* Frankfurt/Main, West Germany: Posev, 1968.

"Soviet Café's Cleaning Day Thwarts Writers' Gathering." *New York Times,* January 24, 1979, p. A7.

"Soviet to Publish 'We.'" *New York Times,* June 25, 1987, p. C25.

Spieker, Sven. "Andrei Bitov's Bookish Landscapes: Travelling through the Texts in 'Uroki Armenii,'" *Wiener Slawistischer Almanach,* 24 (1989), 171–85.

"S raznykh tochek zreniia." *Literaturnoe obozrenie,* 10 (1973), 40–5.

Ssachno, Helen von. "Formkunste sind dem Zensor suspekt. Andrej Bitows Roman 'Das Puschkin-Haus' erschien in Amerika." *Süddeutsche Zeitung,* January 10, 1979, p. 29.

"Metropol feiert Premiere." *Süddeutsche Zeitung,* August 8, 1979, p. 8.

"Tauziehen hinter den Kulissen. Was haben die russischen Metropol-Autoren zu erwarten?" *Süddeutsche Zeitung,* March 7, 1980, p. 35.

Stepanian, K. "Kak zhit', chtoby zhit'?" *Literaturnaia gazeta,* April 1, 1987, p. 5.

Strehler, Bernard L. *Time, Cells, and Aging.* San Francisco, California: Academic Press, 1977.

Struve, Gleb. *Russian Literature under Lenin and Stalin 1917–1953*. Norman, Oklahoma: University of Oklahoma Press, 1971.

Surovtsev, Iurii. "Puteshestvie k liudiam." *Literaturnaia Rossiia*, July 21, 1967, p. 8.

Takuboku, Ishikawa. "Insolvable Discord" in *A Handful of Sand*. Trans. Shio Sakanishe. Westport, Connecticut: Greenwood Press Publishers, 1976.

Terepelova, A. A. "Geroi i zhanr (O nekotorykh osobennostiakh povesti 50–60-kh gg.)." *Russkaia literatura XX veka. Sovetskaia literatura. Moskovskii gosudarstvennyi pedagogischeskii institut. Uchënye zapiski*, 456 (1971), 244–57.

Tinbergen, N. *Social Behavior in Animals*. London: Chapman and Hall, 1975.

Tolstoi, L. N. "Smert' Ivana Il'icha," in *Polnoe sobranie sochinenii*, vol. XXVI (Moscow, 1936).

Trefilova, G. "Rabochii moment." *Literaturnoe obozrenie*, 10 (1973), 40–4.

Triapkin, Nikolai. *Gusi–lebedi. Stikhi*. Moscow, 1971.

Zlatoust. Izbrannye stikhi. Moscow, 1971.

Trifonov, Iurii. "Sredi knig." *Iunost'*, 4 (1964), 74.

Truehart, Charles. "The Den of the Literary Lions." *Washington Post*, April 25, 1987, pp. B1, B5.

Truffaut, François. *The Films in My Life*. Trans. Leonard Mayhew. New York: Simon and Schuster, 1978.

Turbin, V. "Listopad po vesne." *Novyi mir*, 4 (1972), 259–64.

Turgenev, I. S. "Russkii iazyk." *Polnoe sobranie sochinenii i pisem v dvadtsati vos'mi tomakh*. vol. XIII (Moscow–Leningrad, 1967), p. 198.

Turkov, A. "Protivnik pritaivshegosia sna." *Molodaia gvardiia*, 8 (1964), 309–12.

Tvrdíková, Sylva. "Modifikace hrdiny a žánru (Andrej Bitov)." *Bulletin ruského jazyka a literatura*, 20 (1976), 49–58.

"Two Leading Soviet Writers Plan to Emigrate to the West." *New York Times*. April 17, 1980, p. A10.

Tynianov, Iurii. *Arkhaisty i novatory*. Leningrad, 1929.

Poètika. Istoriia literatury. Kino. Moscow, 1977.

Pushkin i ego sovremenniki. Moscow, 1969.

Tynianov. Iu. and Kazanskii, B., eds. *Fel'eton. Sbornik statei*, Leningrad, 1927.

Ueda, Makoto, *Modern Japanese Poets and the Nature of Literature*. Stanford, California: Stanford University Press, 1983.

Ugrešić, Dubravka. "Udio eksperimenta (Proza Andreja Bitova)," in

Nova ruska proza. (Zagreb: Znanstvena biblioteka Hrvatskog filoškog društva, 1980), pp. 75–110.

Ul'iashov, Pavel. "I mif, i skaz, i pritcha." *Literaturnaia gazeta*, March 8, 1978, p. 5.

Updike, John. "Doubt and Difficulty in Leningrad and Moscow." *New Yorker*, September 12, 1988, 108–14.

Urban, Adol'f. "Filosofichnost' khudozhestvennoi prozy." *Zvezda*, 9 (1978), 209–21.

"V nastoiashchem vremeni." *Zvezda*, 7 (1973), 214–16.

"V razmyshlenii i deistvii." *Zvezda*, 12 (1971), 185–202.

"U.S. Authors Protest Suppression of Soviet Authors." *New York Times*, August 12, 1979, p. 5.

Ushakov, Nikolai. "Sviaz' vremen." *Literaturnaia gazeta*, June 10, 1970, p. 3.

Vail, Petr and Genis, Aleksandr. "Khimera simmetrii. Andrei Bitov." *Sintaksis*, 18 (1987), pp. 80–91.

Vertlib, Evgenii. "Andrei Bitov. *Pushkinskii Dom.*" *Russian Language Journal*, XXXIV, no. 117 (1980), 225–8.

Voevodin, Vsevolod. "Otvetstvennost' talanta." *Literaturnaia gazeta*, March 24, 1964, p. 3.

Vorontsov, Yuri and Rachuk, Igor. *The Phenomenon of the Soviet Cinema.* Moscow, 1980.

Vospominaniia o Rubtsove. Compiled by V. A. Oboturov and A. A. Griazev, Arkhangel'sk, 1983.

Waddell, L. A. "The Buddhist Pictorial Wheel of Life." *Journal of the Asiatic Society of Bengal*, LXI, no. 1 (1892), 133–55.

"Wheel." *The Hindu World. An Encyclopedic Survey of Hinduism.* Benjamin Walker. New York: Frederick A. Praeger, 1968, 597–9.

Whitney, Craig R. "Soviet Rebuffs Top Authors Seeking to Get Censored Works Printed." *New York Times*, January 28, 1979, p. 14.

"Writers Say Soviet Yields in a Dispute." *New York Times*, October 24, 1979, p. 9.

Zarzycka, Ewa Berard. "Le vent de Petersbourg souffle à nouveau sur Leningrad." *La Quinzaine littéraire*, no. 525, Feb. 1–15, 1989, pp. 6–7.

Zeno of Elea. A Text, with Translation and Notes by H. D. P. Lee. Cambridge, England: Cambridge at the University Press, 1936.

Zlochevskaia, Liubov'. "'Iz punkta A ...'" *Studencheskii meridian*, 8 (1988), 30–1.

Zolotusskii, Igor'. *Chas vybora.* Moscow, 1976.

"Ostriëm vnutr'. *Moskovskii komsomolets*, December 22, 1967, p. 4.

"Poznanie nastoiashchego." *Voprosy literatury*, 10 (1975), 3–37.
Teplo dobra. Moscow, 1970.
Zoshchenko, Mikhail. *Izbrannye proizvedeniia v dvukh tomakh*. vol. I.
Leningrad, 1968.

Index

CAMBRIDGE STUDIES IN RUSSIAN LITERATURE

General editor: MALCOLM JONES
Editorial board: ANTHONY CROSS, CARYL EMERSON,
HENRY GIFFORD, G. S. SMITH, VICTOR TERRAS

In the same series
Novy Mir
EDITH ROGOVIN FRANKEL
The enigma of Gogol
RICHARD PEACE
Three Russian writers and the irrational
T. R. N. EDWARDS
Word and music in the novels of Andrey Bely
ADA STEINBERG
The Russian revolutionary novel
RICHARD FREEBORN
Poets of modern Russia
PETER FRANCE
Andrey Bely
J. D. ELSWORTH
Nikolay Novikov
W. GARETH JONES
Vladimir Nabokov
DAVID RAMPTON
Portraits of early Russian liberals
DEREK OFFORD
Marina Tsvetaeva
SIMON KARLINSKY
Bulgakov's last decade
J. A. E. CURTIS
Velimir Khlebnikov
RAYMOND COOKE
Dostoyevsky and the process of literary creation
JACQUES CATTEAU
translated by Audrey Littlewood
The poetic imagination of Vyacheslav Ivanov
PAMELA DAVIDSON
Joseph Brodsky
VALENTINA POLUKHINA

STUDIES OF THE HARRIMAN INSTITUTE

Selected Titles in Russian Literature and Culture

Through the Glass of Soviet Literature. Views of Russian Society by Ernest J. Simmons (Columbia University Press, 1953).

Russian Classics in Soviet Jackets by Maurice Friedberg (Columbia University Press, 1962).

Red Virgin Soil. Soviet Literature in the 1920s by Robert A. Maguire (Princeton University Press, 1968; reprint Cornell University Press, 1987).

Mayakovsky. A Poet in the Revolution by Edward J. Brown (Princeton University Press, 1973).

The Familiar Letter as a Literary Genre in the Age of Pushkin by William Mills Todd III (Princeton University Press, 1976).

Sergei Aksakov and Russian Pastoral by Andrew A. Durkin (Rutgers University Press, 1983).

Leo Tolstoy. Resident and Stranger by Richard Gustafson (Princeton University Press, 1986).

Andrey Bely. Spirit of Symbolism, edited by John Malmstad (Cornell University Press, 1987).

Russian Literary Politics and the Pushkin Celebration of 1880 by Marcus C. Levitt (Cornell University Press, 1989).

Russianness: In Honor of Rufus Mathewson, edited by Robert L. Belknap (Ardis Publishers, 1990).

In Stalin's Time by Vera Dunham (Cambridge University Press, 1976; reprint Duke University Press, 1990).

Folklore for Stalin by Frank Miller (M. E. Sharpe, 1990).

Vasilii Trediakovsky. The Fool of the New Russian Literature by Irina Reyfman (Stanford University Press, 1990).

Ilya Repin and the World of Russian Art by Elizabeth Kridl Valkenier (Columbia University Press, 1990).

The Genesis of "The Brothers Karamazov" by Robert L. Belknap (Northwestern University Press, 1990).

Autobiographical Statements in Twentieth-Century Russian Literature, edited by Jane Gary Harris (Princeton University Press, 1990).

The Paradise Myth in Eighteenth-Century Russia. Utopian Patterns in Early Secular Russian Literature and Culture by Stephen Lessing Baehr (Stanford University Press, 1991).